MAPPING
STRATEGIC
KNOWLEDGE

MAPPING STRATEGIC KNOWLEDGE

Edited by

Anne Sigismund Huff and Mark Jenkins

SAGE Publications
London • Thousand Oaks • New Delhi

First published 2002

Decision Explorer is a registered trademark of Banxia
Software Ltd

 SAGE Publications Ltd
6 Bonhill Street
London EC2A 4PU

SAGE Publications Inc
2455 Teller Road
Thousand Oaks, California 91320

SAGE Publications India Pvt Ltd
32, M-Block Market
Greater Kailash - I
New Delhi 110 048

British Library Cataloguing in Publication data

A catalogue record for this book is available from
the British Library

ISBN 0 7619 6948 9
ISBN 0 7619 6949 7(pbk)

Library of Congress Control Number available

Typeset by SIVA Math Setters, Chennai, India
Printed in Great Britain by The Cromwell Press Ltd,
Trowbridge, Wiltshire

CONTENTS

LIST OF TABLES
AND FIGURES

TABLES

FIGURES

NOTES ON CONTRIBUTORS

Fran Ackermann is a Professor in the Management Science Department at Strathclyde University, Scotland. She is interested in the role that group decision support systems and cause mapping can play in supporting the development and implementation of strategy. She has worked extensively with both public and private organizations from a consultancy/action research basis, helping groups work together more effectively, develop a sense of shared meaning and begin to negotiate towards action. She has written widely in strategy, operational research and information systems arenas. With Colin Eden she is the author of *Making Strategy: The Journey of Strategic Management* (Sage, 1998).

Véronique Ambrosini is a Research Fellow in the Strategic Management Group at Cranfield School of Management, UK, working in association with Professor Cliff Bowman. She joined Cranfield in April 1994, prior to which she was an assistant manager working for McDonald's Restaurants. She holds an MBA from the University of Birmingham and studied for her first degree at the ISEG, a French Business School. Her research interests include the resource-based theory of the firm, tacit knowledge, organizational routines and competitive advantage. Her PhD considered the role of routines in organizational performance. Her most recent journal articles can be found in the *Journal of Management Studies, British Journal of Management, European Management Journal,* and *Journal of Management Studies.*

Michel Bougon is Professor of Strategy at Bryant College, Rhode Island, USA, a private undergraduate and graduate AACSB-accredited school of business. His research centres on ontology and cognition applied to the cognitive mapping of sense making by individuals and by congregations of individuals. His published work includes the conceptual unification of organization theory and strategy. He also researches the mapping of strategizing by organizations and individuals. He has created several techniques to support his research, such as the 'self-Q interviews'. He has also developed several conceptual tools to extend cognitive mapping, such as the 'cryptic labels' and the 'congregate map' of small groups and teams. His publications include a chapter in Anne Huff (ed.), *Mapping Strategic Thought* (Wiley, 1990).

Cliff Bowman is Professor of Business Strategy at Cranfield School of Management, UK. He has published several books on strategy. His research interests include resource-based theory, corporate strategy and strategy processes. Recent publications include 'Strategy in Practice' (Prentice Hall, 1998) and 'Competitive and Corporate Strategy' (Irwin 1997, with D. Faulkner).

Nardine Collier is a Research Assistant in the Strategic Management Group at Cranfield School of Management, UK. Nardine joined Cranfield in 1998 and is currently undertaking a part-time PhD on the relationship between strategy development processes and the innovation performance of organizations. Recently, with Frank Fishwick and Gerry Johnson, she published 'The processes of strategy development in the public sector', in G. Johnson and K. Scholes (eds.) 'Exploring Public Sector Strategy', Prentice Hall (2000).

John R. Doyle is Distinguished Senior Research Fellow at Cardiff Business School, University of Cardiff, Wales. He is currently researching the meanings that people extract from (and attach to) visual forms. Such forms may be 3-D, as in cognitive sculpting, or flat, as in advertising material or brand logos. He is eclectic in research method, ranging from conversation and 'mere' observation of people's attempts to 'cognitively sculpt' their thoughts and feelings, through to controlled psychological experimentation in which the font, colour, name and image appearing in presentational material may be manipulated.

Colin Eden is Director of the University of Stratchclyde Graduate School of Business, Scotland, and Professor of Management Science and Strategic Management. He has written over 200 articles published in management, operational research and strategy journals, and published seven books in the field of management science, managerial and organizational cognition, group decision support and strategy making. His most recent book, with Fran Ackermann, *Making Strategy: The Journey of Strategic Management* (Sage, 1988), introduces qualitative modelling to a strategic management audience. Recently he has been a consultant to the senior management teams from many settings including the Scottish Natural Heritage, Bombardier Inc., the Northern Ireland Office, Elsevier Science and the Royal Ulster Constabulary. As well as a continuing interest in strategic problem solving and strategy making, he is currently conducting research into strategic risk. With Fran Ackermann, he is the developer of the cognitive mapping software 'Decision Explorer' and the group support software 'Group Explorer', each of which is now used worldwide by researchers and practitioners.

Roger I. Hall is a Senior Scholar at the I.H. Asper School of Business, University of Manitoba, Canada. His prime research interest is in explaining the rise and fall of organizations from the way policies are formed through the collective decision-making behavior of managers who seek to control a dynamic complex system, such as a business, that is only partially understood. He holds degrees in physics, production management and business administration and studied under Joan Woodward (a pioneer in the field of organization theory) and Arnold Tustin (an important figure in the founding of the system dynamics discipline). He received his practical training in electronics and control theory in the Royal Naval Electrical School (H.M.S. *Collingwood*), and also as an apprentice, and later a production manager, in the British electronics industry (Siemens Edison Swan). He is a founding member of the System Dynamics Society, a Past President of the Administrative Sciences Association of Canada and won First Prize in the 1984 International Competition for the Most Original New Contribution to the field of Organizational Analysis, sponsored by the College on Organization of the Institute of Management Sciences. Hall's research has been published in *Administrative Science Quarterly, Management Science, System Dynamic Review* and the *Journal of Business Research*.

Nick Henry was recently appointed to a Readership in Urban and Regional Studies in the Centre for Urban and Regional Development Studies (CURDS), University of Newcastle, UK. Previously, he was Lecturer in Economic Geography at the University of Birmingham. He has been involved in a number of Economic and Social Research Council-funded projects on regional development in the advanced economies. His most recent publications include an interdisciplinary edited collection on *Knowledge, Space, Economy* (Routledge, 2000, with J. Bryson, P. Daniels and J. Pollard) and *The Economic Geography Reader* (Wiley, 1999, with J. Bryson, R. Martin and D. Keeble). He is the author and joint author of numerous academic articles on the motor sport industry and *In Pole Position: Motor Sport Success in Britain and Its Lessons for the World's Motor Industry* (Euromotor Reports, Ludvigsen Associates Ltd, 1999).

Gerard P. Hodgkinson is Associate Dean (Research) and Professor of Organizational Behaviour and Strategic Management at Leeds University Business School, The University of Leeds, UK. A Fellow of the British Academy of Management and a fellow of the British Psychological Society, his principal research interests centre on the psychological analysis of strategic management processes, especially cognitive processes in strategic decision making and business competition. His work has appeared in a range of scholarly international journals including *Strategic Management Journal, Journal of Management Studies, Journal of Occupational and Organizational Psychology,* and *Human Relations.* He is co-author (with Paul R. Sparrow) of *The Competent Organization: A Psychological Analysis of The Strategic Management Process* (Open University Press, forthcoming).

He has also published a number of chapters in edited volumes, including: 'Cognitive Processes in Strategic Management: Some Emerging Trends and Future Directions, in N. Anderson, D.S. Ones, H.K. Sinangil and C. Viswesvaran (Eds.), *Handbook of Industrial, Work and Organizational Psychology* (Sage, 2001). He is Editor-in-Chief of the *British Journal of Management* and a Consulting Editor of the *Journal of Occupational and Organizational Psychology*. A practising Chartered Occupational Psychologist, he has conducted numerous consultancy assignments across a wide range of private and public sector organizations.

Anne Sigismund Huff is a Professor in Strategic Management at the University of Colorado, Boulder, USA, with a joint appointment at Cranfield School of Management in the UK. Her research interests focus on strategic change, both as a dynamic process of interaction among firms and as a cognitive process affected by the interaction of individuals over time. Her publications include the book *Mapping Strategic Thought* (Wiley, 1990) and co-edited volumes of *Advances in Strategic Management* (JAI Press, 1990–7). In 1998–9 she was President of the Academy of Management, an international organization of over 12,000 scholars interested in management issues.

Dale W. Jasinski is an Associate Professor of Management at Quinnipiac University in Hamden, Connecticut, USA. He came to Quinnipiac to launch the first Bachelor and Masters degree programs in entrepreneurship in the state. A successful entrepreneur before earning his PhD from the University of Colorado at Boulder, USA, he teaches both entrepreneurship and strategic management at the undergraduate, graduate and executive level. His research interests include how individual and collective cognitive processes affect firm growth, especially as they relate to the identification and recognition of strategic options. Current research papers include the impact of strategic vision on employee performance, and an exploration of the role of options in promoting firm growth.

Mark Jenkins is Professor of Competitive Strategy and Director of the DBA programme at Cranfield School of Management, UK. Prior to joining Cranfield he worked for the Lex Service Group and Massey Ferguson Tractors Ltd. His teaching focuses on the areas of competitive strategy, knowledge management and innovation. His consulting activities reflect these specializations, where he has worked throughout Europe, the USA and in parts of the Far East and Middle East. In addition to his work at Cranfield he has been a visiting Professor in Strategic Management at the University of Colorado and has contributed to the MBA programme at Warwick Business School. He is currently researching the role of knowledge and innovation in the development of Formula One motor sport. He has published and presented a wide range of work in the areas of strategy and marketing. He is a founding editor of the *Journal of Marketing Practice,* a member of the editorial review board for the *European Journal of Marketing* and is author of *The Customer Centred Strategy* (Pitman, 1997).

Gerry Johnson is Professor of Strategic Management at the University of Strathclyde Graduate School of Business, Scotland. After graduating from University College London, he worked for several years in management positions in Unilever and Reed International before becoming a management consultant. He taught at Aston University Management Centre, where he obtained his PhD, and Manchester Business School before joining Cranfield School of Management in 1988, where he remained until taking up his current appointment in 2000. Professor Johnson is co-author of Europe's best-selling strategic management textbook, *Exploring Corporate Strategy* (Prentice Hall, 5th edn, 1999) and co-editor of a book series that develops themes in that text. He is also author of *Strategic Change and the Management Process*, editor of *Business Strategy and Retailing, The Challenge of Strategic Management* and *Strategic Thinking*, author of numerous papers on strategic management and a member of the editorial board of the *Strategic Management Journal.* His research work is primarily concerned with processes of strategy development and change in organizations. He also works extensively as a consultant at a senior level on issues of strategy development and strategic change with UK and international firms and public sector organisations.

Phyllis Johnson is a Research Fellow at the Graduate School of Business, University of Strathclyde, Scotland. She gained her MSc and PhD from Cranfield University. Her PhD addressed shared thinking in top management teams and its impact on the strategic decision-making process. She is a chartered psychologist and works as a psychotherapist for HM Naval Base Clyde. Her areas of interest are top team interaction and emotional life in organizations, in particular in the corporate board. She has presented her work at many international conferences and contributed chapters to several key research texts in the field. She acts as a reviewer for the *British Journal of Management,* the *Journal of Management Studies* and the *Journal of Occupational and Organizational Psychology.*

A. John Maule is Senior Lecturer in Management Decision Making at Leeds University Business School, UK. His research focuses on how people make judgements and take decisions in the face of risk and uncertainty, focusing, in particular, on how individuals model strategic choice and the effects of time pressure and stress on decision making. He has recently been assisting UK government departments to develop strategies for communicating food and health risk to the public.

Yuri Mishina is a doctoral student in organizational behavior with a minor in strategic management at the University of Illinois at Urbana-Champaign, USA. His research interests lie in the intersections of strategy, entrepreneurship and cognition. Current projects explore the social construction of capabilities, symbolic protests within an institutional framework, the tactics of challenge and delegitimation, and the effects of resources, strategies and environments upon rates of growth.

Heidi M. Neck is currently pursuing a PhD in Strategic Management and Entrepreneurship from the University of Colorado at Boulder, USA. Her research focuses on young, high-growth firms, and her dissertation seeks to link strategic alternatives and organizational slack to the growth of high-technology IPOs. She has published in *Frontiers of Entrepreneurship Research*, the *Journal of Developmental Entrepreneurship* and the *Journal of Leadership Studies*. Neck has recently been appointed as an Assistant Professor of Entrepreneurship at Babson College, which commences in the Fall, 2001.

Steven Pinch is a Professor in Geography at the University of Southampton, UK. His primary research interests are in the changing geography of the welfare state and in the growth dynamics of agglomerating industries. His main books are *Cities and Services: The Geography of Collective Consumption* (Routledge and Kegan Paul, 1985), *Worlds of Welfare: Understanding the Changing Geographies of Social Welfare Provision* (Routledge, 1997) and (with Paul Knox) *Urban Social Geography: An Introduction* (Prentice Hall, 4th edn, 2000).

Timothy G. Pollock is an Assistant Professor in the Management and Human Resources Department at the University of Wisconsin-Madison, USA. Pollock's research focuses on the role that social and political factors, such as reputation, social networks and power, play in shaping executive compensation, corporate governance activities and market transactions. He is also interested in exploring how the cognitive processes of managers interact with firm resources to affect the performance and survival of high-growth firms. Pollock's research has been published in *Administrative Science Quarterly, Human Communication Research*, the *Journal of Organizational Behavior*, the *Corporate Reputation Review*, the *British Journal of Management* and the *Academy of Management Executive*.

Joseph F. Porac is a Professor of Organization and Management and the Senior Associate Dean for Faculty and Research at the Goizueta Business School at Emory University, USA. His research interests centre on the cognitive bases of markets and organizations, and he is currently pursuing research on minivans, motorcycles, the US paper industry and the use of information technologies. His research has appeared in a variety of organizational journals. Recent papers include 'Industry categories and the politics of the comparable firm in CEO compensation', with James Wade and Timothy Pollock (*Administrative Science Quarterly*, 44: 112–144),

'Sociocognitive dynamics in a product market', with Jose Antonio Rosa, Jelena Runser-Spanjol and Michael S. Saxon (*Journal of Marketing*, 63: 64–77), *Cognition, Knowledge and Organizations* (Stamford, CT: JAI Press, 1999) with Raghu Garud and 'Strategy and cognition' with Howard Thomas, in A. Pettigrew, H. Thomas and R. Whittington (eds), *Handbook of Strategy and Management* (Sage, 2001).

Olaf G. Rughase is a partner with Panlogos GmbH, Offenbach, Germany, a strategy consulting firm. Prior to his consulting activities, he worked for Deutsche Bank Germany, Dresdner Bank Brazil and several other companies in Germany and the United States. He is completing his doctoral studies at the University of Witten-Herdecke, Germany. His research interests include strategic change, issue management and cognitive contributions to strategy theory.

David Sims is Professor of Management Studies, Brunel University, UK, and Head of the School of Business and Management. He has an academic background in operational research and organizational behaviour, and has been a consultant to organizations in the oil, power, computer, publishing, airline, hotel and engineering industries, as well as in the public sector. His research interests are in management thinking and learning, in particular in agenda shaping, problem construction and managerial story telling. He is editorial advisor of the journal *Management Learning*, and is author or co-author of some sixty books and articles (including the textbook *Organizing and Organization* [Sage, 2000]) and a further forty or so international conference papers, though he cannot remember what they all say.

INTRODUCTION

This book explores the connection between two interesting and important conversations in the study of strategic management. The first involves questions of how knowledge is generated and managed in organizations. A central issue in this literature has been how informal, social mechanisms affect knowledge development and use. For example, 'communities of practice' (Brown and Duguid, 1991) have been identified as important social contexts sheltering knowledge development. 'Knowing' exemplified in action has been distinguished from more rhetorical knowledge (Cook and Brown, 1999), and found to be more important to practice. Both observations expand on the idea that tacit understanding is different from, and often bolsters, explicit knowledge (Nonaka, 1994; Nonaka and Takeuchi, 1995; Polanyi, 1966).

Interest in the informal and less articulated aspects of knowledge is closely connected with the resource-based theory of the firm (Conner and Prahalad, 1996; Grant, 1991; Penrose, 1995; Peteraf, 1993; Wernerfelt, 1984), which emphasizes that competitive advantage comes from resources that are difficult to imitate (Barney, 1991; Lippman and Rumelt, 1982). Organizational routines that embed knowledge in shared practices have been particularly salient in this theory, because they are much more problematic for outsiders to understand, buy or copy (Nelson and Winter, 1977).

While many people believe that organizational knowing is particularly valuable, analysts are left with the difficulties of identifying these more obscure knowledge assets, and strategists are further encumbered by significant problems managing them. It seems obvious that both exploitation of current capabilities, and exploration that might lead to the development of new capabilities (March, 1991), are hindered if informal, tacit knowing cannot be united with more explicit, formal understanding.

We feel this juncture invites use of cognitive mapping, a tool developed in the study of managerial and organizational cognition (Walsh, 1995). A 'map' makes conceptual entities more visible. While early maps were sometimes taken as direct reports on cognitive processes, later studies adopted a more modest, and more appropriate, position: maps are intermediate tools – they facilitate the discussion of cognitive processes that can never be directly observed (Eden, Jones and Sims, 1979). Mapping tools are thus potentially as attractive to consultants and practitioners as they are to academics. In fact, we regard mapping work as an especially strong vehicle for moving between theory and practice – a frequently desired but rarely achieved goal in professional fields.

Neck and Collier's annotated bibliography at the end of this volume shows that cognitive mapping research and practice has significantly grown in size and scope since the publication of Colin Eden's pioneering work (e.g. 1988, 1992) and Huff's *Mapping Strategic Thought* (1990). Interest in mapping has been fuelled by advances in mapping methods, especially computer-based instruments that facilitate data collection and analysis. Concurrently, experience with cognitive mapping has highlighted the limitations of remaining rigidly within a cognitive perspective. Over time, work on managerial cognition and cognitive mapping has become more closely integrated with research on affect and social interaction. This move makes it more compatible with the knowledge-mapping tasks that interest us in this volume of original readings.

The purpose of our book is three-fold. We want to:

- demonstrate the range of strategically relevant knowledge questions that can be approached from a mapping perspective;
- illustrate the varied mapping tools that are now available; and
- address methodological and theoretic issues that are raised by efforts to map strategic knowledge.

WHAT IS A MAP?

Drawing on common language uses of the term, we suggest that a 'map'

- is a visual representation that,
- establishes a landscape, or domain,
- names the most important entities that exist within that domain, and
- simultaneously places them within two or more relationships.

A more complex map has two further characteristics. It

- facilitates images of being 'within' the established domain, and
- encourages mentally moving among entities.

The last two characteristics clarify the importance of location and perspective and promote consideration of change in entities and relationships – two issues of increasing importance as strategic management comes to be seen as an ongoing, dynamic process.

In this book we are interested in a broad family of 'maps', which rarely (with the exception of Chapter 6, by Henry and Pinch) have a geographic referent. Each of the characteristics in our definition therefore deserves further explication.

Represents Visually

At heart, a map is a visual way of thinking that many people, though not all, find compelling. The image can be a useful 'transitional object' (Eden and Ackermann, 1998) that provides perspective for the individual. It can be equally helpful in a group context by creating distance between ideas and their initial sponsors. A map can also be a mnemonic, which serves to resurface connections considered in the past. Equally, maps often suggest new connections.

Those who are able to use a map as a thinking tool find that it can organize and simplify ideas, even complex ones, in much the same way that an urban subway map clarifies complex underground connections. The visual impact of a 'good' simplifying map makes it a useful means of communicating knowledge, and a useful repository for collecting knowledge.

Alternatively, however, current knowledge can sometimes be more easily elaborated once its skeletal form is revealed in visual form. The map then becomes useful ground for making the simple more complex and thus moving beyond what was known in the past. The map's visual form can reveal 'holes' in current information. Its structure also facilitates comparison with other maps that can be used as possible templates for modifying content. The map then becomes a helpful record of emerging knowledge.

Defines Domain

A map does not exist without establishing a 'domain'. While interpretive and related academic arguments insist that everything is defined by context, a map highlights this critical aspect of knowledge. By its very existence, a map 'frames' a particular landscape, and makes it more clearly the subject of consideration. What is included in the frame is much easier to identify, and challenge. Alternative frames are easier to imagine once a first alternative is made more explicit. Maps even make the absent more obvious.

Names Distinct Entities

The names or labels found on a map also deserve explication. The mapmaker is typically well advised to use some well-known names as an orienting device, even if the map is a private thinking tool. Just the word 'Paris', for example, establishes a great deal in a geographic map. Almost all of us would expect other names in France, or the rest of Europe if the scale is large, though we might be wrong if the map were of Texas, which also incorporates a place called 'Paris'. This example indicates how much the way knowing is 'parced' (Weick, 1979) affects subsequent sense–making. Categorization is thus a major map-making task (Porac and Thomas, 1994).

Again, what is not named can be as important to the course of subsequent thought as what is named. Map makers must make choices. But as consumers of maps in many different settings (driving an automobile, using a subway, trying to find an unfamiliar constellation), we understand that choices have to be made, and we can imagine highlighting other aspects of the terrain.

Establishes Multiple Relationships among Entities

Perhaps the most distinctive attribute of a map is that it establishes relationships. Size distinctions are a common but important way of relating map entities. Thus, in geographic maps we find rivers, streams and creeks; highways and secondary roads; major metropolitan areas, smaller cities and towns.

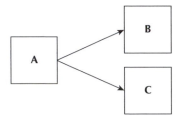

Figure 1 A basic visual statement of connection

A list could make the same distinctions among entities, but the information conveyed on a geographic map establishes relationships in a two-dimensional coordinate system. The simple box and arrows diagram shown in Figure 1, for example, is a basic visual statement of connection. This map can be understood in several different ways. Drawing on the Western convention of 'reading' from left to right, it suggests that A precedes B and C in some ordering scheme. Often a map of this sort is intended to read that A 'causes' B and C, while B and C are not causally linked (except through A). But perhaps the relationship is merely temporal, or spatial. Able map makers understand these alternatives, and make their intentions clear in legends and accompanying text.

Design, colour, sound cues, computer links and other options can be used for clarity and to add additional categorization schemes. As a relatively simple example, consider the map of competitor relationships in the pharmaceutical industry in Figure 2. The 'north–south' coordinate indicates relative expenditures on R&D. Companies of different size (the entities mapped) are made comparable by dividing their actual expenditures by total sales revenue, though raw data might be more informative for some purposes. On the east–west coordinate, expenditures on advertizing are similarly normalized. The vertical dimension, sales

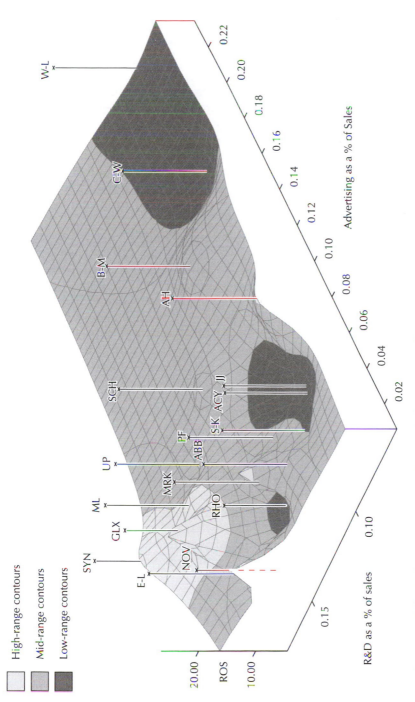

Figure 2 Return on Sales (RoS) performance surface, 1970 (Huff and Huff, 2000:188)

growth, makes it possible to assess possible performance implications of these two strategic investments.

Facilitates Images

We are particularly interested in cognitive maps because we believe their visual form makes it easier to consider the implications of 'standing' at different points on the map. Though this is particularly obvious with a map such as that shown in Figure 2, where some firms' performance positions are clearly better than other competitors, even a simple diagram like the one shown in Figure 1 can be used to speculate about the differences between interpreting a knowledge domain from point A, or point C.

Suggests Options for Movement and Change

Visual maps of this sort thus invite speculation about strategic moves, which is why the map in Figure 2 was created. The map clarified the difficulty some firms in the industry are likely to have in 'moving to' more profitable positions. Other maps might be compared with this map. For example, how would the relative attractiveness of firm positions change if a different performance measure were used, or if firms were placed on coordinates defined by other strategic decisions? Even maps that are less explicitly geographic invite such speculation, as the authors of the following chapters make clear.

OVERVIEW OF THE BOOK

In defining and discussing the characteristics of a map, we have sought both to emphasize the open architecture of the mapping concept, and also to establish that we do not see maps as a direct portrayal of individual or collective knowledge. Maps are tools that we can simplify or enhance. In this volume we have brought together a diverse collection of empirical studies that illustrate three uses of knowledge-mapping tools.

Part I: Methods for Directly Discovering Managerial Knowledge

The first three chapters of the book illustrate the range of approaches available to surface managerial knowledge. The chapters are united by the practical motive of understanding knowing in context, and by reliance on direct interaction with managers to collect information, as shown in Table 1.

TABLE 1 Part I: Methods for directly discovering managerial knowledge

Strategic issue(s)	Cognitive, knowledge and mapping questions addressed	Data source/Level of analysis	Method of analysis/ Purpose of map	Contribution/Key finding(s)	Knowledge management implications
1. Ambrosini & Bowman Mapping successful organizational routines.	How top management teams can identify and explore the tacit routines that create competitive advantage.	How can routines be identified and examined, if they are not readily discussed, go beyond standardized procedures, and involve multiple individuals?	Uses individual interviews, requests for metaphors and stories, and causal mapping in an eight-hour interactive workshop with the top management team of a British mutual organization.	Self-Q technique (Bougon) and other more open-ended techniques used to elicit primary information for workshop discussion. Decision Explorer software used to display and store data on the causal sources of advantage in current practice.	Proposes that organization-level tacit knowledge is best understood as tacit routines. Provides an empirical example of one organization's attempt to identify the routines that underlie *its* success.	Describes the 'digging process' required to surface rarely discussed activities. Provides practical advice for other researchers (e.g. helping participants focus on what is being done rather than what should be done).
2. Rughase Linking content to process: how mental models of the customer enhance creative strategy processes.	How to facilitate customer-focused strategic change.	How do our customers see us? How do we build consensus for strategic action?	Consultants draw cognitive maps from stories told by customers. Discussion in the TMT (Top Management Team) develops understanding of the maps and uses them for further strategizing.	SENSOR® process uses maps derived from customers to challenge top management thinking.	Change can be facilitated by connecting customer thinking with current managerial assumptions. Provides an empirical example from a German warehousing firm.	Illustrates value of a story-based methodology for sharing knowledge between key shareholders.
3. Doyle & Sims Enabling metaphor in conversation: a technique of cognitive sculpting.	Accessing highly embedded knowledge.	How to understand deep knowledge?	Individual and group interaction with physical objects.	Physical objects placed in relationships are used as an intervention tool.	Chapter describes the use of 'cognitive sculpting' as a tool for developing metaphoric thinking.	Everyday, unexamined physical metaphors can be a powerful basis for surfacing undiscussed knowledge.

Chapter 1, by Véronique Ambrosini and Cliff Bowman, proposes that routines should be examined as a particularly important repository of tacit organizational knowledge. Resource-based theory supports the view that organizations benefit from knowledge that is dispersed among participants, and sustained by their joint efforts, without being widely codified. With this definition as a premise, Ambrosini and Bowman individually interviewed top-level managers in a financial services firm, then worked with the team to identify the tacit routines that managers thought could be causally linked to their company's competitive advantage. Consistent with resource-based theory, some effort was required to 'tease out' beliefs about competitive advantage in a team context. In addition, the routines managers initially identified as the basis for their competitive advantage rarely survived sustained conversation. The simple mapping process used supported the identification of underlying, more sustainable sources of advantage from the managers' perspective.

Olaf Rughase, in *Chapter 2*, raises a potential problem with the managerial perspective, however. This chapter examines the disparity between what managers think they know about their customers and their customer's experience of product offerings. In the consulting engagement reported, an initial customer survey by a German warehousing firm was difficult for managers to interpret. Rughase describes how the tacit knowledge of customers was discovered in the stories they told about their experiences with the firm. Though these stories almost always seemed trivial to the storyteller, and rarely directly covered the issues found in the survey, the consultants were able to aggregate and map the data gathered into two quite different accounts. Tape recordings from the interviews then were used to introduce map relationships to the management team. In the case study reported, the conversation supported reinterpretation of the previously obscure survey data, and led to re-segmentation of the firm's market.

Chapter 3 moves even more deeply into tacit knowledge by describing a method of engaging managers with a 'toy box' of physical objects. John Doyle and David Sims call their technique 'cognitive sculpting'. It is designed to elicit understanding so embedded that it is not accessible via interactive query or storytelling (the data-gathering methods used in Chapters 1 and 2). The authors demonstrate how rearranging evocative physical objects enables a group of individuals to surface and debate more deep-rooted issues arising from strategic change programs as an example of their technique.

This work is an innovative and distinctive addition to the repertoire of mapping techniques. It pushes the definition of a 'map' by making it more transitory and plastic, which fits many obervers' definitions of organizational knowledge very well. At the same time, using physical, visual tools makes tacit knowing more explicit, which potentially facilitates knowledge management.

Part II: Inferring Managerial Knowledge

Part I suggests the wide range of mapping methodologies that might be used to directly interact with managers. Part II provides an equally wide repertoire for mapping organizational knowledge from less direct sources, as summarized in Table 2.

The first approach, taken by a pioneer in the cognitive mapping field, Roger Hall, is reported in *Chapter 4*. Hall's retrospective analysis of decision making by managers of the *Old Saturday Evening Post* (1976) was an early indicator of the potential impact of managerial cognition. In Chapter 4, he more completely illustrates how a highly structured map – in this case an AI program – can be developed to represent the decision-making process of a group of senior managers. Hall defines the behavioural rules applied by a specific top management team, the leaders of a sports club. Although managers are consulted at ambiguous junctures, the researcher is surfacing and reflecting on managerial knowledge, then testing the model against subsequent behaviour.

Joseph Porac, who made important contributions to the field of organizational and managerial cognition with his work on the Scottish knitwear industry (1989), reports on a new study of entrepreneurial growth strategies in *Chapter 5*. This work, which is carried out with co-authors Yuri Mishina and Timothy Pollock, uses a series of propositions developed from resource-based theory to draw out different growth strategies across industries. The data were collected by the Kaufman Foundation. Five different growth strategies, each with multiple components, are identified from the data. This is particularly interesting because it suggests that knowledge crosses industry boundaries.

The question of transorganizational knowledge is more completely explored in *Chapter 6*, by Nick Henry and Stephen Pinch. This chapter draws on the principles of 'untraded interdependencies' between firms (Storper and Salais, 1997). The study more specifically considers a 'technological knowledge cluster', the motor sports industry in England, and demonstrates how mapping approaches can be used to identify knowledge flows at the inter-organizational level. The value of considering differing levels of abstraction (individual, firm and cluster) is emphasized, and, once again, this is an approach to knowledge mapping that depends on researcher framing and interpretation.

Part III: Theoretic and Methodological Issues

The third section of our book has a theoretic and methodological focus, as summarized in Table 3.

Colin Eden and Ackermann, the authors of *Chapter 7*, have extensive experience in using mapping techniques. They also developed 'Decision

TABLE 2   Part II: Inferring managerial knowledge

	Strategic issue(s) and theoretic sources	Cognitive, knowledge and mapping questions addressed	Data source/Level of analysis	Method of analysis/ Purpose of map	Contribution/Key finding(s)	Knowledge management implications
4. Hall Mimicking collective interpretation of complex cause–effect relations using simple behavioural rules embodied in an AI program.	Complex causes and consequences of policy decisions are rarely discussed by managers, even though dynamic systems cannot be adequately explained without them.	Can an AI program mimic the decision-making logic of a policy group? Can managers use such a program to understand and work with greater complexity?	Sport club executives provided information about political entities and variables actively influencing decision making within their organization. At points of path indeterminacy in the model they provided additional input on causal beliefs within the group.	The author developed the AI program based on behavioural rules from the research literature. Group policy making is mimicked by running trials of the AI program on the causal map developed from users' initial inputs.	Policies resulting from the AI program corresponded to executive decision making in the sports club at two points in time.	AI programs provide a structure for discussing the consequences of alternative causal assumptions, along with the implications of adopting more or less complex causal arguments.
5. Porac, Mishina & Pollock Entrepreneurial narratives and the dominant logic of high-growth firms.	Explain 'cognitive proposition' from resource-based theory that firm growth and direction is determined by the interaction of available resources, capabilities and managerial mental models.	How can individual strategies and an overarching 'growth logic' be identified in entrepreneurial firms? Can similar growth logics be discerned across firms?	Open-ended narrative data from 54 entrepreneurial founders collected by the Kaufman Foundation were used as the data for firm-level analysis.	Content analysis with ATLAS/ti™ software used to identify growth strategies; cluster analysis used to compare multiple strategy patterns across founder narratives.	Study finds evidence of multiple growth strategies within firms. Five clusters or 'growth logics' that combine different strategies are identified across the data set.	Evidence of distinctive yet dispersed knowledge and beliefs within a broad entrepreneurial community.
6. Henry & Pinch Spatializing knowledge: placing the knowledge community of Motor Sport Valley.	Empirical investigation by two economic geographers of the proposition articulated by Storper and Salais (1997) and others that 'untraded interdependencies' underlie economic activity.	What are the sources of shared meanings and understandings that support world-wide economic dominance of producers found within a specific geographic region?	Specialist publications; 50 in-depth interviews; site tours in the British Motor Sport Industry.	Geographic maps and 'genealogical trees' used to locate and track movement of suppliers, designers and services	Describes how knowledge is continually transformed as players observe, and more importantly move among, specific work locations.	Provides an example of the 'microfoundation' of knowledge production within a greater socio-political/ economic system.

TABLE 3   Part III: Theoretic and methodological issues

Strategic issue(s) and theoretic sources	Cognitive, knowledge and mapping questions addressed	Data source/Level of analysis	Method of analysis/ Purpose of map	Contribution/Key finding(s)	Knowledge management implications
7. Eden & Ackermann Mapping strategy: a framework for facilitating strategy making.	The creation of a development processual (socio-political) model of strategy formulation.	How to use causal mapping technologies to elicit and subsequently structure involvement from multiple participants in the strategy development process?	Shared and negotiated perspectives within a group process.	Decision Explorer™ computer software, computer groupware or pencil-and-paper procedures described as alternatives for eliciting and relating concepts.	Illustrates 'teardrop' method for connecting strategic goals and actions.	Summary of an extensive project using interactive and computerized mapping tools to help top managers and other stakeholders map their environment, specify mutually agreed goals and define strategy.
8. Hodgkinson & Maule The individual in the strategy process: insights from behavioural decision research and cognitive mapping.	Experimental cognitive psychology and behavioural decision theory has generated a large and consistent body of laboratory evidence on 'bounded rationality' (Simon, 1956). Research on managerial cognition has worked more closely with managers to develop more complex but disparate models.	Can work associating positive decision frames with risk-averse choice be replicated with more managerial-relevant materials and analytic tools?	Laboratory study using undergraduate subjects replicated using 52 senior managers from a banking organization.	Participants completed a causal map from a comprehensive list of variables relevant to a case vignette, justifying investment decisions.	Study using more complex and strategically relevant investment decisions replicated and expanded on previous studies of biased decision making. Subjects asked to complete a cognitive mapping task prior to receiving the prompt did not show the same bias.	Preliminary analysis suggests there may be statistically significant differences among mapping methods that provide the basis for overcoming some decision biases.

(Contd.)

TABLE 3　(Contd.)

	Strategic issue(s) and theoretic sources	Cognitive, knowledge and mapping questions addressed	Data source/Level of analysis	Method of analysis/ Purpose of map	Contribution/Key finding(s)	Knowledge management implications
9. Johnson & Johnson Facilitating group cognitive mapping of corporation core competencies.	How to develop insight of unit core competences that might support corporate strategizing.	How can expert intervention improve use of mapping tools?	Group cause mapping process developed from Ambrosini and Bowman.	Group mapping procedures facilitated by consultants.	Draws on a large-scale corporate attempt to identify sources of advantage to discuss theoretic and practical difficulties with causal mapping.	Questions validity of unfacilitated mapping methods.
10. Jaskinki & Huff Using a knowledge-based system to study strategic options and researchers' mental models.	Identification and development of strategic options in a volatile and uncertain high-tech environment.	How to describe mental models? How to document change in mental models over time?	Study of strategic options used to illustrate researchers' mental models.	ATLAS/ti™ software used as a knowledge-based system to code data, build connections among codes, visually document the conceptual structure and generate attending propositions.	Chapter uses case study of an entrepreneurial organization seeking new options to illustrate the use of ATLAS/ti as a methodological tool.	Suggests that computerized mapping programmes have the capacity to track researcher's mental model.

Explorer', a widely used computer mapping program we offer to readers on the last page of this book. In this chapter, Eden and Ackermann provide a very practical description of their mapping technology. A particularly interesting aspect of the chapter, from our point of view, is the authors' sensitivity to the political aspects of mapping exercises. Their account also illustrates the importance of identifying issues that are salient to strategy development in a specific context.

Chapter 8 by Gerard Hodgkinson and John Maule, is theoretically oriented in a very different way. These authors champion the cause of experimental research methods to elicit and develop maps, and provide an innovative approach to testing the effect of different mapping approaches. An initial study of undergraduate decision making is replicated with senior managers from the banking sector. The results suggest why maps need to be carefully framed as a basis for managerial understanding to avoid biases. In fact, the authors suggest there are some situations in which mapping may be dysfunctional.

Care in testing methodologies must be matched by care when working with managers to elicit knowledge maps; this issue is tackled in *Chapter 9*, by Phyllis Johnson and Gerry Johnson. Their report focuses on theoretical, methodological and practical difficulties of applying mapping techniques to elicit managers' views on the sources of competitive advantage. The chapter explores some of the particular issues raised by using maps to improve and aggregate local knowledge and raises some important questions regarding the nature of cognition itself.

The need to reflect specifically on the *researcher's* mental models is then discussed in *Chapter 10*, by Dale Jasinski and Anne Huff. This chapter uses coding decisions made in Jasinski's dissertation on option theory to discuss issues of validity and reliability in qualitative work. The chapter is also interesting because it uses Atlas/ti., a knowledge-based computer system, to assist in the analysis of textual data.

Finally, the volume ends with an annotated bibliography constructed by Heidi Neck and Nardine Collier. This bibliographic reference illustrates the breadth and depth of the mapping field and provides a useful starting point for those scholars and practitioners who wish to explore further.

The bibliography is followed by an order form for a CD by Michel Bougon. Bougon discusses the rapidity of change in the new economy and uses Decision Explorer – a tool intitially developed by Eden and Ackermann and described most fully in Chapters 1 and 7 – to illustrate the nested logic of several well-known firms from web and news sources. A free copy of the program is available on the CD.

SUMMARY

We believe the chapters in this book make a strong case for mapping strategic knowledge. The case is further elaborated in six interrelated points. First, *maps can connect and organize dispersed organizational knowledge*. Organizations generate complex knowledge but much of it is difficult to capture and communicate. As organizations push to deliver higher-quality goods more quickly and more cheaply, they have less time for the necessary management of these resources. Yet knowledge from past experience is critical for a variety of purposes, from training new employees to updating current practices. The global imperatives of corporations mean they are dealing with more complex processes, market segments and product offers across geographic and cultural boundaries, which makes the need for the connection and linking of organizational knowledge even greater.

Second, *knowledge maps can facilitate organizational activities by simplifying inevitably complex domains*. One of the enduring mantras of strategic management is the need to achieve clarity and logic in the central rationale of the strategy. With increasing complexity, this becomes increasingly challenging. Methodologies that distil complexity help strategists maintain coherence whilst, at the same time, grounding their ideas in the operational reality of the organization.

Third, *maps also have the capacity to represent knowledge at various levels of abstraction*. They therefore can be used to connect the idiosyncratic detail of one context with other conditions that either cannot or need not be represented in such detail. Computer-based maps, in particular, can collapse or hide some portions of a knowledge domain while other portions are examined, developed and transferred. Thus a map might show how a 'simple' strategy connects with more 'complex' organizational activities, and vice versa. Links between macro and micro phenomena are often vague or missing from the strategic logic of an organization and maps, potentially, can bridge this gap. Different levels of detail in a family of maps similarly can make the complex more simple, and the simple more complex.

A fourth compelling reason to pay attention to maps and mapping technology is that *maps can surface and organize concepts and relationships that are normally taken for granted*. This agenda is a dominant one in the chapters that follow. One of the most widely discussed ideas in the knowledge field is the difference between explicit and tacit knowledge (Nonaka and Takeuchi, 1995). Recognizing and surfacing tacit knowledge is important (though competitively risky) for further strategizing, yet embeddedness makes clarity problematic. Maps are a tangible but flexible tool that can help reveal that which has not been articulated in the past. Source data can come from the organization, but about competitors, partners, suppliers and other actors.

Fifth, *maps also have the ability to facilitate communication in group settings and help aggregate opinions within a group*. This is particularly important as the boundaries around individual tasks, specific formal and informal groups, and larger organizational entities become more permeable and transient. The engagement of many different individuals in the strategic task has become more important, and attention is turning not only to coordinating rational and creative thought but also to the impact of issues previously seen as more peripheral, such as politics, emotion and values. Maps are useful tools for transferring knowledge and developing new knowledge among individuals in all of these areas.

Knowledge can only be transferred if those intended to receive it are able to understand the way in which it is coded or structured. More subtle knowing also requires shared coding schemes. Maps provide a basis for dialogue on these issues.

While other benefits of mapping technology might be explored, we will content ourselves with a final, especially critical, sixth point – *maps have the capacity not only to catalogue but also to **generate** knowledge*. Mapping exercises facilitate 'what if' revisions in a knowledge domain. When they record beliefs about causal or other relationships, they extend the insights available from other sources, including quantitative spreadsheets (which are, of course, explicit, first-order maps in themselves). By providing a basis to make knowledge more explicit and more likely to be shared, debated and revised, maps become a dynamic basis for knowledge creation. As organizations face increasingly demanding environments, we believe the mapping tools we present for generating knowledge may be the greatest contribution of the book.

REFERENCES

Barney, J. (1991) 'Firm resources and sustained competitive advantage', *Journal of Management*, 17: 99–120.

Brown. J.S. and Duguid, P. (1991) 'Organizational learning and communities of practice: towards a unified view of working, learning and innovation', *Organization Science* 2: 40–57. Notes: cited in Brown & Duguid, 1998.

Conner, K.R. and Prahalad, C.K. (1996) 'A resource-based theory of the firm: Knowledge versus opportunism', *Organization Science,* 7: 477–501.

Cook, S.D.N, and Brown, J.S. (1999) 'Bridging epistemologies: the generative dance between organizational knowledge and organizational knowing', *Organization Science* 10: 381–400. Notes: cited in EGOS 2000 paper.

Eden, C. (1992) 'On the nature of cognitive maps', *Journal of Management Studies,* 29: 261–265.

Eden, C. (1988) 'Cognitive mapping', *European Journal of Operational Research* 36: 1–13.

Eden, C. and Ackermann, F. (1998) *Making Strategy: The Journey of Strategic Management.* London: Sage.

Eden, C., Jones, S. and Sims, D. (1979) *Thinking in Organizations.* London: Macmillan.

Grant, R.M. (1991) 'The resource-based theory of competitive advantage: Implications for strategy formulation', *California Management Review,* 33: 114–135.

Hall, R.I. (1984) 'The natural logic of management policy making: Its implication for the survival of an organisation', *Management Science,* 30: 905–927.

Huff, A.S. (ed.) (1990) *Mapping Strategic Thought.* Chichester: Wiley.

Huff, A.S. and Huff, J.O. (2000) *When Firms Change Direction.* Oxford: Oxford University Press.

Lippman, S.A. and Rumelt, R. (1982) 'Uncertain imitability: An analysis of interfirm differences in efficiency under competition', *Bell Journal of Economics*, 13: 418–438.

March, J.G. (1991) 'Exploration and exploitation in organizational learning', *Organization Science*, 2: 71–87.

Nelson, R.R. and Winter, S.G. (1977) 'In search of useful theory of innovation', *Research Policy*, 6: 36–76.

Nonaka, I. (1994) 'A dynamic theory of organizational knowledge creation', *Organization Science*, 5: 14–37.

Nonaka, I. and Takeuchi, H. (1995) *The Knowledge-Creating Company*. New York: Oxford University Press.

Penrose, E. (1995) *The Theory of the Growth of the Firm*. 3rd edn. Oxford: Oxford University Press.

Peteraf, M.A. (1993) 'The cornerstones of competitive advantage: A resource-based view', *Strategic Management Journal*, 14: 179–191.

Polanyi, M. (1966) *The Tacit Dimension*, Garden City, NY: Doubleday.

Porac, J.F., Thomas, H. and Baden-Fuller, C. (1989) 'Competitive groups as cognitive communities: the case of Scottish knitwear manufacturers', *Journal of Management Studies* 26: 397–416.

Porac, J.F. and Thomas, H. (1994) 'Cognitive categorization and subjective rivalry among retailers in a small city', *Journal of Applied Psychology*, 79: 54–66.

Senge, P.M. (1990) *The Fifth Discipline: The Art and Practice of the Learning Organization*. New York: Doubleday.

Simon, H.A. (1956) 'Rational choice and the structure of the environment', *Psychological Review*, 63: 129–138.

Storper, M. and Salais, R. (1997) *Worlds of Production: The Action Frameworks of the Economy*. Cambridge, MA: Harvard University Press.

Walsh, J.P. (1995) 'Managerial and organizational cognition: Notes from a trip down memory lane', *Organization Science* 6: 280–320.

Weick, K.E. (1979) *The Social Psychology of Organizing*. Reading, MA: Addison-Wesley.

Wernerfelt, B. (1984) 'A resource-based view of the firm', *Strategic Management Journal*, 5: 171–180.

I

METHODS FOR DIRECTLY DISCOVERING MANAGERIAL KNOWLEDGE

1

MAPPING SUCCESSFUL ORGANIZATIONAL ROUTINES

Véronique Ambrosini and **Cliff Bowman**

ABSTRACT

It is widely acknowledged in the strategy field and in the literature on the resource-based view of the firm in particular that tacit knowledge can be a source of sustainable advantage. However, despite the attention that has been dedicated to resource-based theory and to tacit knowledge at the conceptual level, there is little empirical research on the topic. In this chapter we explore how cause mapping can help bridge this gap.

We first briefly define tacit knowledge and argue that organizational-level tacit knowledge is best understood as tacit routines. Secondly, we suggest that causal mapping is a simple but powerful technique that can help managers elicit the routines that are central to their organization's success. We argue that causal mapping is a digging process that can facilitate the elicitation of less explicit causes for success, especially when coupled with techniques such as metaphors and storytelling, which have been argued to help express the inexpressible. In the last part of the chapter we report on an empirical study we carried out in a British mutual organization, in which we used causal mapping to uncover tacit routines. We describe the study and set out our findings concentrating on one of the issues that emerged from the study: the apparent lack of management attention towards activities that are critical in delivering advantage. We conclude by arguing that researching tacit routines is valuable and may even be critical for managers who want to understand better how their organization works in order to help them sustain advantage.

INTRODUCTION

In the strategy literature, and the resource-based view of the firm literature in particular, tacit knowledge has been argued to be a source of competitive advantage largely because it is difficult to express, it generates causal ambiguity, it is practical, and it is context-specific (Grant, 1993; Nonaka, 1991; Sobol and Lei, 1994; for a more complete discussion please refer to Ambrosini and Bowman, 1998). This implies that tacit knowledge possesses all the requirements that a 'resource' needs to have to be a source of sustainable competitive advantage (Barney, 1991): it is valuable, rare, imperfectly imitable and imperfectly substitutable.

The main interest in strategy resides in organizational tacit knowledge rather than individual tacit knowledge. However, when tacit knowledge is being discussed, very often the distinction between individual tacit knowledge and organizational tacit knowledge is not made, or it is blurred. We believe that this confusion may be reduced by employing the expression 'tacit routines' rather than 'organizational-level' tacit knowledge.

Several authors (Grant, 1996; Nelson and Winter, 1982; Spender, 1996) have argued that organizational knowledge resides in routines. They have suggested that organizations are social systems, that is, that they are more than the sum of their parts and that these parts are interdependent (Gharajedaghi and Ackoff, 1994). This means that an organization is conceived as a set of interrelated routines.

This view can be traced back to Nelson and Winter (1982). According to them, it is the establishment of routines that codifies and preserves memories and knowledge. Thus specialized knowledge becomes embedded in ongoing organizational activities. They suggest that organizations remember through informal and formal routines: they 'remember by doing'. Nelson and Winter's position is unambiguous; they argue that 'to view organizational memory as reducible to individual memories is to overlook, or undervalue, the linking of those individual memories by shared experiences in the past, experiences that have established the extremely detailed and specified communication system that underlies routines performance' (1982: 105).

However, Grant explains that routines are often tacit: 'organizational routines involve a large component of tacit knowledge which implies limits on the extent to which organization's capabilities can be articulated' (1991: 110). These types of routines are firm-specific, taken for granted, path-dependent and complex. This is precisely what gives them value – they are unique and difficult to imitate.

Accepting these arguments, we are actually concerned with studying tacit routines when we study tacit knowledge at the organizational level. Tacit routines are not standard operating procedures; they are not codified or prescribed ways of doing things. They are activities involving more than one organizational member that cannot readily be talked about and that are happening without having been deliberately and explicitly established. The expression 'tacit routines' can be seen as synonymous with 'organizational tacit knowledge' as both phenomena are difficult to verbalize. They are about doing, and they are context-specific.

Tacit

Once we specify what we mean by 'organizational-level knowledge', it is important that we clarify what we mean by 'tacit'. From the literature (Nonaka, 1991; Polanyi, 1962; Reber, 1989; Spender, 1996), it can be implied that there are various degrees of tacitness. Hence we could have the following:

1 Tacit routines that are totally unavailable. They are not accessible because they are deeply ingrained in organizational members.
2 Tacit routines that could be accessed but that cannot be expressed through the normal use of words. They might be articulated differently, for example through the use of metaphors and storytelling.
3 Tacit routines that are unarticulated but that could be articulated readily if organizational members were simply asked the question: how do you do that? In this case routines are tacit simply because nobody ever asked the right question.

We concentrated in an exploratory study on the last two cases of tacitness (2 and 3): knowledge not yet articulated but that could be. As indicated earlier, the claim that tacit knowledge occupies a central role in the development of competitive advantage is widespread. However, despite the attention that has been dedicated to the issue, there is little empirical research to support these theoretical assertions. One of the main reasons why there have been very few attempts to research tacit routines empirically is that research instruments such as surveys and structured interviews are likely to be inappropriate insofar as individuals cannot be asked to state what they cannot readily articulate. The main challenge that may have to be faced is finding ways of expressing what could be but has not been expressed (Nonaka, 1991).

INVESTIGATING TACIT ROUTINES:
METHODOLOGY[1]

In the next few pages, we set out the methodology we used to research tacit routines empirically. We begin by describing a research proposal based on our review of the literature. Then we outline what we did and what we learnt from it.

Cognitive Maps

We shall not explain here what cognitive maps are about as this has been done extensively elsewhere (Huff, 1990). Let us just say that cognitive maps are the representation of an individual's personal knowledge, of an individual's own experience (Weick and Bougon, 1986), and they are ways of representing individuals' views of reality (Eden et al., 1981).

There are various types of cognitive maps (Huff, 1990). One of them is the cause map or causal map: 'a cause map is a form of cognitive map that incorporates concepts tied together by causality relations' (Weick and Bougon, 1986: 106).

Causal maps are probably the most pertinent type of cognitive maps to use in this research primarily because causal mapping allows us to focus on action (Huff, 1990). When assessing its appropriateness in this context, we should restate that tacit routines are about doing things, they are goal-oriented. Jenkins noted that 'causality provides a potentially higher level of procedural knowledge (how it works, and how to do it) than other sets of relationships' (1995: 53), which implies that causal maps are likely to be appropriate for studying tacit routines. Another reason for using such maps is that the question 'Are tacit routines a source of competitive advantage?' is by nature causal.

Furthermore, causal maps can be particularly useful for eliciting factors that are context-dependent, as tacit routines are, because, 'by virtue of the time spent in a particular department or function, managers develop a viewpoint that is consistent with the activities and goals of that department or particular function' (Walsh, 1988: 875). As Bougon et al. (1977) highlight, this knowledge is stored in the minds of managers in the form of cognitive maps, and cause maps in particular. In short, causal maps reflect what is understood to be happening in an organization. One of the main benefits of using cognitive maps is that they 'place concepts in relation to one another, ... they impose structure on vague situations' (Weick and Bougon, 1986: 107). Cause maps are therefore a way of ordering and analysing something that is 'fuzzy'. These maps are also useful in eliciting tacit routines because they allow us to study issues at a micro-level; they can also represent multiple explanations and consequences, show interrelationships between factors, and potential dilemmas (Eden and Ackermann, 1998).

Researching Tacit Routines: proposed Method

Similarly to Eden et al. (1992), in this study causal maps are not assumed to be models of cognition as such. We adopt Eden's view that 'the only reasonable claim that can be made of cognitive maps as an artefact ... is that ... they may represent subjective data more meaningfully than other models' (1992: 262). They are simply used as a technique that would allow us to elicit tacit routines.

There are different ways of building so-called 'group' or 'collective maps'. They can be an average of individual maps, a composite of individual maps (Weick and Bougon, 1986) or they can be derived from group discussion (Nelson and Mathews, 1991). However, because a group map may encompass more than the common content of the individual maps (Langfield-Smith, 1992), we suggest that construction of the causal map should be a group activity, a group discussion. By looking at the views of others and reconsidering their own views, group members should be able to reflect on their own and others' behaviours in the light of the group-level interaction and discussion. Moreover, a group map 'as a visual inter-active model, acts in the form of a ... transitional object that encourages dialogues' (Eden and Ackermann, 1998: 71). This approach could be a convincing element when appealing for organizations to participate in research, as 'the process of constructing a consensus around causal factors influencing the organization can be a useful diagnostic exercise' for the organization (Nelson and Mathews, 1991: 381).

The group discussion could take the format of focus groups. To dis-cover which tacit routines are valuable and to follow the resource-based view of the firm's line of questioning 'Is X a source of sustainable com-petitive advantage?', the discussion should focus on a more straight-forward, if less precise, question like: 'What makes your organization successful?' Respondents could be asked to identify concepts and express the relationships between them. The relations could be estab-lished not only on what the participants 'know' but also in their atti-tudes, reactions, feelings, and so on. The advantage of a focus group format is that 'the inherent group dynamics tend to yield insights that ordinarily are not obtainable from individual interviews' (Schiffman and Kanuk, 1991: 52).

Eliciting Tacit Routines: The Process

The causal mapping system should be powerful in revealing tacit routines because the process is about continuously asking the respon-dents to reflect on their behaviours, on what they do. They would ordi-narily not do so. During the mapping, they are encouraged to explain what they do and in that process they reveal to themselves aspects of their behaviour that up to that point were tacit (in terms of degree 2 and 3 above). The in-depth probing that allows the map to develop taps the routines that go unspoken in the organization. While mapping, the researcher should be able to catch instances where individuals say things such as 'Oh yes, that's right', 'Aha! I hadn't realized that'. The 'Oh, yes' experience suggests that something that was tacit has just been made explicit by an individual. This shows that managers are gaining insights from the session and are becoming aware of their, up-to-now tacit, routines.

starting the causal map

As mentioned earlier, we start with the broad question: what causes success in your organization? The first few answers are likely to be well-known, general causes for that success. We describe how we move toward a more specific map in the next few paragraphs.

There are several ways of constructing a map. For example, Walsh (1988) uses a predefined list, Axelrod (1976) derives constructs from texts, Markóczy and Goldberg (1995) draw material from interviews. As we are looking at taken-for-granted tacit knowledge, prescribed checklists or structured interviews are likely to be inappropriate. There is a need for 'creat[ing] a situation in which cognitive maps can emerge as fully as possible with a minimum of influence' (Bougon, 1983: 182), that is, we should 'avoid suggesting anything to the individual that might become part of an eventual cognitive map' (Cossette and Audet, 1992: 332). So, we believe that the map should ideally be built without predetermined constructs. The constructs should be established during the mapping session itself.

However, we are aware that starting a causal mapping session from scratch could be time consuming and hence we believe that preliminary interviews are a way to elicit constructs that can be used as a basis for the maps. From the literature we concluded that two different methods could be appropriate to elicit those constructs. They could be uncovered through self-Q interviews, a technique that limits the influence of the researcher (Bougon, 1983), or through semi-structured interviews, with storytelling. We designed a study in which we interviewed each participant once. Half of the group was interviewed using one technique and half using the other. The results of both methods are included in what follows. The motive for using two separate methods is to 'make sure that the ground is well covered' (Markóczy and Goldberg, 1995: 310). The interviews to elicit the constructs that are to be used to start the causal map are to be carried out on an individual basis. These interviews should provide us with an opportunity to establish rapport with the participants. This is paramount as 'close rapport with respondents opens doors to more informed research' (Fontana and Frey, 1994: 367).

self-Q

Self-Q is a non-directive mapping technique developed by Bougon (1983). It is a self-interviewing technique that draws on the respondent's account of his/her beliefs to generate constructs. The reason why tacit routines could be elicited through self-Q questioning is best given by this quote:

> in self-Q interviews, participants essentially interview themselves. The first key idea is that participants are the experts on the personal knowledge that guides their social behaviour. The second key idea is that participants formulate their questions on the basis of their own personal knowledge ... and on

the basis of their own thinking ... about the situation they are questioning. (Bougon et al., 1989: 328–329)

Bougon et al. also assert that with the self-interviewing technique 'the events, objects, and concepts [the participants] use to express their questions ... reveal their tacit and explicit knowledge' (1989: 329).

As mentioned previously, this technique could be applied to elicit the constructs used to start building the group cause map. The technique involves 'people ask[ing] themselves questions about whatever topic is being mapped and the concepts are then extracted from the questions' (Weick and Bougon, 1986:115). Here the questioning is to be focused on the respondents' views about what they do that makes the organization successful. Practically,

the Self-Q technique uses a framing statement and a ... diagram. The framing statement is read by participants and is intended to set the stage for self-questioning and to provide the subject with enough information to begin the self-questioning process. ... The diagram is intended to be used by participants to cue themselves to ask additional questions. (Sheetz et al., 1994: 37)

This technique is appealing because it lowers the participants' resistance to respond: 'people are not practiced in defending against questions that they ask themselves and over which they have control. Furthermore, since the person is asking questions rather than making assertions, the questions themselves seem harmless' (Weick and Bougon, 1986: 115). Another benefit of this technique is that the researcher does not hinder the production of constructs by his/her lack of knowledge of the organization under observation. The fact that 'often a researcher ... does not really know enough to ask the right questions' (Bougon et al., 1989: 353) is not an issue when using the self-questioning technique.

semi-structured interviews

The second method we used to start uncovering constructs is semi-structured interviews. The interviews are semi-structured in the sense that their purpose and structure is pre-determined: for example, we wanted to know what the causes of success were, and we wanted participants to give examples, to tell stories about this success.

We believe that it would be useful to encourage the interviewees to tell stories because 'stories are one of the many forms of implicit communication used in organizational contexts' (Martin, 1982: 257). People 'manage the collective memory of the organization through storytelling' (Boje, 1991b: 9). Martin explains that stories are used in organizations to 'explain "how things are done around here"' (1982: 256). It is also an appropriate device for studying tacit routines because people frame their experience in stories (Wilkins and Thompson, 1991). Moreover, 'stories are contextually embedded' (Boje, 1991a: 109), they 'can reflect the complex social web within which work takes place' (Brown and Dugruid, 1991: 44). In other words, through storytelling, participants can express what is done in the organization, and hence some tacit routines may be uncovered. This means that through stories people say more than they would normally: 'stories permit researchers to examine perceptions that are often filtered, denied, or not in the subjects' consciousness during traditional interviews' (Hansen and Kahnweiler, 1993: 1394).

The stories could be generated through interviews, with the participants being asked to tell maybe two stories, one positive and one negative, concerning what has in the past caused organizational failure and organizational success. (This is based on the critical incident technique developed by Flanagan [1954].) As recommended by Ford and Wood (1992), the interviews should, if possible, take place in the participants' organization as the familiar surroundings can serve as cues.

metaphors

Martin (1982) argues that both stories and metaphors can serve to transmit tacit knowledge. Metaphors are interesting as a way of eliciting tacit routines, for a variety of reasons. They may, for example, elicit tacit routines because 'metaphorical language gives tacit knowledge voice' (Munby, 1986: 198). They ... 'communicate meaning when no explicit language is available, especially in regard to complex ambiguous experience' (Srivastava and Barrett, 1988: 60).

Among the reasons behind the claim that metaphors can help express what is not easily articulable is that metaphors can generate new meaning. They can 'render vague and abstract ideas concrete' (Sackmann, 1989: 482). Because they allow different ways of thinking, people may be able to explain complex organizational phenomena metaphorically (Tsoukas, 1991). Metaphors can 'transmit an entire story visually using one image' (Sackmann, 1989: 468). This idea of image is central in understanding the argument concerning the articulation of tacit knowledge through metaphors. Because metaphors are vivid images, they may substitute for a large number of words (Sackmann, 1989) and they are 'useful in coping with a large amount of data' (Hill and Levenhagen, 1995: 1068). Images also allow us to speak about process because they are not discrete. This matters because tacit routines are capabilities; they are a *process* (they are about how to do things).

The procedural aspect of tacit routines is a factor in why it is difficult to communicate routines through words. This is explained by Ortony:

> language [is a] discrete symbols system ... words partition experiences. [However] experience does not arrive in little discrete packets, but flows, leading us imperceptibly from one state to another. Thus the task we have to perform in communication is to convey what is usually some kind of

continuum by using discrete symbols. It would not be surprising if discrete symbol systems were incapable of literally capturing every conceivable aspect of an object, event or experience that one might wish to describe. ... This deficiency is filled by metaphor. (1975: 46)

Metaphors are a means of capturing the continuous flow of experience, hence they can be a means of capturing tacit knowledge. 'They allow the transfer of concrete bands of experience whereas literal discourse segments experiences' (Tsoukas, 1991: 581). 'One can say through metaphor what cannot be said in discrete, literal terms, especially when words are not available or do not exist' (Srivastava and Barrett, 1988: 37).

All the above suggests that it is worth considering metaphors when attempting to elicit tacit routines. However, capturing metaphors may not be trouble-free. One of the problems is obviously to make sure that a metaphor is not used when more direct language could easily be available. It is necessary to ensure that the metaphor is employed where no appropriate words are accessible. One way of making sure that a metaphor is used in such a manner is by asking the individual to express his/her metaphor in another way. If another metaphor is used rather than literal, usual, basic terms, then one may be inclined to think that the use of metaphor is appropriate. The second problem is that not every individual may be ready or able to use metaphors during a discussion.

the mapping process

The interviews we have just described, whether based on self-Q or semi-structured interviews, allowed us to know the participants better, raise their confidence in the process and of course elicit a few 'success' factors. This being done, the tacit-skill elicitation process can begin in earnest. The map can start with 'success' and previously revealed factors. The goal of the mapping is now to find the reasons for the success. The questions that can help the participants to do so could be, for instance: How does that happen? What causes that? Who is involved? What influences that? By answering these questions, the participants can start eliciting more particular, precise reasons for success. The best image to describe the mapping process is an 'onion' metaphor. By peeling away layer after layer of the reasons for success, participants get to the less explicit causes for success. These are causes they could not have readily surfaced without prompting and probing. It is important throughout the session to insist that we are only interested in what they are currently doing, even if it is perceived to be trivial or irrelevant, and not in what they believe they *should* be doing, though this is an understandable concern of organizational members.

As the process moves from the explicit reasons for success to the point where participants have to reflect on what they do not usually think about, the flow of factors is likely to slow down. In this case we encourage participants to think of examples of how they perform the factor they have just elicited, or tell stories about the factor, or use metaphors to explain how the factor works. In each case, as we explained previously, answering questions helps express the inexpressible.

Throughout the mapping process participants are encouraged to speak about what they do. The factors should be written as actions, if possible, rather than abstract statements, because tacit routines are about doing and not verbalizing what is done. It is not about 'knowing about' or reciprocally 'not knowing about'. Asking participants to use verbs and 'I' is one useful way of making sure they are discussing what they are doing.

The map will stop when the respondents, despite being pressed for more examples and encouraged to say more, cannot reveal more factors.

This was how we envisaged using causal mapping to elicit tacit knowledge. Let us now examine how we applied this method and what we learned from the experience.

Empirically Investigating Tacit Routines

It was with the definition and methodology just established in mind that we began to elicit the tacit routines of a UK-based organization. Our aim was to elicit the tacit routines that generate success in the organization, that is, we wanted to explore whether theoretical claims that tacit routines are a source of sustainable competitive advantage could be substantiated empirically.

The organization we approached can be said to have achieved competitive success. It is a UK-based mutual organization (called case A in what follows). The full top management team (TMT) participated in the study. We invited the TMT to take part in a one-day causal mapping session aimed at uncovering the routines that make them successful. We asked them to concentrate only on what they were currently doing and to focus on what causes recent or current success.

Case A: Methodology

Figure 1.1 summarizes the methodology used in this study.

In order to start the process of uncovering the routines that mattered for case A's success, we first interviewed each TMT member about what they believed the reasons for their organization's success were. We interviewed two members using Bougon's self-Q technique. For the other three members we used semi-structured interviews, including storytelling.

After analysis of these interviews, a list of factors that contribute to the success of the organization was drawn up. The list contained 63 elements. This was too many to explore in a one-day workshop. We

1. Preliminary interviews about what causes success in the organization to elicit constructs to start the map (A, B and C).

2. Set up the map with the preliminary constructs as starting points

3. Begin the mapping process with questions such as:
   What causes that?
   How does it happen?

4. If the flow of constructs stops, ask questions such as:
   Could you give us an example of how that happened?
   Could you tell us a story?

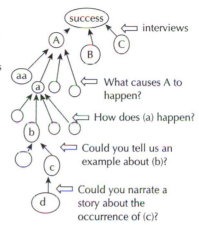

Figure 1.1   Researching tacit routines: a summary of the proposed method (adapted from Ambrosini and Bowman, 2001)

therefore decided to only examine the nine most frequently cited factors (see Table 1.1).

Four weeks later we invited the whole top team to take part in a one-day causal mapping session aimed at uncovering the routines that make them successful. At the start of the workshop we provided the top team with the nine primary causes of success that were elicited during the interviews. The purpose of the workshop was to ask the team to uncover the factors that caused these to happen – basically, to uncover what they do that leads to success. We were only interested in what they were currently doing, even if it was perceived to be trivial or irrelevant. We insisted that we were not interested in what they believed they *should* be doing. In accord with the resource-based view of the firm, we also asked them to concentrate on what they thought was unique to their organization. Finally we asked them to establish links between the various routines they identified.

In order to keep the mapping process going, we kept asking questions of the participants when they were struggling to find reasons for success. The questions we asked included, for instance: How does that happen? What causes that? Who is involved? What influences that? Could you please give us an example? The questions were kept simple and to the point. We insisted that anything could (and should) be said, even it is was perceived as 'trivial', as it was likely that what makes the difference between firms was likely to reside not in obvious, generic factors but in detail, in the idiosyncratic ways of doing things in the organization.

To help us with this process, we used the Decision Explorer™ software developed by Colin Eden, Fran Ackermann and their colleagues at the

TABLE 1.1   Initial list of factors contributing to the organization's success used during the casual mapping session

Big clients joining
CEO
Charity market
Customer focus
Ethos
Investment returns
Services offered
Staff commitment
Trustees

University of Strathclyde. The causal map being built was displayed on a screen so that participants could see it evolving. Because of the amount of data we collected, we could not manage to work on one whole map and therefore we worked on only a few factors at a time. At the end of the workshop each individual was given all the maps that were generated (see Appendix).

Because whether a routine is tacit or not can only be assessed by the individuals concerned, we needed more information from participants. For instance, if during the group session it was surfaced that the routine 'speaking to customers without recording the message' is a source of success, we needed to ask whether the managers explicitly 'knew' that before the session. This implies that the maps generated should be coded. Hence at the end of the causal map session, each TMT member was requested to individually code the maps using three categories:

A   routines that are well known to you;
B   routines that are known about but that you find difficult to deal with; and
C   routines that were tacit to you up to the group session.

Discussion

case A: results

We did not receive all the coded maps from all TMT members. Because of the amount of data, the TMT concentrated on only a few maps (see Appendix for a couple of examples), and only three sets of maps were returned to us: the Chief Executive's, the Human Resources Director's and the Business Development Director's.

Before carrying out any analysis all routines that were not positive (in other words factors that were a hindrance to the organization's success or factors that were about what it wishes to do rather than what it does) were removed.

As this study was totally exploratory and to our knowledge there is no empirical research that has looked at the link between tacit routines and competitive advantage, we had very few hypotheses. Our view was that a large majority of the factors to be coded would be found as belonging to category A (well-known) and that only one or two of the factors to be coded would be found as belonging to category C (tacit before the group session).

The coding was different from one member to another. Two of them coded the majority of the factors in category A (53.7 per cent and 54.4 per cent). One (the CEO) coded all the factors as A or B, and another member coded 89.5 per cent of the factors in these categories. The results of the third member were significantly different. Indeed, he categorized only 28.6 per cent of the factors as belonging to category A and altogether only 37.3 per cent as belonging to either A or B or both. In other words, for him a large number of the factors were tacit (40.5 per cent vs 10.5 per cent and 0 per cent for the others). The divergence in responses was to a certain extent surprising, as the TMT is small and has been together for a while. This would indicate that perceptions of tacitness are personal and not organizational. As each TMT member has a different functional background and occupation, the differences could be functionally biased (Walsh, 1988).

The analysis of the coding also revealed that a fair portion of the factors that were perceived to cause success in the organization were categorized as B, 'difficult to deal with'. The Chief Executive of the organization classified 46 per cent of the causes for success in this category, the Business Development Director 35 per cent and the Human Resources Manager 31 per cent. We explained to the participants that by this category we mean the things they know are going on in the organization and that they recognize as being important, but which tended to be left alone, or unmanaged. This could be because no one really knows how to manage or change the activity. Examples of statements that fell under the B category include: 'We can go on gut-feel; we don't take a commercial view'; 'We accept different modes of behaviour in different areas of the organization'; 'We write customers a ten-page letter instead of a two-page one'; 'The way managers and team leaders behave'.

comment

We would like to add that from the comments we received from the TMT it seems that the experience has been useful for them as a way of uncovering elements to their success factors that they do not know how to deal with, how to manage. They believed that the experience was an 'eye opener' as far as realizing that part of why their organization is successful is beyond their immediate management. If anything, this study revealed that researching tacit routines is indeed valuable and that it may be critical for a management team to understand better how their organization works in order to help the organization sustain advantage.

methodological lessons

Case A was our first attempt at eliciting tacit routines. We drew a number of lessons from the experience.

pre-causal mapping

- Self-Q is difficult to use. It is not a natural process, and we found that even if the participants understood the idea, they had problems asking questions spontaneously. We never reached any kind of flow in the interviews and very few factors were generated in comparison with the semi-structured interviews. This interview technique is also time consuming, as the participants need to be briefed in-depth. Considering these problems, we decided to abandon self-Q in our subsequent studies.
- The interviews are a useful 'ice-breaker' for the subsequent workshop. They allow the participants to know the researchers and the researchers to know better the business the participants operate in. They also allow the researchers to introduce the concept of tacit knowledge, routines and causal mapping. However, we believe that they are not essential. We think we could have managed without them. This would have meant spending more time before the mapping session to discuss the exercise and talk about the obvious reasons why the business is successful, and then start the exercise as such, rather than going straight into data from the interviews.

causal mapping

- Trust and confidence matter a lot during the mapping. Participants must be relaxed and feel confident and comfortable expressing themselves. They need to feel that they won't be made to feel a fool. Otherwise they are unlikely to air their intuitive understandings and feelings and more likely to concentrate on tangible aspects of their organization. Hence the exercise could be a waste of time, as only well-known and well-defined aspects of the organization would be discussed.
- As explained earlier, metaphors seem to be a powerful tool to capture tacit knowledge, but their capture is in practice troublesome. We discovered that they were very difficult indeed to capture 'live'. In the flow of the discussion during the mapping exercise they are difficult to spot, and if spotted they are difficult to analyse. We believe that it is still worth trying to capture them as they can be a powerful means of expression. The researcher needs to take note of them and come back to metaphoric language for further explanation. This can sometimes be done straightaway.
- This first study made us realize that while we need to keep the causal mapping session informal, insofar as we do not want to disturb the

flow of ideas, we also need to be directive. It is especially important to insist on individuals dealing with what they *currently* do. We also need to ensure that, if we want to explore success, participants stay focused on success. This is important. There was a tendency for some TMT members, first, to mention what they thought should be done in the organization rather than actual current or past behaviour, and, secondly, to delve into what was not working in the organization and what should be done to remedy that.

- We would like to stress that asking participants to think of particular examples, to tell a story, is a powerful trigger. Many constructs were revealed this way. Asking for examples pushes participants to explain what is really happening, it forces them to give details, and also it triggers other thoughts and stories and hence keeps 'the ball rolling'.

- We do not think, in retrospect, that the Decision Explorer software should be used 'live'. It is a technical aid, and we found in our case that it slowed the session, distracted the audience and researchers, and also that we were too dependent on the technology working perfectly. Any hitches were disruptive. We suggest instead the use of 'Post-it' notes and large sheets of paper. Notes are easy to use, they can be easily moved and should be reliable whatever the situation. We would advocate the use Decision Explorer for analysis and presentation of the maps. The maps can be keyed in after the session.

- We all found the mapping process very tiring. It went on for almost eight hours, and the participants were quite exhausted at the end. They did not expect this, as they thought that the exercise was going to be quite straightforward.

coding

- Another conclusion we drew from Case A is that it is important to keep the coding individual. From one manager to another there was a wide difference in the number of factors coded and which factors were coded as tacit. This highlights that tacitness is personal (Polanyi, 1962; Ravetz, 1971) and not always shared across a team of managers, even if they have been together for a long time.

- The previous point begs the question of whether the factors coded as tacit were really tacit. It seems likely that some of the factors were simply not known by respondents. This suggests that we may need to add a new category: 'routines you did not know about'. Not knowing that something is done is not the same as not realizing *that what is done matters*. We are returning here to the initial definition: tacit knowledge is about doing and not verbalizing what is done; it is not about 'knowing about' or reciprocally 'not knowing about' (Nonaka, 1991). Hence we need a coding category that would allow us to deal with ignorance, rather than tacitness.

- At the start of the analysis we encountered one problem we had not fully anticipated: a fair number of factors were not coded. This is something we need to address. There are various reasons why all the factors might not have been coded:

  - The coding categories proposed may not have been adequate. (This might mean we have to ask the respondent to tell us why he or she chose *not* to code a particular factor.)
  - Some of the participants simply refused to code the factors because they did not want to admit that they did not understand everything that is happening in the organization. To admit that may have been uncomfortable. This appears to be what happened in the case of one TMT member who refused to give the maps back and who commented that he had learnt nothing from the day, despite his displaying great enthusiasm to us at the end of the causal mapping session itself about the value of the exercise. Participants are justifiably afraid of losing some of their status. We now believe we have to insist that the exercise is a challenge, that there is no right or wrong. Our experience reinforces the view that a high degree of trust is required within the team, and between the team and researchers.
  - The lack of coding, as we learnt from speaking to the team afterwards, can also be due to the fact that it is time consuming.
  - Participants may also see little value in the coding *per se*. Creating categories is very much of an academic interest; it is of little concern for managers. They do not need to know what the nature of the constructs they have surfaced is. What matters to them is what generates success in their organization, why it is so and how it can be sustained and developed, and not who knew what and what type of routine it was. Perhaps another round of interviews would be more fruitful.

further insights into the causal mapping process

Following the session we discussed with the participants what they thought of the process and what they learnt from it. We also used mapping with groups of managers attending short courses. These managers engaged in a limited mapping exercise for their own firm and shared their insights and experiences of the technique in small groups. Their thoughts are also included in the following.

The benefits of the process of mapping organizational success, as seen by managers, are as follows:

- It fosters understanding; it gives insights into what is happening in the organization.
- It places value in the detail; it forces the respondents to deal with specifics.

- It highlights how difficult it is to know what causes success.
- It reveals the 'hot buttons', the key contributors to success.
- It helps in understanding the uniqueness of the organization; the success factors identified are mostly context-specific.
- It shows the hidden strengths of the organization.
- It crystallizes connectivity; it shows interrelationships.
- It highlights that responsibility for what causes advantage in organizations is not obvious.
- It is not attributable to one division, one function or one specific person.
- It shows the importance of people as the bases of success, not equipment, and so on.
- It focuses on the positive, which is not often done in organizations.
- It identifies critical processes that are unmanaged, that are not planned, that participants did not realize mattered and that sometimes are not well respected in the organization.
- It shows what the organization needs to keep doing.
- It gives new ways of discussing strategy, of discussing the business process.

difficulties that emerged from the process

Similarly we discussed problems that were perceived to be attached to the process. The main comments were as follows:

- Participants need to be honest for the session to be valuable.
- It is difficult to open up, it can be personally uncomfortable, because it makes some participants realize they don't know something potentially important. They may not want to admit it, because it shows that they are not in control.
- The map is very complex, there are a lot of interrelationships, and so it is difficult to focus, and to find which connections really matter. You may not see the wood for the trees.
- It is easy to get bogged down in the detail.
- It may get too complicated. Where do you end the map?
- It is a bit reductionist. It is all about the people involved in the process, hence it may be biased, too subjective. Maybe a lot of people need to be involved in identifying success factors.
- Who controls the mapping process? Is there a dominant personality? Is the map a representation of the view of one specific group or individual?
- Participants may have a preconceived idea of where the map is going to go.
- How do you take the process forward as a researcher? What do you do with the maps? How do you report back to the organization?

Considering the pros and cons, and considering that so far we have not come across any method that seems to be as suitable and as fruitful in eliciting tacit routines, we believe that it is a worthwhile effort to explore causal mapping further as a means of uncovering the idiosyncratic aspects of organizations.

TACIT AND UNMANAGED ROUTINES:
IMPLICATIONS FOR MANAGERS AND STRATEGIC MANAGEMENT

The results showed that among all the factors that cause success in an organization, some of them are often left 'unmanaged'. This certainly raises questions in terms of the fragility of competitive advantage and the role of managers and strategic management in sustaining advantage.

If tacit and unmanaged routines are important success factors in an organization, rather than, say, tangible resources, one can conclude that the main sources of differential value between firms may be at the margin of managerial understanding. A major implication of this is that sustainable competitive advantage based on those routines is most likely to be vulnerable. We can express several hypotheses about why this may be so.

One of the first reasons comes from the nature of tacit routines. Tacit routines generate causal ambiguity and, consequently, organizations may not know precisely which routines or set of routines are at the source of their advantage (Reed and DeFillipi, 1990). This means that managers may inadvertently change or destroy a fundamentally important routine. This appears to have happened in some organizations that embarked on a business process re-engineering programme or decided to downsize or delayer.

Another reason why competitive advantage may be vulnerable arises from the managers' disposition towards routines: they may not know that routines matter or they may not care about them. Top managers may pay scant attention to the detail of what is happening in the organization. They are encouraged and expected to address the 'big picture', the strategic agenda of the organization. They are not encouraged or expected to engage in the detail of the organization.

Two implications may flow from this. First, the detail of how things are done may not be recognized as having 'strategic value'. Details tend to be perceived by managers as peripheral or even trivial. They are seen as things that are of concern for the shop floor, which senior managers do not need to consider. The detailed running of the operation is usually not seen as being 'strategic' because strategy is not understood as looking into the routines of the organization, rather it is understood as 'analysis and strategy formulation'. In brief, this means that routines are of little concern for senior managers and, consequently, one can easily understand that superior performance based on routines may be vulnerable. If those routines are not perceived as being of value, they will not be protected and nurtured, and hence can easily be inadvertently annihilated. The consequence of this lack of attention to detail by managers is that what may make the difference between organizations is very much at the margin of managerial interest.

These points suggest that the role of the 'manager' and of the 'strategist' and her/his vocabulary has to change. Maybe one needs to start to understand 'strategy' as 'recognizing organization routines' and maybe the word 'manage' needs to be replaced by words like 'protect', 'nurture' and 'leverage' rather than 'control', 'direct', 'monitor' or 'plan' (Bartlett and Ghoshal, 1997). Indeed managers need to start understanding that details matter, that the details, the activities that create value, need to be nurtured and maybe leveraged to other parts of the organization where they could be of even greater value.

However, the deliberate search for tacit routines may in itself be dangerous, and that is where the paradox of tacit knowledge lies. If tacit routines become manageable, then they may become imitable, even if we can argue that the risk is limited because of the idiosyncrasy of tacit routines: that is, they work in one specific context with specific people, the interrelationships between them, their environment, the equipment, and so on. We believe the risk is worth taking if it means that managers can better understand what makes the firm successful today and have better insights into what to protect when undertaking change.

More broadly, the critical role that routines may play in the generation of organizational success leads us to question the role of the most 'rational' approaches to strategic management and strategic change. It is indeed an extremely arduous, if not impossible, task to plan and analyse something that one does not understand very well. Moreover, planning or controlling routines may destroy them as their informality may be part of what makes them successful. Such actions may also render them imitable and hence in turn nullify their effects.

It is also interesting that the Industrial Organization economics-based approach of strategic management appears to be of limited use to managers trying to find competitive advantage. This theoretic approach focuses on what is happening outside the firm to explain performance (Mosakowski, 1998). In contrast, the resource-based view of the firm concentrates on what is happening inside (Barney, 1995) and what is unique to each organization. If routines are a source of advantage, what causes success in an organization is idiosyncratic to each organization: that is, one cannot copy a 'recipe' (Spender, 1989) from one firm to another. 'Generic strategies' (Porter, 1980) become the equivalent of tangible resources. They are available to any organizations, and cannot lead to advantage.

Idiosyncrasy and the limitations of generic strategies may make us realize that, for example cost cutting is not a tactic that is going to have long-term benefits. Cost cutting is easy to understand, relatively easy to implement, it lends itself to measurement and control and as such is a tactic that managers like. Cost cutting does allow managers to avoid uncertainty and ambiguity, however cost cutting is a well-trodden 'recipe'. Everybody knows how to do it and hence it can be executed by all, with benefits achieved by most firms. In other words, cost cutting will only help an organization to stay in competition rather than help it move ahead of competition.

CONCLUSION

In this chapter we have suggested that organizational tacit knowledge could be understood as tacit routines. We have also suggested that there are different degrees of tacitness. Routines may be unarticulable because they are deeply ingrained in the unconscious; they may be only imperfectly articulable; or they may be articulable, if the researcher finds the right trigger to allow organization members to express them. We have suggested that, considering our lack of knowledge on tacit routines, managers and their facilitators should concentrate on those routines that are not yet articulated but could be, even if imperfectly.

We have proposed an avenue for empirical research that uses causal mapping as a useful method to elicit tacit routines. This technique allows participants to reflect on what they are doing. Continually asking managers what they do that causes success teaches them to uncover skills that they would not normally talk about. The discovery process is facilitated by encouraging participants to tell stories and employ metaphors.

We would also like to acknowledge some of the limitations of our research. Clearly, one cannot establish a unique and direct link between tacit routines and competitive advantage. There is no single factor that determines performance; tacit routines may be just one contribution of many. Moreover, our broad aim is to map organizational success, but it goes without saying that we can only map part of the routine processes that might cause success in organizations.

There are quite a few reasons why this is so. First, the maps reflect inputs by a certain group of managers. We can therefore only register the routines they are able to access. Ideally everybody in the organization should take part. Second, there is a time constraint: mapping a full organization would take weeks if not months. Outsider researchers are rarely granted such access. Third, the principal reason why tacit routines have been argued to be a source of sustainable advantage is that they are immobile and inimitable. By surfacing them, organizations take the risk of making tacit routines accessible and hence losing their advantage. However, this argument can be reversed by saying that if an organization is aware of the real source of its superiority, it can attempt to protect and nurture it.

Next steps are also problematic. Recognizing the existence of a phenomenon is just a first step in moving to a resource that can be better managed and replicated. Factors that are difficult to articulate can also be difficult to manage. In fact, do they need to be managed, or merely protected? Up to now, these factors had not been surfaced and hence nothing was consciously done to manage them. The primary goal of the workshops was to identify factors associated with success to make sure that they were not destroyed when implementing changes in the organization, or rather, to make sure that the organization was well aware of why it had so far been successful. Of course what has worked in the past is not guaranteed to work in the future. However, it is good to understand the real basis for current and past success before trying to establish a new one.

APPENDIX

Extracts from the map generated during the causal mapping session.

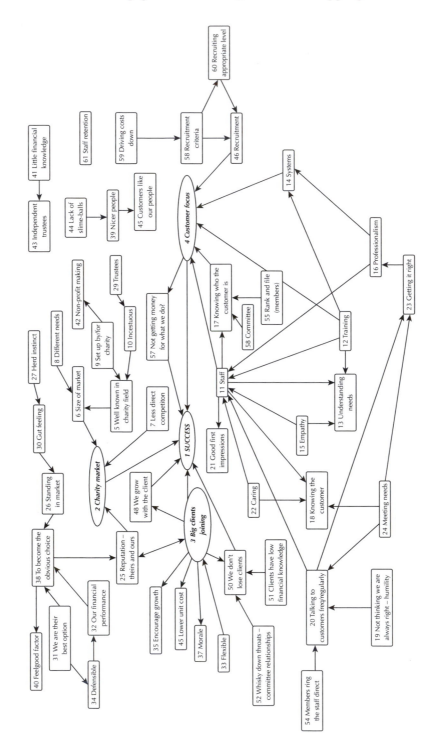

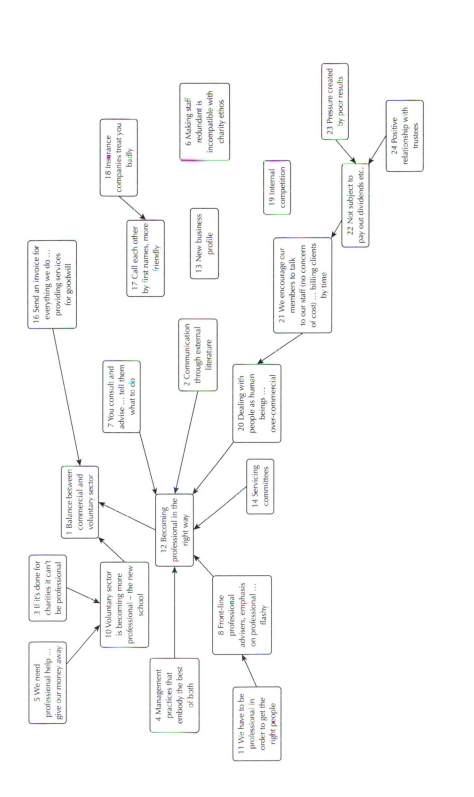

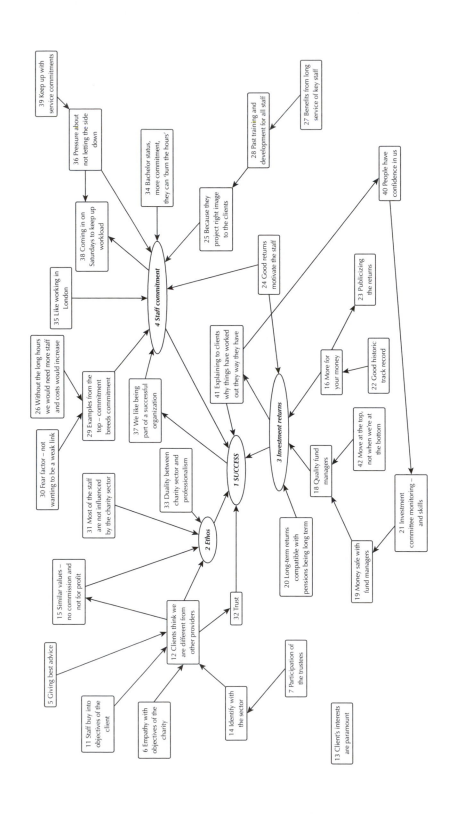

39 Keep up with service commitments

36 Pressure about not letting the side down

34 Bachelor status, more commitment, they can 'burn the hours'

28 Past training and development for all staff

27 Benefits from long service of key staff

38 Coming in on Saturdays to keep up workload

25 Because they project right image to the clients

40 People have confidence in us

35 Like working in London

24 Good returns motivate the staff

23 Publicizing the returns

4 Staff commitment

26 Without the long hours we would need more staff and costs would increase

29 Examples from the top – commitment breeds commitment

37 We like being part of a successful organization

41 Explaining to clients why things have worked out they way they have

16 More for your money

22 Good historic track record

30 Fear factor – not wanting to be a weak link

3 Investment returns

42 Move at the top, not when we're at the bottom

31 Most of the staff are not influenced by the charity sector

33 Duality between charity sector and professionalism

1 SUCCESS

18 Quality fund managers

15 Similar values – no commission and not for profit

2 Ethos

20 Long-term returns compatible with pensions being long term

19 Money safe with fund managers

21 Investment committee monitoring – and skills

5 Giving best advice

12 Clients think we are different from other providers

32 Trust

11 Staff buy into objectives of the client

7 Participation of the trustees

6 Empathy with objectives of the charity

14 Identify with the sector

13 Client's interests are paramount

NOTE

1. This methodology section is adopted from Ambrosini and Bowman (2001).

REFERENCES

Ambrosini, V. and Bowman, C. (1998) 'The dilemma of tacit knowledge: Tacit routines as a source of sustainable competitive advantage', paper presented at the British Academy of Management Conference, refereed track, Lancaster.

Ambrosini, V. and Bowman, C. (2001) 'Tacit knowledge: Suggestions for operationalization', *Journal of Management Studies*, November, 38(6): 811–829.

Axelrod, R.M. (ed.) (1976) *The Structure of Decision: Cognitive Maps of Political Elites*. Princeton NJ: Princeton University Press.

Barney, J.B. (1991) 'Firm resources and sustained competitive advantage', *Journal of Management*, 17 (1): 99–120.

Barney, J.B. (1995). 'Looking inside for competitive advantage', *Academy of Management Executive*, 9 (4): 49–61.

Bartlett, C.A. and Ghoshal, S. (1997) 'The myth of the generic manager: New personal competencies for new management roles', *California Management Review*, 40 (1): 92–119.

Boje, D.M. (1991a) 'The storytelling organization: A study of story performance in an office supply firm', *Administrative Science Quarterly*, 36: 106–126.

Boje, D.M. (1991b) 'Consulting and change in storytelling organisation', *Journal of Organizational Change Management*, 4 (3): 7–17.

Bougon, M.G. (1983) 'Uncovering cognitive maps: The self-Q technique', in G. Morgan (ed.), *Beyond Method*. Beverly Hills, CA: Sage. pp. 173–188.

Bougon, M., Weick, K. and Binkhorst, D. (1977) 'Cognitions in organizations: An analysis of the Utrecht jazz orchestra', *Administrative Science Quarterly*, 22: 606–639.

Bougon, M., Baird, N., Komocar, J.M. and Ross, W. (1989). Identifying strategic loops: The self-Q interviews. In A.S. Huff [ed.], *Managing strategic thought*. Chichester: Wiley. pp. 327–354.

Brown, J.S. and Dugruid, P. (1991) 'Organizational learning and communities-of-practice: Toward a unified view of working, learning and innovation', *Organization Science*, 2 (1): 40–57.

Cossette, P. and Audet, M. (1992) 'Mapping an idiosyncratic schema', *Journal of Management Studies*, 29 (3): 325–347.

Eden, C. (1992) 'On the nature of cognitive maps', *Journal of Management Studies*, 29 (3): 261–265.

Eden, C. and Ackermann, F. (1998) *Making Strategy: The Journey of Strategic Management*. London: Sage.

Eden, C., Jones, S., Sims, D. and Smithin, T. (1981) 'The intersubjectivity of issues and issues of intersubjectivity', *Journal of Management Studies*, 18 (1): 37–47.

Eden, C., Ackermann, F. and Cropper, S. (1992) 'The analysis of cause maps', *Journal of Management Studies*, 29 (3): 309–324.

Flanagan, J.C. (1954) 'The critical incident technique', *Psychological Bulletin*, 51: 327–358.

Fontana, P.A. and Frey, J.H. (1994) 'Interviewing: The art of science', in N.K. Denzin and Y.S. Lincoln (eds), *Handbook of Qualitative Research*, Thousand Oaks, CA: Sage. pp. 361–376.

Ford, J.M. and Wood, L.E. (1992) 'Structuring and documenting interactions with subject-matter experts', *Performance Improvement Quarterly*, 5 (1): 2–24.

Gharajedaghi, J. and Ackoff, R.L. (1994) 'Mechanisms, organisms and social systems', in H. Tsoukas (ed.), *New Thinking in Organizational Behaviour*. Oxford: Butterworth and Heinemann. pp. 25–39.

Grant, R.M. (1991) 'The resource-based theory of competitive advantage: Implications for strategy formulation', *California Management Review*, 33 (3): 114–135.

Grant, R.M. (1993) 'Organizational capabilities within a knowledge based view of the firm', paper presented at the annual meeting of the Academy of Management Conference, Atlanta, Georgia.

Grant, R.M. (1996) 'Towards a knowledge based theory of the firm', *Strategic Management Journal*, 17: 109–122.

Hansen, C.D. and Kahnweiler, W.M. (1993) 'Storytelling: An instrument for understanding the dynamics of corporate relationships', *Human Relations*, 46 (12): 1391–1409.

Hill, R.C. and Levenhagen, M. (1995) 'Metaphors and mental models: Sensemaking and sensegiving in innovative and entrepreneurial activities', *Journal of Management*, 21 (6): 1057–1074.

Huff, A.S. (1990) 'Mapping strategic thought', in A.S. Huff (ed.), *Mapping Strategic Thought*. Chichester: John Wiley. pp. 11–49.

Jenkins, M. (1995) 'Subjective strategies for small business growth: An evaluation of the causal maps of small independent retailers', unpublished PhD dissertation, Cranfield School of Management.

Langfield-Smith, K. (1992) 'Exploring the need for a shared cognitive map', *Journal of Management Studies*, 29 (3): 349–368.

Markóczy, L. and Goldberg, J. (1995) 'A method for eliciting and comparing causal maps', *Journal of Management*, 21 (2): 305–333.

Martin, J. (1982) 'Stories and scripts in organizational settings', in A.H. Hastorf and A.M. Isen (eds), *Cognitive Social Psychology*. New York: Elsevier. pp. 255–305.

Mosakowski, E. (1998) 'Managerial prescriptions under the resource-based view of strategy: The example of motivational techniques', *Strategic Management Journal*, 19 (12): 1169–1182.

Munby, H. (1986) 'Metaphor in the thinking of teachers: An exploratory study', *Journal of Curriculum Studies*, 18 (2): 197–209.

Nelson, R.E. and Mathews, K.M. (1991) 'Cause maps and social network analysis in organizational diagnosis', *Journal of Applied Behavioral Science*, 27: 379–397.

Nelson, R.R. and Winter, S.G. (1992) *An Evolutionary Theory of Economic Change*. Cambridge, MA: Belknap Press.

Nonaka, I. (1991) 'The knowledge-creating company', *Harvard Business Review*, 69 (6): 96–104.

Ortony, A. (1975) 'Why metaphors are necessary and not just nice', *Educational Theory*, 25 (1): 45–53.

Polanyi, M. (1962) *Personal Knowledge: Towards a Post-Critical Philosophy*. London: Routledge and Kegan Paul.

Porter, M.E. (1980) *Competitive Strategy: Techniques for Analysing Industries and Competitors*. New York: Free Press.

Ravetz, J.R. (1971) *Scientific Knowledge and Its Social Problems*. Oxford: Clarendon Press.

Reber, A.S. (1989) 'Implicit learning and tacit knowledge', *Journal of Experimental Psychology*, 118: 219–235.

Reed, R. and DeFillipi, R.J. (1990) 'Causal ambiguity, barriers to imitation and sustainable competitive advantage', *Academy of Management Review*, 15 (1): 88–102.

Sackmann, S. (1989) 'The role of metaphors in organization transformation', *Human Relations*, 42 (6): 463–485.

Schiffman, L.G. and Kanuk, L.L. (1991) *Consumer Behavior*. Englewood Cliffs, NJ: Prentice Hall.

Sheetz, S.D., Tegarden, D.P., Kozar, K.A. and Zigurs, I. (1994) 'A group support systems approach to cognitive mapping', *Journal of Management Information Systems*, 11 (1): 31–57.

Sobol, M.G. and Lei, D. (1994) 'Environment, manufacturing technology and embedded knowledge', *International Journal of Human Factors in Manufacturing*, 4 (2): 167–189.

Spender, J.C. (1989) *Industry Recipes: The Nature and Sources of Managerial Judgement*. Oxford: Blackwell.

Spender, J.C. (1996) 'Organizational knowledge, learning and memory: Three concepts in search of a theory', *Journal of Organizational Change Management*, 9 (1): 63–78.

Srivastava, S. and Barrett, F.J. (1988) 'The transforming nature of metaphors in group development: A study in group theory', *Human Relations*, 41 (1): 31–64.

Tsoukas, H. (1991) 'The missing link: A transformational view of metaphors in organizational science', *Academy of Management Review*, 16 (3): 566–585.

Walsh, J.P. (1988) 'Selectivity and selective perception: An investigation of managers' belief structures and information processing', *Academy of Management Journal*, 31 (4): 873–896.

Weick, K.E. and Bougon, M.G. (1986) 'Organizations as cognitive maps', in H.P. Sims (ed.), *The Thinking Organization*. San Fransisco: Jossey-Bass. pp. 125–135.

Wilkins, A.L. and Thompson, M.P. (1991) 'On getting the story crooked and straight', *Journal of Organizational Change Management*, 4 (3): 18–26.

2

LINKING CONTENT TO PROCESS

How Mental Models of the Customer Enhance the Creative Strategy Processes

Olaf G. Rughase

ABSTRACT

We at Panlogos Consulting and the University of Witten-Herdecke consider customers to be the most relevant source of information for guiding the strategy process. For this reason, we have developed an analytical tool – called SENSOR®[1] – that helps managers explore the 'world of the customer'. Using a storytelling approach, this instrument expands the insights of research findings from the Cognitive School. SENSOR®, introduced as a consulting tool in 1997, has already been used in numerous business applications in engineering, financial services, publishing, consulting, trading, personnel services and manufacturing firms. In this chapter we provide one case example as an indication of how this knowledge tool can be used to facilitate strategic change.

IDENTIFYING PITFALLS IN THE STRATEGIC LEARNING PROCESS

The Cognitive School in strategic management has gained importance in recent years with empirical findings and theory now widely recognized by both academics and practitioners. One important branch of the Cognitive School takes a subjective, interpretive view of strategy and information processing (e.g. Daft and Weick, 1984). Recently, this branch has become increasingly recognized in strategic management research (Kemmerer and Narayanan, 2000; Walsh, 1995).

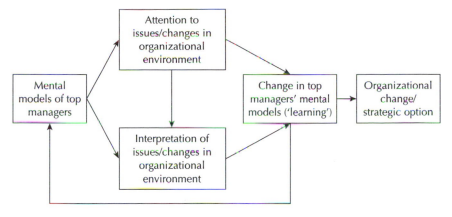

Figure 2.1   A cognitive model for organizational change

Cognitive researchers using an interpretive approach have developed a number of models to describe how managers and organizations deal with highly significant information. In 1983, Dutton et al. proposed that an interpretation (diagnosis) of strategic issues has three elements: inputs (such as cognitive maps, political interests or issue characteristics), process (recursiveness, retroductivity and heterarchy) and outcomes (such as assumptions, cause–effect understanding, predictive judgements).

Interpretation is the key factor that links changes in strategic action to changes in top managers' reading of the environment (Dutton and Jackson, 1987). Many researchers, including Barr et al. (1993), propose that organizational renewal depends on learning, which means additions to or changes of managers' mental models (see Figure 2.1). These mental models and interpretations may change in a recursive process, for example by redefinition of meanings after receiving additional information. As a result, the process of data (issue) interpretation is seen as less systematic and unidirectional than it is when derived from purely rationalistic schools (Dutton et al., 1983). Nevertheless, interpretation of strategic alternatives affects what commitments are made in organizations.

Despite theoretical and empirical contributions, there has been little effort to integrate analytical tools (e.g. environmental scanning, market research, competitor analysis) into a cognitive strategy model with the aim of combining content *and* process. For instance, Eden and Ackermann (1998) developed techniques to facilitate strategic conversations in order to enhance strategic action in organizations. But as with most techniques, they tend to stick to the 'inside-out' perspective. Van der Heijden (1996) similarly uses the scenario technique as a powerful learning tool for managers to enable strategy creation by creative interpretations. He refers mainly to external scenarios that are derived from managers' shared and agreed-upon mental models of the external world (the 'inside-out' perspective). A striking blind spot, theoretical as well as empirical, involves the inattention to customers as an 'outside' source of information.

How can it be sufficient only to learn within a defined group, within limited contexts? Learning in regard to strategy development is a discovery-driven process that definitely needs additional information (content) for an in-depth understanding of changes in the environment – both from inside (e.g. core competences) and from outside of the organization (e.g. trends, markets, environment). Change of a manager's mental model or an addition to it is very unlikely without any specific external or internal trigger of information (content).

At first glance, this challenge seems to be easy to cope with. But what exactly does trigger the learning process? As shown in Figure 2.2, top managers face many issues and symptoms. In almost every industry, typical symptoms or issues might be that:

- purchase patterns of customers become unpredictable;
- target groups are disappearing after a short period of time;
- competitive advantages are non-persistent;
- revenue decreases dramatically;
- a new competitor has changed the 'rules of the game', and so on.

In responding to these issues and symptoms, each manager draws on different personal experiences and knowledge, which in turn respond to a diversity of contexts that exist in the minds of the managers. This diversity of contexts generates different interpretations about issues, symptoms, events and situations. Multiple interpretations based on different contexts are then being discussed within the group of top managers (and beyond) by 'calibrating' their underlying assumptions. Do the contexts lead to different meanings? Are these contexts related to each other? This conversational 'calibration' process is not necessarily a formal one. 'Often much more important is the informal "learning" activity, consisting of unscheduled discussions, debate and conversation about strategic questions that goes on continuously at all levels in the organization' (van der Heijden, 1996: 273). Following this important process, top managers build consensus for strategic action based on an agreed in-depth understanding of issues and symptoms.

In practice this learning process harbours three major pitfalls. First, there is possibly *no diversity of contexts* among the top managers at all. That does not mean that homogeneous contexts are counter-productive for holding an appropriate strategic position in general, but homogeneity is unlikely to lead to a learning process or to strategic change. From our consulting experience, some currently successful companies get stuck in this situation for too long, as they tend to read the environment only through their (still) profitable products, processes and outcomes.

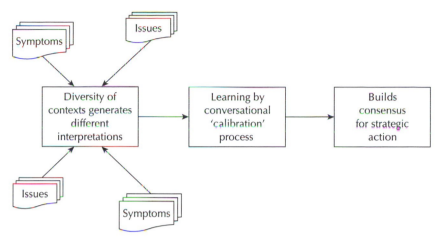

Figure 2.2 The strategy learning process

Second, there is perhaps a *lack of contexts* among the top managers. Very often managers are surprised by unmanageable consumers, who show unpredictable buying behaviour, and by societal demands, which were formerly unknown. At that very moment, managers lack appropriate contexts in order to achieve an in-depth understanding of the issues.

Third, top managers may have *no willingness or ability to drive a conversational 'calibration' process*. In fact, many discussions and debates are limited to an exchange of superficial statements. Accordingly, managers may persuade others, but do not convince them. On the contrary, a change-producing conversation is based on an exchange of contexts and related arguments in order to 'understand' your conversation partner and to find solutions and/or a level of common agreement. If managers don't calibrate their contexts, strategy implementation is likely to fail, because different interpretations (creating hidden agendas) allow inconsistent strategic action by the management team.

As contexts play a major role in the learning process, the Cognitive School typically views analytical tools with scepticism because many of these tools are still embedded in an orderly strategic planning framework. Planning models approach strategy development as a designed and conscious process that must be kept simple (e.g. Andrews, 1987; Eden and Ackermann, 1998). However, as revealed by many researchers, this traditional strategic planning concept has been proven to be inappropriate in times of hyper-competition (e.g. Brown and Eisenhardt, 1998; Mintzberg, 1994). Moreover, these analytical tools tend to provide lots of numbers (e.g. market share, turnover, customer satisfaction measures). The quantitive data tend to be seen as conclusions that present an 'objective' view of the world. Very often, this information excludes contexts that are actually needed.

THE CASE STUDY: A WHOLESALE FIRM

In order to elucidate the shortcomings of many efforts at strategy development, the following case study gives an example of a company that initially lacked contexts to understand the data that were available to them. The company is a German wholesale firm offering articles that can only be differentiated to a certain degree. At the time we were first involved with the firm it was faced with decreasing profit margins and disappearing target groups. The customer base included large to small businesses that needed the products for further processing. The competitive environment in this market can be described as an oligopoly – relatively constant over many years.

The top management team (TMT) were trapped in pitfall number two of the learning process previously described: they were surprised by symptoms and issues, and the team lacked appropriate contexts to make sense of them. In order to cope with these demanding issues the TMT wanted to (a) find new products and services for their existing target groups and (b) differentiate themselves from their competitors. As an increasing number of their customers were turning away, the TMT decided to begin with their existing and lost customers by initiating a customer satisfaction survey. The wholesale company interviewed about 2,500 representative customers with a standard questionnaire.

The results of this survey were extremely surprising to the TMT: 91.4 per cent of their customers were 'always satisfied' or 'mostly satisfied' with the company's performance; 7.7 per cent of the customers rated the performance 'variable'; and only 0.9 per cent were 'mostly unsatisfied'. On the contrary, as can be seen in Table 2.1, 35.87 per cent of the customers classified competitors 'much better' or 'better', 58.42 per cent classified the competitor's performance as 'even', and only 5.71 per cent considered competitors 'poor' compared to their current supplier. In addition to these irritating outcomes, the TMT received lots of ambiguous data about specific topics. For example, in some cases, the frequency of field service visits was too high. On the other hand, many customers were asking for additional service and sales support. As a result, the TMT ended up with more questions than they originally had – and were still lacking contexts to understand the issues highlighted by the survey.

There was one piece of apparent good news: the TMT were reassured that their company was often able to satisfy its customers. However, the data seemed to suggest that it no longer had any sustainable competitive advantages. Even more dramatic, conflicting information made a search for new products and services almost impossible for the TMT.

How can an analytical tool be created to support the mental process of strategy development and implementation under conditions like these? The purpose of the cooperation between Panlogos Consulting and the University of Witten-Herdecke is to develop analytical tools that reflect

TABLE 2.1   Customer satisfaction with competitors (per cent)

Competitor is ...	Much better	Better	Even	Poor	Very poor
Competitor A	1.63	11.41	21.74	1.09	0
Competitor B	1.63	10.86	15.76	2.17	0
Competitor C	0.54	3.53	8.42	1.36	0
Competitor D	0.83	2.72	8.15	0.82	0
Competitor E	0.27	2.45	4.35	0.27	0
Total	4.90	30.97	58.42	5.71	0

the insights of the research findings of the Cognitive School. The key seems to be to link content to process.

SENSOR®: A STORY-BASED TOOL
FOR STRATEGIC ANALYSIS

We developed an analytical approach that brings content into a strategy process by considering the interpretation and learning process. We consider the customer to be the most relevant source of information for strategy processes. Firms need to annex the 'thinking of the customer' with their own thinking to strategically position products and services in the future. Porter (1980) already claimed that uniqueness does not lead to differentiation unless it is valuable to the consumer. In other words: competitive advantages are only created in the minds of the customers. To develop innovative products and services, companies need to find what customers will value in the future. But there is a significant difference between what customers want and what they need. In fact, companies have to provide something that the customers would like to have, even though they never knew that they were looking for it; afterwards telling them (the companies) that they always wanted to have what they finally got (Liebl, 2000). For this reason, it is necessary to understand the 'world of the customer' in detail, in order to surprise customers with valuable products and services they never thought of before.

Of course, managers already have a mental model about customers and their 'world', according to their experiences with customers and other information. But from our experience, these models are likely to be incomplete. Managers tend to focus only on those parts of the 'world of the customer' that are directly linked with their existing business. In addition, the mental map is often inaccurate, because managers are often left to indirect information sources. In consequence, an analytical tool should give managers food for thought in order to change their mental models about the 'world of the customer' or enhance them with elements that they 'learn' from the customer. Our analytical approach – which is called

SENSOR® – helps managers to explore the 'world of the customer' by making patterns within this 'world' visible. In addition, it gives a deep understanding for customer behaviour and customer attitudes.

A critical element in acquiring an in-depth understanding of customers is the stories they tell (Liebl, 1999). Customers' positive and negative stories represent unique experiences with organizations, and thereby form an organization's strategic identity (Gabriel, 2000). Actually, there are many techniques that describe customers' perception and expectations, including buying criteria (Porter, 1980) and experiences of customer value (Woodruff, 1997). But single techniques are barely able to describe a complex competitive advantage based on a set of different activities, services, attributes or values that are in interaction with each other (Porter, 1996).

Storytelling, on the other hand, is the 'preferred sensemaking currency of human relationships' (Boje, 1991). Among customers and organizations it is an excellent candidate for connecting more specific techniques. Empirical evidence shows that information has significant impact on judgements and understanding when it is conveyed in the form of a narrative. For example, Pennington and Hastie's (1992) research focused on the role of stories in making juridical decisions. They found out that participants favoured the side (prosecution or defence) whose testimony was provided in story-order. The participants were also more confident of their decisions when the testimonies were in story-order than when they were not. Adaval and Wyer (1998) made the same findings with consumers who estimated the attractiveness of vacations described in two different travel brochures. Customers generally preferred a narrative form of events to a simple list of features. An example of using storytelling in strategic management is given by 3M (Shaw et al., 1998), where abstract business plans replaced by narrative texts further employees' comprehension and sustainable commitment.

Stories matter not only in information processing, but also in remembering (Bartlett, 1932). As Schank and Abelson (1995) claim, all of the important knowledge that people acquire and retain in memory is based on stories constructed around past experiences. What's more, the 'content of story memories depends on whether and how they are told to others, and these reconstituted memories form the basis of the individual's *remembered self*' (Schank and Abelson, 1995: 1). In other words, 'stories provide the basis for (a) comprehending new experiences; (b) making judgements and decisions about the persons, objects, and events to which the story refer; and (c) developing general attitudes and beliefs concerning these referents' (Adaval and Wyer, 1998: 208). Stories not only represent detailed descriptions of perceptions, they also elicit values as well as the identities of storytellers (Conway, 1996; Meyer, 1995; Taylor, 1996). Frames and meanings can be identified as well as the background of motivation and acting. This is particularly important in order to understand customers' perception in-depth. Further, stories are easy to receive from customers. It is easier by far for customers to tell stories than to transfer their experiences into the abstract value categories of questionnaires.

In order to absorb customers' stories, our analytical instrument, SENSOR®, contains qualitative elements that are heavily influenced by cognitive science. An in-depth interview (narrative/problem-oriented) represents the heart of the instrument (Patton, 1990; Witzel, 1985). This interview contains elements of ethnographic interviews (Spradley, 1979; Woodruff and Gardial, 1996) and of means–end theory (Claeys et al., 1995; Reynolds and Gutman, 1988).[2] During these interviews, customers are given the opportunity to express their experiences in their own words (stories). Within these stories, they talk about their perceptions, the way they use the product or service, general beliefs and especially *how* they perceived their experiences by describing related meanings and motivations.

For example, one customer of the wholesale firm we are using for our case study told us the following story (extract):

> Well … [*pause – 30 seconds*] Yes, I can remember a remarkable story! Just three months ago, we had severe problems with one of their products. We had – as always – a time-critical order from one of our best customers. Only two days before the day of delivery, we found out that 5 tons of the required material in stock was bad quality and that it was impossible to process it with our machines. These problems occur from time to time in our industry, but normally we immediately check the quality when we get the material. Now, we really had a problem! First of all, the whole production plan was in danger – our machines need to run 24 hours. But not only that, this customer especially is always very pig-headed when it comes to delays. My boss put me under enormous pressure to solve the problem. First thing I did, I called the wholesaler and explained the situation to him. You know, we are not a big customer and 5 tons is extremely difficult to get within one day, even for a professional wholesaler. What is there to say – they got it fixed in only one day. What a job! I can't tell you how happy I was. [*laughing*] Thanks to Mr Lange, who took care of it immediately, we didn't lose one of our best customers. I mean, the way he handled it was very professional; just a few questions and Mr Lange knew what to do. In my opinion, that really makes a difference and really surprised me. [*pause – 1 minute*] You know, talking is cheap in our industry – everybody promises anything. But what really counts is that you can rely on your supplier, who knows you and will help you in critical situations. Most of the wholesalers just want to sell, I mean, I understand that, but afterwards they don't care anymore. Losing a good customer leads us into a tough situation. However, on that particular evening I bought a bottle of champagne, went home a little bit early, and shared the rest of the evening with my family. [*pause – 15 seconds*] Hey, talking about wholesalers that brings me to another thing ….

Customers know many stories to tell that refer to experiences with certain products, services or companies. During these stories they change topics quickly, ask themselves questions (and give answers), or jump from beliefs to associations to other related stories. Normally, such an interview takes from 45 minutes up to one and a half hours. Of course, all interviewees are kept anonymous. There is no written guide or manual for the interviewer, who needs to be well trained and experienced in passive interview techniques, such as supportive or describing questions ('Did I understand you right ...?' or 'Could you describe to me what do you mean by ...?'), as the interviewee should ideally talk for over 95 per cent of the time. All interviews are tape-recorded, so the interviewer can focus on the customer and the development of the narrative instead of making notes.

There are two important indicators for the success of these non-standardized interviews. The first indicator is given by the customers themselves. After describing detailed perceptions, beliefs, complex associations, meanings and motivations, in many cases customers do not know what has happened during the talk. A common feedback from customers is: 'It was real fun and somehow interesting, but all I did was talk. There was no structure at all. I doubt that you will get anything concrete from that!' In fact, that is the best feedback we can get when aiming to reveal the unconscious by means of an ethnographic interview. The second indicator is given by the interviewers. After a certain amount of interviews, they tend to say: 'I am getting bored. Each time, I hear the same stories over and over again!' By then, you know that you are on the right track as patterns have already become visible.

ANALYSING STORY-BASED DATA

During evaluation, each qualitative interview is analysed by an inter-subjective, systematic and focused content analysis. During this process each story is deconstructed into its elements. The elements of the story are brought into relation to each other or into relation to other expressions, meanings and motivations that were amplified by the customer.

In order to achieve this, every tape-recorded interview is analysed three times by a specially trained analyst. The first time, the analyst tries to get a general understanding of the basic structure of the interview. The second time, the analyst begins to write down and draw all elements of the stories (in the words of the customer) on a blank sheet of paper using simple tools like a pencil and rubber. The analyst relates the elements to each other as the customer creates linkages during the interview. This session is very time-consuming, as the analyst needs constantly to evolve and change an expanding network. The third time, the analyst verifies all the elements and completes details which she/he might not have heard during the second session. In order to get intersubjective results, other analysts run random tests to compare results. Through this process, a net of stories is created for each customer eliciting the contexts of his or her 'worldview'.

Having such a validated network for each interview, the analysts begin to process a 'qualitative content analysis' (Mayring, 1997). When comparing these single networks to each other, by creating categories for similar or equivalent contexts, descriptions, meanings, attitudes or perceptions patterns become visible very quickly. Usually, only 15 to 25 interviews per segment are sufficient to reveal detailed patterns (Bushko and Raynor, 1997). These distinct patterns can be consolidated into detailed cognitive maps (Huff, 1990; Laukkanen, 1998). Not only are the elements within these cognitive maps important, but so are the relations between the elements. The relations depict the customer's associations and complex perception of unique values (e.g. competitive advantages). As a result, SENSOR® provides cognitive maps that are networks of stories within the 'world of the customer' – revealing customers' values, attitudes and reasons.

However, the instrument itself and its results are not sufficient to enhance the strategy process. In order to link content and process, the cognitive maps are not presented to the managers as traditional research outcomes in a unidirectional way. Considering the use of stories for better information processing, many examples and voice-recorded sequences from different interviews are used to give managers the experience of detecting patterns themselves during a workshop. Managers are first asked to make their own pattern construction of the voice-recorded sequences they have heard. Then, step by step, parts of the cognitive map that resulted from analysis are revealed. During this process, managers create a piecemeal understanding of linkages within the cognitive map. In the course of the workshop, the complete cognitive map is (re)constructed by the management. Moreover, they begin to tell stories of their own experiences with customers, which are in accordance with some of these linkages. By then, you know that the cognitive map's information has become useable knowledge for management.

By the end of the workshop, managers are able to 'read' and understand the cognitive maps in detail. Of course, many managers have heard a lot of stories and anecdotes from customers before, but redesigning these fragments and constructing linkages between them gives them a different perspective on the 'world of the customer'. This is exactly the kind of information (content) that triggers an interpretation and learning process.

In our consulting experience, the mental map of the customer is different from the mental map of the manager about the customer. Often the difference is considerable. We believe that important 'outside-in' information is lacking if a strategy process only relies on 'inside-out' perspectives. However, differences between the mental maps of the customer and the mental maps of managers about the customer immediately bring new creative ideas and new opportunities to the minds of managers. Our SENSOR® approach provides detailed information about the customer's cognition to enhance this learning process. The 'outside-in' perspective interacts with the 'inside-out' to create new knowledge from which new strategy can be generated.

DISCUSSION OF RESULTS AND THE STRATEGIC LEARNING PROCESS IN PRACTICE

To illustrate the outcomes of the analytical tool, we return to the case study. After accomplishing the customer satisfaction survey, the German wholesaler initiated a SENSOR® study in order to get contextual patterns from stories its customers tell. To get a selection of interviewees from its broad customer base, the company followed its existing segmentation by customer's company size and turnover. Thirty customers were chosen within three different segments, plus five non-customers. Among customers and non-customers, interviews were made with the chief executive or the head of purchasing department. As a result of the interviews, we acquired two distinct cognitive maps (patterns) from the stories customers told (Figures 2.3 and 2.4). In addition, non-customers told stories in the same contextual patterns as did customers. In consequence, there was no difference between customers and non-customers in regard to their existing 'worldviews'.

Usually cognitive maps are very complex. For the purpose of demonstration, the cognitive maps shown here are kept as simple as possible. For instance, all arrows in the maps are only cause–effect relations.[3] Some arrows are bold, indicating that these cause–effect relations were named by at least 85 per cent of all interviewees who created this contextual pattern. The first pattern (Figure 2.3) is based on narratives of 13 customers, and the second pattern (Figure 2.4) is derived from stories of 22 customers. In order to 'read' the map, follow single paths of connected elements. For example, in Figure 2.3 take 'quality of product' as a starting element. More than 85 per cent of the customers were telling stories around these core cause–effect relations to the effect of (simplified):

> The *quality of the product* is important, because we *don't* want to *have any problems* in the manufacturing process with the product due to our *machine-time optimization*. This optimization is necessary, because we always get *extremely time-critical orders* from our customers. You need to know that our *customers* are always under enormous *time pressure* to get the final product. Therefore, we need to provide *flexibility* for our customers.

In accordance with our experiences, the TMT of the German wholesaler had a far different mental map about their customers than SENSOR® revealed. Most importantly, the TMT suddenly recognized that there were two contextual patterns (Figure 2.3 and Figure 2.4) instead of one to be taken into account. The first contextual pattern (Figure 2.3) was well known to them. The customers in this pattern are under extreme competitive pressure. Perceiving their own business as highly standardized, this group of customers try to achieve cost leadership by machine-time optimization and low purchasing costs in order to survive. They mainly forced the wholesaler to lower prices – which raised the issue of decreasing profit margins.

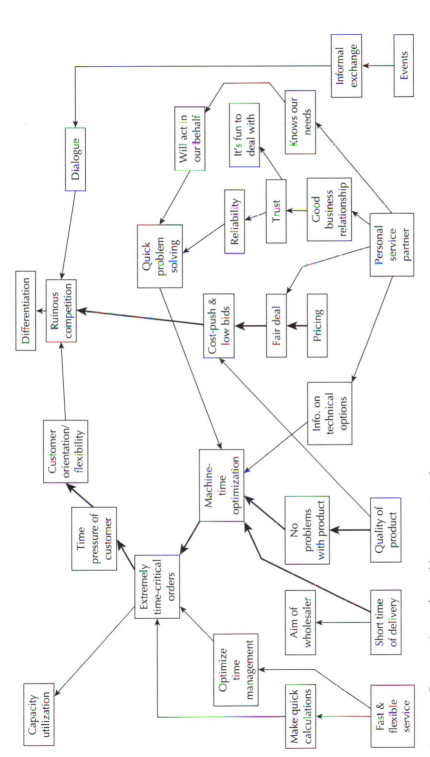

Figure 2.3 Customers' causal cognitive map: pattern I

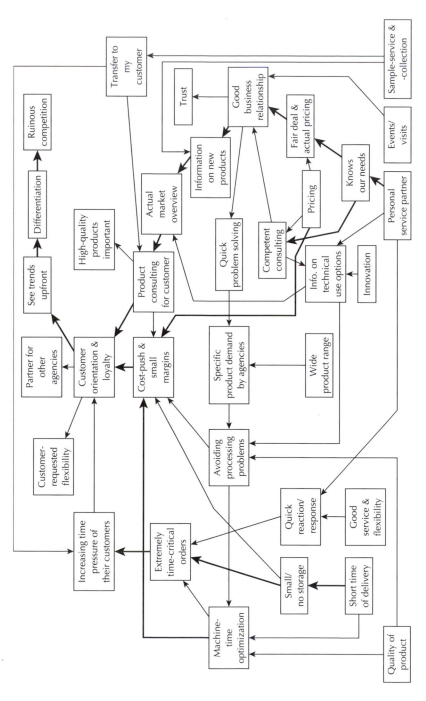

Figure 2.4 Customers' causal cognitive map: pattern II

Taking a closer look at the patterns, the TMT found out that a major part of their target group had not disappeared. In reality this target group had developed a new contextual pattern (Figure 2.4), which was formerly unknown to the TMT. The second group of customers perceive their business quite differently. As shown in the figure, they are trying to get out of ruinous competition by focusing on the use of innovative, high-quality (high-price) products of the wholesaler and of competitors. In consequence, these businesses reduced the turnover volume of standard products with their wholesalers. Before knowing these contexts, the TMT had the impression that many customers were just 'disappearing'.

During a full-day workshop, the TMT calibrated their interpretations of the contexts by using examples and stories, while referring to linkages in the cognitive maps. Our experience is captured directly by Barry and Elmes: 'From a practitioner's viewpoint, the narrativist stance can encourage people to explore strategic issues in more meaningful ways' (1997: 431).

An immediate indicator of the workshops' value was that by its conclusion the TMT were able to interpret every single piece of information from the customer satisfaction survey they had earlier found so difficult to understand. As mentioned, the frequency of field service visits was perceived as too high by customers. The first group of customers (Figure 2.3) needed fewer visits, because their interest was limited to pricing and time of delivery. They can get this information by phone or online. Only when problems arise do they require personal service to find a solution as quickly as possible. The second group of customers (Figure 2.4) need and ask for more visits, because their interest is focused on information about new, innovative products and actual market situations. Intense personal support would help them to improve their own service to end-users. In reality, however, current field service visits were limited to information about existing standard products so that even this group requested a reduction in the frequency of personal visits.

CONCLUSIONS FOR STRATEGIC REORIENTATION

The last task for the TMT was to build consensus for strategic action. They decided to give up their existing customer segmentation and replace it with the two segments that were detected by the storytelling approach. The decision was made to focus primarily on the second group of customers (Figure 2.4), because their knowledge-based core competences allowed them to provide lots of new services and products, improving customers' professional aims. Several reasons supported this decision, for example (a) higher profit margins, (b) no competitor in this field, (c) an increasing number of customers in the future, and (d) ruinous competition in the other customer group leading to a decreasing customer base.

This dramatic change in strategy was made possible by annexing the 'thinking of the customer' to the knowledge of the managers. The

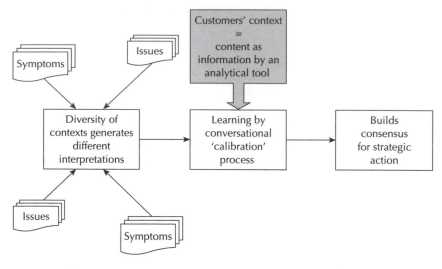

Figure 2.5   The strategy learning process: linking content to process

customers' contexts were a critical content in enhancing a creative strategy process (Figure 2.5). The wholesaler gained substantially more than it would have by, for instance, just hiring a sales consultant to increase sales power in traditional customer segments. It finally found a new sustainable strategic position.

In conclusion, bringing the content of analytical tools into a mental strategy process is necessary in order to combine 'inside-out' and 'outside-in' perspectives in strategic management. Analytical tools should be carefully adapted to the insights of the research findings of the Cognitive School. Experience has shown that in order to gain these contents, the same methodologies and techniques (such as cognitive mapping) can be used (see, e.g., Eden and Ackermann, 1998). These methodologies and techniques already consider the interpretive view of information processing and they are suitable to demonstrate differences of interpretations from external sources, compared to those of managers inside the organization, thus triggering the learning process by conversational calibration.

NOTES

I would like to thank Franz Liebl for his help in clarifying these ideas and his thoughtful comments on earlier drafts.

   1. Registered trademark in Germany.
   2. In specific cases the qualitative interview is followed by a quantitative questionnaire. Sometimes the management would like to verify certain competitive advantages that they think play a major role for the customer. The interviewer will then present only those questions to the interviewee that were not covered in the qualitative part of the interview. Using

a special form of questioning based on Kano (1984) and Berger et al. (1993), these results indicate whether the described performance would be perceived as a 'must-be' or as an 'attractive' element. The quantitative results should only be interpreted together with the results of the qualitative interviews.

3. Owing to the purpose of the SENSOR® study, the linkages may also describe non-directive associations (A reminds me of B), time-order of elements (after A I make B) or relations (A is better/worse than B).

REFERENCES

Adaval, R. and Wyer, R.S. (1998) 'The role of narratives in consumer information process-ing', *Journal of Consumer Psychology*, 7 (3): 207–245.

Andrews, K.R. (1987) *The Concept of Corporate Strategy*. (3rd edn). Homewood, IL: Irwin.

Barr, P.S., Stimpert J.L. and Huff, A.S. (1993) 'Cognitive change, strategic action, and organi-zational renewal', *Strategic Management Journal*, 13 (special issue: summer): 15–36.

Barry, D. and Elmes, M. (1997) 'Strategy retold: Toward a narrative view of strategic dis-course', *Academy of Management Review*, 22 (2): 429–452.

Bartlett, F.C. (1932) *Remembering: A Study in Experimental and Social Psychology*. New York: Macmillan.

Berger, R.B., Boger, D., Bolster, C., Burchill, G., DuMouchel, W., Pouliot, F., Richter, R., Rubinoff, A., Shen, D., Timko, M. and Walden, D. (1993) 'Kano's methods for under-standing customer-defined quality', *Hinshitsu (Quality): The Journal of the Japanese Society for Quality Control*, Fall: 3–35.

Boje, D.M. (1991) 'The storytelling organization: A study of story performance in an office-supply firm', *Administrative Science Quarterly*, 36: 106–126.

Brown, S.L. and Eisenhardt, K.M. (1998) *Competing on the Edge: Strategy as Structured Chaos*. Boston: Harvard Business School Press.

Bushko, D. and Raynor, M. (1997) 'Consulting's future, game theory, and storytelling', *Journal of Management Consulting*, 9 (4): 3–6.

Claeys, C., Swinnen, A. and van den Abeele, P. (1995) 'Consumers' means–ends chains for 'think' and 'feel' products', *International Journal of Research in Marketing*, 12 (3): 193–208.

Conway, M.A. (1996) 'Autobiographical memory', in E.L. Bjork and R.A. Bjork (eds), *Memory*. San Diego: Academic Press. pp. 165–194.

Daft, R.L. and Weick, K.E. (1984) 'Toward a model of organizations as interpretation systems', *Academy of Management Review*, 9 (2): 284–295.

Dutton, J.E. and Jackson, S.E. (1987) 'Categorizing strategic issues: Links to organization action', *Academy of Management Review*, 12 (1): 76–90.

Dutton, J.E., Fahey, L. and Narayanan, V.K. (1983) 'Toward understanding strategic issue diagnosis', *Strategic Management Journal*, 4: 307–323.

Eden, C. and Ackermann, F. (1998) *Making Strategy: The Journey of Strategic Management*. London: Sage.

Gabriel, Y. (2000) *Storytelling in Organizations: Facts, Fictions, and Fantasies*. New York: Oxford University Press.

Huff, A.S. (ed.) (1990) *Mapping Strategic Thought*. Chichester: Wiley.

Kano, N. (1984) 'Miryoku-teki hinshitsu to atarimae hinshitsu', *Hinshitsu (Quality): The Journal of the Japanese Society for Quality Control*, 14 (2): 39–48.

Kemmerer, B. and Narayanan, V.K. (2000) 'A cognitive perspective on strategic management: Contributions and implications', paper presented at Strategic Management Society (SMS) 20th Annual International Conference, Vancouver, Canada.

Laukkanen, M. (1998) 'Conducting causal mapping research: Opportunities and challenges', in C. Eden and J.-C. Spender (eds), *Managerial and Organizational Cognition*. London: Sage. pp. 168–191.

Liebl, F. (1999) 'Was ist schon einmalig?', *econy*, 2: 116–117.

Liebl, F. (2000) *Der Schock des Neuen: Entstehung und Management von Issues und Trends*. Munich: Gerling.

Mayring, P. (1997) *Qualitative Inhaltsanalyse: Grundlagen und Techniken*. 6th edn. Weinheim: Deutscher Studien Verlag.

Meyer, J.C. (1995) 'Tell me a story: Eliciting organizational values from narratives', *Communication Quarterly*, 43 (2): 210–224.

Mintzberg, H. (1994) *The Rise and Fall of Strategic Planning*. New York: Free Press.

Patton, M.Q. (1990) *Qualitative Evaluation and Research Methods*. 2nd edn. Newbury Park, CA: Sage.

Pennington, N. and Hastie, R. (1992) 'Explaining the evidence: Testing the story model for juror decision making', *Journal of Personality and Social Psychology*, 62: 189–206.

Porter, M.E. (1980) *Competitive Strategy: Techniques for Analyzing Industries and Competitors*. New York: Free Press.

Porter, M.E. (1996) 'What is strategy?', *Harvard Business Review*, November/December: 61–78.

Reynolds, T.J. and Gutman, J. (1988) 'Laddering theory, method, analysis and interpretation', *Journal of Advertising Research*, 28 (1): 11–31.

Schank, R.C. and Abelson, R.P. (1995) 'Knowledge and memory: The real story', in R.S. Wyer (ed.), *Advances in Social Cognition: Vol. 8 Knowledge and Memory: The Real Story*. Hillsdale, NJ: Lawrence Erlbaum Associates. pp. 1–85.

Shaw, G., Brown, R. and Bromiley, P. (1998) 'Strategic stories: How 3M is rewriting business planning', *Harvard Business Review*, May/June: 41–50.

Spradley, J.P. (1979) *The Ethnographic Interview*. New York: Holt, Reinhart, Winston.

Taylor, D. (1996) *The Healing Power of Stories: Creating Yourself Through the Stories of Your Life*. New York: Gill & Macmillan.

van der Heijden, K. (1996) *Scenarios: The Art of Strategic Conversation*. Chichester: Wiley.

Walsh, J.P. (1995) 'Managerial and organizational cognition: Notes from a trip down memory lane', *Organization Science*, 6: 280–321.

Witzel, A. (1985) 'Das problemzentrierte interview', in G. Jüttemann (ed.), *Qualitative Forschung in der Psychologie: Grundfragen, Verfahrensweisen, Anwendungsfehler*. Weinheim: Beltz.

Woodruff, R.B. (1997) 'Customer value: The next source for competitive advantage', *Journal of the Academy of Marketing Science*, 25 (2): 139–153.

Woodruff, R.B. and Gardial, S.F. (1996) *Know Your Customer: New Approaches to Customer Value and Satisfaction*. Cambridge, MA: Blackwell Business.

3

ENABLING STRATEGIC METAPHOR IN CONVERSATION

A Technique of Cognitive Sculpting for Explicating Knowledge

John R. Doyle and **David Sims**

ABSTRACT

The chapter describes our way of operationalizing the concept of metaphor for organizational intervention and research purposes. It describes cognitive sculpting, a technique we have developed to enable people to build physical metaphors for whatever they are trying to talk about (Sims and Doyle, 1995). The technique has turned out to be effective both for the expression of existing metaphor and for the production of new metaphor. We discuss possible reasons for this effectiveness and suggest some implications for surfacing and generating organizational knowledge. In particular, we are concerned with how attention seems to be differently directed when discussion centres on a cognitive sculpture, and how aspects of knowledge that are normally less honoured in a propositional, entirely verbal and more digital conversation may come into play when a sculpture is involved. We raise some of the questions that seem to us to be begged by our work so far, and conclude by considering the potential of facilitating strategic knowledge via sculpting.

We think in metaphors. This is true whether we are talking about thinking that is abstract and creative, or about thinking that might appear mundane and commonplace. At either of these extremes, and everywhere between, our knowledge is built on metaphor and analogy. For example, the idea that knowledge could be 'built' on something is metaphorical, though you may not have registered it as such when you read the previous sentence. It is noticeable how often metaphorical expression arises from primitive, concrete thinking using body-kinaesthetic and image schemas to represent what we take to be our knowledge of the world, both inner and outer.

The word metaphor is derived from the Greek 'to carry' or 'transfer'. A colleague tells me that in Greece the word for 'house removals' derives from the same root. This image is reminiscent both of Monty Python (removal men with a highbrow interest in metaphor) and of homunculi in the head, for in the same way that household goods are carried from one place to another, in metaphor a set of symbolic relationships is 'carried' from one place (technically known as the vehicle or, in research on analogy, the source domain) to another (the topic, or the target domain when applied to analogy). On arrival, this set of symbolic relationships collects a meaning. (These terms are themselves a set of mixed metaphors: topics, vehicles, domains, sources, targets and arrival.)

THREE KINDS OF METAPHOR

In this chapter it will be helpful to distinguish three kinds of metaphor. In the first, the metaphor consists of a main theme with elaborations. TIME IS MONEY is the main theme of a metaphor with which we are all familiar. But since people have found the metaphor useful, we have a collection of related metaphors around this same theme – these are the elaborations. Money can be spent, wasted, saved; so too can time. Here metaphor is much more than the metaphor heading (TIME IS MONEY); metaphor transfers many of the uses associated with the source domain to the target domain. We do not mean, by the isolation of a main theme, as distinct from elaborations of the theme, that the former necessarily pre-dates the latter in the evolution of a metaphor. Rather, we mean that the main theme acts as a kind of category heading for the elaborations, and thus allows the basis of the metaphor to be more explicitly seen in the language.

The uses that do or don't get transferred via metaphor implicitly define those aspects of the source domain that are relevant to the target domain. For instance, the TIME IS MONEY metaphor makes no use of the physical appearance of money, or the fact that different countries have different currencies. The metaphor presumably originates in the fact that people receive money for time worked. It is then a short step to equate time not working with money not earned, which is one of the connotations of the statement 'Time is money'. The identification of money and time is very close in this metaphor: we would not think twice if someone said 'three hours is £60'. It is worth reflecting that there is an underlying idea here: time is a resource, and within our culture most resources are compared with each other in terms of one relatively quantifiable and convertible resource: money. Hence the phrase 'Time is money' may be more a convenient statement of an underlying theme than a root theme in itself.

Another kind of metaphor is the one-shot metaphor, for instance when a metaphor has just been coined for the first time (e.g. TIME IS A COMPUTER PROGRAM). The new metaphor would probably first appear in a single elaboration that picked out the particular sense in which the metaphor is to be understood (e.g. 'Time's algorithm will determine which of us is right'). If the metaphor were to catch on, we might find elaborations similar to the above (e.g. NIGHT IS DOWN-TIME) appearing in common usage. But as we shall see, many metaphors are just one-shot metaphors.

The third category of metaphor is when there appears to be a family resemblance of metaphors that lack an explicit statement of the main theme. Uses such as:

- The prize giving is only a short way off.
- My partner's birthday is close to my own.
- In the distant past…
- What length of time will it take?

These, and many more related usages, seem to be examples of a metaphor TIME IS DISTANCE, which is not an explicit metaphor in its own right in English. It is this third kind of metaphor that Lakoff and Johnson drew attention to in their book *Metaphors We Live By* (1980), and it consists of elaborations without a statement of the main theme. Because these metaphors are not grounded in an explicit main metaphor that holds them together, we could equally well describe them as implicit metaphors.

METAPHOR, ANALOGY AND SIMILE

Metaphor is sometimes contrasted with analogy (e.g. Miller, 1979; Tsoukas, 1991) in that the latter focuses on the relation between objects (A is to B as X is to Y), and that analogy may be made between objects within the same domain. (E.g. it would be perfectly acceptable to draw the analogy between the toes' relationship to their feet and the fingers' relationship to their hands, where both source and target are clearly from the same domain – parts of the body.) Metaphor, on the other hand, applies only when the domains are quite different (e.g. *Spies are a nation's ears*). An additional way that metaphor differs from analogy is that it is purely a linguistic device, though it clearly implies the existence of sophisticated cognitive models, to make the cross-domain transfer of meaning possible.

On the other hand, simile, which is also a linguistic device, differs from metaphor in such an apparently insignificant way that many commentators have sought to conflate metaphor with simile as cognitively equivalent (Ortony, 1975). At a surface level simile is signalled by the words 'is like'. To use a simile such as 'Time is like money' differs from metaphor, first, because the verbal formula 'is like' draws attention to the figurative. With simile we expect the speaker to carry on and tell us exactly how time is like money.

Second, simile differs from metaphor (most notably from the third kind of metaphor) in the degree of awareness invoked in the hearer about the figurative nature of the utterance. By contrast, implicit metaphors seem to go undetected by most speakers, because they are so taken for granted. Whereas the simile emphasizes that meaning is being transferred, metaphor hides this fact. In asserting that A *is* B, rather than merely *like* B, a fusion of meanings is invited. The linguistic conventions surrounding metaphor also make it possible for elaborations to be used quite naturally. If A is B, then we may talk about A in much the same way we would talk about B. In this way metaphor is allowed to become embedded in our language.

Analogy, simile and metaphor are all primarily cognitive devices, and the last two are realized in characteristic language conventions. Symbols are also not to be taken literally, but usually convey their content in a more overtly affective, rather than cognitive, manner, and are more likely to be visual objects or enacted ceremony than linguistic devices. The relation between the symbol and what it symbolizes may be totally arbitrary, as in a country's flag, or an exclamation mark. Saluting the flag or desecrating the flag are both gestures to the essential meaning behind the symbol.

THE UBIQUITY OF METAPHOR

The various particular metaphors scattered throughout this chapter are intended to give an impression of the prevalence of metaphor. In addition, we now report on two studies that shed further light on this matter.

In a review of the neglect shown by cognitive psychology to figurative language, Pollio et al. note that 'speakers as varied as politicians engaging in public rhetoric, to patients and therapists engaging in psychotherapy, produce an average of about 1.5 novel and 3.4 clichéd figures of speech per 100 words spoken' (1990: 143). (In our typology of metaphors, above, only the one-shot metaphors could *not* be described as clichéd.) They go on to estimate that speakers will produce an average of 15 million or so figurative uses in a lifetime.

Martin (1994) used text from the *Wall Street Journal* (*WSJ*), which in some ways must be closer to 'business talk' than Pollio et al.'s corpus. He found overall frequencies consistent with Pollio's for the incidence of figurative language: 4.3 metaphors per 100 words of text. That is approximately one metaphor per sentence.

But Martin also analysed the metaphors into clusters (themes), and found that over half of all metaphor instances were accounted for by just five metaphor themes. By far the most popular metaphor in the *WSJ* is

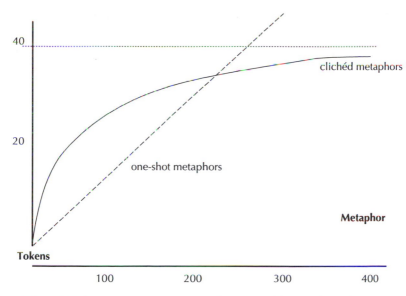

Figure 3.1   Metaphor types (instances) as a function of the number of metaphor tokens met for one-shot metaphors (dashed line) and clichéd metaphors (continuous line). NB: The sequence AABCBCA has three types (A, B, C) but seven tokens

what Martin calls 'Value-as-location/value-change-as-movement', which might occur in phrases such as *house prices have fallen sharply, the index finished down 12.3 at 2078.4*, and *turbulent trading on the floor*. This elaborated metaphor, by itself, accounted for a quarter of all uses.

Martin further divided the clusters into those that occurred once, and those that occurred more than once. (This latter cluster are presumably 'clichéd', in Pollio et al.'s terminology.) We have schematically reproduced his findings in Figure 3.1. The number of clichéd metaphors in the *WSJ* seems to asymptote at about 40. However, the rate of production of one-shot metaphors increased constantly with the amount of text met.

METAPHOR TYPES

While the study was limited in the amount of text it analysed, it is interesting to speculate that metaphors can be divided into two distinct classes. For any given area of discourse we suggest there are a relatively small number of metaphors that account for most of the instances – for the *WSJ* it accounted for nearly 90 per cent – and that provide the basic means of talking about the domain. These metaphors are part of the background that goes largely unnoticed, as evidenced by the fact that the five most popular metaphors were of the third kind listed above, namely elaborations without explicit heading.

On the other hand, people continue to coin new metaphors at a rate that does not seem to decline, and that enables them to talk creatively. By their novel connecting of disparate domains, these, presumably, are the kinds of metaphors we would most likely notice as metaphors.

METAPHOR AND SCIENTIFIC THINKING

In his 'Catechism of Cliché', Myles na Gopaleen (perhaps better known as Flann O'Brien, author of *The Third Policeman*) makes fun of the apparently arbitrary nature of prepositions in English.

> What can one do with fierce resistance, especially in Russia?
> Offer it.
> But if one puts fierce resistance, in what direction does one put it?
> Up.
> In what direction does the meeting break in disorder?
> Up.
> In what direction should I shut?
> Up. (1997)

Yet the use of prepositions in English is not as arbitrary as might seem from this examples. Lakoff and Johnson (1980) suggest that the metaphor MORE IS UP (as indicated by: a *rise* in salary, a *higher* rate of taxation, *lower* inflation) may be based in the everyday experience of adding more to a pile or container, and observing that the level of the pile goes up. They list a dozen or so other metaphors centred on the concept of verticality (e.g. HAPPY IS UP, DISORDER IS UP, CONSCIOUS IS UP, etc.), each plausibly grounded in physical experience.

Along with a renewed interest in metaphor has gone a parallel debate about its usefulness (or lack of) in theorizing within the social sciences. The traditional view (e.g. Miller, 1976; Pinder and Bourgeois, 1982) sees metaphor as, at best, a useful starting point, but to be eliminated as soon as possible in favour of scientific thinking. The other view is that metaphor is inescapable.

We take the Lakoffian view that all thinking, whether scientific thinking or not, is inextricably bound up with figurative thinking. Scientific thinking merely takes the basic 'metaphors we live by' more seriously, more systematically, and perhaps more literally(!), than does non-scientific thinking. As an example, we have already described two metaphors TIME IS DISTANCE and MORE IS UP. Consider their appearance as labels on a graph (Figure 3.2), typical of the conventions adopted in scientific work. It is clear that the conventions implied by this labelling are only a refinement of the two metaphors TIME IS DISTANCE (*x*-axis) and MORE IS UP (*y*-axis), and not an escape from them.

Not only is metaphor fundamental to thought in general, but a particular facility with analogy may have its own advantages. In a series of studies

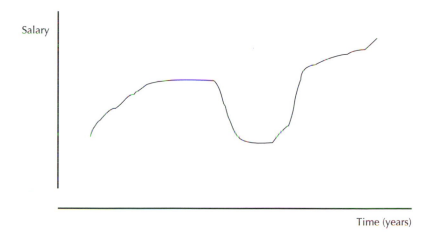

Salary

Time (years)

Figure 3.2   Illustrating that typical scientific conventions are often based on metaphors. Someone's salary has gone UP, then DOWN, then UP again (just as the line does)

Klemp and McClelland (1986) used peer evaluation to identify 'outstanding managers' in a number of organizations. They found that one of the features that distinguished the outstanding manager from the merely very good manager (these were all managers who by most people's standards had succeeded) was their ability to use unusual analogies.

This may be connected with the notion of analogue and digital thinking (Watzlawick et al., 1967). Their distinction is probably best understood by thinking of analogue and digital watches. The analogue communicates in a way that is somehow recognizable as a picture of that which it communicates. The digital communicates without the use of such pictures. The use of gesture, posture, voice tone and diagrams in most forms of complex communication bear testimony to the idea that most people value analogue communication, and that this still applies when the material being communicated is scientific or technical. Metaphor is essentially an extension of Watzlawick's analogue communication to the level of ideas, and Klemp and McLelland could as well have referred to 'metaphor' as 'analogy' in their work.

THE IMPORTANCE OF THE PHYSICAL

Why is the use of metaphor so important in our thinking? It seems that there are understandings that we can form on the basis of our physical relationships with objects that cannot be formed without making use of these relationships. We can maybe understand more of the diversity of thinking and why people might need metaphor to convey their meaning if we consider one of the more extreme groups of metaphor makers, dancers, talking about their work. Isadora Duncan said 'If I could tell you what it is, I would not have danced it' – an elegant summary of the sentiments of metaphor makers everywhere, but all the more convincing from a dancer because it is so clearly 'grounded' in the physical world of the body. Gardner quotes the dancer Martha Graham as saying: 'I have often remarked on the extreme difficulty of having any kind of conversation with most dancers which has any kind of logical cohesiveness – their minds just jump around (maybe like my body) – the logic – such as it is – occurs on the level of motor activity' (1993: 225). By extension, the variety of forms of expression that we engage in may come from a deep level, and the restriction of thinking to abstract, digital, ungrounded language may disempower most of what Gardner refers to as our 'multiple intelligences'.

IMAGE SCHEMAS

The theoretical perspective that links the literature on metaphor with our technique of cognitive sculpting (Sims and Doyle, 1995) is the role of image schemas. We have already seen the conceptually basic notion of UP/DOWN in metaphors that connected UP with increase and DOWN with decrease. This would be an example of an image schema. Mandler (1992) describes image schemas as condensed redescriptions of perceptual (and to a lesser extent motor) processes. How many such image schemas do humans typically have? Martin (1994) estimates a few hundred, Lakoff (1989) describes a handful, and Johnson (1987) gives a 'partial list' of thirty or so, some of which he analyses in depth. They include: container, linkage, part–whole, blockage, balance, near–far, superimposition. It is not appropriate to go through the whole list; instead we shall briefly describe the first two examples to give an idea of how image schemas and metaphor may be related.

Containers fall into three types: those that typically contain us (such as rooms, caves); those that typically do not contain us (such as cups, bags); and our own bodies (clearly a special case). The main features of a container are that it has an inside, an outside and a boundary, so that objects can be *in* or *out of* the container, and can *come into* the container if we are also in it or *go into* it if we are not, and so on. The boundary prevents free movement of objects.

'Container' is used in very many metaphors. Here are some examples of the metaphor MIND IS A CONTAINER:

- I have an idea *in* mind.
- I try to put thoughts of failure right *out of* mind.
- It suddenly *came into* my mind.
- He is *out of* his mind.

These examples also rely on the related metaphor IDEAS ARE OBJECTS (*Where did you pick that idea up from?*; *I dropped the idea into the conversation*; *We bounced ideas off each other*; *He stole her best ideas*) and the source-to-target mapping between 'in mind' = conscious of and 'out of mind' = not conscious of, as in the saying: 'out of sight, out of mind'.[1]

Our second example of an image schema is *link*. A link connects two objects that are a distance apart. The connection is not rigid, so that if I move one object the other is likely to move, but not necessarily. Therefore linkage, or connection, is often used to denote causality or relationship between two entities, where the nature of the relationship is somewhat imprecise:

- He was *linked* with the Watergate scandal wasn't he?
- Smoking has been *linked* to lung cancer.
- Surely there is some *connection* between the two events.

Look again at the first two sentences after the heading 'Image Schemas' on page 70. Metaphors *are* ubiquitous. We suggest that metaphors based on the link schema will be popular with all those who are concerned with the non-obvious relationships between events, things or people. This would be true for academics, but also for the creators of business deals, the managers of complex enterprises, and physicians working with poorly understood diseases in the complexity of the human body, among others.

COGNITIVE SCULPTING

We have argued that much of our knowledge is based in (or on?) metaphor, and much of our metaphorical thinking is based in or on our representation of objects and their relationships with each other and with ourselves. The facility to think metaphorically or analogically is highly valued in many fields.

If metaphor is underpinned by an abstracted understanding of objects and our bodily relationship with them, then it may make sense to use objects explicitly to facilitate the use of metaphor and analogy. As we have argued, this is the essence of metaphor: we wish to talk about an abstract, complex and difficult-to-understand domain, where common meanings are not necessarily shared; instead of doing so directly we talk about the complex domain *as if* we were talking about a concrete, simple and well-understood domain, where common meanings *are* shared. Such well-understood domains are typically connected with everyday experience in the world of bodies and objects – an understanding we built up in the first few years of our lives. These understandings are extremely schematic representations of simple relationships between objects: things can be near or far away, things can be inside a container or not, things can balance or not, and so on (these are image schemas). If one wants to think about a complex issue, one will need to enable more of one's abilities in thinking to be used, and this will necessitate the use of metaphor.

It is obvious that it is easier to do complicated arithmetic on paper than in your head, or that the minutes of a meeting are a more faithful record than our own memories, or that a complex argument is easier to follow and review if it is written down rather than spoken. In an analogous manner we suggest it will be helpful to have an externalized representation of people's metaphors to work with. Similarly, it is often helpful for these externalized representations to attempt to capture the metaphoric rather than the literal; the drawn map is often more helpful to the driver than a list of instructions, even if both are only hazy memories. Even for numerical calculations, a considerable proportion of the world's population is happier with the metaphoric abacus than the literal pencil and paper. Our suggestion for an effective externalized, metaphoric representation of knowledge is *cognitive sculpting*, which we now describe.

In cognitive sculpting, people are involved in a conversation or discussion about issues that may be complex or emotionally charged – certainly difficult to talk about in one way or another. We have a box (toy box) to hand that contains a collection of objects that the participants are free to lay out on a table in front of them, ostensibly to illustrate what they are saying. Participants are also free to adjust the arrangement of the objects in order to make a point, or even to remove objects from the table altogether. It can be seen that we mean 'sculpture' in a very broad, modern sense. The sculpture is shared by all participants, who may adjust any part of it.

Let us imagine a session in full swing. Three people sit around a 2′ × 4′ coffee table which at first glance already has a number of objects haphazardly strewn across it. A closer inspection reveals a small wooden person looking out from inside an upturned glass tumbler. The wooden person has a piece of string tied around its foot; the string is trapped under the tumbler, so that the person is pressed up against the glass.

A light-bulb rests on the title page of a report. (The report is actually a highly controversial internal report). A piece of electrical wire almost reaches the bulb, but not quite. Tracing it back we see that it is trapped under a large block of wood. On top of the wood sits a chess piece – not a white knight but a black one. Elsewhere drawing pins surround a crowd of pawns. A bunch of keys sit on a chair at some distance from the table. A credit card and a calling card from a management consultant are propped against the keys. This is the state of the sculpture so far. It has been gradually added to, subtracted from and otherwise altered. Here is a reconstructed snippet of a conversation among three managers that takes place about and through the sculpture (see Figure 3.3).

X   I get into this helpless state of mind [*points to the upturned tumbler*], so that I can't do anything about the problem. I'm tied so closely to this state of

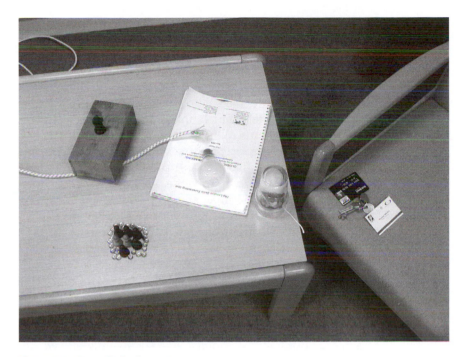

Figure 3.3   Example Sculpture A

mind that I don't even see the glass. I mean, most of the time I don't even see that it is a state of mind I'm in. If I weren't so tied to it, I could at least look away.

Y   But have you ever thought that your state of mind also protects you? If you removed the tumbler – got into a different state of mind – you might wander around and get trapped under this weight of authority [*taps the block of wood*]. Or worse…

X   Yes, but someone has to connect up the bulb to the wiring and show people what this report is really about.

Z   But if you're not careful you might find it's you that makes the circuit and get fried for your pains!

Y   No. FIRED!

[*Laughter. One of the three rummages around and comes up with a knife and fork, which he places on either side of the light-bulb, as if setting the table for a meal. More laughter.*]

Months later these three cognitive sculptors still share the joke (insight) about 'making the circuit'.

This interchange is, of course, highly condensed and selective. It is none the less quite typical of the kind of conversation that takes place. Meanings are negotiated, and the symbolic world of objects is a fertile arena for metaphor, symbolism and reconceptions, which sometimes emerge as jokes. By acknowledging the element of risk (fried, fired, or just trapped under the weight of authority) in being a visionary (i.e. outside the glass), and by enacting in this small world some of the visionary processes (i.e. re-visions of interpretation), the participants are legitimizing to each other (particularly in the use of good-natured humour) a larger visionary activity. Since one of the most effective blocks to creativity is self-censorship for fear of ridicule, the group is signalling, with an immediacy that words alone could rarely match, that it *will* support creativity/ strategic thinking/change, and thus making it more likely to happen.

One may keep tangible records of cognitive sculpting by video-taping the session. In the absence of a video a couple of instant photographs to chart the progress of the sculpture (certainly one photograph at the end of the session), together with an audio-tape, should be sufficient to capture most of the significant turns of the conversation, and to enable the participants to re-create some of the insights and the knowledge from the time of the conversation.

Choice of Objects

We have participated in, and facilitated, cognitive sculpting sessions in which we had access to our toy box, and also in sessions in which we did not have such access, and instead made use of objects in the immediate locale. We have compared groups working with objects from the toy box with groups working from a box made up of a similar number of objects of similar size gathered from the surfaces of our offices with little consideration for their symbolic qualities, and we have found that having a carefully selected set of objects on hand is a benefit. In any case the toy box can always be supplemented by local objects, which, like the knife and fork in the above sketch, may come to have particular significance.

Our toy box is continually changing through both additions and losses as objects are reclaimed for their 'proper' use. But there is a stable core of objects that we have come to know and that our research participants seem to love.

One criterion of choice was to select objects that seemed to support ready (perhaps even stereotypical) associations. In this category we find:

- light-bulb   –   inspiration, an idea;
- dice   –   chance, fate;
- passport   –   credentials, identity;
- chess pieces   –   especially pawn (obvious), king (boss) and knight (unpredictable);
- chain   –   lack of freedom, shackles;
- tangled string   –   a knotty problem, etc.;
- key   –   solution;
- pair of glasses   –   seeing something, insight;
- torch batteries   –   energy, power;

- a credit card — a variety of financial associations;
- farmyard animals — (pig, cow, bull, sheep): the usual;
- toy people — people;
- calculator — computer, the accountant;
- red bill — itself, debt, arrears of various kinds.

There were also objects that seem less stereotypical, but are none the less constrained:

- a ruler/tape-measure;
- a spirit-level;
- old coinage;
- foreign coinage;
- stone;
- block of wood (circa 10 cm × 15 cm × 25 cm);
- a small picture frame.

As an example of the greater variety in meanings that these objects have supported, the block of wood was often used to represent a blockage (stereotypical); but if placed upright it also came to signify a pedestal (see Figure 3.4), and, especially for the authors, a pedestal that people could get trapped on top of, which is the down-side of succeeding at something when you find afterwards that you didn't really want to succeed at it (see Figure 3.5). Also, because of its relative size and weight, it sometimes represented things that were threatening, and could crush; again, some-times it represented a vantage point to look down from.

We also chose some objects that would defy neat categorization, and, à la Rorschach, support a variety of different projections:

- metal lattice-like grill;
- driftwood;
- a clump of melted metal rescued from a fire.

Curiously, each were often stereotyped as 'something amorphous, hard to understand'. Some objects were chosen to support the representation of vigorous action within the sculpture:

- hammer;
- hacksaw;
- scissors;
- screwdriver, etc.

Their very presence in our toy box may have suggested that these tools were the least useful in someone's toolbox – and if he or she did not want to use them, why should the participants want to use them? Whether for this reason, or because the vigorous actions these tools denote just do not

Figure 3.4   Example Sculpture B

'fit' with the style of cognitive sculpting, these objects have been used less frequently by participants than we originally anticipated.

Finally, although many image schemas can be represented by their relationship to other objects in the sculpture (e.g. near–far, contact, part–whole, centre–periphery, blockage, etc.), others benefited from purposefully ensuring enough props to support that schema. Examples are:

- Link   –   chain, string, electrical wiring;
- Container   –   cup, tin with lid (so things could be hidden and/or kept), perspex box (see-through).

Other schemas that we have not properly supported but could, and clearly should, are:

- Balance   –   scales, or a set of pieces that could readily be assembled into a balance;
- Attraction   –   magnet, sloping surface.

We do believe that some schemas are more problematic. Source–path–goal, for instance, so strongly implies movement as to make natural

Figure 3.5   Example Sculpture C

expression within cognitive sculpting difficult. Perhaps we should add a diagrammatic arrow? Catapult? Similarly, there are a number of other objects that would prove useful additions to the toy box (often because participants told us so):

- magnifying glass   –   looking closer;
- mirror   –   seeing something about yourself;
- egg timer   –   limited time ('time running out');
- plug   –   being 'plugged in';
- phone   –   communication.

ATTENTION

The overt objective of cognitive sculpting, as described above, is to support metaphoric and symbolic productions in conversation. In the next two sections we investigate additional aspects of conversations that use cognitive sculpting that may not be shared by normal conversation. In this section we deal with attentional effects.

First, cognitive sculpting does support a different view of the conversation, quite literally. The general course of the conversation may be comprehended by all participants at-a-glance from the objects on the table. Thus what was said half an hour ago can exert much more of an influence on the present flow of ideas and expression than in a normal conversation – the extant sculpture has a mnemonic effect. We have noticed what we call the long loop of conversations: a theme may be abandoned and the objects associated with it left untouched only to return much later. We have noticed that the accompanying feeling, rather than one of exasperation ('I have the feeling we have been going round in circles'), is more like a musical theme returning at the right moment. Like the musical theme, ideas in cognitive sculpting do not often literally repeat; they are more likely to return varied and developed, or at least to be repeated with a different interpretive emphasis. One might say that cognitive sculpting tends to turn the normal serial conversation into more of a parallel one; the wandering conversation into a focused one.

The second attentional effect concerns social self-presentation. In normal conversation one spends a lot of time and mental energy in maintaining one's social self to others. One tries to maintain the right amount of eye-contact, one inspects the other participants' faces for reactions to one's words, one works to signal the right expression to their words. Part of the reason for this activity is the lack of anything else to focus on. In cognitive sculpting there *is* something else to focus on. Conversation takes place through the sculpture. One speaks about the sculpture as much as to anyone in particular. The other participants' attention also tends to be focused on the hands that are doing the manipulating, rather than the lips that are doing the talking, or the eyes that are the 'windows to the soul' of the other.

We suggest that there are two freedoms won by this deflection of attention from the private face to the public sculpture. The first of these is, to use a crude information-processing metaphor, that the effort of social self-presentation is diverted, and one has spare capacity to think about what is being said and done. Anyone who has given a lecture that was not going down well will be aware of the release felt by putting a slide on. I am no longer talking to you the audience, I am talking about it, the slide, and your attention can be on it rather than on my face and my persona. For the time that the slide is up we share a common focus of attention; our gaze is united, and we are not confronting each other.

Of course, in cognitive sculpting the participants do not always focus on the sculpture. Sometimes the conversation will revert to normal for a while. The participants will talk over the top of the sculpture, perhaps sitting back away from the table, with a change of posture. One notices this as a distinct change in 'footing' to the conversation (Goffman, 1981).

The second way in which focusing on the objects and not the person frees the participants has to do with the attribution process. It is known from attribution research (e.g. summarized in Hewstone and Antarki, 1988, or Ross and Nisbett, 1991) that if a speaker is made perceptually salient in a conversation (e.g. by allowing the observers to see the speaker's face full on rather than seeing the speaker from behind), observers will make more dispositional attributions to that person's words (espoused opinions). That is, the observers will believe the speaker's words are a reflection of her personality rather than a reflection of the situation she finds herself in. The less perceptually salient the speaker, the more her words are attributed to the situation, and not to her personality.

In cognitive sculpting, we have argued, each speaker is made less perceptually salient since the participants focus on the sculpture rather than the speaker. This means we should expect fewer dispositional attributions. In other words, as a participant in a cognitive sculpting session, I will not imagine that the words you say necessarily reflect enduring attitudes, opinions or traits, and so I will not try to hold you to your words. Also, we have found that a cognitive sculpture on a table seems to permit people to have the kind of conversation they might have in an art gallery – a sharing of interested comments in response to a physical object, which is often very different from the purportedly rational, linear comments of purposeful discussion, where you are expected to 'get it right'. If the speaker becomes aware that she is not required fully to believe everything she says, then we can see that the conditions are right for the kind of 'let's imagine' conversation that would otherwise have to take place in a remote conditional or subjunctive tense, and thus be difficult to sustain. In cognitive sculpting one can try out meanings in ways that would not normally be sanctioned.

A final benefit is that associating ideas with objects is an effective mnemonic technique that was known to the ancient Greeks (Norman, 1976), which entails remembering things by associating them with memory of a physical arrangement. Normally people who want to practise the technique have to make a conscious effort to do so. However, in cognitive sculpting it comes as a by-product of the process itself. There is no extra effort needed to make the conversation live longer in memory, for the ideas have already been associated with objects.

SPEAKING WITH THE MUTE HAND

In the previous section we outlined some ways in which conversations using cognitive sculpting might differ from normal conversations. In this section we substantiate the hypothesis that cognitive sculpting gives a medium of expression to kinds of knowledge that are often difficult to access and communicate.

The human brain is divided into two hemispheres. Each hemisphere of the brain is specialized to deal with different kinds of material (Springer and Deutsch, 1989). In the normal right-handed person, the left hemisphere (which also controls the right hand) specializes in logic, language, things analytical. Right-handed lawyers, who need to argue cases eloquently and rigorously, have well-developed left hemispheres. The right hemisphere (which controls the left hand) specializes in things spatial, analogical and metaphorical. Sculptors (at least those who are right-handed) have well-developed right hemispheres. The right hemisphere is often described as mute, in that it does not have any control of speech. People who suffer a stroke to the right hemisphere (identified by loss of control of the left side of the body) rarely lose the ability to speak. If damage is to the left hemisphere, speech loss can be severe or total.

In the normal person the two hemispheres are connected by a massive bundle of fibres called the corpus callosum, which allows information to flow between centres. Despite this connexion, it appears that communication between the hemispheres is not always unimpeded. For instance, in *The Language of Change*, Watzlawick (1978) describes 'blockages' to the functioning of the right hemisphere, and methods to remove the blockages. His general approach may be described as blocking the left hemisphere (e.g. through paradox) in order to free up the right hemisphere.

Cognitive sculpting, on the other hand, relies on the co-operative, rather than competitive, use of both right and left hemispheres. Our approach is to facilitate the flow of information across the corpus callosum in both directions. At the start of a cognitive sculpting session we could say that the participant allows the right hemisphere the indulgence of some kind of visual-metaphorical 'commentary' on the conversation. But as the session progresses a different source of control sometimes takes over, namely the mute right hemisphere. After all, spatial relationship is the right hemisphere's forte. It is also possible that, outside of our normal locus of control and awareness, the right hemisphere arranges messages in the sculpture (perhaps the 'accidental' but apposite juxtaposition of two objects) that the speaking self incorporates into *its* commentary. Any facilitator of cognitive sculpting should recognize the different feel that the functioning of each hemisphere has, and understand that it is balance and interplay between the hemispheres, rather than overthrow of one by the other, that is desired.

Replaying the videos of a cognitive sculpting session, one notices the pace of speech slowing, presumably as the left hemisphere begins to give up some control and allows the apparently accidental work of the right hemisphere to influence the arrangement and contemplation of the objects. The pauses lengthen; each move, as in a game of chess, seems to require long, silent thought. Then, quite suddenly, the mode may shift as ordinary commentary again takes over.

Insofar as we experience blockage of direct communication across the corpus callosum, cognitive sculpting works to enhance the co-operation of both hemispheres (speech and space) in exploring complexity through the medium of an external display to which they can both contribute.

UNANSWERED QUESTIONS

We have presented cognitive sculpting as a method of helping people to think through issues, for example strategic questions for their organization. In other words, our orientation has been to produce something that is helpful to the participants in the immediate term in the progress of their discussions. We also believe that participants take longer-term gains of other kinds away with them. At a simple level there is the experience, and the symbolism that the participants share, which can resurface months later. This may be especially significant in the discussion of strategic issues, which have enough longevity for the development of this new, metaphoric, visually referenced language to be of real significance. We also believe that participants who engage in cognitive sculpting are able to internalize the process, even to the extent of performing it in an imaginary world of objects in their heads, thus enriching their metaphorizing. After all, it is not always possible, or indeed appropriate, to pull out a bag of *objets trouvés* and get to work. Those who have had explicit experience of cognitive sculpting might also be more willing to illustrate a point in an otherwise normal conversation with reference to objects that come to hand (a kind of 'barefoot' cognitive sculpting). Or since some people do this kind of thinking with physical props naturally, once exposed to cognitive sculpting, someone who had previously been unreceptive might be more willing to enter into his or her 'object world'.

Another question is whether there are 'good' and 'bad' cognitive sculptors. Certainly some participants take to the process more readily than others. Why should this be? Can we distinguish them in advance?

A further question is whether what we have described is sculpture, theatre or something else. Perhaps we should be pleased, rather than worried, that cognitive sculpting is more than merely cognitive, and includes dramatic, symbolic, social and sometimes entirely whimsical elements. But labels *are* important. Our name for the technique does justice to its model-building aspect, but insufficient justice to the dramatic element. The term 'cognitive sculpting' sets up expectations in the participants of how they 'should' behave, which might be different had we adopted alternative terms such as 'dramatic sculpting', 'cognitive theatre', or 'strategic knowledge sculpting'. Part of our orientation is that the objects do remain and are important, hence the focus on the sculpture. The objects as configured at any time in a session are meant to represent a significant part of the conversation to date, whereas in drama the props are just props that come and go with the scenes.

We also wonder whether the metaphor of 'sculpture' emphasizes stability rather than change, statics rather than dynamics. Sculptures tend to be relatively enduring, to imply something that expresses itself without movement. How different would the participants' experience have been if we had worked instead on 'kinetic cognitive sculpture', and emphasized movement rather than the stasis of objects?

Having a tangible representation of the session is particularly useful if two or more groups have worked independently on a common theme. At the end of the session each group can explain the genesis of their sculpture, and receive questions and other comments. For those who have experienced an 'art crit' – the session in which students and staff at an art college gather round to discuss the work of different students or groups of students – the resulting ruminations have something of the same atmosphere. Long silences are tolerated that give time for mature, and probably non-verbal, reflection.

A final question is to what extent the two authors have developed an idiom of usage that is peculiar to themselves. For instance, other users of cognitive sculpting have found an important role for animals in the toy box, which we have not emphasized. As one example, the psychologist Tina Kotzé was working on team development with a multi-racial group in South Africa, but had failed to get the energy and commitment she usually got with other groups. Ready to give up, she decided to have one more try, this time with cognitive sculpting. Because of the place of animals (as she saw it) in the life and metaphors of South Africa's indigenous peoples, she introduced quite a lot of animals into her toy box. They had a superb session, with blacks enthusing about what they could demonstrate with the animals; whites enjoying being shown a different way of symbolizing; blacks enjoying the fact that whites were interested in their symbolic language; and none of the issues about who was comfortable in which language, or who was literate, which had plagued them previously.

In a second example from another user, the executive team of a UK company were introduced to cognitive sculpting. Early on they characterized one board member, a rather tall, aloof man who happened to be absent that day, as a giraffe. In the course of the afternoon the giraffe came to take on a number of interconnected meanings. The absent member aspect of the giraffe came to represent the outsider (also their more serious selves), looking in over the fence at some very strange goings-on. Yet the giraffe itself is rather droll, with its ridiculously long neck. So it also came to represent the entire wacky nature of what they were doing that afternoon, a lightness in their dealings with each other that they wanted to encourage. The giraffe was inside each of them, as both creator and observer of the alternative behaviours.

For a third example, Baocheng Li has used cognitive sculpting in his work with managers in a major international airline in discussing issues to do with the environmental effects of the airline. His work has been different from most of what we have described in that he has been working with individual sculptors, expressing themselves to themselves and to him as interviewer, rather than in a group. Also, he describes the sculptures we have been talking about so far as 'complex', while he has been working with what he calls 'simple' sculptures. Participants in his work have been picking up an object from the toy box, handling it, and commenting on the issues he wanted to know about, i.e., they play with just one or two objects. However, the effect of having a selection of toys to pick up and use, and of being able to hold them and play with them while talking, seems to have been very similar to the effects we have talked about with more complex structures and with groups of participants.

The first two examples illustrate that the right symbol(s) at the right moment can have a dramatic effect in resolving opposites. In the former, the opposites were inter-personal (the black/white divide, compounded by differences in language, literacy and status). In the latter, the opposites were intra-personal (expected *serious* behaviour/desired *fun* behaviour). The third example illustrates a way in which the core ideas of cognitive sculpting can be the basis for many different forms of practice in permitting people to talk about issues, often strategic ones, where they might have had no way of articulating their knowledge without the sculpting devices. Also, for all three examples, some of the knowledge that they articulated may not have pre-existed their words; the knowledge may be new learning that only arose in the interaction between the hands and the object(s) during play.

COGNITIVE SCULPTING AND STRATEGIC KNOWLEDGE

We have discussed the rationale and practice of cognitive sculpting. We and the others mentioned in the chapter who have used the technique have done so without differentiating the kind of knowledge being expressed or created. Having said this, Kotzé would not have taken the trouble to enable lengthy conversations through the metaphors of animals if the issues under discussion had not been seen as of major significance. Similarly, Li's conversations with airline managers would not have been worth having had not both he and they seen the issues of a matter of environmental strategy.

Strategic thinking consists of preparing for an uncertain future by rehearsing a deep reflection on the present and on ways in which the future might unfold from the present. It consists not so much of making plans as of rehearsing and getting to know the current world and anticipated worlds so as to be able to respond as a skilled and competent improviser in whatever world then unfolds. In working circumstances where there is always something more urgent than reflection, how might one achieve this?

We suggest that cognitive sculpting is uniquely appropriate here. Our futures are controlled by the metaphors we bring to them, and we have argued that cognitive sculpting is a good way of explicating and developing metaphor. The development of a shared metaphoric language within a group may enable such explication and development of metaphor to happen at a group level, thus preparing the whole group for the necessary discourse to respond to new situations with shared strategic knowledge.

They will have formed metaphors together and built up a history of discussion through them, which will prepare them particularly well for responding opportunistically together to unanticipated events in a more or less anticipated world.

The approach implies that strategic knowledge is not solely cognitive, but employs what Gardner (1993) would term 'other intelligences'. However, no-one who has ever felt the urge to pace up and down, to move their hands, or to draw a diagram while contemplating strategic issues would dispute this; cognitive sculpting is perhaps practised more widely than is often acknowledged, and part of our purpose in this chapter is to argue for making more purposeful and explicit use of something that is often used less deliberately and formally.

We have argued that metaphor is a way of talking about complex domains in terms of simpler, better understood domains, which are usually concrete. We have described and related our technique of cognitive sculpting to metaphor, via the intermediate concept of image schemas. We have examined work on the separation of functions within the cerebral hemispheres, and related the activity of cognitive sculpting to them. We suggest that cognitive sculpting is a device to help integrate the two hemispheres, and to bring the metaphorical into a profitable dialogue with the analytical. It also brings a more playful aspect to discussions that can get too serious for their own good, and enable people to articulate futures otherwise unspoken.

NOTE

1. It is interesting to note the change in sense when the related metaphor is PERSONS ARE OBJECTS, and hence could be contained by their minds, or alternatively be regarded as dangerously unbounded when they are 'out of their mind'.

REFERENCES

Gardner, H. (1993) *Frames of Mind*. 2nd edn. London: Fontana.

Goffman, E. (1981) *Forms of Talk*. Oxford: Blackwell.

Hewstone, M. and Antarki, C. (1988) 'Attribution theory and social explanation', in M. Hewstone, W. Stroebe, J.-P. Codol and G.M. Stephenson (eds), *Introduction to Social Psychology*. Oxford: Blackwell.

Johnson, M. (1987) *The Body in the Mind*. Chicago: University of Chicago Press.

Klemp, G.O. and McClelland, D.C. (1986) 'What characterizes intelligent functioning among senior managers?' in R.J. Sternberg and R.K. Wagner (eds), *Practical Intelligence*. Cambridge: Cambridge University Press.

Lakoff, G. (1989) 'Some empirical results about the nature of concept', *Mind and Language*, 4: 103–129.

Lakoff, G. and Johnson, M. (1980) *Metaphors We Live By*. Chicago: University of Chicago Press.

Mandler, J. (1992) 'How to build a baby: II. Conceptual primitives', *Psychological Review*, 99: 587–604.

Martin, J.H. (1994) 'MetaBank: A knowledge-base of metaphoric language conventions', *Computational Intelligence*, 10 (2): 134–149.

Miller, G.A. (1979) 'Images and models, similes and metaphors', in A. Ortony (ed.), *Metaphor and Thought*. Cambridge: Cambridge University Press.

Miller, R.N. (1976) 'The dubious case for metaphors in educational writing', *Educational Theory*, 26: 174–181.

na Gopaleen, M. (1977) *The Best of Myles*. London: Picador.

Norman, D.A. (1976) *Memory and Attention*. New York: Wiley.

Ortony, A. (1975) 'Why metaphors are necessary and not just nice', *Educational Theory*, 25: 45–53.

Pinder, C.C. and Bourgeois, V.W. (1982) 'Controlling tropes in administrative science', *Administrative Science Quarterly*, 27: 641–652.

Pollio, H.R., Smith, M.K. and Pollio, M.R. (1990) 'Figurative language and cognitive psychology', *Language and Cognitive Processes*, 5 (2): 141–167.

Ross, L. and Nisbett, R.E. (1991) *The Person and the Situation: Perspectives of Social Psychology*. New York: McGraw-Hill.

Sims, D.B.P. and Doyle, J.R. (1995) 'Cognitive sculpting as a means of working with managers' metaphors', *OMEGA*, 23 (2): 117–124.

Springer, S.P. and Deutsch, G. (1989) *Left Brain, Right Brain*. 3rd edn. New York: W.H. Freeman.

Tsoukas, H. (1991) 'The missing link: A transformational view of metaphors in organizational science', *Academy of Management Review*, 16 (3): 566–585.

Watzlawick, P. (1978) *The Language of Change*. New York: Norton.

Watzlawick, P., Bavelas, J.B. and Jackson, D.D. (1967) *Pragmatics of Human Communication*. New York: Norton.

INFERRING
MANAGERIAL
KNOWLEDGE

4

GAINING UNDERSTANDING IN A COMPLEX CAUSE–EFFECT POLICY DOMAIN

Roger I. Hall

ABSTRACT

An artificial intelligence (AI) program that contains simple behavioural rules is used in this study as a surrogate for the socio-cognitive and socio-political protocols employed by a group to make sense collectively of a complex system of cause–effect. A formal corporate cause–effect map of the operations of a sports club is used as a surrogate for the 'real-world' complex web of cause–effect that converts policy decisions into outcomes affecting corporate survival goals. Group policy making is mimicked by running trials with the AI program on the causal map of the sports club to see what policies are formed and why. The resulting policies compared favourably to those adopted by the executive of the club at two different periods in its history. The resulting discussion focuses on: (a) employing formal corporate cause–effect maps to improve group policy making; (b) the missing feedback causal paths in the collective map of the group; (c) whether managers can be trained to handle more causal complexity; (d) why different starting beliefs might affect the future histories of identical organizations in the same industry; and (e) the puzzle of exceptional organizations.

INTRODUCTION: CAUSE–EFFECT
COMPLEXITY AND POLICY MAKING

Speculating and arguing about the causal influences determining successful outcomes comprises an important part of the work of policy groups empowered to make weighty decisions committing the resources of an organization. However, the true system of causal relations at work in determining the outcomes of policies is rarely known to the group in complete detail; particularly if the causal relations perceived by the management have been learnt from *outcome-irrelevant learning structures* (Einhorn and Hogarth, 1978), or have been subjected to *judgement biases* (Kahneman and Tversky, 1982) or *conditioned beliefs* (hypothesized cause–effects validated solely on the basis that policies based on them worked in the past), or have been selectively biased to support the cause of the dominant coalition for internal political reasons (Pettigrew, 1973), or have just gone unseen. Even if the group has a good understanding of the causal relationships or has commissioned experts to uncover the 'true' relationships, the map may still be complicated by *multiple chains of causality* (many causal arguments) from policy decision to outcomes, *indeterminacy* (opposing arguments about the effects of the causal chains) and *feedback loops* (confounding circular chains of causality imparting dynamic properties to outcomes).

Even quite simple organizational operating systems can give rise to a relatively large number of chains of cause–effect paths from policy variables to organizational goals and many potentially confounding feedback loops. For example, the rudimentary formal map to be used in this study was found to contain 24 direct causal influences among 15 active variables representing chains of cause–effect in the operations of a sports club. Two of the active variables were identified by club policy makers as beginning policy variables under their aegis, and two other variables were likewise identified as ending outcome survival-goal variables. On analysis with a Path-Finding programme, the map was found to contain 21 chains of influences (paths) from beginning policy to ending goal variables (13 chains containing arguments for increasing the value of the policy variables and 7 arguing the opposite) and 8 feedback loops.

The executive committee of the club was comprised of volunteer members enamoured of the sport, but with limited comprehension of the causal influences and limited resources to unravel the causal system. Under such circumstances, how could they gain an understanding of the cause–effect system on which to base their policy decisions?

HOW MANAGERS COLLECTIVELY DEAL WITH CAUSAL COMPLEXITY USING SIMPLE BEHAVIOURAL RULES

In order to make the policy process manageable, policy-making groups will resort to activities of a socio-political nature for collectively negotiating what is to be believed and accepted (Eden, 1990), including the ostracizing of apostates (Steinbrunner, 1974). A kind of administrative *natural logic* (Hall, 1981, 1984, 1989 and 1990) is applied by the policy-making group to simplify the emerging collective map so as to avoid equivocality (Weick, 1969), uncertainty (Cyert and March, 1992) and conflict (Coser, 1964), and to attempt to correct unsatisfactory performance of the corporate survival goals and, at the same time, satisfy subunit goals (Cyert and March, 1992). This process usually results in some kind of a simple shared cognitive map of the major causes and their effects thought to be active within and between the organization and its significant environments; complete with attendant biases and misattributions. Policy problems are then inferred from the movements of key performance indices that result in identifiable performance gaps. Policies can then be invoked from the shared cognitive map to rectify or take advantage of the perceived problems.

The notion that programs based on simple rules can be built to think and act like people is borrowed from the field of artificial intelligence (Newell and Simon, 1966; Schank and Colby, 1973). From this perspective it is argued that the group processes for simplifying the complex cause–effect relations for policy making can be represented by a limited set of interlocking behavioural rules, such as the following:

- Policy elites will usually agree on the key policy variables, such as prices and promotion expenditure, directly affecting policy outcomes, such as revenue growth and profit (after Roberts, 1976).
- Policy makers readily accept pairs of influence relations (simple arguments of direct cause and effect of one variable on another – e.g. promotion expenditure influences sales positively [Axelrod, 1976]).
- Policy makers formulate arguments from the pairs of causal relations to connect policy variables to their effects on goals (after Roberts, 1976).
- Policy makers' cause–effect maps are characterized by a few short determinate causal paths. For example, higher prices lead to higher revenue – the more complicated causal argument linking loss of customers to higher prices is ignored (after Axelrod, 1976).
- The political entities within an organization, such as the departments of marketing, operations and finance, will each identify and pursue their own status-enhancing goals, such as the number of customers, volume of production and total revenue (after Pettigrew, 1973).
- The top political entity of the organization, such as the governing body or board of directors, will focus its policy-making efforts primarily on corporate survival goals, such as revenue growth and net revenue or profit.
- Each political entity will form its own preferred policies – the marketing department may seek to increase the promotion budget (after Pettigrew, 1973).
- The top political entity will form its preferred corporate policies (increased promotion expenditures to increase revenues and increased prices to increase profits).
- As corporate problems arise, each political entity will seek to use the situation to pursue its preferred policies or will be faced with defending its status (after Pettigrew, 1973). Corporate problems are defined by unsatisfactory performance of the survival goals, usually associated with growth, profit or both together, or by their over-achievement (how to absorb the slack in the system; after Cyert and March, 1992).

- Where there is consensus of all political entities on a policy action to overcome a corporate goal shortfall (such as increasing prices to shore up a sagging profit), it will be implemented.
- Where there is not consensus, the dominant entity or coalition of entities will unilaterally implement policies to protect the corporate goals. This will give rise to tension and conflict within the organization.
- Where there is an impasse (conflicting corporate policies), a 'sequential attention to goals' rule is applied – for example, first increase promotion expenditures to bolster revenue growth and, second, increase prices to shore up profit (after Cyert and March, 1992).

These rules for group policy making can be likened to decision-making protocols stored in the brain to interpret its physical domain and make decisions on how to move the body to a new location. However, the mind requires the body to enact its decisions and some knowledge of how the body can be expected to react to its decisions. In like fashion, the group 'mind' requires policy-making protocols to interpret its policy domains and some knowledge, such as a cause–effect map, of how it can be expected to react to its policy decisions. The artificial intelligence (AI) that I have programmed to mimic group policy making similarly requires a corporate system cause–effect map or model. The AI treats the cause–effect map as its policy territory upon which it applies its protocols. In effect, the map acts as a surrogate for the real-world complex of causal relationships, and the AI acts as a surrogate for the socio-cognitive and socio-political rule-based processes employed by a group of policy makers as it attempts to fathom the causal system and make decisions to move the organization to some new state. The question is whether this rule-based approach will generate policies that are similar to those observed in the real organizations, and what insights this might afford us.

HOW THE BEHAVIOURAL RULES EMBEDDED IN AN ARTIFICIAL INTELLIGENCE PROGRAM EMULATE MANAGEMENT POLICY MAKING

The prototype AI is programmed in HyperCard™ and HyperTalk™ as a Graphic User Interface program for the Macintosh computer. Reprogramming in VisualWorks™ for the MacOS, Windows and Unix environments is currently in progress. The processes programmed in the AI are designed to read in the corporate system cause–effect map in mathematical representational form and to work interactively with a user conversant with the organization that supplies information about departments, their goals and their current beliefs in policy-to-goal causality. The AI program then synthesizes a simplified group cause map and analyses it to form policies for certain problem situations such as poor revenue growth or financial loss, but in a way that emulates the management group decision processes. The behavioural rules listed above are

TABLE 4.1   A summary of the behavioural rules and matching AI policy inference procedures used to mimic group policy-making behaviour

Behavioural rules	AI procedures
[What cause-effect map of an organization is to be studied?]	Prompt the user to select the file containing the equations representing the organization's cause-effect map. Import the file. Parse the equations.
Policy elites can usually agree on the key policy variables (e.g. prices and promotion expenditure) directly affecting financial results (Roberts, 1976).	Form an *alphabetic list* of all variables in the equations representing the corporate system. Prompt the user to select those to be categorized as *policy variables*.
Organizations are made up of political entities (e.g. departments of marketing, operations and finance) each pursuing its own status-enhancing goal (after Pettigrew, 1973).	Prompt the user to name the dominant political entities (departments, divisions, groups, etc.) and to select the *goal variable* for each entity from the alphabetic list.
The governing body of the organization (board of directors) will be concerned primarily with the survival goals of growth or decline and profit or loss.	Prompt the user to select the *corporate survival goal variables* from the alphabetic list.
Policy maker's readily accept pairs of influence relations (simple arguments of direct cause and effect of one variable on another; e.g., promotion expenditure influences sales positively [Axelrod, 1976]).	Parse the equations representing the corporate system into bivariate correlational influence relations of the form: *variable x influences variable y positively or negatively*.
Policy makers formulate arguments from the pairs of causal relations to connect policy variables to their effects on goals (after Roberts, 1976).	Launch a path-finding algorithm to find all paths of causal relations from each *policy variable* to each *goal* by concatenating the bivariate relations and computing their total path correlations.
Policy makers' maps are characterized by a few short determinate causal paths (e.g. higher prices leads to higher revenue – the more complicated causal argument linking higher prices to loss of customers is ignored (after Axelrod, 1976)).	Select the two shortest paths of opposing policy representing opposing arguments of the effect of each policy variable on each goal. The user is prompted to select one of these argument as the current belief.
Each political entity will form its own preferred policies (e.g. the marketing department may seek to increase the promotion budget (after Pettigrew, 1976)).	Form a table of the *desired movement of each policy variable* (increase, decrease or indifferent) to favour the goal of each political entity.
As corporate problems arise, each political entity will seek to use the situation to pursue its preferred policies or will be faced with defending its status (after Pettigrew, 1973). Corporate problems are defined by unsatisfactory performance of the survival goals of growth, profit or both together, or by their over-achievement (i.e. how to absorb the slack in the system; after Cyert and March, 1992).	Form a table of the *movements of each policy variable* (*increase, decrease, indifferent, impasse*) *for solving the corporate problems*. Produce an *index of dissension* (e.g. number of dissenting departments) for each policy. Choose the policies where consensus is found (no dissent), otherwise select the policies most favourable or least damaging to the dominant group (political entity).
Where there is an impasse (conflicting corporate policies), use a sequential attention to goals (after Cyert and March, 1992).	Select a revenue growth policy first and a profit-correcting policy next.

Source: Reprinted from Hall, R.I., 'A Study of Political Formation in Complex Organizations', *Journal of Business Research*, 45(2): 162 (1999) with permission from Elsevor Science.

incorporated in the AI as matching procedures, as shown in Table 4.1 and described next. These procedures constitute the 'guts' of the AI program.

The user is first prompted to select the corporate cause–effect system to study. The map must be in a suitable mathematical equation form of either a set of assignment equations representing an Axelrod (1976) or Eden-type (Eden and Huxham, 1988) cognitive map, or a set of time-difference equations representing a System Dynamics model (Hall, 1976/1996).[1] A parsing routine in the AI converts the equations into (a) a list of variables in alphabetic order, and (b) a list of bivariate links (pairs of variables) in the form: variable x influences variable y positively or negatively in a direct causal sense.

Next, the user is prompted to name the political entities (e.g. departments, divisions, influential coalitions, boards of directors and executive groups) and the dominant goal of each. The user then is asked to identify the policy variables and the goals of each political entity from the alphabetic list of variables provided by the program. The AI program then searches the cause–effect relations to find paths made up of the bivariate links starting from those variables named by the user as *policy variables* to those named *goals*. A *depth-first with backtracking* path-finding algorithm (after Tarjan, 1972) is used to identify all the paths (representing lines of arguments) from the named policy variables to the named goals.[2] It also finds the feedback loops embedded along the paths, but since these are usually oblivious to the management (Axelrod, 1976), they are not used in the subsequent AI process for forming policies.[3]

The AI program then identifies the two shortest paths of opposing cause–effect as representing the simplest counter-arguments for how each policy variable effects each goal variable. These are candidates for policies to remedy unsatisfied goals. Where two paths of opposing influences exist, the user is asked to choose one as representing the current causal belief of the policy-making group, perhaps learnt from prior environment conditioning, or based on current preference for socio-political reasons.[4] From these paths, the desired policies of each department are formed (which policy variables to change and in which direction). In this way, the AI mimics, albeit in a simplistic fashion, the socio-psychological and socio-political processes that groups employ to make sense of complex and potentially conflictful situations. In the next section, a simple corporate system cause–effect map of a sports club will be described. It will be used to illustrate how the AI program works and to compare simulated policies with those adopted by the club's executive.

A CAUSE–EFFECT SYSTEM MAP OF A SPORTS CLUB

The corporate cause–effect relations are represented in three different, but corresponding, ways: (a) a *directed digraph* arrow diagram; (b) a set of assignment equations; and (c) a verbal description.

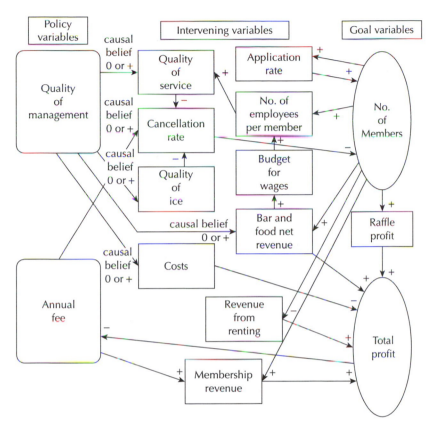

Figure 4.1   An Axelrod-type mapping of the system of cause–effect of the operations of a sports club (adapted from Hall and Menzies, 1983/1990)

(a) Directed Digraph Representation

The relations are depicted diagrammatically in Figure 4.1 by an Axelrod arrow-type of cause–effect system map. The map is a simplified version taken from a previously published study of a failing prestigious curling club approaching its 100th anniversary (Hall and Menzies, 1983/1990).

Figure 4.1 was constructed from interviews with the club's policy elite backed up by club documentation such as membership and accounting statements. (For a detailed description of the corporate system of influences, see Hall and Menzies, 1983/1990.) Referring to Figure 4.1, the survival goals of the curling club, as defined by the club's executive, are to maintain the *NumberofMembers* and make enough *TotalProfit* to remain viable. The policy decision variables under the aegis of the club executive were identified as *AnnualFee* and *QualityofManagement*.

TABLE 4.2 Assignment equations and documented
explanations representing the Axelrod-type
mapping of the sports club system of Figure 4.1

Policy Variables

AnnualFee=–TotalProfit
{annual membership fee is negatively influenced by the total profit, i.e. when profit declines, fees are increased}

QualityOfManagement=1
{quality of club management is a variable changed by executive fiat and is not influenced by other variables, i.e. it is an exogenous variable in this conceptualization on the club operating system}

Intervening Variables

ApplicationRate=+NoOfMembers
{application rate of new members is positively influenced by the number of current members, i.e. club members recruit more new members}

CancellationRate=[0 or +]AnnualFee–QualityOfIce–QualityOfService
{the number of members cancelling their membership is influenced negatively by quality of ice and services and [not to be influenced or to be influenced positively] by fees, i.e. lower club quality will cause more members to quit and higher fees [will or will not] cause more members to quit}

QualityOfService=[0 or +]QualityOfManagement+NoOfEmployeesPerMember
{quality of services is influenced [not at all or is positively] by quality of club management and is influenced positively by the number of employees relative to members, i.e. quality of services is perceived to have [either no effect or to increase] with better management and/or a better ratio of service employees to number of club members}

QualityOfIce=[0 or +]QualityOfManagement
{quality and consistency of the curling rink ice surface [is not or is] directly related to the quality of club management, i.e. good management [will not or will] ensure higher-quality conditions for playing the game of curling}

NoOfEmployeesPerMember=–NoOfMembers+BudgetForWages
{the ratio of employees to club members is reduced by a bigger membership and/or increased by a larger budget for wages}

BudgetForWages=+BarAndFoodNetRev
{monies available for wages are directly related to revenue from the bar and food services}

BarAndFoodNetRev=[0 or +]QualityOfManagement+NoOfMembers
{net revenues from bar and food services [are not or are] directly influenced by the quality of the club management, and/or are directly influenced by the number of members, i.e better management [will or will not] increase the net profit from the bar and food facility, and more members will result in higher usage and hence a higher profit from the food and bar services}

RaffleProfit=+NoOfMembers
{more members will increase the profit from the annual raffle}

RevenueFromRenting=–NoOfMembers
{revenues from renting out the facilities to outsiders are negatively influenced by the current number of members, i.e. fewer members leads to less use of the facilities and more time available for leasing it out, and vice versa}

MembershipRevenue=+NoOfMembers+AnnualFee
{revenues from membership fees are directly related to the current number of members and the level of fees they are paying}

(Contd.)

TABLE 4.2   Contd.

Costs=[0 or +]QualityOfManagement
{costs of running the sports side of the club are mostly overhead expenses [not related or directly related] to the quality of management}

Goal Variables
NoOfMembers=+ApplicationRate–CancellationRate
{the current number of members is increased by new members joining and decreased by those quitting}

TotalProfit=+RaffleProfit+BarAndFoodNetRev+RevenueFromRenting+MembershipRevenue– Costs
{total profit is increased by profits from the annual raffle and the bar and food services, and by revenues from renting out facilities and membership fees, and decreased by costs for running the sports facilities}

Legend

$y=x+z$	denotes x & z both influence y positively (in a correlational sense).
$y=+x-z$	denotes x influences y positively & z influences y negatively.
$y=1$	denotes that y is not influenced by any other variables in the map.
$y=[0$ or $+]x$	denotes that x can either have no (zero) influence on y or x can influence y positively. The sign '0' will, in effect, remove (cut) the the influence of x on y.

(b) Assignment Equations Representation

Table 4.2 shows the same relationships as a set of documented symbolic assignment equations. These assignment equations are in the form of:

the variable on left of the '=' sign is influenced by the variable(s)
on the right side either positively (+) or negatively (–).

That is, if the influence is '+', this means that an increase in the value of the variable on the right side will bring about an increase in the value of the variable on the left, and vice versa. And if the influence is '–', this indicates the reverse, namely an increase in the value of the variable on the right will cause a decrease in the value of the variable on the left, and vice versa. To simulate the management's blindness to a particular influence, a '0' sign is used to zero it; in effect, to cut the cause–effect link. The AI requires these equations in order to compute the paths from policy variables to goals.

(c) Verbal Description Representation

The verbal descriptions of the cause–effect relations are contained in the documentation following each equation in Table 4.2. The documentation details the causal arguments for each equation and its associated directed arrow of influence in Figure 4.1 and is intended to aid the reader in following the skein of causal influences throughout the map from policy variables through intervening variables to goals.[5]

TRIALS WITH THE AI AND CORPORATE SYSTEM MAP OF THE SPORTS CLUB

The AI program imports the data file containing the assignment equations of Table 4.2, after prompting the user for its name and location. By following the routines outlined in Table 4.1, the AI produces an alphabetic listing of all variables and prompts the user to identify the policy and goal variables from this list. *AnnualFees* and *QualityOfManagement* were chosen for the policy variables and *TotalProfit* and *NumberOfMembers* were chosen for goals in accordance with Table 4.2. Trials with the AI program were then run for two levels of comprehension by the club executive of the complexity of the influence relations represented in Table 4.2 and Figure 4.1.

Elementary Level of Comprehension

At first, because of the past success of the club, the executive committee demonstrated little understanding of the direct effect of the *AnnualFee* and the indirect effect of *QualityOfManagement* on the *CancellationRate* of members. Traditionally, when a financial loss was incurred, the management raised the annual fee. The missing influences are treated as *causal beliefs* to which the club's executive was blinded in the first instance. In Table 4.2 and Figure 4.1, these *causal beliefs* affect: (a) the influence of the *AnnualFee* on *CancellationRate* of club members, and the influences of *QualityOfManagement* on (b) *QualityofServices,* (c) the *QualityOfIce* and (d) the *Costs* of running the club. When asked by the AI program whether any changes to the causal relations are required, the above influences were given a zero assignment value that, in effect, negates their effects and severs the links. From the memory of former executive committee members, it appears that the concept of *QualityOfManagement* and its possible effects never came up for conscious discussion at executive committee meetings at that time.

When prompted by the AI program to enter the names of political entities within the club, there was only one political entity identified – namely that of the president and executive committee of the club – due to the small size of the organization.[6]

Results of the Trial with the Elementary Level of Comprehension

The results of running the AI program with the modified cause–effect relations are shown in Tables 4.3 and 4.4.

In Table 4.3 only one causal path was identified by the AI program, namely *AnnualFee* influences *MembershipRevenue*, which in turn influences *TotalProfit*. It is a path of **positive** influence from the policy variable

TABLE 4.3   Results of the AI policy inference procedure:
Trial 1: Policy-to-goal cause–effect paths
found with the elementary comprehension
level of cause–effect beliefs

Causal path from policy variable	to corporate survival goal variable	Perceived effect of policy on goal along causal path	No. of links in causal path
AnnualFee	NoOfMembers	Zero	N/A
AnnualFee	TotalProfit	Positive	2
QualityofManagement	NoOfMembers	Zero	N/A
QualityofManagement	TotalProfit	Zero	N/A

TABLE 4.4   Results of the AI policy inference procedure:
Trial 1: Desired policies for improving the
achievement of club goals derived with the elementary
comprehension level of cause–effect beliefs

	Corporate survival goals variables	
Policy variables	Desired direction of policy variable to increase goal of NoOfMembers	Desired direction of policy variable to increase goal of TotalProfit
AnnualFee	No connection seen	Increase
QualityOfManagement	No connection seen	No connection seen

AnnualFee to the goal variable of *Profit*; that is, an increase in *AnnualFee* will cause an increase in *TotalProfit* (*ceteris quietus* – all other influences remaining dormant). There are no causal paths from *QualityOfManagement* to *TotalProfit* or *NoOfMembers*. Cutting all the links emanating from the policy variable *QualityOfManagement* in effect made them unseen in the emulated collective map of the club executive committee.[7]

These relationships are translated by the AI program in Table 4.4 into a desired policy to increase *AnnualFees* to improve the goal *TotalProfit*, since the causal path from *AnnualFee* to *TotalProfit* has a 'positive' correlation. There is an indifference to all other available policies. This is exactly the policy adopted by the club executive at that time to correct financial losses. These simple and straightforward results might be considered intuitively obvious. However, one has to take into account the comprehension of the committee at that time (its collective map) of the complexity of the 'real' cause–effect system. For larger organizations with several divisions or departments and more convoluted and complex maps of causal relationships, the results are not so intuitively obvious. The simple club example, however, does serve to illustrate how the AI program works.

Trials with a Higher Level of Comprehension

Later, in response to the declining membership, brought about by high fees and a critical financial loss, a new executive committee of the club undertook a study of the situation. It led to a better understanding of the effects of *QualityOfManagement* and *AnnualFee* on membership decline and financial viability. To reflect this improved understanding, the causal beliefs previously cut were restored. The AI program now found multiple paths from policy variables to goals. Many of the paths exhibit *indeterminacy*, representing counter-arguments for raising or lowering the values of the policy variables to enhance the goals.

Resolving Path Indeterminacy

It is not now apparent whether a policy variable influences a goal variable positively or negatively, in a causal correlational sense. The AI program deals with this by listing the two shortest paths of opposite cause–effect linking each policy variable to each goal. The pairs of paths are listed in Figure 4.2 and represent the two simplest causal arguments of the effect of each policy variable on each goal: one arguing to *increase* the policy variable to *increase* the goal variable and the other to ***decrease*** the policy variable to ***increase*** the goal variable. This is where the user's knowledge of the particular situation is required.

To resolve this indeterminacy, the user is requested to choose which one of each pair of paths will best represent the current beliefs in causality of the policy-making group. For the #1 causal paths (in Figure 4.2) from *AnnualFee* to *TotalProfit*, the shortest path of ***positive*** correlation (*AnnualFee, MembershipRevenue, TotalProfit*) is now countered by a path of ***negative*** correlation (*AnnualFee, CancellationRate, NoOfMembers, BarAndFoodNetRev, TotalProfit*). The latter path is predicated on the argument that higher fees will increase member cancellations, leading to fewer club members and reduced revenues from the bar and food services and lower profit. It has more causal links and so might be more difficult to argue in an executive meeting without strong supporting evidence to counter the more direct and persuasive accounting logic of higher fees bringing in more revenue and profit. The study conducted by the club executive indicated that higher fees had increased the cancellation rate of members to the point where it exceeded the application rate of new members, thus causing the observed decline in the number of club members. This leads us to the choice of the second (negative) path as representing the new belief of the group.

For the #2 causal paths (Figure 4.2) from *AnnualFees* to *NoOfMembers*, the AI could find no paths of ***positive*** correlation since increasing *AnnualFee* leads only to an increase in *CancellationRate*, which, in turn, has a negative causal correlational effect on *NoOfMembers*. So, by default, the path of ***negative*** causal correlation is chosen.

For the #3 causal paths (Figure 4.2) found from *QualityOfManagement* to *TotalProfit*, the shortest path of positive correlation (*QualityOfManagement, BarAndFoodNetRev, TotalProfit*) is now countered by a path of negative

#1 Causal Paths: *from AnnualFee to TotalProfit*   Select one

either **Path:** AnnualFee, MembershipRevenue, TotalProfit **No. of links:** 2   **Path causal correlation:** positive   ◯
or **Path:** AnnualFee, CancellationRate, NoOfMembers, BarAndFoodNetRev, TotalProfit **No. of links:** 4   **Path causal correlation:** negative   ⦿

#2 Causal Paths: *from AnnualFee to NoOfMembers*   Select one

either **Path:** *none* **No. of links:** 0   **Path causal correlation:** positive   ◯
or **Path:** AnnualFee, CancellationRate, NoOfMembers **No. of links:** 2   **Path causal correlation:** negative   ⦿[†]

[†]chosen by default

#3 Causal Paths: *from QualityOfManagement to TotalProfit*   Select one

either **Path:** QualityOfManagement, BarAndFoodNetRev, TotalProfit **No. of links:** 2   **Path causal correlation:** positive   ⦿
or **Path:** QualityOfManagement, Cost, TotalProfit **No. of links:** 2   **Path causal correlation:** negative   ◯

#4 Causal Paths: *from QualityOfManagement to NoOfMembers*   Select one

either **Path:** QualityOfManagement, QualityOfService, CancellationRate, NoOfMembers **No. of links:** 3   **Path causal correlation:** positive   ⦿
or **Path:** QualityOfManagement, Cost, TotalProfit, AnnualFee,   CancellationRate, NoOfMembers **No. of links:** 5   **Path causal correlation:** negative   ◯

Figure 4.2   User responses requested by the AI program to solve indeterminancy found in the opposing cause–effect path correlations

The shortest policy-to-goal paths of opposing correlation, found by the AI program, are displayed above. These represent the simplest arguments for raising or lowering the value of each policy variable to enchance each goal.

For each pair of policy-to-goal paths, select the path that best reflects the group's belief in the causal correlation (either positive or negative).

correlation (*QualityOfManagement, Cost, TotalProfit*). The executive committee came to understand that a good club manager could guarantee to manage the club's services efficiently, to contain costs and turn the loss on Bar and Food operations into a profit. So the ***positive*** path correlation was chosen to represent the new belief in the effect of *QualityOfManagement* on *TotalProfit*.

For the #4 causal paths (Figure 4.2) found from *QualityOfManagement* to *NoOfMembers*, the shortest path of positive correlation (*QualityOfManagement, QualityOfService, CancellationRate, NoOfMembers*) is now countered by a path of negative correlation (*QualityOfManagement, Cost, TotalProfit, AnnualFee, CancellationRate, NoOfMembers*). The executive committee also came to the understanding that good club management could provide both improved services to members and consistent ice quality for the game of curling. It was argued that these improvements would further stem the loss of members. So the path of *positive* correlation linking *QualityOfManagement* to *NoOfMembers* was chosen to represent their belief. As mentioned previously, these choices to resolve the indeterminacy in the AI program's causal map of the operations of the club require a person with local knowledge of the situation.

Results of the Trial with the Higher Level of Comprehension

Once all the policy-to-goal paths have been cleared of indeterminacy, the AI program summarizes in Table 4.5 the now deterministic paths as *negative* influences of policy variables *AnnualFee* and ***positive*** influences of *QualityOfManagement* on the *TotalProfit* and *NoOfMembers* of the club. These relationships are translated by the AI program (shown in Table 4.6) into a desired policy to ***decrease*** *AnnualFees* to improve the goals *TotalProfit* and *NoOfMembers*, and, likewise, to *increase QualityOfManagement* to improve the goals *TotalProfit* and *NoOfMembers*. There is, also, no impasse since the policies for increasing membership and profits are the same. As described in Hall and Menzies (1983/1990), policies identical to these were adopted and vigorously pursued by a new executive that took over the running of the club, which adds further to the credibility of the AI program in emulating the logic used by a group in policy making.

FEEDBACK LOOPS OF CAUSALITY

Lastly, in Table 4.7, the AI lists the feedback (circular) paths of cause–effect buried in Figure 4.1. These loops can create unintended outcomes if they go unnoticed. The positive loops can lead to uncontrolled growth or decline resulting in instability and loss of control. For example, for Path #1 in Table 4.7, any increase in the *NoOfMembers*, through its effect on

TABLE 4.5   Results of the AI policy inference procedure:
Trial 2: Policy-to-goal cause–effect paths with the higher
comprehension level of cause–effect beliefs

Causal path from policy variable	to corporate survival goal variable	Effect of policy on goal along causal path	No. of links in causal path
AnnualFee	NoOfMembers	Negative	2
AnnualFee	TotalProfit	Negative	4
QualityOfManagement	NoOfMembers	Positive	3
QualityOfManagement	TotalProfit	Positive	2

TABLE 4.6   Results of the AI policy inference procedure:
Trial 2: Desired policies for improving the achievement
of club goals derived with the higher comprehension level
of cause–effect beliefs

	Corporate survival goal variables	
Policy variables	Desired direction of policy variable to increase goal of NoOfMembers	Desired direction of policy variable to increase goal of TotalProfit
AnnualFee	Decrease	Decrease
QualityofManagement	Increase	Increase

increasing the *ApplicationRate*, will, in turn, further increase *NoOfMembers*, resulting in an exponential escalation of members over time. The opposite can also happen. If *NoOfMembers* **decreases**, resulting in a decrease in *ApplicationRate* and, in turn, a further decrease in *NoOfMembers*, a downward spiral of *NoOfMembers* ensues. One can infer from this that 'positive' feedback cause–effect paths are critical to growth, but can also lead to uncontrolled decline if not monitored and quickly acted upon. There are five 'positive' feedback paths listed in Table 4.7, any one of which could take the club operations for a roller-coaster ride!

Path #4 in Table 4.7 provides an example of a 'negative' feedback path. It indicates that if the *NoOfMembers* increases, the *NoOfEmployeesPerMember* (an index of service) declines, reducing the *QualityOfService* perceived by club members, thus increasing the *CancellationRate* and decreasing the *NoOfMembers*. It forms a self-regulating loop that, *ceteris quietus*, offsets an increase in *NoOfMembers* with a decrease at a later time, and vice versa. It suggests that any increase in membership will be limited if the service capacity of the club is not improved. There are three 'negative' feedback paths in total in Table 4.7. Any one of these could limit the growth of the club or, in unison with other feedback paths, create unstable behaviours such as oscillations of operations. Yet these feedback paths go largely unseen because the group policy-making protocols are fixated on finding linear policy-to-goal paths and do not include the search for circular paths. Also, circular paths so confound the simple cause–effect predictions as to require a more rigorous dynamic analysis beyond what could be expected from a group meeting in committee.

TABLE 4.7 Results of the AI policy inference procedure: feedback loops path buried in the cause–effect system map that can create unintended outcomes

#	No. of causal links	correlation	Feedback loop paths found in sports club cause–effect map			
1	2	Positive	NoOfMembers	ApplicationRate	NoOfMembers	
2	3	Negative	AnnualFee	MembershipRevenue	TotalProfit	AnnualFee
3	4	Negative	NoOfMembers, CancellationRate	NoOfEmployeesPerMember, NoOfMembers	QualityOfService	AnnualFee
4	5	Negative	NoOfMembers, CancellationRate	RevenueFromRenting, NoOfMembers	TotalProfit	AnnualFee
5	5	Positive	NoOfMembers, CancellationRate	MembershipRevenue, NoOfMembers	TotalProfit	AnnualFee
6	5	Positive	NoOfMembers, CancellationRate	BarAndFoodNetRev, NoOfMembers	TotalProfit	AnnualFee
7	5	Positive	NoOfMembers, CancellationRate	RaffleProfit, NoOfMembers	TotalProfit	AnnualFee
8	6	Positive	NoOfMembers, NoOfEmployeesPerMember, NoOfMembers	BarAndFoodNetRev, QualityOfService	BudgetForWages, CancellationRate	

DISCUSSION

Limitations of the Study

The causal system map of the operations of the sports club may not trap all the requisite richness of the real-world cause–effect system it is intended to represent. As in any qualitative research study, the researcher has to avoid pitfalls such as interviewing the wrong person and asking the wrong questions, leading to the building of a map of how the corporate system of cause–effect is thought to work or is supposed to work rather than how it does work (Hall, 1978).

Similarly, the AI procedures are based on generic behavioural protocols garnered from the literature. Some may be situation- or era- or national-culture-dependent, or just may not represent all the complexity of human group decision making. Nevertheless, given the interwoven complexity of causal relations within the system map and the relatively parsimonious set of simple generic behavioural protocols built into the AI, the similarities between the predicted and adopted policies by the club's executive are quite startling. The explanations generated by the analysis into how the policies became adopted adds further to the credibility of the model.

Bearing in mind the above limitations and the fact that we have only a sample of two corporate operating systems (this study of a club and another study of a magazine publishing firm [Hall, 1999]) to compare the polices adopted with the AI program predictions, the following discussion is put forward.

Can Formal Methods of Cause–Effect Mapping Improve Group Policy Making?

The detail and precision required in the building and analysis of corporate system cause–effect maps is not to everyone's liking. The subsequent analysis can alienate policy makers because it potentially confounds their relatively simple linear maps and may question their policies, without necessarily posing any better policies. Extracting more reliable policies from the analysis of a formal corporate system map can take considerable time and effort. This is not the stuff for action-oriented managers who wish to make quick decisions and get on with other things. Yet in my experience, there are a growing number of managers (in some organizations, at least) with the patience and interest to follow the convoluted logic of causal diagrams without getting too upset!

As an example, the effect of walking a class of senior managers from a large furniture manufacturing firm through an elaborate cause–effect system map was quite unexpected. It concerned a complex map built around employee commitment that showed graphically why some productivity improvement programmes, such as Total Quality Management

(TQM), can lead to bankruptcy.[8] The presentation concentrated on sensitizing the class to the feedback cause–effect paths that usually go unseen yet bring about the unintended side-effects of layoff decisions. Immediately after the class, the managers convened a meeting and reversed a policy decision made previously concerning laying off surplus employees resulting from a successful company TQM programme. One might draw the conclusion that something in the map enriched the group's comprehension, thus tipping the balance from one policy to the other.

The Implications of the Unseen Feedback Cause–Effect Paths

Positive and negative feedback loops working in unison can form configurations giving rise to behaviours such as the *limits to growth* and the *quick fix* (Senge, 1990: App. 2). For instance, the *limits to growth* scenario could arise if the membership of the club declines due to the lack of service capacity and/or quality of management and/or high fees. The frequent raising of fees to rectify the profit position without realizing the deleterious side-effects it was having on membership could be labelled a *quick fix*. It would appear that both scenarios were involved in the long-run decline of membership and financial viability of the sports club,[9] yet the feedback cause–effect paths causing it went unseen by the club executive committee.

The study provides insight into how feedback cause–effect paths become overlooked in the organizational behaviour processes of building a group cause–effect map; a characteristic noted by other researchers (Axelrod, 1976; Forrester, 1970). It means that a group would be unlikely to perceive the system dynamics giving rise to growth and decline and to unintended side-effects of their policies. It is akin to forecasting the weather without an understanding of the thermal feedback dynamics that can suddenly turn an unstable air mass into a raging storm. The absence of recursive causal paths in the thinking of managers and policy makers is of particular concern to members of the System Dynamics and Organizational Learning movement (*European Journal of Operational Research*, 1992; Senge, 1990). Without the inclusion of feedback relations, even improvements leading to more accurate group cause–effect maps would not necessarily provide any better policies. How can policy makers fathom which of the numerous feedback loops hidden in a formal corporate systems map could possibly destabilize the system? Even with this knowledge, it is rarely immediately obvious what policies to invoke. A rigorously developed System Dynamics simulation model (see, for examples: Hall, 1976/1996; Hall and Menzies, 1983/1990; Morecroft and van der Heijden, 1992) is capable of providing this analysis.

Can Managers be Trained to Handle More Causal Complexity?

A relevant question concerns how trainable managers are in cause–effect mapping. Jacques and Carson (1994) argue that managers fall naturally into categories in their mental ability in handling complexity. They identify four types of complexity of mental processing (*declarative, cumulative, serial and parallel*) working on either *symbolic* or *conceptual* information; the highest order obtainable by managers being *conceptual parallel*-level reasoning. Is system cause–effect thinking a special kind of *conceptual parallel* reasoning or is it of a yet higher *universal* order? Should we concentrate only on those managers who exhibit the potential to reason at this level? Can system thinking be moved down to the *symbolic* information level so that managers with the capacity for this type of reasoning could benefit? This seems to be the approach taken by Senge (1990) when describing the archetypal feedback loops present in organized systems using vignettes, such as the *fix that fails* and the *limits to growth*, mentioned before, that might help such managers perceive certain configurations of feedback paths, appreciate their effects and know what to do or what not to do about it. In this regard, the AI program used in this study is capable of exposing the hidden feedback loops to facilitate this kind of learning.

Do Different Starting Beliefs Lead to Different Future Histories?

As explained before, the AI program finds the two shortest paths from policy-to-goal of opposing cause–effect path correlation. The user is asked to choose which one (the 'positive' or 'negative' path) represents the current belief of the group. Suppose that instead of choosing, say, the 'positive' sign of correlation, a 'negative' sign is chosen as the belief, and supposing the resulting policy is just as successful with the 'negative' sign under the current circumstances. Would the organization applying the policy experience a quite different future? That is, different starting beliefs could explain why different organizations in the same industry, with similar cause–effect policy domains, might evolve in quite different ways. This is consistent with the theory of 'Order Out of Chaos' (Prigogine and Stengers, 1984), which postulates that the kind of organization evolving in closed-feedback cause–effect systems is very dependent on the initial starting conditions. This suggests that the method employed in this study might be used by a policy group to check out its current beliefs to see if it is missing out on more attractive future histories!

The Puzzle of Exceptional Organizations

The logic encoded in the AI program aids the selection of the shortest paths from policy-to-goal representing the cause–effect arguments with the most immediate effect. This is argued to be the most realistic situation in group policy making, where simple arguments would more likely carry the day. There is growing evidence that exceptional organizations adopt policies that are premised on more complex arguments that relate less tangible policy variables, such as training the workforce, to relatively long-run goals, such as developing the potential of the organization, that run counter to the conventional wisdom of their industries at the time (Doman et al., 1995; Starbuck, 1993). How different are the collective policy maps in such organizations, and how does this difference come about? Is it culturally determined by a founder and passed down to succeeding generations of managers to apply blindly? Or by chance did the group start with different beliefs to other organizations in the same industry? Or is there some higher level of group policy map comprehension responsible for the phenomenon? The answers to these questions could be most illuminating!

SUMMARY

In this study I have presented a process model of group policy making based on a relatively small number of behavioural rules garnered from the literature on how a policy-making group makes sense of its complex cause–effect policy domain. These rules were embedded in an AI program to mimic the collective decision-making behaviours of policy-making groups. A cause–effect system map of a club was used as a surrogate policy domain. The map was interpreted by the AI for two levels of comprehension of the cause–effect system of relationships among the concept variables in the map. The resulting policies were compared with those adopted by the club executive committee at two separate periods in the club's history that corresponded to the two levels of comprehension. The identical policies observed add credence to the AI program emulating the collective cognition of the policy makers. The AI program affords an explanation for the missing feedback paths of cause–effect in the policy maps of managers observed by others. Questions are addressed of whether formal cause–effect maps can help policy groups enhance their maps to make better policy decisions, whether it might be possible to train managers in this kind of system thinking, and what the implications are of the missing feedback paths in group cause–effect maps. The way policies are chosen and the closed-feedback nature of the cause–effect system of the policy domain suggest that organizations are subject to 'Order out of Chaos Theory'. This might explain why different starting beliefs in cause–effect path correlations result in quite different time paths or histories. It might also cast some light on the phenomenon of exceptional organizations.

NOTES

This is a revised and expanded version of working papers presented at the Symposium on Strategic Implementation and Assessment Research, Montreal, 1996, the Colloquium of the *European Group for Organizational Studies* on Contrasts and Contradictions in Organization, Istanbul, 1995, and the International Workshop on Rationality and Organization of the European Institute for Advanced Studies in Management, Brussels, 1993.

I wish to acknowledge the support received for this study by a Strategic Research Grant No. 804-94-0007 from the Social Sciences and Humanities Research Council of Canada, and by a Visiting Fellowship from the University of Warwick Business School.

I am indebted to my colleagues Peter Aitchison, Department of Applied Mathematics, and Bill Kocay, Department of Computer Science, University of Manitoba, for providing the path-finding algorithm used in this study.

1. For a discussion on methods for eliciting formal cause–effect maps from managers, see Hall et al. (1994).

2. See Hall et al. (1994) for a more detailed description of the path finder.

3. Axelrod (1976) notes that the cognitive maps of managers are characterized by a few short determinant causal paths (arguments) with few or no feedback loops (circular arguments) that would complicate the map and confound the analysis.

4. Pettigrew (1973) notes that group status enhancement or defence can have a powerful influence on a group's preferences in decision making.

5. Different modes of presentation, it would seem, appeal to different people. For instance, a corporate lawyer attending a company in-house seminar pleaded with me to use words rather than diagrams to explain a complex cause–effect system map. The other participants, on the other hand, much preferred the visual display in arrow diagram form.

6. For a more complex organization with several political entities each pursuing its own goals, see the analysis contained in Hall (1999).

7. This does not mean that all the members of the committee were blind to the missing relations, but that those who had insight may have chosen not to challenge the group's implicit understanding, for whatever reasons.

8. Taken from Sterman et al. (1997).

9. For a more detailed explanation of the effect of the feedback loops on the performance of the club, see Hall and Menzies (1983/1990).

REFERENCES

Axelrod, R.M. (ed.) (1976) *The Structure of Decision: Cognitive Maps of Policy Elites*. Princeton, NJ: Princeton University Press.

Coser, L.A. (1964) 'The termination of conflict', in W.J. Gore and J.W. Dyson (eds), *The Making of Decisions*. Glencoe, IL: Free Press.

Cyert, R.M. and March, J.G. (1992) *A Behavioral Theory of the Firm*. 2nd edn. Englewood Cliffs, NJ: Prentice-Hall.

Doman, A., Glucksman, M., Mass, N. and Sasportes, M. (1995) 'The dynamics of managing life insurance companies', *System Dynamics Review*, 11: 219–232.

Eden, C. (1990) 'Strategy development as a social process', *Journal of Management Studies*, 29: 799–811.

Eden, C. and Huxham, C. (1988) 'Action-oriented management', *Journal of the Operational Research Society*, 39: 889–899.

Einhorn, H.J. and Hogarth, R.M. (1978) 'Confidence in judgment: Persistence of the illusion of validity', *Psychological Review*, 85: 395–416.

European Journal of Operational Research (1992) Special edition on Modelling for Learning. 59 (1).

Forrester, J.W. (1970) 'Counterintuitive behavior of social systems', *Technology Review*, 3: 52–68.

Hall, R.I. (1976) 'A system pathology of an organization: The rise and fall of the *Old Saturday Evening Post*', *Administrative Science Quarterly*, 21: 185–211. Reprinted (1996) in G.P. Richardson (ed.), *Modelling for Management I: Simulation in Support of Systems Thinking* (The international library of management series). Aldershot, UK: Dartmouth Publishing. pp. 251–277.

Hall, R.I. (1978) 'Simple techniques for constructing explanatory models of complex systems for policy analysis', *Dynamica*, 3: 101–144.

Hall, R.I. (1981) 'Decision making in a complex organization', in G.W. England, A.R. Negandhi and B. Wilpert (eds), *The Functioning of Complex Organizations* (selected papers from the specialized conference of the International Institute of Management of the Science Center, Berlin). Cambridge, MA: Oelgeschlager, Gunn & Hain. pp. 111–144.

Hall, R.I. (1984) 'The natural logic of management policy making: Its implications for the survival of an organization', *Management Science*, 30: 905–927.

Hall, R.I. (1989) 'An artificial intelligence approach to building a process model of management policy making', in M.C. Jackson, P. Keys and S.A. Cropper (eds), *Operational Research and the Social Sciences* (selected papers from the 1989 IFORS specialized conference, Queen's College, Cambridge University). New York: Plenum Press. pp. 439–444.

Hall, R.I. (1990) 'Building an artificial intelligence model of management policy making: A tool for exploring organizational issues', in M. Marsuch (ed.), *Organization, Management and Expert Systems: Models of Automated Reasoning* (selected papers from the international workshop of the Management Center, University of Amsterdam). Berlin: de Gruyter. pp. 103–121.

Hall, R.I. (1999) 'A study of policy formation in complex organizations: Emulating group decision making with a simple artificial intelligence and a system model of corporate operations', *Journal of Business Research* (special edition on Strategy Implementation and Assessment Research), 45: 157–171.

Hall, R.I. and Menzies, W.B. (1983) 'A corporate system model of a sports club: Using simulation as an aid to policy making in a crisis', *Management Science*, 29: 52–64. Reprinted (1990) in R.G. Dyson (ed.), *Strategic Planning: Models and Analytical Methods*. Chichester: Wiley. pp. 183–197.

Hall, R.I. Aitchison, P. and Kocay, W.L. (1994) 'Causal policy maps of managers: Formal methods for eliciting and analysis', *System Dynamics Review*, 10: 337–360.

Jacques, E. and Carson, K. (1994) *Human Capability*. Falls Church, Victoria: Carson Hall & Co.

Kahneman, D.S. and Tversky, A. (1982) *Judgment Under Uncertainty: Heuristics and Biases*. Cambridge: Cambridge University Press.

Morecroft, J.D.W. and van der Heijden, K.A.J.M. (1992) 'Modelling the oil producers: Capturing oil industry knowledge in a behavioral simulation model', *European Journal of Operational Research*, 59: 102–122.

Newell, A. and Simon, H.A. (1966) 'Computer simulation of human thinking', *Science*, 134: 2011–2017.

Pettigrew, A.M. (1973) *The Politics of Organizational Decision Making*. London: Tavistock.

Prigogine, I. and Stengers, I. (1984) *Order Out of Chaos*. London: Heinemann.

Roberts, F.S. (1976) 'Strategy for the energy crisis: The case for commuter transport policy', in R.M. Axelrod (ed.), *The Structure of Decision: Cognitive Maps of Policy Elites*, Princeton, NJ: Princeton University Press. pp. 414–426.

Schank, R.C. and Colby, K.M. (1973) *Computer Models of Thought and Language*. San Francisco: W.H. Freeman.

Senge, P.M. (1990) *The Fifth Discipline: The Art and Practice of the Learning Organization.* New York: Doubleday.

Starbuck, W.H. (1993) 'Keeping a butterfly and an elephant in a house of cards: The elements of exceptional success', *Journal of Management Studies*, 30: 886–921.

Steinbrunner, J.D. (1974) *The Cybernetic Theory of Decision.* Princeton, NJ: Princeton University Press.

Sterman, J., Repenning, J.N. and Kofman, F. (1997) 'Unanticipated side effects of successful quality programs: Exploring a paradox of organizational improvement', *Management Science*, 43: 503–521.

Tarjan, R. (1972) 'Depth-first search and linear graph algorithms', *SIAM Journal of Computing*, 1: 146–160.

Weick, K.E. (1969) *The Social Psychology of Organizing.* Reading, MA: Addison-Wesley.

5

ENTREPRENEURIAL NARRATIVES AND THE DOMINANT LOGICS OF HIGH-GROWTH FIRMS

Joseph F. Porac, Yuri Mishina and **Timothy G. Pollock**

ABSTRACT

Our focus has been on extracting information from narrative data about the 'dominant logics', or mental models, of entrepreneurial teams. It is based upon the assumption that open-ended narrative data about firm competences, founder characteristics, corporate values and future plans represent a rich source of information about the mental models of a company's management. In this study we focus on what managers view as the feasible growth strategies available to their firms and the linkages among these strategies. We show that there are inter-industry patterns in the clustering of growth strategies that summarize distinctive cognitive representations of management regarding firm expansion. The patterns are evidence of macro-level entrepreneurial knowledge with both public policy and strategic implications.

INTRODUCTION

Uncovering the mental models of managers is a topic of primary interest for managerial cognition researchers. Examining the cognitive frameworks of managers can provide insights into the motivations behind managerial actions and subsequent firm performance (Fiol, 1995; Penrose, 1959). However, 'thoughts are, by definition, unobservable through any direct means' (Fiol, 1995: 522). As a result, researchers face the difficult task of attempting to deduce managerial beliefs by examining the verbal communications of managers. To this end, a variety of cognitive mapping techniques have been used by researchers to assess the implicit mental models of managers. Most research on cognitive mapping has examined causal beliefs (Bougon, 1983; Cossette and Audet, 1992; Eden et al., 1992; Langfield-Smith, 1992; Laukkanen, 1994; Pitt, 1998) and/or categories of competitors (Calori et al., 1994; Porac et al., 1995; Reger and Palmer, 1996). While research of this type has been interesting and valuable, cognitive mapping is applicable to more than causal beliefs and environmental categorizations. One area in which cognitive mapping has not previously been used is in understanding the linkage between firm growth and entrepreneurial cognitive frameworks.

Entrepreneurs are cognitive agents who operate in turbulent, equivocal environments such as new industries or new industry segments (Hill and Levenhagen, 1995). In these uncertain competitive environments, changes in technology shift knowledge streams so that knowledge gaps are constantly being opened and closed. Whenever knowledge gaps are created, uncertainty and ambiguity are perceived. Entrepreneurs reduce this perceived uncertainty by 'bridging and closing gaps between different streams of knowledge' (Levenhagen et al., 1993: 77). In doing so, they are able to create potentially sustainable competitive advantages. However, aside from their ability to implement their ideas and erect barriers to imitation, there are several things that entrepreneurs must do in order to succeed in finding and filling gaps. First, they must stay abreast of fundamental changes in various knowledge streams in order to be able to recognize the opening and closing of knowledge gaps (Levenhagen et al., 1993). Second, they must challenge pre-existing assumptions and beliefs in order to be able to generate the new conceptualizations or recombinations of existing knowledge and resources that are required to fill these gaps (Levenhagen et al., 1993). Finally, entrepreneurial leaders must create compelling 'stories' and arguments to reduce ambiguity and uncertainty for their stakeholders and thereby gain credibility and legitimization for their new conceptualizations (Levenhagen et al., 1993). As a result, entrepreneurs' mental models are instrumental in determining their success in discovering and bridging gaps in knowledge in order to create value for their organization.

This suggests that one difference between entrepreneurs and non-entrepreneurs may be in their respective cognitive structures. Palich and Bagby (1995), for example, found that while entrepreneurs do not have a higher risk propensity than non-entrepreneurs, the former perceive situations as being more positive and filled with opportunities than do the latter. Similarly, Jenkins and Johnson (1997) found that entrepreneurial success was associated with specific types of causal attributions that entrepreneurs make.

While researchers have examined entrepreneurial characteristics and behaviours associated with the successful start-up of a business (Gatewood et al., 1995), differences between entrepreneurs and non-entrepreneurs (Chen et al., 1998; Jenkins and Johnson, 1997; Palich and Bagby, 1995) and corporate entrepreneurship (Russell, 1999), research on entrepreneurial cognition has generally stopped at the point a business is started. Therefore, little attention has been given to the way in which the perceptions and beliefs of entrepreneurs affect the continued growth of the firm. In addition, cognitive mapping techniques have been applied to the study of the entrepreneurial mind in only a few studies (e.g. Jenkins and Johnson, 1997; Russell, 1999). Therefore, not much is known about the linkages between cognitive mapping, entrepreneurial cognition and growth strategies. To address this deficit in the literature, we examine entrepreneurial beliefs using the resource-based view of the firm and its underlying cognitive proposition as a theoretical lens and present a new method for mapping managerial logics for organizational growth.

The Cognitive Proposition Underlying Resource-Based Views of Growth

The resource-based view of the firm provides a useful framework for understanding the role of managerial cognitive structures in shaping entrepreneurial strategies for growth (Mahoney and Pandian, 1992; Peteraf, 1993). Tracing the origins of their work to Penrose (1959), resource-based theorists argue that a firm's unique portfolio of tangible and intangible resources influences the rate and direction of its growth and diversification. The rate of growth is influenced by how the management team conceptualizes and uses the firm's resource base. The direction of expansion is controlled by path dependencies inherent in imperfect resource substitution, the indivisibility of the firm's assets, and what management considers to be the firm's feasible growth strategies. All of these 'internal' forces interact with the competitive environment to determine economic performance. A firm can capture sustainable profits and grow to the extent that its key value-creating activities, or core competences (Hamel and Prahalad, 1994), cannot be easily imitated by competitors (Barney, 1991; Lippman and Rumelt, 1982).

The ability to sustain profitability in the face of competition has received the bulk of attention in the resource-based literature (Peteraf, 1993). No doubt, this has been due to the theoretical and practical importance of understanding firm performance within competitive markets. However, as Penrose (1959) noted, the way in which competitive forces impact a firm's profit stream depends in part on the 'image' (in Penrose's terms) that its managers have of both the firm itself and the competitive environment in which it operates. Managers will pursue competitive actions and deploy resources in ways that are consistent with their images of their firms' capabilities and the competitive threats that they believe the firm faces. In fact, Penrose suggests that this is the key entrepreneurial role of the management team. Thus, the Penrosian competitive environment is a subjective one as management teams from different firms survey the competitive landscape from their own idiosyncratic vantage points, use their market knowledge to define firm-specific productive capabilities, and then shift their firm's activities toward unique market opportunities that *they believe* their productive capabilities make possible. It is the combination of these managerial images of the firm and the competitive environment with what Penrose calls the 'entrepreneurial ambition' of a management team (its risk propensity and desire for growth) that defines the set of growth strategies that the management team deems feasible and attempts to enact.

One of the key insights of the Penrosian view is that it is not the actual resources themselves that determine the growth and direction of a firm. Rather, growth is a function of the productive capabilities that are engendered by resources interacting with managerial cognitive frameworks. To our knowledge, the 'cognitive proposition' (Mahoney and Pandian, 1992) described by Penrose, which underlies the resource-based view of organizational growth, has not been the subject of any systematic, scholarly inquiry in the entrepreneurship literature. Although a resource-based view of entrepreneurship has begun to receive some attention (Brush and Radha, 1997; Brush et al., 1997; Chandler and Hanks, 1994; Greene and Brown, 1997; Hart et al., 1995), the study of growth strategies from a cognitive perspective has not been the subject of much quantitative empirical research. The purpose of this study is to begin to investigate the cognitive bases of entrepreneurial dominant logics among a group of high-growth and successful firms. In particular, the research attempts to determine the extent to which underlying patterns of dominant growth logics exist across a sample of entrepreneurial firms from widely varying industries.

Dominant Growth Logics as Clusters of Growth Strategies

The probability of adopting a given set of growth strategies will vary given the unique conditions of a firm. Each combination of strategies can differ in its cost, a firm's ability to implement them, and the time they will take to provide a return on the company's investment. At the same time, however, research in strategic management has shown that there are systematic patterns of strategic similarity within and across industries (McGee and Thomas, 1986). These results have been generalized to the entrepreneurship arena by Carter et al. (1994), who found clear clusters of competitive strategies among new ventures across six different industries. These results make it clear that firms are not completely unique in the strategies that they enact, and uncovering similarities in strategies is an important line of research in the strategic management field.

Our study expands this line of research in two ways. First, most research on strategic similarity has focused on competitive strategies rather than explicit strategies for expanding a firm's business. In our research, we seek to uncover patterns of similarity among firms in their logics and strategies for growing the business. Second, our approach is explicitly cognitive in nature in the sense that we focus on the belief systems of entrepreneurs regarding their growth plans, what we have called growth 'logics'. Although some research has been conducted on strategic similarity from a cognitive perspective (Porac et al., 1995; Reger and Huff, 1993), this work was not focused on growth logics or on entrepreneurial firms *per se*. Putting these two contributions together, the goal of the present research is to determine the extent to which inter-industry similarities exist in the beliefs of entrepreneurs regarding their firms' feasible expansion paths, such that clusters of differing growth logics can be discerned across firms. To answer this question, we coded open-ended statements by entrepreneurs regarding their plans for future expansion and then used cluster analysis techniques to uncover inter-industry patterns in these growth statements.

RESEARCH METHOD

Data

Our statistical sample of entrepreneurial firms consisted of 54 firms drawn from the Kauffman Foundation's recently developed database of high-growth firms. This database contains information on regional finalists and winners in the annual Entrepreneur of the Year Competition sponsored by Ernst and Young, the Kauffman Foundation and *Inc.* magazine. Of the 54 firms, 31 per cent are in manufacturing, 48 per cent are service companies, and 11 per cent are retail companies. The remaining 10 per cent of the firms are in construction and real estate. At the time the narratives were written, 54 per cent of the companies in the sample were public. The average number of employees per company was 742, although the numbers ranged from 12 to 5640. The majority of the narratives (72 per cent) were written in 1994 and 1995. The remaining 28 per cent were written in 1993. The average company in our sample had $7.98 million in cash, $11.63 million in fixed assets, $6.71 million in inventory and an average net income, in the year the narratives were written, of $6.08 million. The average company's cash reserves grew by 76 per cent, fixed assets nearly doubled, and after-tax net income grew by almost 80 per cent from the year before the company was nominated for the Entrepreneur of the Year award through the year after the company was nominated. The average company also increased its labour force by 33 per cent from the year before the narrative was written to the year the narrative was written. This suggests that the companies in this sample are indeed high-growth firms.

Of particular significance for this study, the Kauffman database contains narrative information, written by the CEO or a top management team representative, describing both the company and the individual being nominated for the award. The narratives include background information on the nominee and his or her accomplishments, the company's history, its primary products and services, its business practices and its plans for the future. We developed a cognitive map of entrepreneurial dominant logics by content analysing these narratives to identify each firm's intended growth strategies.

Overview of Methodology

Cognitive mapping is a technique that is recognized as a useful way of depicting managerial mental models (Fiol and Huff, 1992). A cognitive map is a depiction of the hidden assumptions and beliefs of managers that represent concepts and the relationships among them (Fiol and Huff, 1992). Managerial cognitive structures must be inferred through managerial verbal or written statements (Fiol, 1995). While most studies on managerial cognition seem to use interviews, other researchers have collected public written statements in order to uncover managerial belief systems. For example, executives' statements in annual reports as well as internal planning documents have been used as sources of data to map the managerial mind (Fiol, 1989, 1995). In this study we continue in this vein by examining open-ended written statements from entrepreneurs. Entrepreneurial narratives are ideal for studying the thoughts and subjective beliefs that a manager may have about his or her environment because they contain 'implicit, personal theories of managerial action' (Pitt, 1998: 387). The statements were then content analysed using a computerized text analysis package, focusing on the sentence as the unit of analysis.

There are several benefits to using computers for qualitative data analysis. Computers can reduce the amount of labour required when organizing and coding ethnographic data without fundamentally changing the nature of the process (Dohan and Sánchez-Jankowski, 1998). However, there are many different types of software packages that can be used to assist researchers in qualitative data analysis, and each type has unique benefits. Dohan and Sánchez-Jankowski (1998) suggest that there are three categories of qualitative analysis software packages: document processors, data organizers and symbolic manipulators. Document processors are used to create and manage ethnographic databases as well as to search and retrieve text strings from these databases. Data organizers, on the other hand, allow the researcher to structure ethnographic databases by organizing and annotating or by coding. In this way, researchers are able more easily to place data in context, maneuvre through large databases and retrieve information based on theoretical mark-ups of the databases. Finally, symbolic manipulators assist researchers in the development and/or testing of theories about the relationships present in the ethnographic database.

The software package that we used, ATLAS/ti™, falls into this last category of symbol manipulators, and was chosen for its applicability to cognitive mapping.

ATLAS/ti is a package that appears to be uniquely suited for the task of cognitive mapping, for three reasons. First, it allows the source data to be in almost any form. Unlike some other packages, which can be used to analyse only textual data, ATLAS/ti allows for the analysis of text, audio, video, graphics or a combination of all four. Second, there is great flexibility in the types of linkages that can be created in ATLAS/ti. For example, both quotations and codes can be annotated, and various types of linkages can be created between the quotations, codes and memos (Dohan and Sánchez-Jankowski, 1998). As a result, several types of cognitive maps, including taxonomies and causal maps, can be drawn from the data using this program. Finally, ATLAS/ti contains a feature that allows for the graphical representation of the codes and linkages. Therefore, it makes the process of drawing a cognitive map less labour-intensive as well.

The content analysis of textual data is an analytic technique that can be used to make inferences regarding the sender of the message, the message itself and/or the intended audience (Weber, 1990). Content categories are developed and used to make analysis of the text more tractable by grouping units of text that have similar meanings. These units may be words, phrases, sentences or other lexical units that the researcher deems appropriate. Past research (Abrahamson and Park, 1994; Wade et al., 1997) has used the frequency with which top management discusses a concept in written narratives as an indicator of the concept's importance. In this study we used the mention of a particular growth strategy as an indicator of the salience of that strategy to the management team of the firm. We assume, therefore, that mentioning a particular strategy at least once implies that the strategy is a component of the entrepreneurial team's growth logic.

The narrative statements from the Kauffman Foundation's database of high-growth firms provide rich and informative interpretations that entrepreneurs have of their environments and the resources available to their firm, as well as perceptions of their ability to influence the performance of their firm (Pitt, 1998). However, there are several potential problems in using such communications as cognitive proxies. The major problem is that there may be a self-serving bias such that the narratives may reflect impression management more than the true feelings and beliefs of the managers (Fiol, 1995; Wagner and Gooding, 1997).

None the less, researchers have demonstrated that even narratives that may have a self-serving bias are useful sources of information on management cognition and strategy (Barr, 1998; Clapham and Schwenk, 1991; Huff and Schwenk, 1990). For example, non-evaluative statements, as opposed to those containing positive or negative evaluations, may be relatively accurate indicators of managerial beliefs (Fiol, 1995). The use of narrative statements from the entrepreneurs is appropriate in this case since we are interested in their mental models. We first analysed the content of each statement made by entrepreneurs in their narratives to separate those statements that referred to future plans for growth from statements that were not about growth. We then generated a map of different firm-growth logics by performing cluster analyses on the growth statements to classify firms into groups that used similar combinations of intended growth strategies. An advantage of content analysis is that the growth strategies and strategy combinations can be inductively derived rather than imposed in an *a priori* way by the researcher (Weber, 1990).

Content Analysis of Narratives

In order to identify the growth strategies that each company considered viable, we conducted two rounds of content analysis on each of the narratives. Two of the researchers performed the content analysis using ATLAS/ti. During the first round of content analysis, we coded each sentence of each narrative into one of six categories: CEO Characteristics, Company Characteristics, Company Capabilities, Growth Strategies, Image of the Market and Other. Less than 1 per cent of the sentences fell into the Other category. Interrater reliability was determined using Cohen's Kappa (Cohen, 1968), which adjusts for random chance in determining interrater agreement. The Cohen's Kappa for this stage of the content analysis, which was calculated on a 20 per cent subsample, was .87. Any disagreements among the raters were resolved.

In the second stage of the content analysis, each growth-strategy sentence was coded using six growth-strategy categories. These categories were derived by moving iteratively between prior theory and the data. The categories that were ultimately identified were consistent with six strategies that the literature on growth suggests can be used to increase revenues and profits (Leonard-Barton, 1995; Lieberman, 1989; Penrose, 1959; Powell et al., 1996; Thompson, 1986). These strategies are: growth through mergers, acquisitions and expansion of the firm's production capacity (Lieberman, 1989; Penrose, 1959); developing alliances or partnerships with other firms (Leonard-Barton, 1995; Powell et al., 1996); expanding into new geographic and customer markets (Leonard-Barton, 1995); developing new products or services to be offered in existing or new markets (Leonard-Barton, 1995); expanding the firm's labour force and/or increasing the capabilities of its employees (Penrose, 1959); and, finally, increasing earnings by reducing costs and/or increasing the productive capacity of existing assets through technical and process improvements (Thompson, 1986). Table 5.1 provides examples of the types of growth strategies that fell into each of these categories.

The first category of growth strategies are those that are 'capital-intensive'. The strategies in this category include building new plants or facilities, expansion of the firm's production capacity, strategic acquisitions,

TABLE 5.1   Expansion path examples

Expansion path category	Activities included
Capital-intensive	Capital expenditures for new plants or facilities Acquisitions and mergers Joint ventures
Alliances and partnerships	Alliances, partnerships, franchising and licensing agreements
Market expansion	Enter new markets (product or geographic) Increase share in existing markets New real estate developments Access new customer base
Product/service	New products and/or services
Human resources	Increased hiring Management team and employee training, education or quality of work life improvements
Technical improvements	Production and administrative process improvements Technological innovations and developments

mergers and joint ventures (Lieberman, 1989; Penrose, 1959). All of these strategies require large capital expenditures, and growth-strategy sentences were coded as 'capital-intensive' when they mentioned such things as 'joint venture', 'construction of … [new facilities]' and 'strategic acquisitions'.

The second category of growth strategies are those that are 'non-capital-intensive'. The strategies in this category include the development of strategic alliances, partnerships with other firms, franchising and licensing agreements (Leonard-Barton, 1995; Powell et al., 1996). Unlike the capital-intensive strategies, these strategies are based upon sharing costs with other firms or otherwise reducing the amount of down-side risk faced by the firm. Growth-strategy sentences in this category mention 'strategic alliances', 'strategic partnerships' and 'licensing agreements'.

The third category of growth strategies are those that involve 'market expansion'. The strategies in this category include entry into new product or geographic markets, increase of market share in existing markets, and accessing new customer segments (Leonard-Barton, 1995). These strategies involve increasing the number of customers served, whether by capturing higher market share or by geographic or product diversification. 'Market expansion' sentences mention 'international expansion', 'seizing opportunities to enter new markets' and 'expansion and diversification … into new fields'.

The fourth category of growth strategies are those that involve 'product or service development'. The strategies in this category include the development of new products as well as services (Leonard-Barton, 1995). Growth-strategy sentences were coded as 'product or service development' when they mentioned things such as 'developing new products', 'increasing the number of product lines' and 'bringing to market new ... products and services'.

The fifth category of growth strategies are those that involve 'human resource improvements'. The strategies in this category include hiring new employees, improving the quality of work life for employees, and enhancing the skill of the management team and employees through training and/or education programmes (Penrose, 1959). Growth-strategy sentences were coded as 'human resource improvements' when they mentioned such things as 'expanding [the company's] workforce', attracting 'additional outstanding employees' and an 'incentive reward system'.

The final category of growth strategies are those that involve 'process improvements'. The strategies in this category include production and administrative process improvement and technological innovation (Thompson, 1986). These strategies are aimed at increasing earnings through enhanced productivity or through cost reduction. Growth-strategy sentences were coded as 'process improvements' when they mentioned things such as 'productivity-enhancing technologies', 'automate numerous processes' and 'development of adaptive process control techniques'.

Table 5.2 provides sample phrases from the growth-strategy sentences that indicated which type of growth strategy was being discussed by the entrepreneur. The Cohen's Kappa for this stage of the analysis, which was calculated using all 274 growth strategy phrases, was .93.

Cluster Analysis

Cluster analysis has been used in various disciplines for the purposes of classification (Aldenderfer and Blashfield, 1984; Bailey, 1994; Romesburg, 1984). In this study, dummy variables were created for the six growth strategies. Since we were interested in the presence or absence of each strategy, as opposed to the relative importance of each growth strategy, a firm's narrative was coded as a '1' if the firm's entrepreneur mentioned his/her intent to use a particular strategy and a '0' if he/she did not. The presence/absence of each of the six strategies was coded in this way. The firms in the study were then clustered along these six binary growth-logic scores using the average-between-groups method (Romesburg, 1984).

The average-between-groups method is one of the most widely used clustering techniques. Romesburg (1984) recommends the use of this technique since there is less distortion in transforming similarities between objects into a tree and because it can be used with any resemblance coefficient. Since we wished to cluster using binary data, the average-between-groups method was the most appropriate choice.

The resemblance coefficient used in our cluster analysis was a simple matching coefficient. The simple matching algorithm calculates similarity based upon the proportion of 1–1 and 0–0 matches along the different attributes between any two cases (Romesburg, 1984). This particular

TABLE 5.2   Sample growth-strategy phrases

Growth-strategy category	Sample phrases
Capital-intensive strategies	'Potential plans for further growth include the acquisition of other companies or technology …' 'Strategic planning for the Company includes acquisitions and mergers …' 'The city facility will increase manufacturing capacity …' 'A newly formed joint venture … should go on stream within twelve months …' 'Fboss also plans continued growth through internal expansion and by the acquisition of businesses …'
Non-capital intensive strategies	'These alliances … strongly position Fcomp for a bright future.' 'Another new division of Fcomp will license in and distribute Pproducts …' '… development of strategic alliances with partners in complementary industries …' 'With this in mind, one of Fcomp's future goals is to build "Strategic Partnerships" with original equipment manufacturers …' 'Future growth will be seen in the use of licensing arrangements now in hand with Ccomp, Ccomp for Pproduct and Ccomp for Pproduct.'
Market expansion strategies	'Fcomp plans to expand geographically …' '… the company intends to expand into related markets …' 'Efforts to penetrate or expand business in the emerging Rregion, Sregion and Tregion markets are a priority and will produce a larger customer base.' '… growth in existing Fcomp markets …' 'Fcomp's Plans for the Future include careful, reasoned expansion and diversification, where needed by clients, into new fields and geographical regions.'
Product and service development strategies	'We will soon expand our services to include …' 'Potential plans for further growth include … developing new products from within.' 'Its vision of the future includes the development of ever more capable versions of the Pproduct and Pproduct xx products.' 'Development continues on these products and associated peripherals.'
Human resource improvement strategies	'To facilitate future growth Fboss has recently added several members to the senior staff.' 'To accomplish this expansion will require a major effort to attract additional outstanding employees to the Fcomp fold.'

(Contd.)

TABLE 5.2   (Contd.)

Growth-strategy category	Sample phrases
	'Fboss believes that employees should be rewarded for good work and plans to structure compensation and career paths at all levels to be closely aligned with performance.' '… improvement and expansion of training through in-house and supported training programs …' '… an incentive reward system that will improve staff motivation …'
Process improvement strategies	'Because [xx] is an ongoing quality system of process improvement, we will undergo a rigorous schedule of external and internal audits to prove we are maintaining and improving our quality.' 'Eliminating and/or reducing re-work through the implementation of Total Quality Management (TQM) techniques …' 'Adaptive process control is one of the many paths Fboss is exploring.' 'In the mid-19[xx]s Fboss plans to invest in productivity-enhancing technologies and quality improvement.'

Note: All identities have been disguised and refer to companies, products and individuals using a letter notation, e.g. Ccomp, Pproduct and Fboss.

resemblance coefficient was chosen for several different reasons. First, it was an association measure and therefore appropriate for binary data.[1] Second, it provides a meaningful proportion since it is the proportion of agreements. Third, based on the nature of the formula used to calculate this coefficient, unlike some of the other association measures, it can be calculated even if there are only 0–0 matches. Finally, simple matching weighs 1–1 and 0–0 matches equally. This was important since we were interested not only in which strategies were mentioned, but also in which ones were not mentioned.

One concern that arises when using cluster analysis is in choosing the appropriate number of clusters. Determining the number of clusters has been problematic and has often been subjective (Aldenderfer and Blashfield, 1984; Bailey, 1994; Milligan and Cooper, 1985; Porac et al., 1995; Romesburg, 1984). One method for determining the optimal number of clusters is to compute correlations between the proximity matrix used to form clusters and a series of structure matrices that correspond to various cluster solutions (Milligan and Cooper, 1985; Porac et al., 1995). The optimal solution occurs when the correlation between the proximity matrix and the structure matrices reaches a maximum. Upon running the cluster analysis, we created structure matrices for two-through ten-cluster solutions and calculated correlations between each structure matrix and the original proximity matrix using the quadratic assignment procedure (QAP) in UCINET IV (Borgatti et al., 1996). From Table 5.3 we can see that the five-cluster solution has the highest correlation and therefore is the

TABLE 5.3   Correlations between proximity matrix
and cluster structure matrices

Cluster solution								
2	3	4	5	6	7	8	9	10
.326	.513	.520	.535	.533	.527	.514	.511	.507

optimal solution. Once the cluster memberships were determined, the narrative statements were qualitatively analysed to search for any commonalties among cluster members that may help explain why entrepreneurs chose a particular set of intended growth strategies. Particular attention was paid to mentions of entrepreneurs' experiences, company experiences and descriptions of their businesses and their environments.

RESULTS

Table 5.4 presents the results of the cluster analysis with five clusters. Figures 5.1 through 5.5 present the five clusters identified in our analysis graphically. Dotted lines indicate that some, but not all, members of a cluster pursued a particular growth strategy. Each cluster has distinct characteristics. The firms in the first cluster focus (Figure 5.1, see page 129) on process improvements and human resources development. The second cluster (Figure 5.2, see page 129) has a focus on market and product expansion, with some of the firms mentioning alliances and partnerships as well. The third cluster (Figure 5.3, see page 130) is focused on human resources and capital-intensive strategies with some market and product expansion. The firms in the fourth cluster (Figure 5.4, see page 131) focus on market expansion, product expansion and capital-intensive strategies. Finally, the firms in the fifth cluster (Figure 5.5, see page 132) mention all six growth strategies. The qualitative analysis of the narrative statements provided some interesting results.

Table 5.5 lists selected sample quotes from the narrative statements that indicate that there are regular patterns within each cluster that reflect the combination of strategies that comprise a cluster's typical growth logic.

The firms in the first cluster (Figure 5.1) seem to focus on expanding product offerings through process improvements and training of employees. The narratives for these firms frequently mention 'quality', 'efficiency' and 'Total Quality Management', and the entrepreneurs' descriptions of their businesses and environments seem to indicate that quality and efficiency are the key ingredients that lead to flexibility and growth. Therefore, these firms evidence a dominant logic of 'expansion of products via continuous improvement'.

The second cluster (Figure 5.2) includes two distinct types of firms. The narrative statements indicate that both types of firms see opportunities

TABLE 5.4   Cluster membership

Clusters	Company ID#		DUMMKT	DUMOUT	DUMPROC	DUMHUM	DUMCAP	DUMNO
1	1	1591	0	0	1	1	0	1
	2	1885	1	1	1	1	0	0
	3	2102	0	1	1	1	0	0
	4	2213	0	0	1	1	0	0
	5	2311	0	1	1	1	0	0
	Total	5	5	5	5	5	5	5
2	1	1652	0	0	0	0	0	0
	2	1808	1	1	0	0	0	0
	3	1814	1	1	0	0	0	0
	4	1818	0	0	0	0	0	0
	5	1859	1	0	0	0	0	0
	6	1868	1	1	0	1	0	0
	7	1888	1	0	0	1	0	0
	8	1940	1	0	0	0	0	0
	9	2066	0	0	0	0	0	0
	10	2100	0	1	0	0	0	1
	11	2109	1	0	0	0	0	0
	12	2112	0	1	0	0	0	1
	13	2120	0	0	0	0	0	1
	14	2140	0	0	0	1	0	1
	15	2141	1	1	0	0	0	0
	16	2152	1	1	0	0	0	1
	17	2155	1	1	0	0	0	1
	18	2226	1	1	0	0	0	0
	19	2227	0	0	0	0	0	0
	20	2233	1	1	1	0	0	0
	21	2244	1	0	0	0	0	1
	22	2297	1	0	0	0	0	1
	23	2506	0	0	0	0	0	0
	Total	23	23	23	23	23	23	23
3	1	1836	1	0	0	1	1	1
	2	1884	1	0	1	1	1	0
	3	1889	1	1	0	1	1	0
	4	1999	0	0	0	1	1	0
	5	2083	0	0	0	1	1	0
	6	2098	0	0	1	1	1	0
	7	2121	1	0	1	1	1	0
	8	2149	0	1	0	1	1	0
	9	2181	0	1	0	1	1	0
	10	2295	0	0	0	1	1	0
	Total	10	10	10	10	10	10	10
4	1	1870	1	0	0	0	1	0
	2	1934	1	1	1	0	1	0
	3	1979	1	1	0	0	1	0
	4	2046	0	0	1	0	1	0
	5	2096	1	1	1	0	1	0
	6	2103	0	1	1	0	1	0
	7	2125	1	1	0	0	1	0

(Contd.)

TABLE 5.4   (Contd.)

Clusters		Company ID#	DUMMKT	DUMOUT	DUMPROC	DUMHUM	DUMCAP	DUMNO
	8	2136	0	1	0	0	1	0
	9	2144	0	0	1	0	1	0
	10	2209	1	0	0	0	1	0
	11	2212	1	1	0	0	1	0
	12	2266	1	0	0	0	1	0
	13	2327	1	1	0	0	1	0
	Total	13	13	13	13	13	13	13
5	1	2090	1	1	1	1	0	1
	2	2271	1	1	1	1	1	1
	3	2314	1	1	1	0	1	1
	Total	3	3	3	3	3	3	3
Total	N	54	54	54	54	54	54	54

for growth into new product and geographic markets, but only one type has identified how to accomplish this growth. The firms that know how they want to accomplish their growth in these new markets generally mention franchising, alliances and partnerships as their intended modes of entry. Since all of the firms see growth opportunities, but only some know how they want to accomplish it, these firms have a 'market and product expansion' logic.

The firms in the third group (Figure 5.3) need to build capacity to serve increasing demand in their current segment or to expand where they have identified 'unmet' market needs and 'under-served' segments. Therefore, these firms have a logic of 'dealing with capacity deficits'.

The fourth group (Figure 5.4) is preparing for future growth through capital expenditures in plant and equipment, mergers, acquisitions and joint ventures. These firms anticipate future growth and are preparing for it by building plants and acquiring other firms. These firms have a logic of 'anticipatory growth'.

The firms from the fifth group (Figure 5.5) follow a 'scattered growth' logic. Each of these firms has experienced growth through a number of different strategies. As a result, they cannot seem to identify which particular growth strategy or combination of strategies is most appropriate for them – everything seems to work. Therefore, the firms in this group state that they are going to follow every single one of the growth strategies. A typical statement will include expansion into new geographic markets, development of new products, improvement of processes, recruitment, strategic acquisitions, partnerships and construction of new plants.

While not all firms in a given cluster choose exactly the same combination of intended growth strategies, it is interesting to note that the narratives indicate that there were dominant logics that led to their choice. For each of the clusters, prior successes with a particular growth strategy seemed to lead to a belief that it was the appropriate strategy to pursue

TABLE 5.5   Sample quotes

Cluster	Quotes
1. Expansion of products via continuous improvement	'total quality control' 'Total Quality Management (TQM)' 'be the most cost-effective, quality leader' 'advocate of total quality management and continuous improvement'
2. Market and product expansion	'find an unfilled niche in the marketplace, create a retail concept to fill that niche, and then grow the business through franchising' 'expand globally by seizing opportunities to enter new markets' 'Future growth will be seen in the use of licensing arrangements now in hand with Ccomp, Ccomp for Pproduct and Ccomp for Pproduct.' 'expanding largely with the money of the franchisees' 'the development of strategic alliances, with partners in complementary industries'
3. Dealing with capacity deficits	'Fboss and Fcomp are at the forefront of the fastest growing segment of the employment market' 'increasing our market share' 'In my opinion the need to provide this service will continue to grow during the next [xx].' 'We are constantly spending time and money on educational seminars to maximize current job competence and readiness for future opportunities.' 'Our group is constantly looking for investment opportunities that we feel are "under"-managed.' '[The newly built plant] … enhances the company's ability to develop and serve its authorized builder organization in those regions.' 'These capacity increases were necessary for Ccomp to meet the demand of its rapidly growing customer base.' 'the company intends to expand into related markets. … Each of these share some common characteristics: they are under-served by their present systems vendors, their requirements are largely met by Fcomp products, and there is no system available today that meets all their needs.'
4. Anticipatory growth	'strategic acquisitions' 'To support this projected growth, annual capital expenditures at Fcomp have risen from approximately [xx] in 19[xx] to over [xx] today.' 'to keep the organization and its resources focused on future challenges and opportunities' 'Fcomp plans to expand geographically by opening new offices or through mergers or acquisitions.' 'Potential plans for further growth include the acquisition of other companies or technology, as well as developing new products from within.'

(Contd.)

TABLE 5.5   (Contd.)

Cluster	Quotes
5. Scattered growth	'continued growth through internal expansion and by the acquisition of businesses with complementary markets or technologies' and 'collaborative efforts with large prime contractors and equipment manufacturers' and 'maintain the high quality of the company's workforce' 'introduction of new products' and 'development of adaptive process control techniques [that will] reduce rework, increase yields and improve quality' and 'eventual acquisition of related companies' and 'strategic alliances with the remaining major equipment [manufacturers]' 'expansion and diversification, where needed by clients, into new fields and geographical regions' and 'focus on recruiting, management training, and developing management information systems'

in the future (Tyler and Steensma, 1998). There are several possible explanations for this bias. If the firm had past experiences with the strategy, the entrepreneur may believe that it is merely the appropriate strategy for the environment. Alternatively, the entrepreneur may believe that there are several appropriate strategies for the environment, but that the firm may have differential ability to implement specific growth strategies. A third explanation is that the entrepreneur believes him/herself to have the appropriate capabilities to implement a particular growth strategy based on past success with it.

DISCUSSION

The resource-based view of the firm argues that the growth and direction of organizations are determined by a complex interaction between available resources, capabilities and managerial mental models (Mahoney and Pandian, 1992; Penrose, 1959). These mental models, or dominant logics, provide subjective constraints to firm actions by limiting the amounts and types of opportunities that a firm will consider. Penrose (1959) has suggested that research on entrepreneurial mental models can be of help in explaining or predicting the behaviour of firms. By qualitatively analysing entrepreneurial narrative statements about growth, we have begun to discern some of the commonalties among firms that share similar dominant logics.

Research in strategy has rarely examined the existence of multiple strategies within an organization, and there appears to be an underlying assumption that a firm will pursue only one strategy at a time. In fact, the only way in which researchers appear to examine multiple strategies is in the context of firm diversification and maintaining coherence among the different lines of business (Grant, 1988; Prahalad and Bettis, 1986). Therefore, while firms may use different competitive strategies in different

Figure 5.1   Growth logic: cluster 1

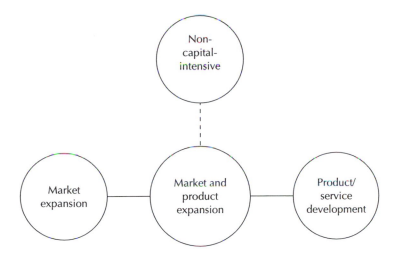

Figure 5.2   Growth logic: cluster 2

businesses, following more than one strategy is seen as generally a bad idea (Porter, 1985). As a result, there has been little research on whether or not organizations will follow multiple strategies or which strategies are likely to co-occur if they do.

However, competitive positioning is based upon the combination of activities that a firm engages in across various markets and lines of business (Porter, 1996). Therefore, it may be more appropriate to think of firms as following a cluster of different types of strategies (growth, marketing, etc.), guided by a single dominant logic about the competitive advantages, resources and capabilities of the firm relative to the competition, as opposed to a single strategy. Since a dominant logic is defined as 'the way in which managers conceptualize the business and make critical resource allocation decisions' (Prahalad and Bettis, 1986: 490), dominant logics are clusters of strategies that the managers see as appropriate for the firm. Since entrepreneurs attempt to reduce uncertainty and create competitive advantage by bridging gaps across multiple streams of knowledge (Levenhagen et al., 1993), dominant logics may be capturing these

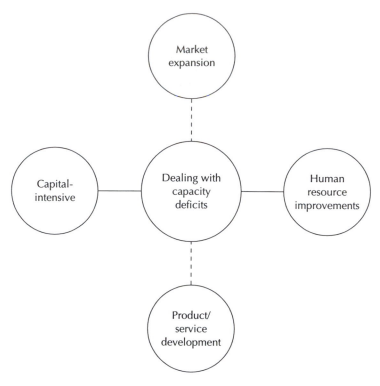

Figure 5.3   Growth logic: cluster 3

attempts to close gaps. The results of this study are consistent with this perspective, and suggest that firms intend to follow multiple strategies for growth, and that these strategies cluster in somewhat predictable ways. As such, dominant logics can be seen as strategy 'portfolios'.

In our study we found five distinct clusters of growth logics, illustrated in Figures 5.1 through 5.5. Each of these growth logic clusters differed in the number and types of strategies that were included. An examination of the narratives suggest that in most of these logic clusters, the entrepreneurs are actively trying to combine multiple strategies to obtain a desired result. Since there has been a wide-spread assumption that multiple strategies are bad and that strategies are inherently unrelated, this may represent attempts to bridge multiple streams of knowledge. However, this is not necessarily the case for all clusters. For example, the market and product expansion logic (Figure 5.2) does not seem to involve an explicit linkage between strategies. Similarly, there does not appear to be any linkage across the strategies in the scattered growth logic (Figure 5.5). Still, it is not entirely clear from the data available in this study if the use of multiple strategies is a way of closing gaps.

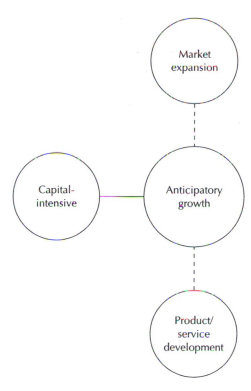

Figure 5.4   Growth logic: cluster 4

Not all of the entrepreneurs discuss whether or not these are multiple, independent strategies or if they anticipate synergies/links among them and are therefore a part of a true 'logic'. One might inquire into the performance effect of following multiple strategies. As stated earlier, strategy researchers have long operated under the assumption that lack of focus is detrimental to firm performance (Porter, 1985). Returning to the resource-based view, growth is constrained by available resources, including managerial capabilities, and attempting to follow too many different opportunities will result in the outstripping of managerial resources (Penrose, 1959). Therefore, growth without focus leads to setting oneself up for failure. As a result, we would expect the number of different strategies included in a firm's dominant logic to be negatively related to performance, with more focused firms having higher performance than less focused firms.

On the other hand, too much focus may leave a firm unable to meet the requirements of the competitive environment (Miller, 1993, 1996; Miller and Chen, 1996). While some amount of focus leads to the development of distinctive competencies, too much focus leads to a skill set that is not capable of keeping up with variation in environmental demands

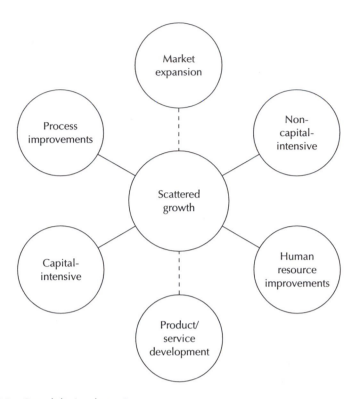

Figure 5.5   Growth logic: cluster 5

(Miller, 1993, 1996; Miller and Chen, 1996). This may limit a firm's ability to compete in all but one small segment of the environment. However, the opportunities available in any one area may be limited, so it may not be possible for firms to maintain a steady rate of growth unless multiple strategies are followed at some point. Also, some entrepreneurship researchers have stated that entrepreneurs search for opportunities beyond their current resource configurations, with the assumption that the required resources will be discovered and acquired along the way (Kirzner, 1985). This suggests that the current resource configurations need not necessarily constrain the number and type of growth strategies chosen, but there may be an optimal level of focus. As a result, we would expect an inverse U-shaped relationship where firms with both low or high numbers of strategies would have lower performance than firms that have an intermediate number of strategies included in their strategy configuration.

While we are unable to clarify the link between the number of dimensions included in a firm's growth logic and their subsequent performance based upon this data set, we are currently pursuing several different directions in our study of entrepreneurial mental models. First, future research will examine the link between growth logics and performance. There are a number of ways in which this could be done. We will try to determine if there are appropriate dominant logics based upon a firm's resource configurations or the environment; if there is 'one best' dominant logic that leads to superior performance; or if there is a link between the number of dimensions included in a firm's dominant logic and its subsequent performance. Second, we seek to study the question of intention versus implementation regarding entrepreneurial growth logics. Argyris and Schon (1974) make distinctions between 'espoused theories' and 'theories in use'. By examining sources of secondary data, we may be able to discover to what extent these entrepreneurs followed the strategies that they discussed in their narratives. Finally, we wish to examine changes in dominant logics. Different theories offer various explanations for why a manager's mental models may change, and we wish to test several explanations against one another to determine which accounts seem to provide valid explanations for strategic change.

While we believe that this study contributes to the resource-based literature by identifying commonalties among entrepreneurs in their dominant logics for growth, there are two limitations of our research that must be recognized.

First, the size and nature of the sample may constrain the ability to make generalizations. With a sample size of only 54, it is difficult to find other systematic relationships among the firms following each dominant logic. For example, it was not possible to see if there was a systematic relationship between industry type and dominant logic. In addition, since the Kauffman database is limited to firms identified as being successful, it is not possible to generalize these findings to firms that are not as successful. This also leaves open the question of how unsuccessful experiences can influence dominant logic development. As a result, larger and more diverse samples should be examined in future research.

Second, the use of narrative statements written by the CEOs or top management team members of the sample firms presents a partial picture of the types of experiences that the firm has truly had. In addition, it is unclear if the sample firms intended to implement the growth strategies they mentioned, or if there may have been some impression management involved on the part of the entrepreneurs. Therefore, it may be worthwhile for future studies to obtain more complete data on firm experiences as well as the actual growth strategies implemented by each firm.

NOTE

1. Association measures are appropriate for binary data (e.g. Aldenderfer and Blashfield, 1984; Bailey, 1994) while Euclidean distance measures are appropriate for data measured on interval or ratio scales (e.g. Romesburg, 1984).

REFERENCES

Abrahamson, E. and Park, C. (1994) 'Concealment of negative organizational outcomes: An agency theory perspective', *Academy of Management Journal*, 37: 1302–1334.

Aldenderfer, M.S. and Blashfield, R.K. (1984) *Cluster Analysis*. Newbury Park, CA: Sage.

Argyris, C. and Schon, D.A. (1974) *Theory in Practice: Increasing Professional Effectiveness*. San Francisco: Jossey-Bass.

Bailey, K.D. (1994) *Typologies and Taxonomies: An Introduction to Classification Techniques*. Thousand Oaks, CA: Sage.

Barney, J. (1991) 'Firm resources and sustained competitive advantage', *Journal of Management*, 17: 99–120.

Barr, P.S. (1998) 'Adapting to unfamiliar environmental events: A look at the evolution of interpretation and its role in strategic change', *Organization Science*, 9: 644–669.

Borgatti, S.P., Everett, M.G. and Freeman, L.C. (1996) UCINET IV Version 1.64. Natick: Analytic Technologies.

Bougon, M.G. (1983) 'Uncovering cognitive maps: The Self-Q technique', in G. Morgan (ed.), *Beyond Method: Strategies for Social Research*. Beverly Hills, CA: Sage. pp. 173–188.

Brush, C.G. and Radha, C. (1997) 'Resources in new and small ventures: Influences on performance outcomes', paper presented at the Babson–Kauffman Conference on Entrepreneurship, Boston, MA.

Brush, C.G., Greene, P.G., Hart, M.M. and Edelman, L.S. (1997) 'Resource configurations over the lifecycle of ventures', paper presented at the Babson–Kauffman Conference on Entrepreneurship, Boston, MA.

Calori, R., Johnson, G. and Sarnin, P. (1994) 'CEOs' cognitive maps and the scope of the organization', *Strategic Management Journal*, 15 (6): 437–457.

Carter, N.M., Stearns, T.M., Reynolds, P.D. and Miller, B.A. (1994) 'New venture strategies: Theory development with an empirical base', *Strategic Management Journal*, 15: 21–41.

Chandler, G.N. and Hanks, S.H. (1994) 'Market attractiveness, resource-based capabilities, venture strategies, and venture performance', *Journal of Business Venturing*, 9: 331–349.

Chen, C.C., Greene, P.G. and Crick, A. (1998) 'Does entrepreneurial self-efficacy distinguish entrepreneurs from managers?', *Journal of Business Venturing*, 13: 295–316.

Clapham, S.E. and Schwenk, C.R. (1991) 'Self-serving attributions, managerial cognition, and company performance', *Strategic Management Journal*, 12: 219–229.

Cohen, J. (1968) 'Weighted kappa: Nominal scale agreement with provision for scaled disagreement or partial credit', *Psychological Bulletin*, 70: 213–220.

Cossette, P. and Audet, M. (1992) 'Mapping of an idiosyncratic schema', *Journal of Management Studies*, 29: 325–347.

Dohan, D. and Sánchez-Jankowski, M.S. (1998) 'Using computers to analyze ethnographic field data: Theoretical and practical considerations', *Annual Review of Sociology*, 24: 477–498.

Eden, C.E., Ackermann, F. and Cropper, S. (1992) 'The analysis of cause maps', *Journal of Management Studies*, 29: 309–324.

Fiol, C.M. (1989) 'A semiotic analysis of corporate language: Organizational boundaries and joint venturing', *Administrative Science Quarterly*, 34: 277–303.

Fiol, C.M. (1995) 'Corporate communications: Comparing executives' private and public statements', *Academy of Management Journal*, 38: 522–536.

Fiol, C.M. and Huff, A.S. (1992) 'Maps for managers: Where are we? Where do we go from here?', *Journal of Management Studies*, 29: 267–285.

Gatewood, E.J., Shaver, K.G. and Gartner, W.B. (1995) 'A longitudinal study of cognitive factors influencing start-up behaviors and success at venture creation', *Journal of Business Venturing*, 10: 371–391.

Grant, R.M. (1988) 'On "dominant logic", relatedness and the link between diversity and performance', *Strategic Management Journal*, 9: 639–642.

Greene, P.G. and Brown, T.E. (1997) 'Resource needs and the dynamic capitalism typology', *Journal of Business Venturing*, 12: 161–173.

Hamel, G. and Prahalad, C.K. (1994) *Competing for the Future*. Cambridge, MA: Harvard Business School Press.

Hart, M.M., Stevenson, H.H. and Dial, J. (1995) 'Entrepreneurship: A definition revisited', *Frontiers of Entrepreneurship Research*, 75–89.

Hill, R.C. and Levenhagen, M. (1995) 'Metaphors and mental models: Sensemaking and sensegiving in innovative and entrepreneurial activities', *Journal of Management*, 21: 1057–1074.

Huff, A.S. and Schwenk, C.R. (1990) 'Bias and sensemaking in good times and bad', in A.S. Huff (ed.), *Mapping Strategic Thought*. New York: Wiley. pp. 89–108.

Jenkins, M. and Johnson, G. (1997) 'Entrepreneurial intentions and outcomes: A comparative causal mapping study', *Journal of Management Studies*, 34: 895–920.

Kirzner, I.M. (1985) *Discovery and the Capitalist Process*. Chicago: University of Chicago Press.

Langfield-Smith, K. (1992) 'Exploring the need for a shared cognitive map', *Journal of Management Studies*, 29: 349–368.

Laukkanen, M. (1994) 'Comparative cause mapping of organizational cognitions', *Organization Science*, 5: 322–343.

Leonard-Barton, D. (1995) *Wellsprings of Knowledge*. Cambridge, MA: Harvard Business School Press.

Levenhagen, M., Porac, J.F. and Thomas, H. (1993) 'Emergent industry leadership and the selling of technological visions: A social constructionist view', in J. Hendry and G. Johnson (eds), *Strategic Thinking: Leadership and the Management of Change*. New York: Wiley.

Lieberman, M. (1989) 'The learning curve: Technology barriers to entry and competitive survival in the chemical processing industries', *Strategic Management Journal*, 10: 431–447.

Lippman, S. and Rumelt, R.P. (1982) 'Uncertain imitability: An analysis of interfirm differences in efficiency under competition', *Bell Journal of Economics*, 13: 418–453.

McGee, J.T. and Thomas, H. (1986) 'Strategic groups: Theory, research, and taxonomy', *Strategic Management Journal*, 7: 141–160.

Mahoney, J.T. and Pandian, J.R. (1992) 'The resource-based view within the conversation of strategic management', *Strategic Management Journal*, 13: 363–380.

Miller, D. (1993) 'The architecture of simplicity', *Academy of Management Review*, 18: 116–138.

Miller, D. (1996) 'Configurations revisited', *Strategic Management Journal*, 17: 505–512.

Miller, D. and Chen, M.J. (1996) 'The simplicity of competitive repertoires: An empirical analysis', *Strategic Management Journal*, 17: 419–439.

Milligan, G.W. and Cooper, M.C. (1985) 'An examination of procedures for determining the number of clusters in a data set', *Psychometrika*, 50 (2): 159–179.

Palich, L.E. and Bagby, D.R. (1995) 'Using cognitive theory to explain entrepreneurial risk-taking: Challenging conventional wisdom', *Journal of Business Venturing*, 10: 425–438.

Penrose, E. (1959) *The Theory of the Growth of the Firm*. Oxford: Oxford University Press.

Peteraf, M.A. (1993) 'The cornerstones of competitive advantage: A resource-based view', *Strategic Management Journal*, 14: 179–191.

Pitt, M. (1998) 'A tale of two gladiators: "Reading" entrepreneurs as texts', *Organization Studies*, 19: 387–414.

Porac, J.F., Thomas, H., Wilson, F., Paton, D. and Kanfer, A. (1995) 'Rivalry and the industry model of Scottish knitwear producers', *Administrative Science Quarterly*, 40: 203–227.

Porter, M.E. (1985) *Competitive Advantage*. New York: Free Press.

Porter, M.E. (1996) 'What is strategy?', *Harvard Business Review*, 74: 61–78.

Powell, W., Koput, K. and Smith-Doerr, L. (1996) 'Interorganizational collaboration and the locus of innovation: Networks of learning in biotechnology', *Administrative Science Quarterly*, 41: 116–145.

Prahalad, C.K. and Bettis, R.A. (1986) 'The dominant logic: A new linkage between diversity and performance', *Strategic Management Journal*, 7: 485–501.

Reger, R.K. and Huff, A.S. (1993) 'Strategic groups: A cognitive perspective', *Strategic Management Journal*, 14: 103–124.

Reger, R.K. and Palmer, T.B. (1996) 'Managerial categorization of competitors: Using old maps to navigate new environments', *Organization Science*, 7: 22–39.

Romesburg, H.C. (1984) *Cluster Analysis for Researchers*. Malabar, FL: Krieger Publishing.

Russell, R.D. (1999) 'Developing a process model of intrapreneurial systems: A cognitive mapping approach', *Entrepreneurship Theory & Practice*, 23: 65–84.

Thompson, R. (1986) 'Understanding cash flow: A system dynamics analysis', *Journal of Small Business Management*, 24: 23–30.

Tyler, B.B. and Steensma, H.K. (1998) 'The effects of executives' experiences and perceptions on their assessment of potential technological alliances', *Srategic Management Journal*, 19: 939–965.

Wade, J., Porac, J. and Pollock, T. (1997) 'Worth words and the justification of executive pay', *Journal of Organizational Behavior*, 18: 641–664.

Wagner, J.A. and Gooding, R.Z. (1997) 'Equivocal information and attribution: An investigation of patterns of managerial sensemaking', *Strategic Management Journal*, 18: 275–286.

Weber, R.P. (1990) *Basic Content Analysis*. 2nd edn. Newbury Park, CA: Sage.

6

SPATIALIZING KNOWLEDGE

Placing the Knowledge Community of Motor Sport Valley

Nick Henry and **Steven Pinch**

ABSTRACT

Within the contemporary world of 'the knowledge economy', understanding the spatial organization of knowledge production has become a key issue. Drawing on recent emphases in economic geography on the cultural construction and social embeddedness of economic success, this chapter outlines an attempt to understand one form of spatial organization of knowledge – the agglomeration or cluster – using the analytical concept of 'the knowledge community'. Using the example of Motor Sport Valley, the chapter provides an empirical and methodological example of how one might place a knowledge community. The British motor sport industry dominates its world of production with a regional agglomeration, Motor Sport Valley, centred on Oxfordshire and stretching into East Anglia and down into Surrey. The chapter provides *empirical demonstration* of the processes of knowledge generation and dissemination constituting the space (and knowledge community) of Motor Sport Valley.

PROLOGUE

The Role of Geography

The sub-discipline of economic geography conveys essentially two major propositions. First, that a simple mapping of economic activity – sectors, trade flows, multinationals, R&D expenditure, labour migration, and so on – reveals the geographically uneven development of economic life. It highlights the realities and interconnections of economic systems at various spatial scales: for example, what Dicken (1998) calls the 'global triad', the 'sunbelt' and 'rustbelt' of the USA (Sawers and Tabb, 1984) or inner-city decline and the rise of commuter belts and dormitory villages. Second, it argues that these changing geographies *matter* economically, politically and socially. Moreover, they matter much more than just shaping (governmental) responses to the uneven processes of economic development. For geographers, space and place matter because the objects and processes of our investigations – the (multinational) firm, markets (e.g. NAFTA), globalization, fair trade, the information highway, commuter belts, sovereignty, and so on – are constituted in, and through, spatial relations (measured in various ways such as distance, proximity, connectivity, presence or absence, borders, etc.). In other words, the outcomes of economic systems and our responses to them are shaped by processes that are inherently geographical in character.

Making 'Maps' in Contemporary Economic Geography

The following chapter on the economic agglomeration or industrial cluster of Motor Sport Valley is an example of the spatial constitution of an economic system. Essentially, the chapter argues for a number of economic processes whose geographies (sometimes referred to in the jargon as 'spatialities') both overlap and intertwine within a particular territory. Labour market and firm formation, technology transfer and knowledge flows have become centred on a geographical region of the UK little known to those outside of the industry who comprise this economic space. Together they constitute, and are partially constituted by, Motor Sport Valley.

Ironically, considering our disciplinary background as geographers, it has needed the editors of this collection to highlight, and reflect upon, the processes of 'mapping' we have undertaken to represent and demonstrate this economic system. The disciplinary history of geography, of course, originates from the first systematic attempts to map the physical features of the world (Livingstone, 1992). Nevertheless, remarkably, the following chapter is distinctive within our sub-discipline by virtue of its attempt to 'track' a set of processes that are arguably growing in significance with the move to centre-stage of 'knowledge' as a key resource of the contemporary economy (Bryson et al., 2000; Castells, 1996; Coyle, 1997; Leadbetter, 1999).

The importance of knowledge as a factor of production has emphasized the social embeddedness of economic activity (Grabher, 1993; Granovetter and Swedberg, 1992; Hodgson, 1999). Within economic geography, the challenge is to represent (and map) the variety of systemic elements ('untraded interdependencies', in the language of Storper and Salais, 1997) that comprise the 'intangibles' of embeddedness. Thus far, as an empirical activity, this mapping has tended towards a concentration on a series of regional economic success stories – for example, Silicon Valley (Saxenian, 1994), the Third Italy (Pyke et al., 1990) and the City of London (Amin and Thrift, 1992) – whose economic dynamism has been attributed to their ability to embed (or make 'sticky' [Markusen, 1996]) regionally distinctive forms of economic activity in the face of economic globalization. Other disciplines, too, recognize the territorial basis of competitive advantage (Castells, 1996; Clark, 1999; Krugman 1991, 1995; Porter, 1990), although fierce debates are ongoing as to the structural basis for such advantage and the level and type of empirical evidence required to deepen understanding (see, e.g., *Economist*, 1999; Martin, 1999). Clearly here, too, the potential of mapping techniques is great.

Mapping Strategic Knowledge: a Geographical Perspective?

In recent years, and as evidenced in our chapter below, geographers have adopted a strongly 'relational' perspective in the conceptualization of the object of study (Allen et al., 1998; Massey, 1993; Massey et al., 1999; Thrift, 1996b). If we can be criticized for often having taken the firm and its decision-making processes as a 'relative given' (notwithstanding an earlier 'behavioural' period in the discipline, see Hayter and Watts, 1983), for stopping at the entrance to the black box if you like, current conceptualizations are likely to highlight the extremely porous and relational nature of the firm in today's economy. Of course, firm boundaries still have important implications for many factors related to legal status, profitability, balance sheets, labour relations, and the like. Nevertheless, firms can increasingly be viewed as mere nodes in a network or web of diverse sets of (spatially constituted) economic relationships; relationships that push and pull and are multi-scalar, diverse, heterogeneous and uneven. In this context, the resource base of the firm could be taken to be its uniqueness as the locus of a particular set of economic flows and relationships, and its strategic knowledge rests with its ability to manage these flows and their internal combination. In this sense, the distributed, differential, partial and complex character of knowledge is emphasized and mapping becomes a key technique for identifying, tracking and monitoring this complexity. Moreover, this mapping becomes focused on the chains (even knowledge chains [ESRC, 2000]) of which the firm is but a part (business to business, value, commodity networks, organizational alliances, labour, technology, etc.) in a greater systematic blurring of environment and firm.

Research themes centred on factors such as knowledge, competitive advantage, clusters, organizational geography, networks, technology transfer, embeddedness and mapping are increasingly oblivious to, if not positively seeking to transcend and refashion, disciplinary boundaries.

We thank the editors for the opportunity they have provided to make a small contribution to this process of development.

INTRODUCTION: KNOWLEDGE, ECONOMY, SPACE

There is now an array of descriptive labels on offer that attempt to capture the heightened role of 'knowledge' within contemporary economies. Initially encompassed within theories of transition such as *post-Fordism* (Lipietz, 1992), *flexible accumulation* (Harvey, 1989), *flexible specialization* (Piore and Sabel, 1984) and *disorganized capitalism* (Lash and Urry, 1987), other entrants on to the scene include *reflexive accumulation* and *economies of signs and space* (Lash and Urry, 1994), *knowledge-based capitalism* (Florida, 1995), *the informational age* (Castells and Hall, 1994), *the learning economy* (Lundvall and Johnson, 1994), *the digital economy* (Pratt, 1998), *the dematerialized economy* (Quah, 1996), *the network society* (Castells, 1996), *soft capitalism* (Thrift, 1996a) and the *weightless world* (Coyle, 1997). With varying emphases, all highlight how 'knowledge' in a variety of overlapping forms (e.g. aesthetic, cognitive, scientific, discursive, digital, information, tacit, etc.) is central to the operation of the contemporary advanced economies. And with varying emphases again, all recognize that the spatial basis of production is being transformed under the imperatives of the 'knowledge economy'. Moreover, it is increasingly clear that this spatial basis is not leading to spatial homogeneity but is generating a distinctive, yet different, pattern of uneven economic development – a new geography of knowledge production. Furthermore, as MacLeod (2000) highlights, and as part of an emergent 'regional political economy', a strong component of this new geography has been an argument for the regional scale as *the* territorial expression of the spatial organization of knowledge production (Castells and Hall, 1994; Cooke and Morgan, 1993; Morgan, 1997; Storper, 1997).

This chapter examines one regional expression of knowledge production in the form of Motor Sport Valley. Elsewhere, drawing on elements of the 'cultural turn' in economic geography, we have argued that a greater understanding of the growth of Motor Sport Valley can be gained from understanding this region as a 'knowledge community': a geographically concentrated node of knowledge production on how to construct the 'best' racing cars in the world (Henry and Pinch, 1997; Pinch and Henry, 1999a, 1999b; Pinch et al., 1997). The aim of this chapter is to demonstrate the processes of knowledge generation and dissemination critical to the constitution of the knowledge community known as Motor Sport Valley. In achieving this aim, the chapter outlines a methodology for tracking how 'knowledge' circulates within a regional world of production. Whilst the regional knowledge network is the main focus, attention is drawn also to the political economy of the world of production of which this network is but a part, albeit an essential one. Drawing on this analysis, the chapter concludes with some thoughts on how the example of Motor Sport Valley might influence our understanding of (a) the 'region' as an organizational mode of production within (b) 'the knowledge economy'.

EXPLAINING MOTOR SPORT VALLEY

Motor Sport Valley (see Figures 6.1 and 6.2),[1] the name given to the regional agglomeration of the British motor sport industry, dominates the world's production of racing cars. It represents a classic example of a world-leading regional agglomeration of small firms (Henry, 1999; Henry and Pinch, 1997; Henry et al., 1996; Pinch et al., 1997). The industry employs well in excess of 30,000 people and consists of scores of small and medium-sized firms clustered in a 50-mile radius around Oxfordshire in southern England. Approximately three-quarters of the world's single-seater racing cars are designed and assembled in this region, including the vast majority of the most competitive Formula One, Championship Auto Racing Teams and Indy Racing League cars. The region is also the base for a large number of the world's rallying teams.

In economic geography, one of the most influential explanatory frameworks for regional agglomeration was the 'Early Californian' 'Approach', which interpreted spatial concentration as an attempt to minimize the transaction costs associated with inter-firm linkage (Scott, 1988; Scott and Storper, 1987). Recently, Storper (1995, 1997) criticized the inadequacy of theories such as these based as they are on analysing the transfer of physical inputs and outputs. Drawing upon what he terms the 'new heterodoxy' of regional analysis, he focuses upon the socially and institutionally embedded character of economic activity, the role of habits and customs in forging technological and production technologies, and the critical and problematic nature of knowledge acquisition in contemporary economies (Storper, 1997; Storper and Salais, 1997). Storper argues that a more effective approach to the enigma of regional concentration may lie in the notion of *untraded interdependencies*. These consist of various conventions, rules, practices and institutions that combine to produce 'frameworks of economic action'. These frameworks structure 'possible worlds of production', that is, frameworks of foreseeable action for economic actors (Storper and Salais, 1997: 20). Possible worlds of production become 'real worlds of production' when they exhibit 'coherence'. For Storper and Salais, coherence in the contemporary advanced economies 'means creating the absolute advantages that propel economic specialization' (1997: 21). Regional agglomerations such as Motor Sport Valley that have come to the fore in recent years are, in Storper and Salais' eyes, successful examples of coherence, real worlds of production identified most especially by their profitable firms and international share of market traded products (1997).

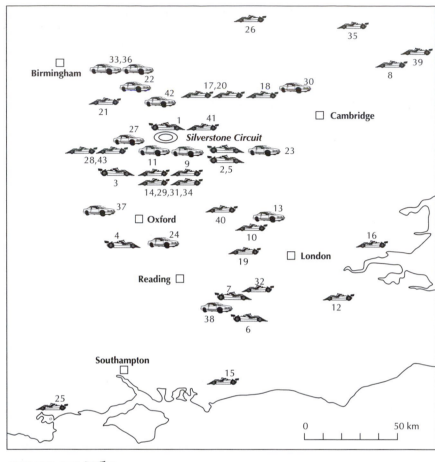

FORMULA ONE

1 Benson and Hedges Total Jordan Peugeot	4 Rothmans Williams Renault
2 Danka Arrows Yamaha	5 Stewart Ford
3 Mild Seven Benetton Renault	6 Tyrrell Racing Organization
	7 West McLaren Mercedes

OTHER FORMULAE and **TOURING/RALLY CARS**

8 Argo Cars	21 Marrow-Jon Morris Designs	34 Spice Racing Cars
9 Audi Sport	22 Mitsubishi Ralliart	35 Spider
10 BMW Team Schnitzer	23 Motor Sport Developments	36 Total Team Peugeot
11 Bowman Cars	24 Nissan Motorsport Europe	37 TWR Racing
12 Elden Racing Cars	25 Penske Cars Ltd.	38 Valvoline Team Mondeo
13 Ford Motorsport	26 Pilbeam Racing Design Ltd.	39 Van Diemen International
14 Galmer Engineering	27 Prodrive	40 Vector Racing Car
15 G Force Precision Engineering	28 Pro Sport Engineering Ltd.	Constructors
16 Hawke Racing Cars	29 Ralt Engineering	41 Vision
17 Jedi	30 Ray Mallock	42 Volkswagen – SBG Sport
18 Lola Cars Ltd.	31 Reynard Racing Cars Ltd.	43 Zeus Motorsport
19 Lyncar	32 Ronta	Engineering
20 Magnum	33 Rouse Sport	

Figure 6.1   Motor Sport Valley: constructors

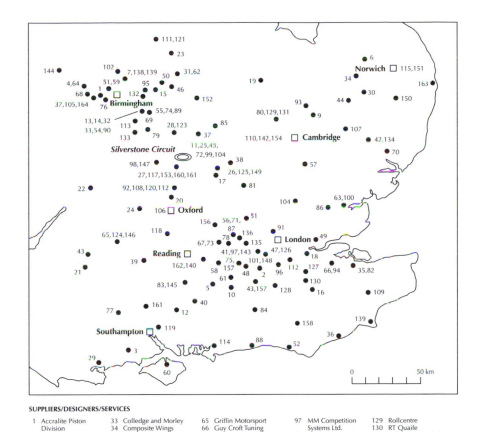

SUPPLIERS/DESIGNERS/SERVICES

1 Accralite Piston Division	33 Colledge and Morley	65 Griffin Motorsport	97 MM Competition Systems Ltd.
2 Activa Technology	34 Composite Wings	66 Guy Croft Tuning	98 Mo Tec (Europe)
3 Active Sensors Ltd.	35 Connaught Competition Engines	67 Hewland Engineering	99 Motorsport Distribution Ltd.
4 ADS	36 Corbeau Seats	68 Hi-Tech Motorsport	100 Mountline Racing Ltd.
5 Aerospace Metal Composites	37 Cosworth Engineering	69 HJS Motorsport Catalysts	101 MSAS Motorsport Division
6 AFS Engineering	38 Cranfield Impact Centre	70 Holbay Racing Engines Ltd.	102 MTEC
7 Alcon Components	39 DCL Components	71 Icore International	103 Mugen (UK Base)
8 Aldon Automotive	40 Dove Composite	72 Ilmore Engineering Ltd.	104 Nimbus Motorsport
9 Aleybars	41 DPS Composites	73 Impact Finishers	105 Omega Pistons
10 Alfred Bull	42 Dunnell Engines	74 Induction Technology Group	106 Oselli Engineering
11 Aluminium Radiators and Cooling Systems	43 Dymag Racing UK	75 James Lister and Sons Ltd.	107 Pace Products
12 Alresford Tectonics	44 Dynamic Suspensions	76 James Lister and Sons Ltd.	108 Pallas Connections
13 Andy Rouse Engineering Ltd.	45 Earl's UK	77 Janspeed	109 Piper Cams
14 AP Racing	46 Eibach Suspension Technology Ltd.	78 Janus Technology	110 PI Research
15 Arrow Race Engine Components	47 Elaborazione Colasuna	79 John Morris Designs	111 Premier Fuel Systems
16 Astratech	48 Electron Beam Processes	80 Kartronix	112 Prisma Design
17 ATL Competition Equipment	49 Engine and Dynomometer	81 KDM Motorsport	113 Proctor and Chester Measurements
18 Auriga	50 Engineering and Motorsport Supplies	82 Kent Aerospace Castings	114 Quantum Racing Service
19 Aurora	51 En Tran	83 Kulite Sensors	115 Quentor Cases
20 Automotive Developments	52 ERL	84 Lane Electronics	116 Racam Precision
21 Avon Racing Division	53 Eurotech Motorsport	85 Langford and Peck Ltd.	117 Race Logic
22 AWF	54 Farndon Engineering	86 Leda Suspensions	118 Raceparts UK
23 Aztek	55 FF Developments	87 Lee Products	119 Race-Tec NAK
24 Berkeley Prowse	56 Flexible Hose Supplies Racing Division	88 Lemo UK	120 Ralt Engineering
25 BM Motorsport Ltd.	57 Fuel Safe UK Ltd.	89 Lifeline	121 Ramair Filters UK Ltd.
26 Bob Sparshott Engineering	58 Genesis Electronic Systems	90 Lifeline Fire and Safety Systems	122 Rapid International
27 Brembo	59 GKN Motorsport	91 McDonald Race Engineering	123 Ravic Engineering
28 BTB Exhausts	60 GKN Westland Aerospace	92 Mag Think Automotiveneco TWlr UK	124 Rayfast
29 C & B Consultants	61 Gomm Metal Developments	93 Mark Dunham Racing	125 Ray Mallock
30 Champion Manufacturing	62 Graham Goode Racing	94 Minister Motorsport	126 RESB International Ltd.
31 Clarendon Eng. & Motorsport Supplies	63 Graham Hathaway Racing	95 Mira	127 Ricardo Consulting Engineers
32 Colinton Engineering	64 Grainger and Worrall	96 Monk Aeroelectronic Design Ltd.	128 Risbridger
			129 Rollcentre
			130 RT Quaife
			131 Safety Devices Ltd.
			132 Samco Sport
			133 SAS Motorsport
			134 Scholar Engines
			135 Serck Marston
			136 Serdi (UK)
			137 Servo and Electrical Sales
			138 Spa Aerofoils Ltd.
			139 Spider Engineering
			140 Spot On Control Cables
			141 Stack Ltd.
			142 Steve Bunkhall
			143 Stone Foundaries
			144 Staubli Unimation
			145 Strain Gauging Co
			146 Swindon Racing Engines Ltd.
			147 The Monogram Co
			148 Think Automotive
			149 Tickford
			150 Tony James Component Wiring
			151 Trick Machinning Ltd.
			152 Trident Racing Supplies
			153 Turbo Technics
			154 TWI
			155 Uniclip Automotive
			156 Universal Air Tool
			157 Universal Grinding Services
			158 Warrior Automotive Research Ltd.
			159 Willans Racing Harness
			160 WP Competition Systems
			161 WP Suspension (UK) Ltd.
			162 X Trac
			163 Zephyr Cams Ltd.
			164 Zeus Ltd.

Figure 6.2 Motor Sport Valley: suppliers

In arguing for untraded interdependencies, frameworks of economic action and worlds of production, Storper and Salais highlight the conceptual frameworks needed to produce knowledges of labour, capital, materials, markets, and so on, and the successful combination required to produce a good. In addition, they highlight the *current* territorialization of such frameworks of knowledge in certain spaces and places. Arguing that this approach bypasses the distinction between notions of 'the economic' and 'the non-economic', Storper and Salais' work, nevertheless, is one of a recent series of attempts at unravelling the 'non-economic' social relations and structures that 'embed' growth (see numerous chapters in Lee and Wills, 1997, for example). Other influential strands of thought within this 'new heterodoxy' or emergent 'regional political economy' include, for example, the concepts of *institutional thickness* (Amin and Thrift, 1994), *learning regions* (Morgan, 1997), *governance* in a variety of forms (Goodwin et al., 1993; Jessop, 1990; Jones, 1998; Peck, 1996; Peck and Tickell, 1994), the *network paradigm* (Castells, 1996; Cooke and Morgan, 1993) and the *associational economy* (Cooke and Morgan, 1998), to name but a few.

Whatever the label, all of the above perspectives are part of a broader conceptual shift in economic geography that recognizes the socially embedded character of production systems; the cultural and discursive aspects of production systems; and the critical importance of knowledge, as a cultural construction, in modern economies. While there has been a great deal of discussion about the role of knowledge in gluing together agglomerations of firms, there have been few demonstrations of the processes through which this knowledge is spread. To some extent, this lack of work is hardly surprising since it is acknowledged that many of these processes of knowledge circulation are untraded, intangible, covert, sometimes immoral (and even illegal). Understanding these processes therefore requires a great deal of work to get 'inside' a particular 'world of production'.

Elsewhere we have argued that a focus upon the process of knowledge generation provides a convincing explanation for the origins and development of Motor Sport Valley (Pinch and Henry, 1999a, 1999b; Pinch et al., 1997). For example, the crucial impetus to the dynamic growth of Motor Sport Valley – the element that glued the contingent factors of club racing, airfields, reduced market competition, tobacco sponsorship, and so on, together – was a radical shift in technological regime or knowledge system. Just as the shift from valves to transistors and semi-conductors was reflected in a spatial shift in the electronics industry from East Coast USA to Southern California (eventually to be labelled Silicon Valley), so the shift to an aerospace-inspired technological trajectory ultimately saw the locus of the world's motor sport industry shift from northern Italy to southern England (eventually labelled Motor Sport Valley). Furthermore, a knowledge-based approach is also important in accounting for the maintenance and growth of the British motor sport industry and Motor Sport Valley as well as its origins. Knowledge generation and dissemination have been crucial to maintaining the dominance of the region and have taken place, we argue, through the medium of 'the knowledge community'. Here we define a knowledge community as a group of people (principally designers, managers and engineers in this case), often in separate organizations but united by a common set of norms, values and understandings, who help to define the knowledge and production trajectories of the economic sector to which they belong. In the case of Motor Sport Valley, the region is synonymous with the knowledge community of motor sport; the core of the community's spatial organization is that of the Valley. The key processes that construct and maintain this community occur on both a traded and untraded basis.

THE METHODS OF PLACING A KNOWLEDGE COMMUNITY

The evidence presented here was collected during the course of a two-year research project which comprised two main parts. Part One was an investigation into the scale, character and geographical location of the British motor sport industry (for example, see Figures 6.1 and 6.2). This was achieved through analysis of specialist literature and interviews with 'key informants'. The specialist literature on the industry is available in large quantities and is of a high quality. For example, there are numerous weekly and monthly magazines on the industry, and dozens of books are produced each year on the sport and the industry that have been collated in several specialist libraries. Although many of these publications are hagiographies and should be interpreted with caution, they provide a wealth of background detail and technical information that few other industries can match. In addition, key informant interviews were undertaken with 10 individuals, including academics, consultants, industry journalists and representatives of the major regulatory bodies of the industry.

The aim of Part Two of the project was to gain knowledge on the nature and geography of both traded and untraded interdependencies in the industry. Part Two therefore involved 50 in-depth interviews with company executives, managers, designers and engineers. Remarkably, we received no refusals to be interviewed. Face-to-face semi-structured interviews took place between June 1996 and January 1997. Each interview, on average, lasted two to three hours and was taped and subsequently transcribed. In many cases, interviews were followed by tours around the premises. The choice of sample followed a 'purposive' sampling approach (Layder, 1998) combining a sample of the most dominant companies in the industry and coverage of the different levels of competition/construction. The aim was to use qualitative methods to cross-check answers in depth and undertake 'triangulation' of findings. In the case of component suppliers, the interviews were continued until 'saturation' was achieved (i.e. the main patterns became established and further interviews were felt unnecessary [Cresswell, 1994]). The level of access achieved meant that the final sample included virtually every major company in the British motor sport industry with every Formula One team in the UK bar one interviewed, every UK-based Indycar manufacturer, five touring car designer/ manufacturers, 10 leading supplier/subcontractor firms, three engine builders, one rally car manufacturer/team and a Formula Ford manufacturer. The project was particularly successful in gaining access to the lead personnel in the industry, including Managing Directors, Technical Directors and Chief Designers as well as Aerodynamicists, Gearbox Engineers and Composites Specialists.

Overall, whilst the methodology was based on well-established qualitative methods, it was innovative in its use of a variety of methods to try to track 'knowledge processes'. The methodology was driven by an attempt to make graphic the 'intangibility' of the world of motor sport production, that is, an attempt to try to delineate knowledge (ideas, information, etc.) and the processes that create, sustain and circulate this through space. Thus, this search meant that as researchers we held uppermost in our minds a particular version of 'culture', in terms of shared meanings and understandings (of say a piece of information) within the industry, and continually investigated the issue of how this was formed as an element of production.

PLACING A KNOWLEDGE COMMUNITY

The methodology produced a number of 'traces' of knowledge processes and their geographies, which are the subject of this major section of the chapter. For the sake of organization, these traces are divided into two major sub-themes on the basis of a rather crude dichotomy between 'knowledge' as embodied literally in people who 'travel' and disembodied ideas and knowledges travelling across space.[2]

Knowledge, Process, Community and Space (1)

A first approach to tracking 'knowledge' was to recognize its embodiment. What is meant here is not the normal view as in embodiment in a piece of machinery, paper or other artefact (although see the recent work on actor-network theory), but literally embodiment as in a thinking, breathing body such as the engineer (see, e.g., Allen and du Gay, 1994; Boden, 1994; Du Gay, 1996; McDowell, 1997; McDowell and Court, 1993; Thrift, 1994, for work that similarly recognizes embodiment in this sense).

staff turnover

One of the most important ways in which knowledge is spread within the motor sport industry is by the rapid and continual transfer of staff (bodies) between the companies within the industry. Especially at the end

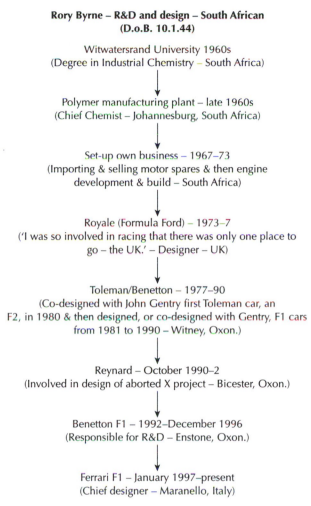

Rory Byrne – R&D and design – South African
(D.o.B. 10.1.44)

Witwatersrand University 1960s
(Degree in Industrial Chemistry – South Africa)

Polymer manufacturing plant – late 1960s
(Chief Chemist – Johannesburg, South Africa)

Set-up own business – 1967–73
(Importing & selling motor spares & then engine
development & build – South Africa)

Royale (Formula Ford) – 1973–7
('I was so involved in racing that there was only one place to
go – the UK.' – Designer – UK)

Toleman/Benetton – 1977–90
(Co-designed with John Gentry first Toleman car, an
F2, in 1980 & then designed, or co-designed with Gentry, F1 cars
from 1981 to 1990 – Witney, Oxon.)

Reynard – October 1990–2
(Involved in design of aborted X project – Bicester, Oxon.)

Benetton F1 – 1992–December 1996
(Responsible for R&D – Enstone, Oxon.)

Ferrari F1 – January 1997–present
(Chief designer – Maranello, Italy)

Figure 6.3   Career history

of every racing season, there is an intense period of negotiation as designers, engineers, managers and, of course, drivers move between teams. As part of the research, the career histories of 100 leading designer/engineers within the industry were mapped (see Figures 6.3 and 6.4 for examples).[3] This mapping revealed a move, on average, once every 3.7 years and an average total of eight moves in a career in the industry. Similarly, a study of advertisements for *technical* posts in Formula One between 1996 and 1997 revealed vacancies for 93 posts, more than 10 per cent of this formula's total employment at that time.

career trajectories

Whilst the above evidence highlights the mobility encapsulated within the labour market, its significance also stems from the geographical

Frank Dernie – Aerodynamicist/Designer
(D.o.B. 3.4.50)

Imperial College late '60s/early '70s
(Mechanical Engineering Degree – London)

↓

David Brown Industries 1970s
(Working with gears)

↓

Garrods 1970s
(Record players – Swindon, Wilts)

↓

Hesketh/Williams 1977–9
(Consultancy work – co-designed 1978 Hesketh with
N. Stroud – Towcester, Northants/Didcot, Oxon.)

↓

Williams 1979–88
(Aerodynamicist & R&D – co-designed 1986–8 cars with
P. Head – Didcot, Oxon.)

↓

Lotus 1988–90
(Chief Engineer – co-designed 1989 car with
M. Coughlan – Norfolk)

↓

Ligier 1990–2
(Technical Director – France)

↓

Benetton 1992–July 1994
(Race engineer & then chief engineer
in 1994 – Enstone, Oxon.)

↓

Ligier July 1994–April 96
(Went back to Ligier after team purchased by Briatore – Technical
Director – France then Oxon.)

↓

Arrows April 1996–7
(Technical Director – moved with T. Walkinshaw's
take-over – Oxon.)

↓

Lola Cars 1998 – present
(Huntingdon)

Figure 6.4   Career history

expression of this labour market. As the sample career histories of Figures 6.3 and 6.4 show, Motor Sport Valley acts as the epicentre of a global, yet highly spatially defined, labour market. In particular, whilst moves occur on an international scale into, and out of, the Valley, overall, the largest number of moves occur between sites *within* the Valley. Moreover, international moves out are invariably followed in quick succession by a return to the Valley, as can be seen in the career history in Figure 6.5. Indeed, these particular career histories introduce a constant and overriding theme of the world of production of Motor Sport Valley. As an individual in motor sport, it is rare that you do not, at some point in your career, spend some time within Motor Sport Valley (and most likely the majority of your career). Essentially, this is about joining *the* knowledge community of motor sport production. Yet opportunities exist in this highly mobile industry to sell your knowledge elsewhere, and many do so. However, the knowledge of the Valley is continually being reconfigured and advanced (see below): it is in effect, a knowledge pool. To move out of the Valley is also to stretch your relationship within the community, to risk your position within the knowledge loop. Thus, few stay away from the Valley for long, returning once more to refigure their position within the community of knowledge. An analogy for the labour market of Motor Sport Valley is that of the dating agency's dinner dance. With each change of course ('racing season') comes a change of seating arrangement with, by the end of the evening, occupants often returning after one or two musical interludes to a seat previously occupied. Furthermore, and skirting the dangers of taking this analogy further, such mixing does not take place only at the level of the individual: *joint career paths* may also be mapped with individuals often moving together, or continually recombining, throughout their careers (see Figures 6.6 and 6.7). Thus, ultimately, as was so graphically illustrated in an article in a trade journal, the industry labour market is made up of people networks such that 'it pays to be well connected' (see Figure 6.8).

firm births and firm deaths

It is important to note, however, that this mobility of the labour market is both voluntary and non-voluntary and it is driven not only by movements of individuals but also by the continual 'movement' of firms. Another significant feature of Motor Sport Valley is the high firm turnover involving both high rates of new firm formation and high firm death rates. Within an industry of several hundred firms, only a handful employ more than 200 people, and there is a widespread feeling within the industry that even this size is dangerous to the competitive edge of the company. Indeed, in a process of growth reminiscent of Silicon Valley (Saxenian, 1994) and the Cambridge Phenomenon (Segal, Quince and Wichsteed, 1985), the hundreds of firms in Motor Sport Valley today can be traced to a few pioneers. For example, Figure 6.9 provides an incomplete family tree for March, a spin-off from Cosworth (Northampton) in 1969.

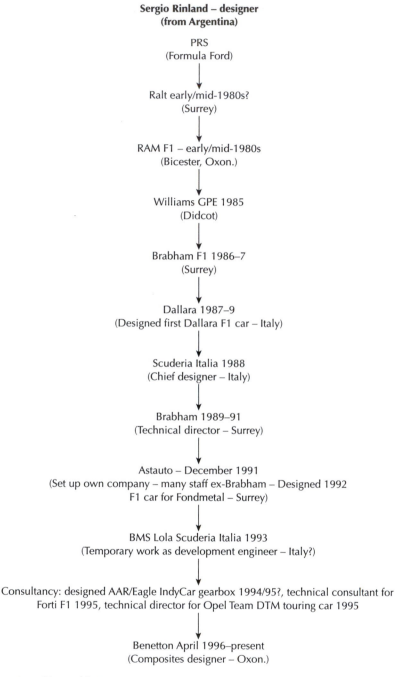

Figure 6.5   Career history

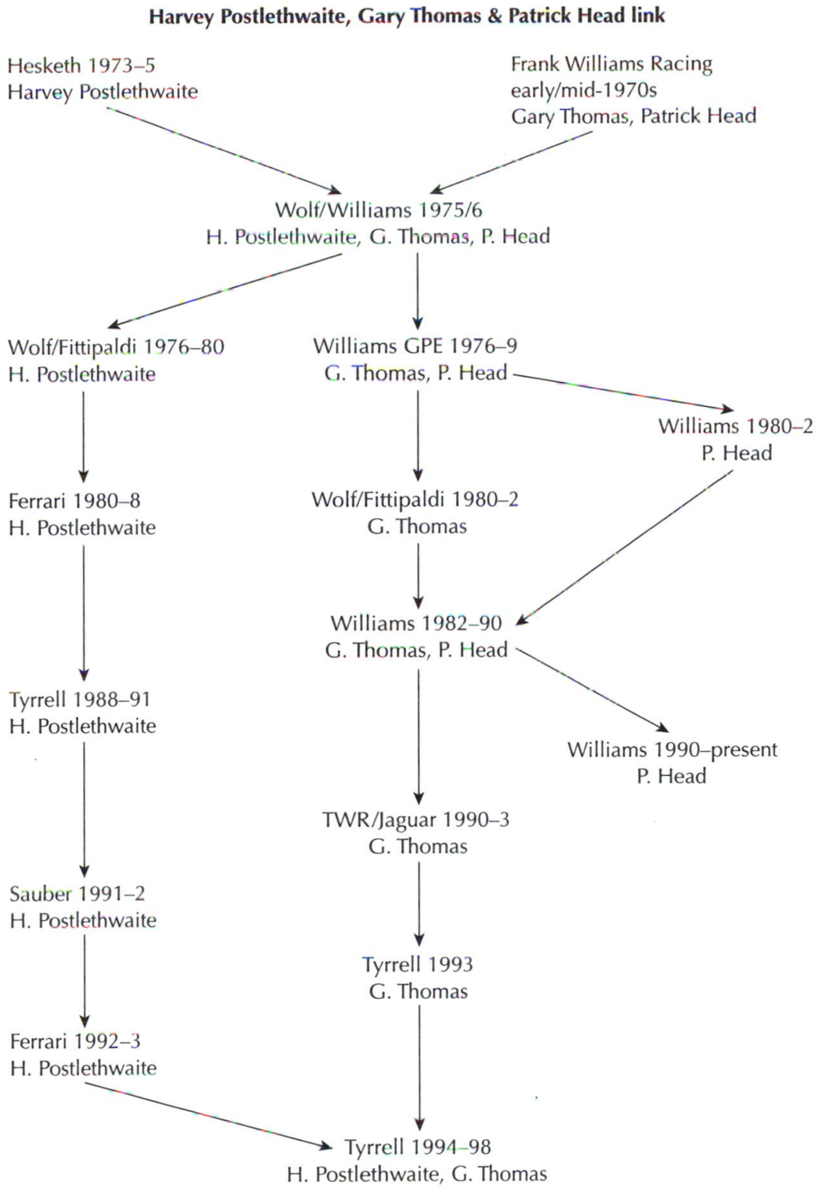

Harvey Postlethwaite, Gary Thomas & Patrick Head link

Hesketh 1973–5
Harvey Postlethwaite

Frank Williams Racing
early/mid-1970s
Gary Thomas, Patrick Head

Wolf/Williams 1975/6
H. Postlethwaite, G. Thomas, P. Head

Wolf/Fittipaldi 1976–80
H. Postlethwaite

Williams GPE 1976–9
G. Thomas, P. Head

Williams 1980–2
P. Head

Ferrari 1980–8
H. Postlethwaite

Wolf/Fittipaldi 1980–2
G. Thomas

Williams 1982–90
G. Thomas, P. Head

Tyrrell 1988–91
H. Postlethwaite

Williams 1990–present
P. Head

TWR/Jaguar 1990–3
G. Thomas

Sauber 1991–2
H. Postlethwaite

Tyrrell 1993
G. Thomas

Ferrari 1992–3
H. Postlethwaite

Tyrrell 1994–98
H. Postlethwaite, G. Thomas

Figure 6.6 Joint career path

March located in nearby Bicester and began a process that has led this small market town to become the world centre for motor sport production. Bringing the tree up-to-date, one of March's spin-offs, Reynard Racing Cars, has itself sponsored a number of internal spin-offs in the town:

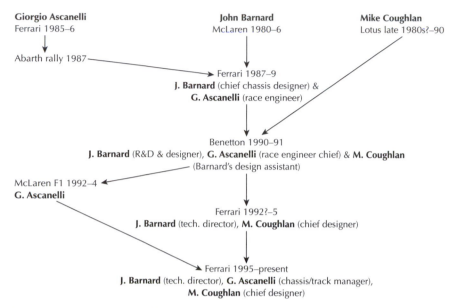

John Barnard, Mike Coughlan & Giorgio Ascanelli link
Barnard, 'I also try to instil my design philosophy in the key development engineers at Ferrari, like Georgio Ascanelli, with whom I have worked in the past at Benetton and Ferrari. I get lots of feedback from him on the practical aspects of operating the cars at the track and on set-up issues.' (Wright, 1996)

Figure 6.7   Joint career path

...the critical mass is about 25 to 30, so when our original company got to 25 to 30 we then bought another factory and we started Reynard Manufacturing and Reynard Racing Cars. ... When that grew to about 60 people, we then started Reynard Composites ... and when that group of companies grew to 90 people we started another company which was designs, and then when that company grew to 120 people we started Reynard's Special Vehicle Projects and that has now grown to 20 people. So we have now got 152 people in the company, but it is made up of separate buildings, some in Bicester and some in Brackley [a nearby small town] (42)[4]

The company opened another large site just outside of Bicester. This site is the production centre for the latest entrant to Formula One, British American Racing, a combination of Reynard Racing Cars and the Tyrrell Formula One team (also within the Valley), which has ended the latter team's twenty-year presence in Formula One racing. In fact, this is a classic example of the process of reconfiguration so characteristic of Motor Sport Valley. One of the longest-running teams in Formula One, Tyrrell will not so much die as be reborn in a modified and reinvigorated version. Thus Tyrrell is one in a long line of Formula One constructors who have come and gone; this includes Pacific, Forti, Simtek and Lola in a field that rarely exceeds a dozen constructors a year. Lola, a major Indycar producer, did not last a season in Formula One, with many commentators suggesting that the company had failed to learn from its previous foray into

It pays to be well connected

F1 is a small world. Everyone knows everyone, and most have worked with each other too. We trace the top careers.

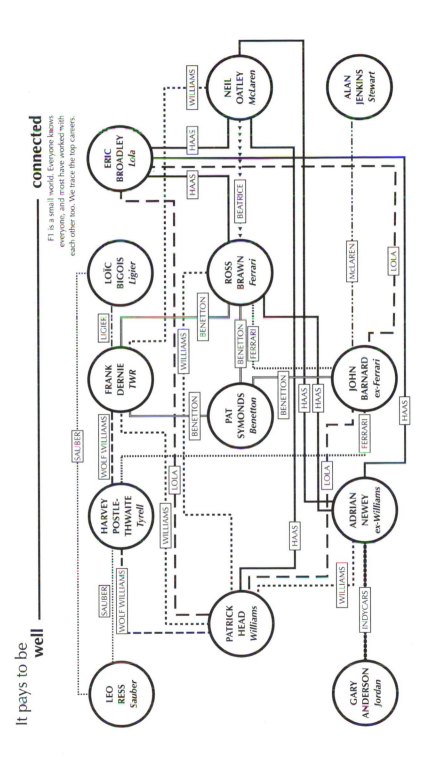

Figure 6.8 It pays to be well connected (adapted from Cooper, 1997)

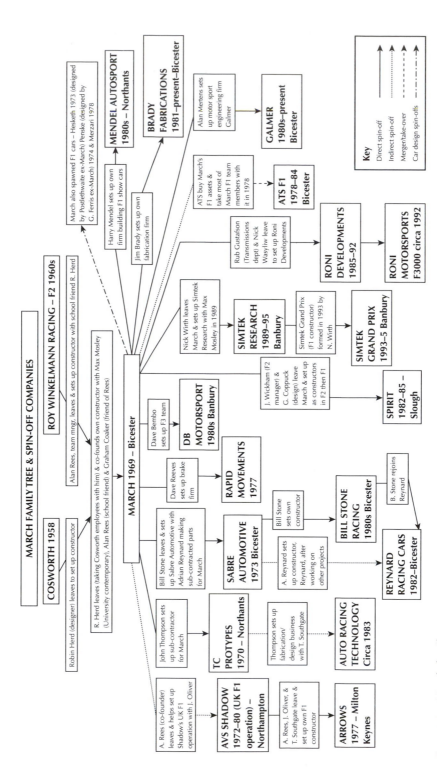

Figure 6.9 March family tree

Formula One a decade ago. This time its entry bankrupted the company, including its Indycar production, only for it to be resurrected once again by a new Irish buyer. Its production of Indycars continues unabated and it still holds ambitions to return to Formula One once again. And it does so from its continued location within Motor Sport Valley, a location held throughout its chequered history.

In similar vein, the recent Formula One bankrupt Simtek Grand Prix provides clear evidence of the entwining of labour movement with firm 'churn' through high rates of firm births and deaths. On its demise, of the top eight individuals employed by Simtek, six were traced to other motor sport jobs within the Valley inside of six months.

The Churning of Knowledge Within the Valley Community (1)

In summary, the evidence above highlights that a key characteristic of the industrial organization and labour market of motor sport is a set of processes leading to the continual 'churning' of people. Fundamental to the argument of this chapter is, first, that this process of 'churning' is centred on, and within, Motor Sport Valley. Second, this churning is a process of circulating and producing embodied knowledge within the knowledge community and regional production centre of Motor Sport Valley. As personnel move, they bring with them knowledge and ideas about how things are done in other firms, helping to raise the knowledge throughout the industry. As one interviewee commented:

> Whoever comes, it doesn't matter from where, he [sic] has to change his ways and adapt, and then once he changes his ways and adapts and he gets part of the system, then someone else comes and learns from him. Then he moves to another team and he takes ways of one team into another, you see. And you go from [leading F1 constructor] to McLaren and say 'at [leading F1 constructor] we did it this way' and they say 'oh really, let's try it'. And then vice versa, someone comes from McLaren to here and someone goes to Williams and you get all these exchanges of people and then we learn from each other all the time. Not trade secrets, obviously, but ways of doing things. If someone used to draw wings at McLaren or Williams or whatever and he comes to draw wings here, he is not going to bring the drawings of McLaren under his arm, but he is going to bring the ways of doing it in here, so he is allowed to explain. He may improve because he is going to see what we have got here, he is going to see the way he did it before and he will say 'ah, I can mix these two and get something even better', and you improve that little bit, and it keeps happening. (43)

The crucial point is that whilst this process may not change the pecking order within the industry, this 'churning' of personnel raises the knowledge base of the industry as a whole within the region. The knowledge community is continually reinvigorated and, synonymous with this, so is production within Motor Sport Valley.

Knowledge, Process, Community and Space (2)

The second approach is to recognize how ideas/knowledge move rather than people *per se*. Thus, this interpretation does move closer to more commonly used concepts of embodiment of knowledge in machinery, for example, although, ultimately, the split between the two interpretations will be seen to be more of a continuum.

suppliers

In this context, an important process of knowledge transfer is through the links constructors and manufacturers have with the numerous component suppliers. Many component suppliers work for more than one constructor making bespoke items of the client's design (but usually with a substantial contribution of their own expertise). Clearly, it is in the interests of these component suppliers not to disclose secrets to other constructors for whom they also undertake work or they would soon be out of business. Nevertheless, as many of our respondents acknowledged, over time, there is a gradual assimilation of the advantages of particular approaches. This knowledge exchange might occur, for example, because a component supplier subtly steers a constructor away from a sub-optimal way of doing something; other examples of the fine lines of this process of knowledge transfer are evident in the quotes from interviewees below:

> There is a difference between confidentiality and the knowledge that one builds up within an environment. (16, Supplier)

> We did have an innovative idea which would solve a problem or improve performance of a particular component, and we did tell the supplier that, and it ended up being on their standard products and sold to everyone else (14, Constructor).[5]

> It is much easier if we have problems to phone somebody and they say, 'yes, we do that for somebody else'. (11, Constructor)

This means that there will inevitably be some 'leakage' of knowledge throughout the industry as a whole. The reason why this is an advantage rather than a problem is because of the very rapid rate of innovation in the industry – as long as a team knows it can keep ahead of its rivals, it is not a major problem if the ideas eventually get transferred throughout the industry. But perhaps more importantly, any individual team probably has more to gain than lose through the skills that components suppliers learn by servicing a number of different racing car companies. The majority of the leading suppliers are based within Motor Sport Valley and these firms and personnel are part of the knowledge community.

gossip, rumour, observation

As economic geographers have come to recognize the importance of 'discursivity' in both the philosophical underpinnings of their work (Barnes, 1996; Bryson et al., 1999; Gibson-Graham, 1996; Martin, 1994; Thrift, 1996b) and its empirical application, the importance of gossip, rumour and observation in defining productive knowledge has been highlighted. In the case of the motor sport industry, particular sites and mediums of this process include the pit lane, test track and race meetings, and the frenzy of speculation encouraged by the large number of specialist magazines and extensive press and television coverage. The role of 'gossip and rumour' in shaping individual careers and, indeed, the uptake of innovations should not be underestimated (see Thrift, 1994, for similar arguments on the City of London):

> F1 mechanics are generally chosen by reputation. Few are picked cold from a business outside racing. They need to know what F1 is about, not simply because of the proficiency that will bring but because it means the mechanic will be aware of precisely what he is letting himself in for. This is not a 9 to 5 job and the motor racing grapevine will let a team owner know whether or not his prospective employee can cope. (Hamilton, 1994: 162)

> I get several calls a week from companies in the same industry asking us if somebody is good for the money or what's happening here or what's happening there. (41)

In terms of observation, teams keep a close eye on their rivals' cars and monitor their performance in test periods. Moreover, all the senses are involved in such monitoring, with, for example, engine noises, gear changes, lap times and the behaviour of the cars when cornering providing important clues – for some – as to the design and construction of a car and its components:

> Spying I do a lot of, I think that's all fair in love and war. So if I get a chance to photograph someone's wing profile or something like that I'm there, and I walk with a camera permanently attached to me. That's so important. (7)

> If you call spying trying to get a look under the bonnet of a car or when the wheels are off quickly ducking your head down, if you call that spying, yes there is, but we all do that. (56)

the discursive aspect of technological innovation

Once analysis moves into the realms of gossip, rumour and observation – understandings between groups of individuals of the meaning of certain things – the understanding of discourse becomes significant. Shared beliefs and understandings comprise, in the terms of Storper and Salais, some of the discursive conventions that make up the framework of action. In turn, in an industry dominated by technical innovation, this highlights the discursive aspect of technological innovation.

Elsewhere, we have discussed the insights the sociology of scientific knowledge (SSK) literature provides in understanding the social construction of technological innovation (Pinch and Henry, 1999a). Thus, for example, concerning the role of discourse, SSK argues that crucial to the generation and dissemination of scientific and technological advances are shared sets of understandings – discourses that help to interpret the world and whose uncertain construction are encapsulated within SSK through the concepts of *interpretive flexibility* and *social closure*. In effect, a version of truth becomes 'winnowed' from the various interpretations that are promulgated (Bijker et al., 1990). Ambiguities are resolved, usually only partially for a limited period, and certain development trajectories are put in place.

Typically in motor sport, considerable uncertainty abounds about the value of any new approach. This uncertainty, and period of interpretive flexibility, can be illustrated by the history of British racing car design in the late 1970s and early 1980s (see also Pinch and Henry, 1999a). This was a period in which British-based teams such as Lotus and McLaren were introducing new approaches at a remarkable rate. Some of these schemes – which in retrospect look 'speculative' and even 'wild' – fell by the wayside, such as four-wheeled drive, six-wheeled vehicles and the double chassis. There were many reasons for their rejections: some approaches were ineffective; some were too expensive; some were too good and were banned by the Fédération Internationale de L'Automobile (FIA), which governed the sport; or the approaches simply did not have enough support from the community of engineers to make them work effectively. Thus even something that today is widespread – carbon fibre – was inevitably greeted with some suspicion in the early days. The properties of carbon fibre had been known for some years previously through work in the aerospace industry and following specialist articles in the motor sport industry press extolling its virtues. Nevertheless, the material was used in a very limited fashion in a few designs. Carbon fibre implied a radical departure from traditional construction metals and a series of questions arose concerning, for example, cost, strength, reliability, weight and, ultimately, would it help win races? Eventually, the leading designers adopted the material, although in different ways and from different supplier sources. Thus it is possible to map the spread of the idea for almost simultaneously Gordon Murray at Brabham, John Barnard at McLaren and Peter Wright of Lotus began using carbon fibre. Barnard's carbon fibre car, MP4, appeared only a few days before the rather different Kevlar-enhanced Lotus 88. Eventually, Barnard's approach became the standard.

Interestingly, at about the same time, some designers were experimenting with another aerospace-inspired technology – 'ground effects'. These involve changes to the aerodynamic profile of the lower part of the racing car through the use of 'sliding skirts' to make the car hug the ground and corner more effectively at high speed. This technology was 'discovered by accident' and virtually ignored in its early days. Later, all the British teams copied the technology, although only a few did so successfully. As with carbon fibre, the spread of this concept can be mapped, but in this case outside of Motor Sport Valley. Ferrari attempted to buy-in the technology (and knowledge of carbon fibre) through the appointment of Harvey Postlethwaite from the (British) March–Wolf team. It is widely acknowledged that Ferrari never fully mastered the technology of ground effects but, instead, were heavily instrumental in the decision to ban the technology in 1981.

Such uncertainty leads to a great deal of blind copying. As one senior engineer commented:

> ...a car might have a particular style or component which sets it out from the rest, but that may not be the reason why it is doing well, but people just blindly copy it because they think... they must have found something, some way of measuring a gain in performance that we can't find, so we'll do it anyway. (33)

Another designer graphically explained:

> ...if painting a race car purple gives it a second a lap, I mean next week they will all be purple. (23)

The outcome is designs led by strong beliefs and discourses about how cars should look and behave as well as the results of testing.

Similarly, it is SSK that can provide insights into the 'embodiment in artefact' of knowledge, as discussed earlier, in examples like supplier components. Knowledge consists of more than materialized ideas (knowledge embedded in physical artefacts, technologies) and includes discourses, understandings and ways of doing things, which highlights the relationship of embodiment as artefacts and embodiment as understandings, meanings and readings of artefacts (see also Gertler, 1994).

Furthermore, SSK highlights the spatiality of these knowledges; how these factors reside in knowledge production centres such as scientific laboratories, research centres and factories and how their transportation is a fraught process. Scientific experiments and technical innovations are often dependent upon knowledges of accepted ways of doing things that are seldom written down (Gertler, 1994; Polanyi, 1967). These forms of knowledge often emerge from sets of people who have undertaken long periods of apprenticeship and are integrated into networks of contacts. For this reason, early scientific experiments are often difficult to replicate in other laboratories. There are so many detailed sets of understandings involved in the formulation of the experiment or in the construction of technological artefacts that not all of these can be incorporated by people attempting replication.

The point is, of course, that both beliefs and discourses about knowledges are debated and determined within the knowledge community, just as they are learnt, and the knowledge community is based in Motor Sport Valley (MSV). Indeed, the (double-faceted) embodied nature of knowledge in the MSV was a theme that was further reinforced on numerous occasions in our interviews. One example was a claim by a designer that although some of the important machine tools of the industry were produced in another country,

> They manufacture the tool but they don't know how to use it for that particular use. (35)

Or as a foreign national working in the Valley put it:

> To make racing cars in southern California was so difficult because the industry is not prepared. So you may find engineers but their mentality is different. They are aerospace so they think different, they organize different, they are not used to our racing mentality. (43)

These examples highlight knowledge as a (community) process, which was summed up by this statement by an English engineer who, whilst based in Motor Sport Valley, was working for a foreign-based constructor whose site overseas he visited regularly:

> We are trying to educate them about the English way of doing things. (11)

Indeed, Ferrari have run courses for their engineers in Maranello, Italy, led by engineers from the UK.

the seamless web of science and technology

Thus, SSK helps us to understand how agreements are forged upon understanding the signs, symbols and conventions of racing car production; the theory underlines how technological trajectories may be put in place as part of worlds of production. Yet a striking element of racing car production is how some of these trajectories end abruptly, or, more precisely, are banned through regulation. One of the key insights from SSK – the seamless web of society and technology – is relevant here. Whilst the above discussion has highlighted the processes of technological discursivity embodied in the designers and engineers of Motor Sport Valley, they are only one of the set of actors involved in the process of creating a 'fast' car. They are not the only members of the knowledge community.

The message of the 'seamless web' is that technologies are political in the sense that they can be designed, either explicitly or implicitly, to open some options and close others. Motor sport illustrates these points very well, for the design of racing cars has been shaped over the years by many competing interest groups: not least the teams, their sponsors, the television companies and the regulators of motor sport. The major sponsors are keen to ensure that racing is exciting, but it must also be relatively safe or the publicity resulting from death or injury to drivers and/or spectators will generally have a negative impact upon the sponsor's image and commercial prospects. Sponsors are all too aware of the historic withdrawal of Mercedes Benz in 1955 after a crash that killed 83 spectators, and there has been an increased emphasis upon enhanced safety features in motor racing in recent years due to untimely (and unexplained) deaths. For example, following the death of Formula One driver Ayrton Senna in 1994, it was suggested that:

> We are much more bothered about all this than we used to be, even as little as quarter of a century ago. When Jim Clark, the British driving hero and two times World Champion, was killed in a Formula Two race at Hockenheim in 1968, the event was front page news, to be sure. But if you look at the *Daily Telegraph* of those times, you do not find the prolonged analysis of the crises in motor-racing or leader page articles agonizing over the future of the sport, or enthusiasts pleading for its continued autonomy. (the *Sunday Telegraph*, 8 May 1994, quoted in Twitchen, 2000 pp. 123–155)

> Clark's death was largely regarded as simply a legitimate consequence of competing in a hazardous sport. The post-mortems were limited and, to a large extent, shrugged aside. A generation later, we live in a very different environment where the freedom of the individual to make a personal choice as to how, or indeed whether, he risks his life is very much hemmed in by wider social constraints. (Henry, 1994, 6; quoted in Twitchen, 2000 pp. 123–155)

These pressures get worked out also through the Technical Panels that regulate the various racing formulae. Within motor sport, the Technical Panels achieve a consensus about the types of cars the various teams can produce. Yet, importantly, the Technical Panels include the key designers in the industry, so reinforcing their presence within the knowledge community (and the presence of Motor Sport Valley within the regulatory framework of racing car production). This means that there is a very strong co-operative, as well as fiercely competitive, element in racing car design and within the Technical Panels. For example, as one engineer noted:

> ... if a team asks FIA [regulatory body in charge of panels] a technical question, the FIA sends a copy of the question and answer to every team. (5)

Yet in competition terms this is significant also because you gain

> some element of understanding of what other people are trying to do by the questions that they ask. (1)

Ultimately:

> I know some of the other designers and, you know, obviously we are all in competition with each other, but you still might well do that [ring them up] and say, 'do you know a good way to...?' or 'do you know a source of this on that information? (27)

The Churning of Knowledge Within
the Valley Community (2)

On the one hand, then, the travelling of people is about the dissemination of knowledge, which in turn generates innovation in one of the most rapidly, incrementally, innovating industries in the world. On the other hand, the travelling of ideas involves their translation into productive knowledge in particular sites (Amin and Thrift, 1992). As one begins to track shared understanding and meaning – the basis of productive knowledge – so the processes of knowledge production and transfer start to become apparent, although their representation is still problematic. In tracking and representing such processes, so do their geographies become apparent. In the productive world of motor sport the sites, the people and the knowledge are first, and foremost, the knowledge community that is Motor Sport Valley.

Furthermore, the message of the 'seamless web' is that to understand a phenomenon such as Motor Sport Valley one needs to be aware of the broader relations of political economy that enable this regionalized knowledge network to flourish.[6] Over many years, and due in large part to the efforts of Bernie Ecclestone – acting as impresario, entrepreneur, political lobbyist and deal maker – the British racing car companies have worked collectively to promote their interests.[7] They have thereby ensured that their competitive position is not threatened by *sudden* changes in the regulations surrounding motor racing that would under-mine their technological trajectory or their economic base of corporate sponsorship.[8] As many have observed, the dissemination of knowledge is intimately bound up with power relations. It involves the capacity of one group to preclude others – or impose upon them a vision or 'worldview' (in this case the acceptable parameters of automotive racing).

CONCLUSIONS

The agglomeration of Motor Sport Valley as a form of spatially constituted knowledge community provides one example of the spatial organization of knowledge production in the contemporary economy. Clearly, many other forms exist, such as the global intranets of the management consultants (Bryson and Daniels, 1998), the array of technopoles of the informational age (Castells and Hall, 1994) and the telecommunications networks of knowl-edge transmission (Warf, 1995). Concerning Motor Sport Valley, we have argued that its formation and reproduction as a knowledge community has been key to understanding its world-wide economic dominance. As a 'real world of production' (Storper and Salais, 1997), Motor Sport Valley has:

> successful systems of conventions, that is, successful real worlds, 'invent' the de facto best products and processes in the sectors in which they operate. Hence, they play a strong role in describing the evolutionary path of those

sectors *tout court*. They produce the supplies of certain objects that lead to the 'social construction of markets'. The economic tests of those sectors are thus themselves path-dependent and subject to strong influence by the generation of products, technologies, and practices from specific conventional systems. It is in this sense that actions, as embodied in conventions, produce the pathway of development of the economy. (Storper and Salais, 1997: 299)

In this sense, Motor Sport Valley should be recognized as the *current* 'pioneer' district in what is a global industry (Amin and Robins, 1990),[9] or an example of one of Amin and Thrift's (1992) neo-Marshallian nodes (Henry and Pinch, 2001). Motor Sport Valley is the site of massive investment by global companies (Ford, DaimlerChrysler, Honda, Mitsubishi, to name but a few), but, in the main, into a network of small and medium-sized independently owned British companies (Henry et al., 1996; Turner, 1998). As a neo-Marshallian node or real world of production, Motor Sport Valley is a centre of 'representation, interaction and innovation in a global filiere' (Amin and Thrift, 1994, 1995; but see also Henry and Pinch, 1998) – a world of convention setting, untraded interdependencies and a framework of action.

In the context of the knowledge economy, we have argued in this chapter that this centre or 'world' is first and foremost constructed through the medium of the knowledge community. Clearly, the concept of 'knowledge' used in this chapter, and in much work by economic geographers on the knowledge economy, is a crude one, yet the aim has been to demonstrate empirically the processes by which some versions of knowledge do get spatialized, and, in this case, spatialized around very particular places. In this regard, the research is a tentative, yet important, step towards the demonstration of concepts of economic geography and agglomeration such as 'industry in the air', 'milieu', 'untraded interdependencies', 'local industrial systems', 'learning regions' and 'institutional thickness'. These are commonly recognized to be an important facet of agglomeration and yet there are relatively few concrete examples of such concepts in action.

In summary, the empirical analysis undertaken in this chapter shows that Motor Sport Valley is a close-knit knowledge community characterized by a complex mixture of co-operation as well as fierce competition. This 'world of production' (Storper and Salais, 1997) includes 'ways of thinking' and 'ways of doing' that transcend individual firms but not the British industry as a whole, and that contribute significantly to its world-beating status. Thus, this chapter, we believe, is an important exemplifier of how to understand the increased salience of agglomerations within the globalizing economy. Furthermore, it opens up further intriguing possibilities about understanding contemporary capitalism and its geographical growth dynamics.

For example, in the British motor sport industry, the paradox of highly secretive companies located close to each other is explained by their vital need to dip into the deep stream of knowledge that keeps being generated and circulated throughout the region largely on an untraded basis.

Recruitment of staff, observation of rival designs, new firm formation, the assimilation of gossip and rumour and discussions with extensive personal contacts, are all facilitated by geographical proximity. In effect, *the region constitutes a 'knowledge pool'* whose internal configuration is continually changing but that, overall, is on a constant learning trajectory. To leave the region is to risk your position within the 'knowledge loop', and it is clear that whilst many British engineers/designers sell their knowledge overseas, very few leave the Valley for any great length of time. Similarly, just as the software engineers of Silicon Valley discuss how they can change firms without changing car parks (Saxenian, 1994), so in the high firm-death industry of British motor sport, engineers know that a location within the Valley is likely to ensure continued employment without the need for a house move, even if the name of the employer is likely to change relatively frequently.

But, as others have argued concerning other regional production systems (Cooke and Morgan, 1993; Saxenian, 1994), this implies that the competitive advantage of the British motor sport industry is integrally bound up with its regional concentration, thus it could be stated that the essential analytical focus should be on *the region as the unit of analysis* and not the firm or industry *per se* (Storper and Walker, 1989). And in this case, the knowledge community is the critical constituent of that region. If one is to capitalize on knowledge, it must be recognized that the motor sport industry is characterized by a high turnover of firms, yet the *industry* goes from strength to strength. In the extreme case, the asset base of the firms themselves is often minimal, involving, for example, some specialist machinery, a (rented?) building and a car that becomes virtually worthless in months, and, critically, the *knowledge of its employees*. It is this knowledge base, and the reputation that this base can command in the eyes of sponsors, that is the key element of the industry. The industry is therefore perhaps best represented as continually shifting networks of people in, and outside of, continually shifting bounded entities called firms. However, it is a knowledge base that is *territorialized*, and this is the crucial competitive advantage of Motor Sport Valley. The question that then arises is whether or not current measures of economic activity, and economic performance, can accurately portray this emergent form of (soft) capitalism. Or is there a need to rethink the objects of study in the economy (e.g. firms, assets, profits, region) to reflect accurately its emergent dynamics?

For example, if the significant unit of competitiveness is the network and region, how do you invest in companies? Furthermore, if that competitiveness is based on 'signs' as well as spaces, exactly what are the assets of any firm/network/region? As the British government recently recognized in its White Paper on competitiveness (DTI, 1998), if the banking system, for example, has always been 'conservative' in its investment policies (i.e. regarding investment in UK small firms rather than 'emerging markets' from Latin America to the Pacific Rim and Eastern Europe), how will it now do its sums when faced with economic growth characterized by a rapid churn of firms and serial entrepreneurs with both firm failures (and successes) to their names?

Finally, a key issue for future studies of agglomerating industries is the relationship between knowledge generation and power relations. Although some of the most innovative racing car companies, and especially the early pioneers such as Coopers, survived on 'shoestring' budgets, there is little doubt that in the contemporary world, competitive success in most racing formulae is dependent upon securing substantial sums of sponsorship money. This funding facilitates the creation of knowledge necessary to produce cars that win races. This competitive success, in turn, enables firms to gain political power to influence the various actors that regulate motor sport: the FIA, various governments, the television companies that transmit the races around the world, and the various sponsors of the sport. As indicated by this chapter (see also Pinch and Henry, 1999a), knowledge is not therefore produced in a vacuum but is an integral part of political economy/society. Industrial agglomerations cannot therefore be understood without appreciating the wider political economy within which they operate. Similarly, relations of power and domination enable certain knowledge communities to construct the technological and production trajectories of particular economic worlds.

NOTES

This is a revised version of a paper published in *Geoforum*, 31 (2), N. Henry and S. Pinch, 'Spatialising knowledge: Placing the knowledge community of Motor Sport Valley', 2000, published with permission from Elsevier Science.

1. The maps in Figures 6.1 and 6.2 represent a snapshot of Motor Sport Valley at a particular point in time – late 1998/early 1999. As discussed later in the chapter, these maps are likely to become outdated in a very short period of time due to the high rate of firm births and deaths endemic to the industry.

2. This is, indeed, a crude distinction as in order for any ideas or knowledge to travel it must do so through some medium or other (i.e. be embodied in some human/non-human artefact).

3. The ability to achieve this came from the vast array of specialist literature within the industry. In addition, a number of these career histories were of individuals interviewed. In these cases, pre-constructed histories were used as part of the interview.

4. The numbers refer to the transcript code. All respondents were assured of anonymity to enable them to speak freely.

5. A constructor is the company that assembles the car using in-house and external supplies. A constructor is, normally, the racing team (e.g. Williams Grand Prix Engineering runs the Rothmans Williams Renault Formula One team) but constructors may also run more than one team (e.g. Prodrive has run a Subaru team and a Nissan team in the World Rally Championship).

6. As another referee commented, the 'cultural-social' perspective of the chapter initiates a certain exclusion of the 'economic' in the sense of, for example, the cohesiveness, competitiveness and employment characteristics of this regional production system. The point is well taken (although see Henry, 1999; Henry et al., 1996; Henry and Pinch, forthcoming) and pleasing in relation to the ultimate aim of the chapter as space is limited to develop fully both strands.

7. We should, nevertheless, bear in mind that this is a fiercely competitive industry, and in the words of Henry 'solidarity between F1 teams is largely built on quicksand' (1990: p. 34).

8. See, for example, the recent, high-profile, ability of the 'industry' to gain exemption from the European ban on tobacco sponsorship of sport for eight years by persuading the UK government to oppose full implementation.

9. As an early paper in the 'geography of post-Fordism/FS (flexible specialization) debate', Amin and Robins (1990) argued that many of the empirical canons of the industrial districts did not provide reproducible paths partly because they included 'pioneer' regions who had, in effect, 'invented' new industries and there can only be one pioneer. Interestingly, Motor Sport Valley wrenched 'pioneer' status in motor sport from the Third Italy.

REFERENCES

Allen, J. and du Gay, P. (1994) 'Industry and the rest: The economic identity of services', *Work, Employment and Society*, 8 (2): 255–271.

Allen, J., Massey, D., Cochrane, A. with Charlesworth, J., Court, G., Henry, N. and Sarre, P. (1998) *Rethinking the Region*. London: Routledge.

Amin, A. and Robins, K. (1990) 'The re-emergence of regional economies? The mythical geography of flexible accumulation'. *Environment and Planning D: Society and Space*, 8: 7–34.

Amin, A. and Thrift, N. (1992) 'Neo-Marshallian nodes in global networks', *International Journal of Urban and Regional Research*, 16 (4): 571–587.

Amin, A. and Thrift, N. (1994) 'Living in the global', in A. Amin and N. Thrift (eds), *Globalization, Institutions and Regional Development in Europe*. Oxford: Oxford University Press, pp. 1–19.

Amin, A. and Thrift, N. (1995) 'Globalisation, institutional "thickness" and the local economy', in P. Healey, S. Cameron, S. Davoudi, S. Graham and A. Madani-Pour (eds), *Managing Cities: The New Urban Context*. Chichester: Wiley.

Barnes, T. (1996) *Logics of Dislocation: Models, Metaphors and Meanings of Economic Space*. New York, Guilford Press.

Bijker, W.E., Hughes, T.P. and Pinch, T. (1990) *The Social Construction of Technological Systems*. Cambridge, MA: MIT Press.

Boden, D. (1994). *The Business of Talk*. Cambridge: Polity.

Bryson, J.R. and Daniels, P.W. (1998) 'Business link strong ties, and the walls of silence: Small and medium-sized enterprises and external business-service expertise', *Environment and Planning C: Government and Policy*, 16: 265–280.

Bryson, J., Henry, N., Keeble, D. and Martin, R. (1999) *The Economic Geography Reader: Producing and Consuming Global Capitalism*. Chichester: Wiley.

Bryson, J., Daniels, P., Henry, N. and Pollard, J. (2000) *Knowledge, Space, Economy*. London: Routledge.

Castells, M. (1996) *The Rise of the Network Society*. Oxford: Blackwell.

Castells, M. and Hall, P. (1994) *Technopoles of the World: The Making of 21st Century Industrial Complexes*. London: Routledge.

Clark, P. (1999) *Organizations in Action: Competition Between Context*. London: Routledge.

Cooke, P. and Morgan, K. (1993) 'The network paradigm: New departures in regional development', *Environment and Planning D: Society and Space*, 11: 543–564.

Cooke, P. and Morgan, K. (1998) *The Associational Economy*. Oxford: Blackwell.

Coyle, D. (1997) *The Weightless World: Strategies for Managing the Digital Economy*. Oxford: Capstone.

Cresswell, J.W. (1994) *Research Design: Quantitative and Qualitative Approaches*. London: Sage.

Department of Trade and Industry (DTI) (1998) *Our Competitive Future: Building the Knowledge Driven Economy*. London: HMSO.

Dicken, P. (1998) *Global Shift: Transforming the World Economy*. 3rd edn. London: Paul Chapman.

du Gay, P. (1996) *Consumption and Identity at Work*. London: Sage.

Economic and Social Research Council (ESRC) (2000) 'The evolution of knowledge: Interaction of research and practice', <http://www.esrc.ac.uk/knowconc.htm>. Accessed 29 March.

Economist (1999) 'Knowing your place', 11 March.

Florida, R. (1995) 'Toward the learning region', *Futures*, 27, 527–536.

Gertler, M. (1994) '"Being there": Proximity, organisation and culture in the development and adoption of advanced manufacturing technologies', *Economic Geography*, 71 (1): 1–25.

Gibson-Graham, J.K. (1996) *The End of Capitalism (As We Knew It): A Feminist Critique of Political Economy*. Oxford: Blackwell.

Goodwin, M., Duncan, S. and Halford, S. (1993) 'Regulation theory, the local state, and the transition of urban politics', *Environment and Planning D: Society and Space*, 11: 67–88.

Grabher, G. (1993) *The Embedded Firm: On the Socioeconomics of Industrial Networks*. London: Routledge.

Granovetter, M. and Swedberg, R. (eds) (1992) *The Sociology of Economic Life*. Boulder, CO: Westview Press.

Hamilton, M. (1994) *Race Without End: The Grind behind the Glamour of the Sasol Jordan Grand Prix Team*. Sparkford: Patrick Stephens.

Harvey, D. (1989) *The Condition of Postmodernity*. Oxford: Blackwell.

Hayter, R. and Watts, H.D. (1983) 'The geography of enterprise: A re-appraisal', *Progress in Human Geography*, 7: 157–181.

Henry, A. (1990) *The Turbo Years: Grand Prix Racing's Battle for Power*. Swindon: Crowood Press.

Henry, A. (1994) *The Darkest Hour*. Autocourse, Vol. 44. London: Hazelton Publishing.

Henry, N. (1999) *In Pole Position: Motor Sport Success in Britain and Its Lessons for the World Motor Industry*. London, Euromotor Reports.

Henry, N. and Pinch, S. (1997) 'A Regional Formula for Success? The innovative region of Motor Sport Valley', School of Geography, University of Birmingham.

Henry, N. and Pinch, S. (1998) '"Motor Sport Valley" and institutional thickness: Thick or thin?', paper presented at the Reflections on the Institutional Turn in Local Economic Development Conference, University of Sheffield, 9–10 September.

Henry, N. and Pinch, S. (forthcoming) 'Neo-Marshallian nodes, institutional thickness and Britain's Motor Sport Valley: Thick or thin'? *Environment and Planning*, 33, 1169–1183.

Henry, N., Pinch, S. and Russell, S. (1996) '"In pole position?" Untraded interdependencies, new industrial spaces and the British motor sport industry', *Area*, 28 (1): 25–36.

Hodgson, G. (1999) *Economics and Utopia: Why the Learning Economy is Not the End of History*. London: Routledge.

Jessop, B. (1990) *State Theory: Putting Capitalist States in Their Place*. Cambridge: Polity.

Jones, M. (1998) *New Institutional Spaces: TECS and the Remaking of Economic Governance*: London, Jessica Kingsley.

Krugman, P. (1991) *Geography and Trade*. Leuven: Leuven University Press.

Krugman, P. (1995) *Development, Geography and Economic Theory*. Cambridge, MA: MIT Press.

Lash, S. and Urry, J. (1987) *The End of Organized Capitalism*. Cambridge: Polity.

Lash, S. and Urry, J. (1994) *Economies of Signs and Space*. London: Sage.

Layder, D. (1998) *Sociological Practice: Linking Theory and Social Research*. London: Sage.

Leadbetter, C. (1999) *Living on Thin Air: The New Economy*. London: Viking.

Lee, R. and Wills, J. (eds) (1997) *Geographies of Economies*. London: Arnold.

Lipietz, A. (1992) *Towards a New Economic Order: Post-Fordism, Ecology and Democracy*. Cambridge: Polity.

Livingstone, D. (1992) *The Geographical Tradition*. Oxford: Blackwell.

Lundvall, B.-A. and Johnson, B. (1994) 'The learning economy', *Journal of Industry Studies*, 1: 23–42.

McDowell, L. (1997) *Capital Culture: Gender at Work in the City*. Oxford: Blackwell.

McDowell, L. and Court, G. (1993) 'The missing subject in economic geography', *South East Programme Occasional Paper Series No. 5*. Faculty of Social Sciences, Milton Keynes: Open University.

MaCleod, G. (2000) 'Re-inventing a region in the age of austerity: Placing knowledge, entrepreneurialism, and reflexive capitalism in Lowland Scotland', *Geoforum*, 31: 29–236.

Markusen, A. (1996) 'Sticky places in slippery slopes: A typology of industrial districts', *Economic Geography*, 72: 293–313.

Martin, R. (1994) 'Economic theory and human geography', in D. Gregory, R. Martin and G. Smith (eds), *Human Geography: Society, Space and Social Science*. Basingstoke: Macmillan. pp. 21–53.

Martin, R. (1999) 'The new "geographical" turn in economics', *Cambridge Journal of Economics*, 23: 65–92.

Massey, D. (1993) 'Power-geometry and a progressive sense of place', in J. Bird, B. Curtis, T. Putnam, G. Robertson and L. Tickner (eds), *Mapping the Futures: Local Cultures, Global Challenge*. London: Routledge. pp. 59–69.

Massey, D., Allen, J. and Sarre, P. (eds) (1999) *Human Geography Today*. Cambridge: Polity.

Morgan, K. (1997) 'The learning region: Institutions innovation and regional renewal', *Regional Studies*, 31: 491–503.

Peck, J. (1996) *Work-Place: The Social Regulation of Labor Markets*. New York: Guilford Press.

Peck, J. and Tickell, A. (1994) 'Searching for a new institutional fix: The after-Fordist crisis and the global–local disorder', in A. Amin (ed.), *Post-Fordism: A Reader*. Oxford: Blackwell. pp. 280–315.

Pinch, S. and Henry, N. (1999a) 'Discursive aspects of technological innovation: The case of the British motor sport industry', *Environment and Planning A*, 31: 665–682.

Pinch, S. and Henry, N. (1999b) 'Paul Krugman's geographical economics, industrial clustering and the British motor sport industry', *Regional Studies*, 33 (9): 815–827.

Pinch, S., Henry, N. and Turner, D. (1997) 'Explaining the supremacy of Motor Sport Valley', School of Geography, University of Birmingham, Working Paper Series 62.

Piore, M. and Sabel, C. (1984) *The Second Industrial Divide*. New York: Basic Books.

Polanyi, M. (1967) *The Tacit Dimension*. London: Routledge and Kegan Paul.

Porter, M. (1990) *The Competitive Advantage of Nations*. London: Macmillan.

Pratt, A. (1998) 'Making digital spaces: A constructivist critique of the network society', mimeo, available from the author, London: Department of Geography, London School of Economics.

Pyke, F., Becattini, G. and Sengenberger, W. (eds) (1990) *Industrial Districts and Inter-Firm Cooperation in Italy*. Geneva: International Institute for Labour Studies.

Quah, D.T. (1996) 'Growth and dematerialisation: Why non-stick frying pans have lost their edge', *Centre Piece*. London: CEP, London School of Economics.

Sawers, L. and Tabb, W. (1984) *Sunbelt/Snowbelt: Urban Development and Regional Restructuring*. Oxford: Oxford University Press.

Saxenian, A. (1994) *Regional Advantage: Culture and Competition in Silicon Valley and Route 128*. Cambridge, MA: Harvard University Press.

Scott, A.J. (1988) *New Industrial Spaces*. London: Pion.

Scott, A.J. and Storper, M. (1987) 'High technology industry and regional development: A theoretical critique and reconstruction', *International Social Science Journal*, 112: 215–232.

Segal, Quince and Wicksteed (SQW) (1985) *The Cambridge Phenomenon: The Growth of High Technology Industry in a University Town*. Cambridge: SQW.

Storper, M. (1995) 'The resurgence of regional economies ten years later: The region as a nexus of untraded interdependencies', *Journal of European Urban and Regional Studies*, 2: 191–221.

Storper, M. (1997) *The Regional World: Territorial Development in a Global Economy*. New York: Guilford Press.

Storper, M. and Salais, R. (1997) *Worlds of Production: The Action Frameworks of the Economy*. Cambridge, MA: Harvard University Press.

Storper, M. and Walker, R. (1989) *The Capitalist Imperative: Territory, Technology and Industrial Growth*. Oxford: Blackwell.

Thrift, N. (1994) 'On the social and cultural determinants of international financial centres: The case of the City of London', in: S. Corbridge, R. Martin and N. Thrift (eds), *Money, Space and Power*. Oxford: Blackwell. pp. 327–355.

Thrift, N. (1996a) 'Knowledge economies: The rise of Soft Capitalism', paper presented to the Institute of British Geographers Annual Conference, University of Stratchclyde, Glasgow, 3–6 January.

Thrift, N. (1996b) *Spatial Formations*. London: Sage.

Turner, D. (1998) 'A study of the relationships between the small firms of Motorsport Valley and multi-nationals', unpublished MPhil., School of Geography, University of Birmingham.

Twitchen, A. (2000) 'The body's second skin: Forming the protective community of grand prix motor racing', in L. McKie and N. Watson (eds), *Organising Bodies*. New York: Macmillan.

Warf, B. (1995) 'Telecommunications and the changing geographies of knowledge transmission in the late 20th century', *Urban Studies*, 32: 529–555.

Wright, P. (1996) 'The designers – John Barnard', *Racecar Engineering*, 5 (6): 41–2.

III

THEORETIC AND METHODOLOGICAL ISSUES

7

A MAPPING FRAMEWORK FOR STRATEGY MAKING

Colin Eden and Fran Ackermann

ABSTRACT

When embarking upon a strategy development process, organizations are often faced with the question of where to start, whom to involve and how to manage the contributions that are surfaced. This chapter provides details of an approach that allows organizations to reflect upon what they have been doing hitherto in order to understand the nature of the organization, its capabilities and aspirations. Our approach helps them explore this understanding, and negotiate an agreement towards a strategic direction. It is, in short, a method for surfacing and sharing current knowledge, and collectively creating new knowledge.

The approach presented is essentially a participative one (rather than being the sole domain of a team of planners), although the extensiveness of participation depends on the culture of the organization, the time available for the exercise, and the resources accessible. It is part of the JOURNEY-making approach to strategy (see Eden and Ackermann, 1998a, for a more detailed explanation), focusing predominantly on the use of cognitive and cause mapping to elicit and work with strategic possibilities.

SURFACING AND EXPLORING CURRENT STRATEGIZING MODELS

Detecting 'emergent strategizing' (Eden and van der Heijden, 1995; Mintzberg and Waters, 1985) is an appropriate starting point for strategy making. Emergent strategizing is what will determine the strategic future of the organization when no deliberate choices are made about that future. What this process entails is asking the group members (whether they be the management team or Board of Directors, or some other group) to reflect on unwritten rules of thumb, taken-for-granted ways of thinking about the strategic issues facing the organization. These are the structures and procedures that will shape the strategic future of the organization should they persist in current activities. Through this part of the JOURNEY-making approach, current concerns as well as implicit or embedded aspirations, knowledge, wisdom and beliefs are surfaced and participants provided with the means to reflect on and debate them. We want to surface that which currently *drives* the organization's direction (the 'theories in use') rather than any espoused and/or published strategy.

The group may, as a consequence of this consideration, agree to let the organization continue 'muddling through' (Lindblom, 1959), resulting in deliberate agreement to this approach as a strategy. Alternatively, they may wish to develop a different strategic future and design the strategic intent to guide the change. Whether or not they are self-conscious of the process, organizations develop and reinforce emergent strategy – as illustrated through the 'recipes' or patterns they adopt (Spender, 1989). Through detecting the underlying recipe(s) and reflecting upon it/them, any strategic management undertaken by the group can be thought of as *'deliberate emergent strategizing'*, as opposed to non-deliberate emergent strategizing. This conscious choice process provides an understanding of the organization's history, capabilities and aspirations, and is a key element to the JOURNEY-making approach. Cognitive and cause mapping – the structuring technique adopted by the process – provides some assistance both in the elicitation and subsequently in the structuring of the contributions surfaced. The resultant model of strategic thinking then facilitates negotiation (strategic conversations) to take place and change becomes more possible because it is politically feasible. We can see our future clearly and wisely only when we know the path that leads to it from the present.

The most powerful conversation that can drive emergent strategic change is that focused on crisis, challenge and 'firefighting' (Mintzberg et al., 1976). Managers attribute *cause and effect relationships* in their attempts to *make sense* (Kelly, 1955) of such crises. Their conversations are usually the starting points for 'issue selling' (Dutton and Ashford, 1993), where each manager seeks to influence his or her colleagues' view of what is important. In crisis, managers fight harder for their views and the drive for action means they reveal – often implicitly – more of their embedded vision, surface more of their assumptions, and take one another more seriously than on 'special' occasions designated for strategy making (e.g. 'away-days'). However, the urgency involved in dealing with strategic crises can mean that whilst each manager surfaces more of his or her strategic assumptions, there is less time for other managers to check out their understanding of these assumptions. Consequently assumptions can be surfaced and missed, or can be severely misunderstood. These misunderstandings occur because the important stage of *sharing meaning* and *making sense* may have been bypassed, and each participant is forced to make untested assumptions about the implicit assumptions embedded in proposals for action coming from colleagues.

Thus a more purposeful strategy development approach must recognize the need for a strategy model to be transparent and understandable to participants (so as to enable them to reflect on one another's assumptions) as well as being appropriate to the task of strategy making. It must capture the subtleties and nuances of meaning, allowing new material to surface and comprehension to build.

The modelling technique – our mapping approach – is a particular form of cognitive mapping (Eden, 1988; Eden and Ackermann, 1998b; Eden et al., 1979) and its developed extensions are cause or strategy mapping. A cognitive map is intended to be a model/representation of a particular person's thinking about the strategic issues facing the organization. The amalgamation of a series of cognitive maps (from a group of individuals) into a computer-based model provides the source for the creation of a *strategy map* as a cause map. This strategy map or model contains the aggregation of the thinking of many people, including conflicting views, subtly different slants on the same issues, and different perspectives on similar views.

The cause- or strategy-mapping model therefore provides a useful device/means for group work through providing a holistic representation. It supports relevant group processes, including the importance of *negotiation* and the significance of *anonymity* (each of these will be addressed below). The model, which is typically a set of embedded maps, provides the means for strategic conversations flushing out the values, assumptions and beliefs of managers (and thus the emergent strategizing), and enables reflection/examination and development of strategic direction. The maps may be created directly by groups (using the 'oval mapping technique' [OMT], or using networked laptop computers and special purpose group support software – 'Group Explorer$^{TM'}$ (www.Phrontis.com). They may also be created during and following interviews with individuals, where the output from the interview is a cognitive map.

Cognitive mapping is used when working with individuals and helps in the elicitation and structuring of each of the participant's distinctive perspectives – how he or she perceives the issue(s) being discussed. The maps strike a balance between (a) providing a device for exploring meaning – through illustrating not just what the facts/issues are but also how they fit together – and (b) ensuring, through their qualitative fuzziness and imprecision, a sufficient degree of *equivocality to facilitate negotiation*. This duality is particularly important when subsequently working in groups.

Cognitive maps are typically used for capturing and exploring the thinking of each member of a senior management team, allowing tacit knowledge, assumptions, assertions, aspirations, values, beliefs and concerns to surface. They are idiographic in nature (Eden and Ackermann, 1998b), reflecting the particular thinking of an individual. However, these individual maps are then woven together to form a group representation, and, following a process of analysis, used to form a group map or model (a 'negotiative device') that can subsequently support the process of developing agreement (the strategic conversation). This process is usually undertaken using software that mirrors the mapping technique ('Decision Explorer'™ [www.Banxia.com]), providing the facility to manage information more effectively through rapid retrieval processes, analytical procedures and flexible displays.

So what actually is a cognitive map and how is it constructed and used during an interview with a senior manager? A cognitive map is essentially a directed graph or causal (option/outcome) network with aspirations/ goals, values and beliefs at the apex, issues/concerns in the centre and detailed actions or assertions supporting these issues (or concerns) at the base. (Figure 7.1 provides an example of a small part of a cognitive map.) In a cognitive map (and later in the strategy map developed by the group), explanations as implicit actions are those statements that are taken to cause a given outcome. However, each explanation or action in turn is informed by other possible actions that support them (explanations), placing the former action *as an outcome*. Therefore, each node on the map is both an explanation and an option for action, and an outcome depending upon the *level* of abstraction required. As part of the mapping process, the maps are deliberately coded with an active verb so that each of the statements/constructs constitutes a call for action as if it were to be taken as an option. The coding process also aims to ensure that the language of the interviewee is captured. Each statement includes an actor as well as action, and, where volunteered, the statement reflects the opposite, contrasting or bipolar element (using the 'rather than' clause).

The 'call for action' also provides an example of statements ('personal constructs', in Kelly's term[1]) as contributors to the process of 'manage and control'. Cognitive maps help by prompting managers to focus on contrasting the current with the past, the current with the aspired future direction, or the past with the future. By focusing on strategic issues rather than the development of idealized scenarios or preferred goals, the process is deliberately designed to get as close as possible to 'theories-in-use' (Argyris and Schon, 1974; Bartunek and Moch, 1987). Doing so helps reduce the possibility of participants discussing 'espoused theories' derived from attendance of management courses or previous strategy documents! This process helps avoid strategy being constructed as 'motherhood and apple pie'. In this chapter we outline several steps that move from individual cognitive maps to the construction of a group 'strategy map'.

METHODOLOGICAL NOTE: THREE WAYS OF MAPPING WITH GROUPS

Alongside the use of individual interviews, group mapping allows members to have a forum for discussing and reflecting upon the organization and its direction (particularly useful where consultation is not a familiar process, or there are no interpersonal issues). Cognitive maps can be constructed from the following two methods for working with

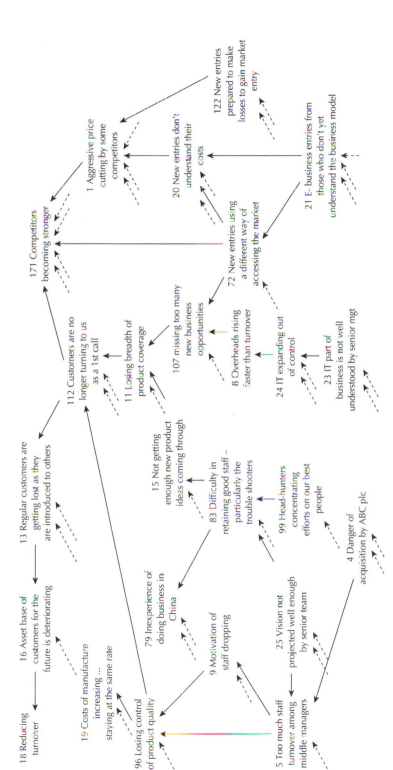

Figure 7.1 A sample of a cognitive map

Note: For clarification, the numbers at the front of the 'concepts' are simply numeric tags provided by the software to aid manipulation of the data. Where there are three dots (an ellipsis), this is shorthand for 'rather than'. Finally, the dotted arrows highlight the fact that there is more material around the concept in question.

mapping in groups. The first, the Oval Mapping Technique (OMT), provides a manual forum for eliciting contributions and structuring them according to the mapping conventions. The second, using computer-supported mapping, allows the group to interact with the map visually and literally. In both cases the techniques support the strategy-making process through aiding conversation and negotiation. However, there are a number of issues that must be addressed in designing such a process: for example, difficulties keeping participants from contributing; the significance of synthesis; enabling enough creativity and fun; and developing strategy maps in real time. We have also used a third, more anonymous method with networked computers, which has its own strengths and weaknesses.

Using the Oval Mapping Technique (OMT)

One approach to producing group maps encourages group members to record and publicly display their views on large 'oval' cards (Bryson et al., 1995; Eden and Ackermann, 1998a). Unlike the production of cognitive maps in a more private environment (with only the interviewer/mapper and one organizational participant), members in a group are able to see the perspectives of the others, add their own contributions, and watch the strategy map unfold. During the process the ovals will be organized by a facilitator following the same guidelines used for building individual cognitive maps – thus concepts will be identified, clusters formed, and inter- and intra-cluster links elicited. Through the process of both surfacing and more significantly structuring the material, participants are able to move towards a model that has the ownership of most of the group. This is achieved as they begin to understand better the different points of view by considering them *in their context*, frequently adding new, subtler, points that can be woven into the overall picture. Through carrying out rough public analyses, identifying clusters of concepts within the context of a structured hierarchy, participants are given the chance to identify and explore the emergent properties of the map.

This public procedure enables group members to begin to *change their mind* as they examine the rationale of alternative viewpoints. They are not required to defend their own viewpoint. It is expected that their own ideas might change as they are seen within the context of the views of others in the group. Moreover, the mapping process promotes synthesis by enabling linkages between and within clusters of inputs. Group maps also encourage creativity through the ability to see alternative points of view, and from this position identify and develop new options and strategies. By encouraging multiple perspectives, providing an environment with enough equivocality to avoid the need for 'face saving', and by structuring the knowledge and insights, the process attends to procedural rationality. It makes sense – which in turn promotes emotional and

Figure 7.2   A strategy group beginning the OMT process

cognitive commitment to the outcomes. The process is designed to encourage social *negotiation*.

To illustrate, Figure 7.2 shows a picture of a small group working on their strategy. The group, who are responsible for providing public transport and information pertaining to its schedule/cost, are in the process of surfacing material on oval cards and beginning to structure it. As they teased out the differences between the various forms of communication they were providing, they also began to negotiate a set of actions to improve and facilitate communication. The group were also responsible for liaising with other transport operators – with the intention of providing an integrated public transport network. Therefore not only did they have to communicate with their own operators but they also provide the public with information on services, including connection possibilities, and so on. Both of these were seen as different requirements from the communication that had to take place within the organization. The debate raised resulted in the organizations goal system being revised.

Using Computer-Supported Mapping

A second way of using mapping with groups is to work with an electronic version of the strategic map – a computer model (Ackermann and Eden, 2001). Although often a starting model has already been generated either through the interviews or through the Oval Mapping Technique, it can also start from scratch. Using the software, either the facilitator enters in participants' comments as they are made or alternatively a group decision support system is used enabling participants to enter their ideas (and links) directly into the model – in a manner similar to writing on the ovals (Ackermann and Eden, 1997). Using the computerized form of mapping (rather than the ovals) allows easy manipulation of the model (e.g. editing, deleting and adding) and encourages participants to play with ideas, explore their context and begin to build up a common understanding. Each of these activities is a precursor to negotiation.

Computerization also supports fast retrieval of material from other parts of the model, should they be seen as relevant to the topic being discussed, and enables rapid analysis to be undertaken, allowing exploration of the model's structural properties. However, computer maps also constrain the amount of material seen at any time to the size of a computer screen – much less material than can be viewed on an OMT wall.

As can be seen from the photo presented in Figure 7.3, the computer-projected model is also attractive because it enables participants to work with the material at their own pace, search the screen for their contributions and, subsequently, read the statements of others. From this process of allowing members to locate their own views in addition to seeing the perspectives of others in context – because the map depicts the surrounding information – a degree of equivocality is possible from the multiplicity of contextual data. Participants are not forced to make immediate responses and so the process of psychological negotiation can proceed without undue influence of emotion. The screen acts as a buffer between a proponent and other contributors, allowing easier negotiation.

In one company this process went a long way to resolving a difficult emotionally charged situation where two coalitions of staff were in dispute about the future. The model's ability to reassure members that their views were captured and taken seriously, along with the opportunity to provide further explanation, was critical to moving beyond deadlock. The strategic problem was that whilst marketing was a central service, the company was understaffed and not providing sufficient service to some of the smaller products seen as significant for the future. Meanwhile because the smaller products still generated overheads, their managers planned to recruit their own marketing staff. The workshop commenced with a clear division between roles, but after both sides had began to appreciate one another's perspectives/difficulties, then it was possible to move to a more collaborative stance.

Whilst each form of mapping has its own specific purpose, both oval mapping and computer modelling (Ackermann and Eden, 2001) are grounded in the same theoretical standpoint – Personal Construct Theory (Kelly, 1955). Regardless of whether they are individual- or group-oriented, the maps provide models that are designed to reflect the thinking, beliefs and aspirations of those whose views have been incorporated.

Figure 7.3   An example of a group using the computer-supported system

Consequently, they provide a means for enabling group members to begin jointly to understand the perspectives of others, reflect on the emergent issues that are surfaced from them, and start to negotiate an agreed strategic direction. Moreover, they promote synthesis through the mapping technique's ability to pull together viewpoints. Both mapping techniques promote creativity that ensues from synthesis and from multiple perspectives. The model itself becomes a socially negotiated reality – 'a transitional object' (de Geus, 1988) – with new meanings being discovered, a common language being developed and an overall understanding and agreement being forged.

Most teams find the process fun as they begin to learn more about their organization and see progress being made. For one group within Shell – who were struggling with developing their own strategic direction – the use of the model to surface, develop and negotiate agreement helped them achieve something that they had not previously been able to do (Galer, 1990). Through the mapping process participants often gain a sense of emotional commitment to the outcome as they find the process both procedurally just (allowing all to have their say) and procedurally rational. In addition, we have found on numerous occasions the act of working together and developing a map and strategic direction helps in the process of building teams (Ackermann, 1992).

The participative aspect of the mapping methods we will describe is critical. First, the process of including staff from around the organization ensures some degree of representation, allowing staff to feel part of the process through influencing or informing the strategic direction taken. From this they are more likely to begin to own the outcomes and understand the final product, thus increasing the chance of effective implementation. Second, by developing a map in a group and thus exploring different perspectives, it becomes possible to persuade the key players to also buy into the outcomes, thus ensuring that the outcomes are *politically feasible*.

Working in Groups using a Networked System of Laptop Computers for the Direct Elicitation of Maps

Not all organizations are comfortable or familiar with participative methods. When working in a part of a Health Authority, it was necessary to start the mapping process using interviews as staff were unused to being asked their viewpoint and apparently unwilling to contribute in a group setting because they were wary of exposing themselves. Finding different ways of eliciting material in a group setting, but also ensuring anonymity, became important. The group support system 'Group Explorer' can provide anonymity (through the direct entry of contributions via a personal laptop computer that is networked to the public screen). Networked computers also allow productivity gains: a group can surface, structure and negotiate towards an agreed direction within half a day, should that be necessary. However, unlike the interviews, starting with a networked system does not promote the same level of deep and reflective thinking at a personal level.

BUILDING THE INITIAL FRAMEWORK FOR STRATEGIC ACTION WITH THE MANAGEMENT TEAM

Step 1: Individual Interviews

All three of the group processes just described here may begin with initial individual interviews. These help group members surface contributions that might otherwise not emerge in a group setting, and also help in furthering reflection and deeper thinking. For example, one organization, unused to participative approaches, used interviews to encourage members to raise their issues, concerns and aspirations because the Chief Executive strongly believed that working directly in a group environment would reduce the knowledge and beliefs elicited and thus diminish the potential of the team and process. The interviews were used to allow members to build up confidence both in the mapping technique and to take more responsibility for decisions and strategic decision making. In other organizations, characterized by more open sharing, initial interviews are still useful because they surface deeper wisdom and so allow for the identification of more of the distinctiveness of the organization during the group sessions and also elicit a wider range of possible strategic options.

Step 2: Developing a Model of Strategic Intent from Individual Interviews

As noted earlier, the mapping process commences with surfacing the organization's emergent strategizing, detecting the patterns of beliefs and values within individual cognitive maps. This effort usually forms the basis for the first part of JOint Understanding and Reflection – an important part of the JOURney-making approach. Using the maps as a vehicle for debate, a social process evolves in which team members explore one another's concerns, assumptions of the world and aspirations for the organization.

The facilitators structure this map as a 'backroom' activity. The composite map takes a hierarchical form similar to the cognitive maps. The possible *aspirations or goals* are at the top of the model; these are supported by (or derived from) emergent *strategic issues*, which in turn are impacted upon by *strategic problems* and possible *strategic options*. This structure is shown by Figure 7.4. The categorization of each of the statements that make up the map into each of these levels is initially a rough one. Typically a first pass will take place following individual interviews, whilst weaving together different cognitive maps. This effort involves carrying out various forms of analysis (explained more fully in Eden et al., 1992, and Eden and Ackermann, 1998a) to tidy the model and subsequently begin to explore its characteristics and thus gain clues for the categorization.

Tidying the model normally takes the form of exploring the 'heads' of the model (statements with no consequences – out-arrows) to check whether these statements, as outcomes, are likely to be taken by the group as 'good or bad in their own right' and therefore as goals or 'negative goals'. They may alternatively be statements requiring further linking into the main body of the model. 'Orphans' (statements currently unconnected) are also identified and woven into the model if appropriate. The weaving process is assisted by the ability of the mapping technique to show not only the concept (statement) but also its context (i.e. the material surrounding it, adding richness and helping determine meaning). Word searches can be conducted to ensure full integration of the different perspectives. This single network/map then provides the basis of a vehicle for strategy negotiation – both psychological and emotional.

Following the tidying process, further analyses are conducted. These include:

- examining the density around the statements (looking for the 'busiest');
- calculating each statement's centrality within the overall structure of the model; and
- searching for feedback loops (showing possible dynamic behaviour).

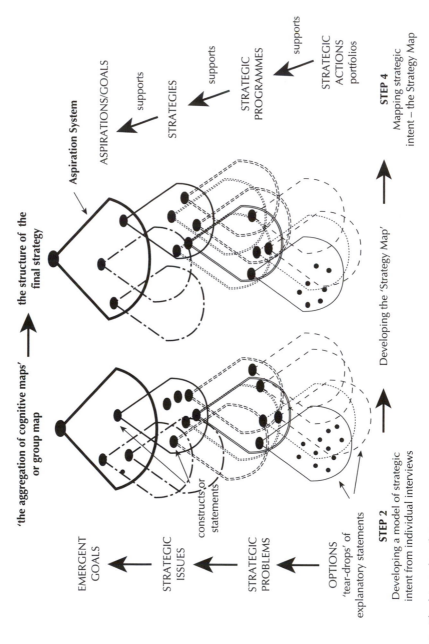

'the aggregation of cognitive maps'
or group map

the structure of the
final strategy

Aspiration System

ASPIRATIONS/GOALS

supports

STRATEGIES

supports

STRATEGIC
PROGRAMMES

supports

STRATEGIC
ACTIONS
portfolios

STEP 4

Mapping strategic
intent – the Strategy Map

Developing the 'Strategy Map'

EMERGENT
GOALS

STRATEGIC
ISSUES

constructs or
statements

STRATEGIC
PROBLEMS

OPTIONS
'tear-drops' of
explanatory statements

STEP 2

Developing a model of strategic
intent from individual interviews

Figure 7.4   The hierarchy of maps

Various forms of clustering are also carried out, slicing the model in different ways and enabling emergent patterns to be detected. For example, hierarchical sets – one of the clustering analyses available in the software – provides valuable assistance during both the 'backroom' work and the subsequent group working. The analysis presents the information as a 'tear-drop' of argument and explanation supporting the statement that acts as the label at its apex – usually a key strategic issue. By cycling around these analyses the modeller is able to gain insights into the structure of the model and develop some sense of confidence in the contents of the various categories. A similar process is undertaken following the generation of a group cause map using either the Oval Mapping Technique or computerized modelling processes, discussed below.

The model of strategy such as the one shown in Figure 7.4 and its associated categories/insights will be further refined by the management team as they work with the model/map. The composite map formed by aggregating individual cognitive maps becomes a 'transitional object' (de Geus, 1988) facilitating conversation. Participants confirm or change the judgments made by the modellers, adding new material and editing existing material. Thus, the group map will either contain the core belief statements that are supported/explained by other statements (options etc.) or provide the rationale for more superordinate goals. From this exploration an emergent aspirations system appears.

These infant candidate goals are the data used by the management team as the basis for the first steps in exploring strategic intent through an analysis of emergent competencies and their coherence in relation to aspirations (Eden and Ackermann, 2000). In some cases these aspirations may appear to be similar to the aspirations of other organizations in the particular industry/area. However, their structure (i.e. the linkages between them and the means of realizing them) is expected to be substantially different. For example, Govan Initiative, an organization in Glasgow (Scotland) dedicated to managing social and economic regeneration, surfaced many of the same goals as have similar organizations dealing with other parts of Glasgow. However, as they negotiated their own strategy, it was through the particular emphasis taken on specific goals/aspirations and their interaction as a network of goals that caused the organization to be differentiated from the others.

REACHING AGREEMENTS

Step 3: Agreeing on the Goal System: the Defining Strategic Intent

This early stage of the JOURNEY-making approach often focuses on enabling the group to begin to explore their emergent aspirations system and to identify the core beliefs that may represent distinctive competencies.

As noted above, the most hierarchically superordinate concepts will provide the first draft of the aspirations or goal system, as in principle the most hierarchically superordinate constructs are assumed to be goals. Following this, each level below is considered in turn – on the basis of whether the concept expresses a desired outcome that at least one member of the management team sees as good 'in its own right'. To be a goal, the concept will not be treated as an option by the individual but will rather be assumed to be a clear aspiration for the group and organization. In addition to surfacing and working with positive statements, these aspirations may be expressed as 'negative goals' – that is, 'We will not allow this outcome to occur. To keep it from happening is as important as attaining other positive goals.' For example, a publishing company seeing one of its key goals as growth in particular aspects of its business, and considering both an increase in product line and marketing effort, also noted that a negative goal could be staff experiencing burn-out. At this time the negative wording is retained.

Following the first identification of goals is an analysis of the group map. Encompassed within this group map are likely to be emergent competencies and distinctive competencies (Eden and Ackermann, 1998a, 2000). The group map evolves by asking the management team to identify distinctive competencies within the model (and add new competencies, if necessary) and subsequently to evaluate them carefully to establish whether they are indeed distinctive or not. Distinctiveness is always a relative 'measure', and so a critical issue, resolved with reference to *all* nodes in the goals/aspirations system, is to determine the 'anchor points' for relativeness. If an organization aspires to have the largest market share in Europe, then distinctiveness is likely to be referred to a European marketplace, whereas if the aspiration relates to France only, then distinctiveness will likely be easier. When considering what is a distinctive competence, questions focus upon (a) whether it is difficult to emulate, (b) whether it can easily be bought, (c) whether there is a high cost of entry, and so on. In addition to agreeing on whether a particular competency is distinctive in its own right, a distinctive competency may also be a particular *pattern of competencies* that are unique to the organization (either as a linked portfolio or as a feedback loop). Thus a loop of competencies may provide competitive advantage as the group believes that even if another organization could acquire the individual competencies, they would not be able to put them together in the same way.

Once a first draft of the process has been undertaken, the results are then viewed alongside the goal system and checks made to ensure that each goal is supported by at least one distinctive competency. Where this is not the case, the group then work on identifying new competencies that must be developed in order to meet the aspiration/goal, or spend effort reviewing the goal and possibly refocusing it. Where competencies are found that do not support the goal system, discussion ensues as to whether they should be dropped, as the energy and resources required to sustain them can be channelled to another area.

The important aspect of this process is recognizing that it is identifying the *systemicity* of competencies (i.e. their relationships with one another) and their relationship (support) with the goal system that provides added value. The mapping process, through its ability to represent the system graphically, can show how a Business Model, or Livelihood Scheme (for public and not-for-profit sector), can be realized. Core distinctive competencies will not emerge until the cycle of exploration for coherence between distinctive competencies and goals (the Business Model) has been undertaken. This cycle usually leads to the identification of strategies for the development of new competencies and diverts attention away from useless distinctive competencies. (For a more detailed description of the process, see Eden and Ackermann, 2000.)

Jointly understanding, reflecting upon and representing beliefs about distinctive competencies and goals/negative goals is the first part of the management team's journey. But which is to be explored first? Our experience suggests that the best starting point is wholly dependent on the particular nature of the organization and its management team. Some teams are issue-focused and can hardly become involved in consideration of strategy without discussion strategic issues/crises first. For many other management teams, starting the discussion by focusing upon developing the draft aspirations/goal system from surfacing issues can be lacking in focus and too abstract. Therefore, for them, the first mapping episode is usually more successful and rewarding if it focuses on an examination and exploration of distinctive competencies, and then use the implicit notion they have of distinctiveness as the basis for developing a draft goal system. Some organizations already have a draft strategy statement – goals and values – and so mapping this draft can act as a starting point for further mapping of issues and competencies.

Step 4: Mapping Strategic Intent: the Strategy Map

We suggested earlier that strategy can be represented as a hierarchical network of elements, or layers, which can become confirmed or redesigned through the journey taken by the organization (Figure 7.4). At the apex is the aspirations (goals) system, supported in turn by the strategies as a system of interconnected statements about future direction. These in turn are supported by strategic programmes as identifiable deliverables, which in turn require the support of portfolios of strategic actions. The important characteristic of the strategy map is that it represents strategy as a hierarchical *systemic network of interconnected statements of strategic intent*. This use of mapping to produce a network provides a range of benefits, including the following:

- It ensures that the final strategic direction is coherent.
- It breaks down the task of agreeing and monitoring the different action portfolios into manageable chunks.
- It assists those working to deliver strategic actions to appreciate how their contribution relates to the strategic programmes and so to strategies and onwards to the organization's goals. Understanding ends and means enables staff to become more engaged in the organization's strategic progress.
- It attains greater leverage through fully appreciating and exploiting the multiple outcomes from each area of effort.
- It provides a focus on the 'arrows' – demonstrating that actions are taken to achieve desired outcomes, rather than taken for their own sake.

The level of detail or elaboration of the strategy (i.e. how comprehensively it is articulated, how extensive the network) is dependent on the organization and its environment. Where there is considerable turbulence, then a clearly articulated set of goals, associated distinctive competencies and attendant strategies may well be sufficient to provide a substantive *framework* for strategic direction without stifling the need to be contingent, opportunistic and flexible – but within a strategic framework. For more stable environments, and in particular for the public sector, where the need for accountability is a significant concern of powerful stakeholders, the development of programmes and action portfolios becomes more important – particularly in light of each action's evaluation. This positioning on a contingency spectrum from *deliberate* emergent strategy to detailed strategic planning (Eden and Ackermann, 1998a) will influence the extensiveness of the network and is therefore a decision the management team must make.

As noted above, developing agreement about strategic intent requires the management team to (re)visit the goal/aspiration system, not only ensuring that all potential goals have been considered, but subsequently examining the goals in relation to the organization's distinctive competencies to develop the Business Model. Where goals are not supported and new competencies need to be grown, the key issues already surfaced (along with any new ones) can be evaluated and the best candidate chosen. These make up the strategies for the organization – each supporting the achievement of either distinctive competences or aspirations. As the team begin to refine the interconnected systems, new insights and a deeper level of understanding are achieved. The network is given extra *meaning* through the context of each statement, rather than relying on an overview with broad 'motherhood and apple pie' statements.

Attending to the connections among goals and between the goal system and the pattern of distinctive competencies often forces the team to confront ambiguities. This leads to developing clarity about what is actually meant by each goal (the context or 'tear-drop' of associated material supporting it). Considering it often forces the management team to take a deeper look at what they are aspiring towards. On a number of occasions this process has brought the management team to a temporary standstill. Their previously held belief that they were all wanting to pursue the same ends, and only wanted assistance as to how to achieve these ends, becomes unravelled and unanticipated differences become apparent.

Early stages of agreeing goals usually involve a draft of 'too many' goals – perhaps over 25 interlinked goals. At the beginning of the negotiating process some form of categorization can be helpful. For example, when Scottish Natural Heritage – a large not-for-profit organization – examined their goal system, the management team found it helpful to begin to weight goals allocating either one, two or three stars to each goal depending on its significance. Another category used was to separate short-term goals from longer-term ideals. Balancing the mix in this way can often provide valuable motivation assistance, as it is easier to demonstrate progress towards the short-term goals. A further useful form of categorization is one that distinguishes facilitative goals from core goals. Here the group seeks to identify those goals that distinctively determine the purpose of the organization and those that exist only to support these outcomes and yet are so important that they must be labelled as goals.

Step 5: Developing Action Programmes

Where it is appropriate to begin to develop action programmes, the strategy map is used to guide action. The aim is to ensure that each strategy is supported by a tear-drop of strategic programmes where any strategic programme may act in support of more than one strategy, and so be potentially more potent. Likewise, each of the strategic programmes represents a 'tear-drop' of options (potential actions), and some of the actions will be particularly potent because they impact the outcomes of several of these strategic programmes. The strategy map as a network therefore provides the basis for *analysis* of action plans through the exploration of the following:

- The *potency* of actions within the network of causality – that is, those actions that are expected to help in the fulfilment of many strategies or goals. This can be undertaken in relation to programme delivery, and thus ultimately in relation to aspirations. From this exploration it is possible to indicate rough priorities, as relative levels of leverage are calculated. This can act as a first stab at option evaluation – however, one that must then be tempered by good judgement.
- The degree to which a set of actions work together as a portfolio and can be used to cluster together *responsibilities for delivery*. For example, the management team may create interdisciplinary teams to involve staff from several divisions, departments or disciplines. This process might commence with having the teams examine the current options,

add or amend them and begin to work on ways forward, taking *ownership* of the outcomes through the process. An alternative approach is to keep responsibility together in one part of the organization. In some cases organizations have been *redesigned* to reflect the structure of the strategy map, so that, for example, particular teardrops become the responsibility of a single division or department.

* Alongside providing insights into the mode of delivery, the degree to which sets of actions work together may give clues as to possible *synergies* where the *combined* effect of the proposed actions yields an outcome greater than the sum of the actions.

Finally a map can suggest the structure of actions within a network. One method is to allow the resource demands of each strategy (as if the strategy levels in the strategy map were 'resource gates' [Eden and Cropper, 1992]) to be checked by tracking *down* the hierarchy. From this point, it is possible to explore all actions that support the strategy and their requirements.

Step 6: Using Maps to Test the Coherency of Strategy

Using mapping as the means of capturing and structuring group contributions to strategy not only supports the process of negotiating and agreeing strategic intent and developing action programmes, but also makes possible coherence checks. The first and most superordinate coherency check focuses upon examining the fit between the desired strategic intention (goal system) and the organization's current and future competencies – formulating the Business Model/Livelihood Scheme. Potential strategies, developed to achieve the goals, can be scrutinized in the light of resources and rationale, increasing their viability and ensuring their relevance. Strategic direction can be further developed by examining its relevance against a number of possible *alternative futures for the organization's environment* (Eden and Ackermann, 1998a: Chapters C8 and P4; Eden and Ackermann, 1999). Not only do future scenarios provide a valuable means of testing options and strategies (Schwartz, 1991; van der Heijden 1996; Wack 1985 a & b: 85), but the process of creating and discussing scenarios also gives rise to new options. These new options can subsequently be incorporated into the map.

Another form of analysis for increasing the coherency of strategic direction is to examine it against the responses of different stakeholders interested in and influential over its delivery. Testing how different stakeholders might respond to the various goals, strategies and actions facilitates responses to lock in those who are positively inclined and ensure their supportive nature, as well as manage those who are likely to cause difficulties (Eden and Ackermann, 1998a: Chapters C7 and P4). For example, within one organization, whose members were from a series of other organizations and mandated to promote economic and social regeneration, the group deliberately considered how the various associated organizations would respond to the strategy direction proposed and in the light of their findings revised certain aspects of the initial map to ensure support.

Each of these episodes of analyses – testing the Business Model/ Livelihood Scheme, exploring alternative futures, and stakeholder analysis – forces coherence within the strategy. As stakeholders are identified, particularly those with power as well as an interest/stake, their identification forces questions about the efficacy of strategies. 'Role thinking' their response to apparently effective strategies sometimes helps in thinking through the potential dynamic disruption stakeholders might do to the effective delivery of strategic outcomes. Futures are identified as important and yet their importance may be difficult to comprehend when seen in the light of the currently agreed system of aspirations.

The strategy map is the continuing reference point for all these considerations. As a network, any conflicting causality will be identified easily and quickly. The map also ensures that the strategy is made up of a coherent set of individual discrete actions in support of a system of goals that are supported as a portfolio by a self-sustaining critical mass or momentum of opinion in the organization. It provides the ability to examine the systemic network and check for its overall, holistic, logic.

DELIVERING STRATEGY: – THE MAP AS A MEANS OF GAINING AGREEMENT AND GIVING MEANING TO ACTION

Step 7: Getting 'Buy in' to Strategic Change

For senior managers and the top management team involved in strategy making, maps can make clear what actions need to be taken in relation to a strategic declaration. However, there may be resistance from the other levels in the organization. This may be as much to do with a lack of clarity about what is expected when, rather than being an outright disagreement with the strategy. Thus, what is an actionable statement for one person may remain ambiguous or meaningless for another. The confusion can be further exacerbated when senior managers, who believe they are acting consistently within a world of complex multiple goals, are perceived to be acting inconsistently by others who are more singularly focused in their tasks. Double messages seem to abound, particularly where a senior manager demands one thing from her subordinates, but appears to pay lip service to it herself by doing the opposite. Providing clarification by presenting extracts of the strategy network – thus reducing ambiguity and demonstrating the multiplicity of objectives – can often alleviate this difficulty to some extent. The network shows what is to be achieved, why and how – this *is* the meaning.

In contrast, one of the reasons why strategic change may be successful is because as strategic conversations unfold as the logic of the map develops and actions are put into place, new ways of doing things appear obvious and old ways are forgotten. Thus, the more successful the change process, through being persuaded by rhetoric *and* logic, the less easy it is to recognize it as change.

Facilitators face a similar situation when they successfully manage the decision-making process of a team of managers by genuinely changing their minds (rather than compromising them into agreement). A genuine change of mind is often largely imperceptible for the person who has changed his mind, and so the role of the facilitator in the process will be difficult to acknowledge. As a consequence the facilitator is not rewarded and so not used again! The facilitator who is acknowledged as successful is often forced to use performance measures that can be counterproductive to the reality of success, where hidden and subtle objectives may be paramount (and only sometimes known to the single client rather than to the management team as a whole). In the same way an organization and its managers may feel pressured to create success measures for strategy that can be, in many ways, counterproductive to successful embedded strategic change.

Step 8: Closure – Using the Map to Build a Strategy Delivery Support System (SDSS) and to Measure Progress

There are two important aspects of closure:– (a) the need (or not) for a routine symbol of strategy, such as the 'mission statement'; and (b) the need for action plans (and their potential for reducing flexibility). The mission statement – often a textual version of the goal system, albeit with a focus on touching the hearts and minds of those who read it – provides an external portrait against which the organization can be compared and judged by those outside of the organization. It is thus often a part of stakeholder management strategy.

Action plans (individual contributions) can be realized through assigning responsibilities and delivery dates (for start, progress or completion) to particular members of staff – often agreed during computer-supported workshops. As these actions are allocated and their time-scales settled, the map allows loads to be ascertained, ensuring that staff are able to undertake the tasks without endangering their current tasks (thus balancing change with continuity). The structure provides ways of analysing the implementation loads on individual staff, departments or divisions. Colour coding can illustrate the amount of progress achieved (e.g. red for no progress, blue for up to half-way, light blue for greater than half-way, and silver for completion).

The use of special computer software for mapping strategy becomes a Strategy Delivery Support System (SDSS). This is a system that can be routinely locked into strategy reviews with individual managers, teams or the senior management team (Ackermann et al., 1992, 1993). The system can also be used with great effect as a Decision Support System (DSS) in the annual performance reviews for staff, so explicitly locking reward systems into strategy delivery. Where progress is not being achieved, further examination is possible in order to detect whether a prior action is outstanding and thus incompletion is someone else's responsibility. Checks can also be made to ensure that the action being pursued (and the progress monitored) matches that being achieved at the level of strategies. Thus, once again, a coherency check is made possible.

Finally, the system acts as an organizational memory allowing regular reference checks to be made as well as informing new members of the organization of the strategic direction.

CONCLUSIONS[2]

Not only can mapping be a powerful means of capturing the knowledge, ideas, beliefs and wisdom of the organization's members embarking on the journey of strategy making, but it can also do so in a manner that structures the resultant material. Maps provide a means of *facilitating conversation and negotiation* in a way that seeks to amplify emotional *and* intellectual commitment. Moreover, as context is provided along with content, participants are able to reflect upon the material being explored, consider alternative perspectives and thus provide the basis for the strategy process to absorb social and political processes endemic in an organization. Through the underlying procedural rationality (the logic of the maps [Simon, 1976]) and procedural justice ([McFarlin and Sweeney, 1992; Thibaut and Walker, 1975] enabling a wider participant set to be involved), the resultant direction becomes something that those involved find themselves becoming committed to.

Maps provide a means of *differentiating one organization's purpose and strategic future from another* through their ability to reflect the management team's deliberate choice in relation to the structure – the linking together of different goals, strategies and actions. Many of the goals of an organization may be similar to those of others. For example, it is likely that for most, if not all, private sector companies, the goal 'increase profit and growth' is evident. None the less, the goals supporting this aspiration *and* their relationships are unique. It is the pattern that drives the distinctiveness of the strategy.

As noted above, mapping also helps with ensuring the coherency of the proposed strategic direction, enabling checks to be made of *the underlying* logic. These checks are made not only across the different elements of strategy (goals, competencies, strategies, etc.) but also with the organization's context – its external and internal environment. Since the map provides context, it is more likely to promote understanding of underlying purpose. Through the sense of involvement that the maps engender, they are more likely to promote 'buy in' to the subsequent results.

Finally, the mapping processes presented in this chapter can provide assistance to *implementation*. In the first instance, this is through ensuring that those responsible for actions are clear about what it is that they are mandated to undertake. The map provides the rationale for action, thus directing the effort more effectively. Second, the map – a form of model – provides the management team with the ability to ensure that the resources (in terms of people and time as well as more tangible assets) are available. Finally, through seeing the strategy as a systemic network, not only can individual items be assessed in terms of their progress, but triangulation can take place where progress on detailed actions is compared with progress on the higher-level concepts they were developed to support.

NOTES

1. The mapping process is substantially informed by Kelly's Personal Construct Theory (Kelly 1955).
2. The proposals summarized here are from *Making Strategy*, (Eden and Ackermann, 1998a), where theory, concepts, practice and sources are brought together in greater detail.

REFERENCES

Ackermann, F. (1992) 'Strategic direction through burning issues: Using SODA as a strategic decision support system', *OR Insight*, 5: 24–28.
Ackermann, F. and Eden, C. (1997) 'Contrasting GDSSs and GSSs in the context of strategic change: Implications for facilitation', *Journal of Decision Systems*, 6: 221–250.
Ackermann, F. and Eden, C. (2001) 'Contrasting single user and networked group. Using decision support systems for strategy making', *Group Decision and Negotiation*, 10: 47–66.
Ackermann, F., Cropper, S. and Eden, C. (1992) 'Moving between groups and individuals using a DSS', *Journal of Decision Sciences*, 1: 17–34.
Ackermann, F., Cropper, S. and Eden, C. (1993) 'The role of decision support in individual performance review', in P.W.G. Bots, H.G. Sol and R. Traunmuller (eds), *Decision Support in Public Administration*. Amsterdam: Elsevier Science Publishers BV. pp. 43–55.
Argyris, C. and Schon, D.A. (1974) *Theories in Practice*. San Francisco: Jossey-Bass.
Bartunek, J.M. and Moch, M.K. (1987) 'First-order, second-order, and third-order change and organization development interventions: A cognitive approach', *Journal of Applied Behaviourial Science*, 23: 483–500.
Bryson, J.M., Ackermann, F., Eden, C. and Finn, C. (1995) 'Using the "Oval Mapping Process" to identify strategic issues and formulate effective strategies', in J. Bryson (ed.), *Strategic Planning for Public and Nonprofit Organisations*. 2nd edn. San Francisco: Jossey-Bass.
de Geus, A. (1988) 'Planning as learning', *Harvard Business Review*, March/April: 70–74.
Dutton, J. and Ashford, S. (1993) 'Selling issues to top management', *Academy of Management Review*, 18: 397–428.

Eden, C. (1988) 'Cognitive mapping: A review', *European Journal of Operational Research*, 36: 1–13.

Eden, C. and Ackermann, F. (1998a) *Making Strategy: The Journey of Strategic Management*. London: Sage.

Eden, C. and Ackermann, F. (1998b) 'Analysing and comparing idiographic causal maps', in C. Eden and J.-C. Spender (eds), *Managerial and Organizational Cognition*. London: Sage. pp. 192–209.

Eden, C. and Ackermann, F. (1999) 'The role of GDSS in scenario development and strategy making', in the *6th International SPIRE/5th International Workshop on Groupware Proceedings*. Cancun Mexico, 22–4 September. IEEE Computer Society Los Alamitos, California. pp. 234–242.

Eden, C. and Ackermann, F. (2000) 'Mapping distinctive competencies: A systemic approach', *Journal of the Operational Research Society*, 51: 1–9.

Eden, C. and Cropper, S. (1992) 'Coherence and balance in strategies for the management of public services: Two confidence tests for strategy development, review and renewal', *Public Money and Management*, 12: 43–52.

Eden, C. and van der Heijden, K. (1995) 'Detecting emergent strategy', in H. Thomas, D. O'Neal and J. Kelly (eds), *Strategic Renaissance and Business Transformation*. New York: Wiley.

Eden, C., Jones, S. and Sims, D. (1979) *Thinking in Organisations*. London: Macmillan.

Eden, C., Ackermann, F. and Cropper, S. (1992) 'The analysis of cause maps', *Journal of Management Studies*, 29: 309–324.

Galer, G. (1990) 'A client's perspective', *International Journal of Strategic Management*, 23: 44–47.

Kelly, G.A. (1955) *The Psychology of Personal Constructs*. New York: Norton.

Lindblom, C.E. (1959) 'The science of muddling through', *Public Administration Review*, 19: 79–88.

McFarlin, D.B. and Sweeney, P.D. (1992) 'Distributive and procedural justice as predictors of satisfaction with personal and organizational outcomes', *Academy of Management Journal*, 35: 626–637.

Mintzberg, H. and Waters, J.A. (1985) 'Of strategies, deliberate and emergent', *Strategic Management Journal*, 6: 257–272.

Mintzberg, H., Raisinghani, H. and Théorêt, A. (1976) 'The structure of unstructured decision processes', *Administrative Science Quarterly*, 21: 246–275.

Schwartz, P. (1991) *The Art of the Long View*. New York: Doubleday.

Simon, H.A. (1976) 'From substantive to procedural rationality', in S.J. Latsis (ed.), *Method and Appraisal in Economics*. Cambridge: Cambridge University Press.

Spender, J.-C. (1989) *Industry Recipes: An Enquiry into the Nature and Sources of Managerial Judgment*. Oxford: Blackwell.

Thibaut, J. and Walker, J. (1975) *Procedural Justice: A Psychological Analysis*. Hillsdale, NJ: Erlbaum.

van der Heijden, K. (1996) *Scenarios: The Art of Strategic Conversation*. Chichester: Wiley.

Wack, P. (1985a) 'Scenarios, shooting the rapids', *Harvard Business Review*, November/December: 131–142.

Wack, P. (1985b) 'Scenarios, uncharted waters ahead', *Harvard Business Review*, September/October: 73–90.

8

THE INDIVIDUAL IN THE STRATEGY PROCESS

Insights from Behavioural Decision Research and Cognitive Mapping

Gerard P. Hodgkinson and **A. John Maule**

ABSTRACT

This chapter draws on the preliminary findings of a project entitled 'Navigating an uncertain world: Strategic cognition and risk.'[1] The primary objectives of this work are two-fold: (a) to develop a more comprehensive understanding of the cognitive processes underpinning strategic decision making; (b) to investigate, under relatively controlled conditions, the prescriptive validity of mapping techniques as a basis for helping executives and other organizational actors to overcome cognitive bias and inertia.

We report findings from two separate experimental studies, using business students in the laboratory and practising managers in an organizational field setting, that demonstrate the efficacy of causal mapping techniques for attenuating the well-documented framing bias. The framing bias occurs when trivial changes to the way in which a problem is presented crucially affect preferences for choice alternatives. A preliminary analysis of our participants' maps illustrates the potential of causal cognitive mapping for gaining key insights into mental representations underpinning this phenomenon. Our findings are interpreted in the context of a dual-process model of strategic decision making, which differentiates situations in which cognitive mapping is likely to be beneficial from those where it is likely to be dysfunctional.

A considerable volume of the burgeoning literature on strategic cognition that has emerged over the past two decades or so has drawn on concepts and theories from the field of behavioural decision making. It has become almost mandatory for cognitively oriented strategy researchers to begin their articles and books with the basic observation that, owing to funda-mental information-processing limitations, or 'bounded rationality' (Simon, 1955, 1956), a variety of heuristics, or 'rules of thumb', such as the 'availability', 'representativeness' and 'anchoring and adjustment' heuris-tics (Kahneman et al., 1982), are deployed by managers in an effort to simplify reality, thus rendering their worlds manageable. Typically, researchers who subscribe to this view go on to observe that an unfortu-nate, latent consequence of the deployment of these heuristics is that they can give rise to cognitive biases such as 'hindsight bias' (the tendency to over-estimate the predictability of past events), 'logical reconstruction' (the logical reconstruction of events that cannot accurately be recalled) and 'wishful thinking' (the tendency to over-estimate the probability of desirable outcomes), which in turn may result in inappropriate/sub-optimal decisions.

For a growing number of writers in the strategy field this stream of work has laid the central conceptual foundations for developing cognitivist accounts of strategic decision processes (Barnes, 1984; Das and Teng, 1999; Schwenk, 1984, 1989, 1995) and there has been a steady accumulation of evidence, within both laboratory and field settings, that suggests that many of the phenomena identified by behavioural decision researchers in other contexts are highly applicable in the context of strategic decision making (Bateman and Zeithaml, 1989a, 1989b; Lant et al., 1992). Others, however, have questioned the appropriateness of this body of knowledge as a basis for advancing understanding of managerial and organizational cognition (MOC) on the grounds that it is essentially *behavioural* in terms of the observational methods and techniques employed and requires clear, logical outcomes against which the observed behaviours of research par-ticipants can be compared in order to assess the nature and extent of bias in their reasoning. As Spender and Eden (1998: 2) observe:

> For us, managerial and organizational cognition must go well beyond what can be deduced from such observations because neither managers nor those who research their behaviours have the logical answers available as reference points. In practice managers make their decisions under conditions of infor-mation inadequacy and other forms of uncertainty.

Thus, an alternative approach to the cognitive analysis of strategic decision processes has arisen over recent years that explores the structure and con-tent of actors' mental representations of strategic problems in a relatively direct fashion. This stream of work, predicated on the assumption that actors construct a simplified representation of reality (or 'mental model') that they use in an effort to navigate an uncertain world, has led to con-siderable innovations among MOC researchers in the development and application of cognitive mapping procedures as varied as repertory grid techniques (Reger and Huff, 1993), card-sort methods (Daniels et al., 1995), multidimensional scaling and clustering techniques (Hodgkinson, 1997a; Hodgkinson et al., 1991, 1996), and the taxonomic interview procedures pioneered by Porac and his associates (Porac et al., 1989). The fruits of this approach are exemplified by the works contained within the present volume and other edited collections published over the past decade (Eden, 1992; Eden and Spender, 1998; Hodgkinson and Thomas, 1997; Huff, 1990; Meindl et al., 1996; Porac and Thomas, 1989).

While this second stream of research has enriched understanding of the nature and significance of MOC in the strategy process, a central contention of this chapter is that the wholesale rejection of the concepts, theories, methods and empirical findings of behavioural decision research at this stage in the development of the MOC field would be profoundly misguided and lead ultimately to its impoverishment. The purpose of this chapter is to argue that there is much to be gained by bringing together these hitherto largely disparate streams of theory and research. The MOC field is entering a period where the timely application of cognitive mapping techniques has the potential to enhance understanding of a variety of phenomena identified originally in the laboratory by behavioural decision researchers. Similarly, scholars whose substantive research focus has been concerned with developing the theory and practice of cognitive mapping potentially have much to gain at this juncture by the judicious application of concepts, methods and techniques from the field of behavioural decision making.

In order to demonstrate the potential mutual enrichment that can be accomplished by bringing these two streams of work closer together, the chapter draws on the preliminary findings of a series of studies that have been conducted by the authors in collaboration with several of their colleagues at the University of Leeds (Hodgkinson and Bown, 1999; Hodgkinson et al., 1998, 1999a, 1999b). Our primary objective in conducting this research is to move beyond the application of experimental methods and cognitive mapping procedures *per se*, in order to develop a more comprehensive understanding of the cognitive processes underlying strategic decision making. Our programme of research is focused on the individual decision maker as the primary unit of analysis, while recognizing fully that the act of strategizing takes place in the context of a socio-political arena (Johnson, 1987; Mintzberg, 1983; Pettigrew, 1973, 1985; Schwenk, 1989) and that strategies are the product of a negotiated order (Walsh and Fahay, 1986), the consequence of which is that the conflicting cognitions of differing stakeholders and stakeholder groups must somehow be reconciled (Forbes and Milliken, 1999; Hodgkinson and Johnson, 1994). Our reasoning is that in order better to understand the cognitive and behavioural dynamics of the strategy process at higher levels of analysis (primary work group/team, the organization as a whole, or inter-organizational network), it is first necessary to illuminate the mechanisms underpinning the judgements and beliefs of the individual strategist as he or she enters the various socio-political arenas in which he or she must operate. This is in much the same way that social cognition scholars have analysed the cognitive processes of individual actors as a necessary precursor to the development of better theory and research on group and social influence processes (see, e.g., Fiske and Taylor, 1991; Tesser, 1995).

DUAL INFORMATION-PROCESSING STRATEGIES IN STRATEGIC DECISION MAKING: TOWARDS
A COGNITIVE MODEL

Drawing on previous research within the fields of strategic management (Barnes, 1984; Hodgkinson, 1997a, 1997b; Reger and Palmer, 1996; Schwenk, 1984, 1985, 1986, 1989, 1995), social cognition (Chaiken, 1980, 1987; Petty, 1995; Petty and Cacioppo, 1986) and behavioural decision making (Kahneman et al., 1982), much of the early effort of the Leeds team has been spent developing a dual-process model of strategic decision making (Hodgkinson and Bown, 1999; Hodgkinson et al., 1998, 1999a). A detailed consideration of our emerging theoretical framework and its underlying rationale lies beyond the scope of the present chapter. Briefly, however, we contend that the way in which individual actors internally represent decision problems and evaluate alternative courses of action in the process of strategizing is accomplished by means of two different, mutually reinforcing information-processing strategies. Type I or heuristic processing, is said to occur when individuals engage in a relatively superficial analysis of stimuli. This is a largely automatic process that lies beyond conscious control. Type II or elaborative processing, by contrast, entails detailed analysis through conscious control.

Faced with complex decision choices under risk and uncertainty, the accumulated body of theory and empirical research evidence suggests overwhelmingly that strategic decision makers employ a range of heuristics in an attempt to reduce the burden of information processing that would otherwise ensue. Drawing on this body of evidence, it is hypothesized that under Type I processing, actors have only limited attentional resources at their disposal and are, therefore, more likely to deploy a variety of heuristics, such as the anchoring and adjustment, availability and representativeness heuristics, in an effort to reduce the burden of information processing upon them. Unfortunately, however, as noted earlier, the deployment of heuristic processing strategies can have a deleterious effect on decision making. To the extent that an individual is reliant on Type I processing strategies, therefore, there is a much greater likelihood that he or she will exhibit biased reasoning. It does not necessarily follow, however, that Type II processing strategies *per se* will result in better-quality decisions. Indeed, a key danger associated with Type II processing strategies is that actors may become overwhelmed by the sheer quantity of information at their disposal. It is precisely for this reason that Type I processing strategies have evolved.

Research Implications

Utilizing this basic distinction between Type I and Type II processing strategies, it is possible to raise a number of non-trivial, descriptive and prescriptive issues that need to be addressed by the cognitive mapping community. At the descriptive level, to what extent do the mental representations of individuals engaged in elaborative processing strategies differ from those adopting heuristic processing strategies? At the very least, if our distinction between Type I and Type II strategies is meaningful, it should be possible to detect differences in the structure and content of actors' cognitive maps elicited under differing experimental conditions designed to induce these alternative processing strategies.

At the prescriptive level, to what extent does the application of cognitive mapping procedures, deployed as an intervention technique, result in changes in processing strategy and, hence, lead to refinements in the judgements of strategic decision makers? In the context of intervention work, one possible outcome of the application of cognitive mapping procedures is that they may cause actors to switch from heuristic to elaborative processing strategies, which in turn may result in significant reductions in cognitive bias. To the extent that our reasoning in this respect is correct, by utilizing experimental procedures it should be possible to demonstrate, under controlled conditions, that the deployment of cognitive mapping techniques leads to significant reductions in a number of cognitive biases, such as those outlined above (see also Barnes, 1984; Bazerman, 1998; Das and Teng, 1999; Goodwin and Wright, 1998; Maule and Hodgkinson, in press; Schwenk, 1984, 1995).

EXPLOITING SYNERGIES BETWEEN COGNITIVE MAPPING AND THE EXPERIMENTAL METHOD:
THE CASE OF FRAMING

In an effort to address these broad research questions the Leeds team has embarked on a series of laboratory and field studies that have utilized the experimental method in conjunction with cognitive mapping techniques. To demonstrate the potential of our approach, preliminary findings from two related studies are reported. As will be seen, encouraging progress has been accomplished in respect of both research questions outlined above.

The studies in question were designed to gain further insights into a particular form of cognitive bias known as 'the framing bias' (Kahneman and Tversky, 1984; Tversky and Kahneman, 1981), a factor known to reduce the quality of decisions in a wide variety of situations (Bazerman, 1998; Goodwin and Wright, 1998) and that previous research has suggested is likely to be applicable in the context of strategic decision making (Bateman and Zeithaml, 1989a, 1989b). This bias arises when trivial changes to the way in which a decision problem is presented, emphasizing either the potential gains or potential losses, lead to reversals of preference, with decision makers being risk-averse when gains are highlighted and risk seeking when losses are highlighted (Kahneman and Tversky, 1979, 1984; Tversky and Kahneman, 1981), as illustrated by the following problem (taken from Bazerman, 1984: 333–334):

A large car manufacturer has recently been hit with a number of economic difficulties, and it appears as if three plants need to be closed and 6,000 employees laid off. The vice president of production has been exploring alternative ways to avoid this crisis. She has developed two plans:

Plan A: This plan will save one of the three plants and 2,000 jobs.
Plan B: This plan has a one-third probability of saving all three plants and all 6,000 jobs, but has a two-thirds probability of saving no plants and no jobs.
Which plan would you select?

Now reconsider this problem, replacing choices A and B, above, with the following choices:

Plan C: This plan will result in the loss of two of the three plants and 4,000 jobs.
Plan D: This plan has a two-thirds probability of resulting in the loss of all three plants and all 6,000 jobs, but has a one-third probability of losing no plants and no jobs.
Which plan would you select?

An analysis of each pair of decision choices reveals that they are objectively identical (Plan A is the same as Plan C, and Plan B is the same as Plan D). Nevertheless, when presented with the first pair of choices, an overwhelming majority of individuals express a preference for Plan A, whereas Plan D becomes the favourite when presented with the second set of choices. Thus, the way in which problems are presented can dramatically alter the way in which outcomes are evaluated.

Kahneman and Tversky (1984) have attempted to account for these systematic departures from rationality by means of 'prospect theory'. According to this theory, actors evaluate potential outcomes as gains and losses relative to a neutral reference point, situated mid-way along an

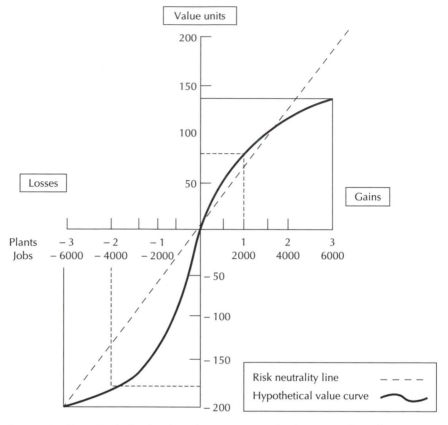

Figure 8.1   Hypothetical value function accounting for framing (adapted from Bazerman, 1998: 49 [© John Wiley & Sons Inc.], based on an original figure by Kahneman and Tversky, 1979 [© The Econometric Society]). Adapted by kind permission of both publishers.

S-shaped value function, as indicated in Figure 8.1. In this figure the units gained or lost relative to the neutral point are plotted along the *x*-axis, while the units of utility associated with these varying levels of gain or loss are plotted along the *y*-axis. The relationship between gains/losses and utility, described by the S-shaped value function, suggests that decision makers are risk-averse when choosing in gains, but risk seeking when choosing in losses. Hence when people build a mental representation of the problem in situations where the outcomes are described in terms of potential gains (number of plants and jobs saved: plans A and B), the potential disaster of losing everything becomes the neutral reference point and outcomes are evaluated along the upper portion of the value function. In consequence, the majority of decision makers express a preference for the safer outcome (a risk-averse strategy). In situations where the problem is framed in terms of job and plant losses (plans C and D), by contrast, the current position of having three plants open becomes the neutral reference point. Under this scenario, the two choices involving job and plant losses are evaluated along the lower portion of the value function in Figure 8.1, and as a result, a risk-seeking strategy becomes the preferred outcome.

Prospect theory not only enables us systematically to identify the ways in which the framing of problems causes decision-making behaviour to deviate from rationality; it also suggests that our response to loss is more extreme than our response to gain. The value function in Figure 8.1 indicates that, ordinarily, the pain of losing $x is generally greater than the pleasure of winning the same amount.

Potentially, prospect theory and the framing-bias phenomenon have a number of important implications for the field of strategic management, both at the level of descriptive theory building and from an interventionist perspective. For example, a key potential danger confronting strategists faced with complex decision choices under risk and uncertainty is that the way in which problems are presented, or framed, may bias their judgements, which in turn may give rise to sub-optimal decisions. Simply stated, the choices adopted by strategists may ultimately be determined by the way in which the options have been framed, or presented, rather than by their objective utility. In situations where riskier options are presented as a glass half full (positively framed), decision makers are likely to adopt a risk-averse strategy and opt for the safer alternative, whereas the same proposal presented as glass half empty (negatively framed) will increase the chances of a risk-seeking strategy being selected. Previous research in the field of strategic management lends credence to this hypothesis.

In a pair of laboratory experiments designed to explore 'the psychological context of strategic decision making', Bateman and Zeithaml (1989a) investigated the impact of decisional frame (positive versus negative future outlook), together with feedback on a past decision (success versus failure) and perceived organizational slack (high versus low) on a re-investment decision. In the first experiment, involving undergraduate students, all three variables were found to have main and interactive effects on the dependent variable (the amount in US dollars participants were prepared to reinvest). The second experiment, involving business executives, combined the decision feedback and organizational slack variables (i.e. failure feedback/low slack versus success feedback/high slack) and investigated the impact of this combined variable and decisional frame on the amount participants were prepared to reinvest. A significant main effect was obtained for decisional frame, together with a significant interaction effect between decisional frame and the combined feedback and organizational slack variable. Although in the predicted direction, the main effect for the combined feedback and organizational slack variable was found to be non-significant.

Taken together, these studies show that the way in which information concerning strategic decisions is presented, or framed, has an impact on individual choice preferences. Merely demonstrating that this phenomenon occurs in the context of laboratory studies involving strategic decision scenarios, however, does not enable us to answer two vital questions: (1) What is the precise cognitive mechanism underpinning this phenomenon? (2) What steps might be taken to minimize its effects? In the following sections we report two of our ongoing studies that address these concerns directly.

Using a variant of causal cognitive mapping (Axelrod, 1976) we have begun to explore actors' mental representations of relatively complex decision scenarios, elicited under controlled, experimental conditions designed to induce a framing bias. In so doing, our aim is to gain insights into the strengths and weaknesses of this particular mapping technique, both as a basis for better understanding why the framing bias occurs and as a means for limiting the potential damage accruing from this phenomenon. Causal mapping techniques are particularly attractive for both of these purposes because, as observed by Huff (1990: 16), they are action-oriented, requiring individuals not only to reflect on events occurring prior to the current situation, in an effort to derive plausible explanations, but also to anticipate future changes.

METHOD

Participants

The first study was an extended pilot study involving a total of $N = 88$ undergraduate students of business and management, nearing the end of their degree programmes. This study examined the feasibility of our methodological approach in general, and tested some of our key hypotheses, in a relatively controlled environment. The second study was a follow-up in the field, involving a sample of senior managers.

It is worth noting at this point that previous investigations into the effects of framing in strategic management (Bateman and Zeithaml, 1989a) have failed to reveal substantive differences in findings between studies using undergraduate students as participants and those using experienced practitioners completing MBA degrees. Nevertheless, in order to ensure that our findings are generalizable to practitioners, hence avoiding the charge of conducting research that is rigorous, but none the less irrelevant (Anderson et al., 2001; Hodgkinson and Herriot, in press; Huff, 2000; Tranfield and Starkey, 1998), our second study was designed to replicate and extend Study 1 in an organizational setting; a banking organization based in the UK. Fifty-two senior managers from a total of 204 initially contacted agreed to take part in this follow-up investigation, a response rate of approximately 25 per cent.

Case Materials

The stimulus materials employed in both studies were based on real-life decision episodes, and in both studies participants were required to draw cause maps in an effort to uncover their mental representations of the strategic decision scenario in question. Both sets of materials comprised a case vignette (*circa* 500–750 words) culminating in a decision involving two choice alternatives.

In both studies elaborate arguments were presented concerning the pros and cons of each alternative. The participants were required to make an investment decision. As per the Bazerman (1984) plant closure problem outlined earlier, two different versions of each problem were developed: a positively framed version, highlighting the potential gains; and a negatively framed version, highlighting potential losses.

The vignette employed in Study 1 described a strategic investment decision facing a manufacturer and distributor of fast paint-drying systems used in the repair of automotive vehicles. A ten-year history of the company, from its inception to the present day, culminating in the decision dilemma, was presented and participants were required to assume the role of a member of the Board and state which of two investment alternatives – 'continue in the domestic market' (the 'safe' alternative) or 'invest overseas' (the 'risky' alternative) – they would recommend. Thus, in the positively framed version, participants were presented with the following choices:

A *Developing a new marketing effort within the domestic market and not attempting to export overseas. Market research indicates that this option would certainly lead to profits of £1 million.*

B *Halting new developments within the domestic market but a commitment to the export market overseas. Market research indicates that this initiative would lead to profits of £3 million with probability one-third, and no profits with probability two-thirds.*

In the negatively framed version, by contrast, they were required to choose between:

C *Developing a new marketing effort within the domestic market and not attempting to export overseas. Market research indicates that this option would certainly lead to profits £2 million below target.*

D *Halting new developments within the domestic market but a commitment to the export market overseas. Market research indicates that this initiative would lead to profits at target level with probability one-third, and profits £3 million below target level with probability two-thirds.*

Apart from these particular variations, the stimulus materials presented to participants were identical in all respects. In this way we were able to impose experimental control on the decision task.

The materials employed in our first study were derived from a careful analysis of documentary sources, chiefly newspaper accounts. In order to further enhance the ecological validity of our work, the materials employed in the follow-up study were based around a 'live issue' and were developed and pilot-tested on the basis of a series of briefing meetings held with members of the senior management team, in conjunction with documentary sources both internal and external to the organization concerned. None of the managers who assisted with the development of the stimulus materials subsequently acted as participants in the main exercise.

The case materials employed in Study 2 were centred on a strategic issue currently facing many financial organizations, namely the extent to which they should continue investing in conventional delivery channels (chiefly high-street branch networks) and/or experiment with new forms of delivery (smart cards and telephone and Internet banking). While there is considerable agreement that present forms of banking have a limited future, there is still great uncertainty regarding which of the various technologies currently under review will ultimately come to dominate the industry. Since each of these technologies is highly capital-intensive, investment in the 'wrong' technology could prove disastrous for the organizations concerned. Building directly on this scenario, the case entailed a fictitious bank (with a similar customer profile to the participants' actual organization) contemplating an investment in two alternative technologies: a telephone banking system involving the use of machine-readable swipe cards; and a networked PC banking system. As in Study 1, elaborate arguments were presented concerning the pros and cons of each alternative and participants were required to make an investment decision. However, following the briefing meetings, it was apparent that a decision involving strictly dichotomous choices would lack realism for the participants. In order further to enhance the ecological validity of this study, therefore, we developed a decision task that required participants to allocate a fixed sum of money (£15 million) to each of the alternatives directly in proportion to their strength of preference. Thus participants in this second study had the option of allocating all the money to one or other of the two alternatives, should they wish to do so. Alternatively, they could split the money across both options, in any proportion, with the proviso that the total amount allocated summed to the full £15 million.

Cognitive Mapping Procedure

The cognitive mapping task entailed the participants completing a cause map, which was drawn by hand, based on a procedure developed by Green and his associates (Green and McManus, 1995; Green et al., 1998).

In both studies participants were presented with a comprehensive list of variables that the research team had identified on the basis of a conceptual analysis of the relevant case vignette. Using only those variables that they had considered as they thought about the decision problem, participants were required to construct a network diagram, with each variable represented as a node. With the proviso that their representations must incorporate both choice alternatives, participants were free to choose as many or few of the variables as they saw fit, but were advised that between three and ten variables are ordinarily incorporated in a typical map.

Within the system employed in these studies, causal relations are represented as linkages between nodes, drawn as lines with an arrowhead depicting the direction of causality and a number (ranging from +3 to –3) depicting the nature and strength of the relationship. Perceived positive causal relations are indicated by positive strength ratings (+3 representing the strongest possible positive effect) and perceived negative causal relations with negative strength ratings (–3 denoting the strongest possible negative effect).

Research Design

In both studies we employed a two (positive vs. negative problem frame) by two (pre- vs post-choice mapping) between-participants experimental design. In other words, participants completed one version only of the research tasks, allocated on a random basis.

FINDINGS

It is convenient to consider our findings under two separate headings: the analysis of choice behaviours and the analysis of the cognitive maps. Although data collection for both studies has been fully completed, analysis of the data pertaining to cognitive mapping is ongoing, so should be regarded as tentative at this time.

Analysis of Choice Behaviours

Thus far, our attention has largely been confined to the testing of two crucial hypotheses:

H1   There will be a significant difference in risk preferences under post-choice mapping conditions. Specifically, significantly greater numbers of participants allocated to the positively framed condition will express a preference for the safe-choice alternative (risk-averse behaviour) as opposed to the risky alternative (risk-seeking behaviour). Conversely, significantly greater numbers of participants allocated to the negatively framed condition will express a preference for the risky-choice alternative (risk-seeking behaviour) as opposed to the safe alternative (risk-averse behaviour).

H2 Under pre-choice mapping conditions there will be no significant differences in risk preferences.

Our first hypothesis is derived directly from previous work on framing (Bateman and Zeithaml, 1989a). Support for this hypothesis would show that the framing bias is not restricted to simple laboratory problems and is a potentially influential factor in more complex strategic situations.

H2 follows directly from our earlier discussion of Type I and Type II processing strategies in the context of interventionist work. If cognitive mapping techniques encourage actors to engage in elaborative thinking consistent with our notion of Type II processing, experimental manipulations designed to induce cognitive biases should no longer be effective when participants are required to engage in a cognitive mapping task prior to decision making. In the context of the present study, this means that the framing bias predicted under H1 should no longer be evident under pre-choice mapping conditions.

As reported in Hodgkinson et al. (1999b), the evidence accumulated from both studies strongly supports each of our hypotheses. As expected, Study 1 revealed a statistically significant association between choice behaviour and framing condition for those participants who were required to complete the cognitive mapping task after deciding which of the two choice alternatives they preferred ($\chi^2_{(df=1; n=44)} = 7.333, p = .007$). This finding provides strong evidence of bias attributable to the framing manipulation. In keeping with the predictions of prospect theory, the number of participants favouring the risk-seeking alternative was higher following exposure to the negatively framed version of the problem ($N = 20$, 45.5%) than the positively framed version of the problem ($N = 12$, 27.3%). Conversely, the number of participants favouring the risk-averse alternative was higher following exposure to the positively framed version of the problem ($N = 10$, 22.7%) than the negatively framed version of the problem ($N = 2$, 4.5%).

Turning to the results of the pre-choice mapping conditions, by contrast, we find no evidence of a framing bias; rather, equal proportions of participants express a preference for the risk-seeking and risk-averse alternatives ($N = 8$, 18.2% vs $N = 14$, 31.8%), irrespective of whether they have been exposed to the positively or negatively framed version of the problem ($\chi^2_{(df=1; n=44)} = 1.00, p = 1.00$).

The findings of our follow-up study in the field tell a similar story. The results indicated that in the post-choice mapping condition the average amount of money allocated to the safe alternative was higher following exposure to the positively framed version of the problem (mean = £6.07 million, mean rank = 16.50) in comparison to the negatively framed version of the problem (mean = £4.31 million, mean rank = 11.31). As expected, the results of a Mann–Whitney U test (corrected for ties) confirmed that this trend is significant ($z = -1.81, p = .035$, 1-tailed), once again providing evidence of a framing bias.

As in Study 1, the data gathered under the pre-choice mapping condition did not reveal any evidence of bias attributable to the framing manipulation. A Mann–Whitney U test (again corrected for ties) indicates that the average amount of money allocated to the safe alternative was no higher following exposure to the positively (mean = £5.67 million, mean rank = 12.40) or negatively (mean = £6.30 million, mean rank = 13.90) framed version of the problem ($z = -0.51, p = .30$, 1-tailed), thus providing corroborating evidence in the field for the findings obtained in our earlier laboratory study.

The fact that a significant association between choice behaviours and problem frame was observed in both the laboratory and the field study under the post-choice mapping conditions confirms that the framing bias is not just restricted to simple laboratory problems and is a potentially influential factor in more complex strategic decisions involving experienced, senior managers. However, no significant association between problem frame and choice behaviour was observed for those participants who completed the cognitive mapping task prior to decision making. This suggests that engaging in the cognitive mapping task prior to decision making attenuated the framing effects observed under the pre-mapping choice conditions. The results of these studies are consistent with a growing body of opinion that effortful thought can attenuate or eliminate the biasing influence of decision frames (e.g. Maule, 1995; Sieck and Yates, 1997; Smith and Levin, 1996; Takemura, 1994).

Analysis of the Cause Maps

To date, our analysis of the participants' cause maps has been limited to a preliminary inspection of their structure and content on a case-by-case basis; nevertheless, sufficient evidence has accumulated to illustrate the considerable potential of our approach to mapping as a basis for investigating the nature and significance of the mental representations underpinning actors' choice behaviours. For ease of presentation, the examples that follow are all taken from individuals whose maps were elicited under the post-choice mapping conditions of our laboratory investigation (i.e. in all cases the mapping exercise was completed once the individual concerned had made his or her decision choice), but are typical of those collected across all four conditions of both studies.

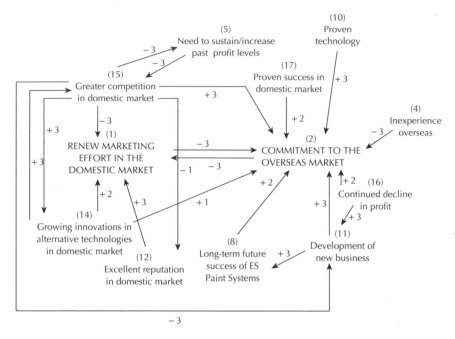

Figure 8.2 Example of a cognitive map elicited from a participant exposed to the negatively framed version of the problem in Study 1, whose decision choice ('commitment to the overseas market') is in accordance with the predictions of prospect theory

Figures 8.2 and 8.3 present the cause maps of two of the individuals who were exposed to the negatively framed version of the problem, while sample maps elicited from participants exposed to the positively framed version of the problem are presented in Figures 8.4 and 8.5. As might be expected, given the nature of the decision task employed in this study, the most striking feature of these maps is the distinctive pattern of activity centred on the choice nodes.

The map presented in Figure 8.2 was elicited from an individual whose decision choice was consistent with the predictions of prospect theory; that is, this individual chose the risky alternative ('commitment to the overseas market'), and this is reflected by a markedly greater number of in-degrees associated with the chosen alternative relative to the rejected alternative (nine vs four). Furthermore, the vast majority of in-degrees (seven out of nine) associated with the chosen alternative are positively valanced.

Figure 8.3, by contrast, presents the map of an individual whose choice behaviour is not consistent with the predictions of prospect theory. Notwithstanding the fact that this individual was similarly exposed to the negatively framed version of the problem, they chose the safer alternative ('renew marketing effort in the domestic market'). As can be seen, this

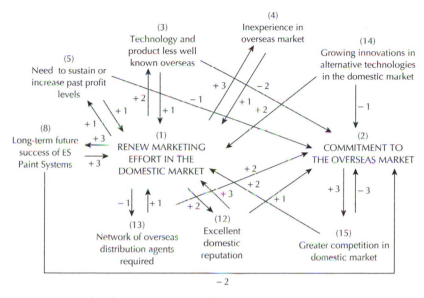

Figure 8.3   Example of a cognitive map elicited from a participant
exposed to the negatively framed version of the problem in Study 1,
whose decision choice ('renew marketing effort in the domestic market')
runs contrary to the predictions of prospect theory

map exhibits a very different structure to that presented in Figure 8.2,
with high levels of activity centred on both choice nodes. Although the
overall number of in-degrees associated with the chosen and rejected
alternatives is almost identical (eight vs seven), in the former case all eight
of the in-degrees are positively valanced, whereas in the latter case five of
the seven in-degrees are negatively valanced.

A similar pattern of findings can be discerned in the maps we have
elicited from participants exposed to the positively framed version of the
problem. The map presented in Figure 8.4, for example, was elicited from
another individual whose choice behaviour conforms to the basic predictions of prospect theory. As expected, this individual chose the risk-averse
alternative ('renew marketing effort in the domestic market') when presented with the positively framed version of the problem. As in the case
of the map presented in Figure 8.2, the bulk of activity in this individual's
map is centred on the chosen alternative relative to the rejected alternative
(four in-degrees and one out-degree vs two in-degrees and one out-degree),
the majority of the in-degrees associated with the chosen alternative being
positively valanced (three out of four) while both of the in-degrees associated with the rejected alternative are negatively valanced.

Turning to the map presented in Figure 8.5, we find a similar pattern to
the map presented in Figure 8.3. Contrary to the predictions of prospect
theory, this individual chose the risk-seeking alternative ('commitment to
the overseas market') when a risk-averse response ('renew marketing

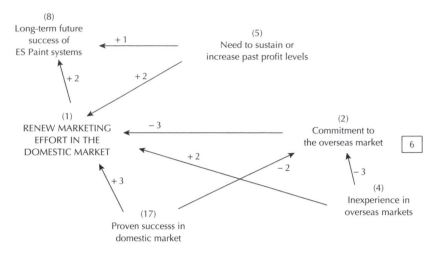

Figure 8.4   Example of a cognitive map elicited from a participant exposed to the positively framed version of the problem in Study 1, whose decision choice ('renew marketing effort in the domestic market') is in accordance with the predictions of prospect theory

effort in the domestic market') was expected to be the favoured outcome. As in the case of the map presented in Figure 8.3, the map of this individual exhibits a relatively balanced pattern of activity across the two choice nodes, with roughly equal numbers of in-degrees associated with the chosen and rejected alternatives (eight vs six). Similarly, in this instance we find that all eight of the in-degrees associated with the chosen alternative are positively valanced, whereas three of the six in-degrees associated with the rejected alternative are negatively valanced.

DISCUSSION

The cognitive perspective on strategic management is still in its infancy. As we have seen, two major streams of research have influenced its development thus far: the first has applied concepts from the heuristics and biases perspective of the experimental cognitive psychology and behavioural decision-making literatures, relying primarily on extrapolation from the laboratory in conjunction with the use of observational methods in the field; the second has utilized cognitive mapping techniques in an attempt to study actors' mental representations of strategic problems in a relatively direct fashion. We began this chapter with the assertion that there is much to be gained for the MOC field as a whole by bringing together these hitherto largely disparate streams of research. The programme of ongoing research reported in this chapter demonstrates the considerable benefits to be attained from such a synthesis.

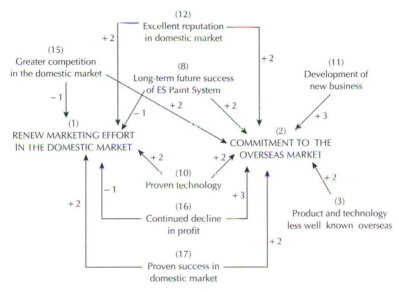

Figure 8.5 Example of a cognitive map elicited from a participant exposed to the positively framed version of the problem in Study 1, whose decision choice ('commitment to the overseas market') runs contrary to the predictions of prospect theory

Our studies confirm that the framing bias, previously identified in relatively simple decision problems given to relatively inexperienced individuals, is also likely to be a feature of the complex decisions taken by experienced individuals in the context of strategy making in business organizations. In addition, perhaps the most important finding of our work to date from an interventionist perspective is that causal cognitive mapping provides an effective means for de-biasing strategists' judgements arising from the effects of framing. Our results indicate that causal mapping is as effective for experienced as for inexperienced decision makers, thus providing strong support for the validity of this technique as a basis for improving the overall quality of decision making.

Work is still underway to identify the precise mechanism(s) by which this de-biasing occurs, and to this end we are in the process of developing several new indices for comparing the participants' cognitive maps in order to test these hypotheses formally, with an appropriate degree of statistical rigour. In the longer term, this should enable us to refine the tools and techniques of causal mapping as a basis for intervening in the strategy process.

FUTURE DIRECTIONS

Our studies have demonstrated the considerable benefits to be gained by utilizing concepts and methods from the field of behavioural decision making in conjunction with cognitive mapping techniques. Additional work is now required in order to explore further these synergies through the investigation of other cognitive biases. One area worthy of immediate investigation in this respect is the well-documented 'escalation of commitment' phenomenon.

'Escalation of commitment', the tendency to commit further resources to a failing course of action (Staw, 1981), has been closely linked not only to the framing bias, but also to a variety of other cognitive biases, including 'illusion of control' and 'over-confidence in judgement' (see, e.g., Huff and Schwenk, 1990; Schwenk, 1986). Extrapolating from our studies of the framing bias, causal cognitive mapping techniques may also prove useful as a means for enriching understanding of the 'escalation of commitment' phenomenon.

On the basis of our framing studies, it is tempting to assume that the greater enrichment of actors' mental models that results from the application of cognitive mapping techniques will invariably lead to better-quality decision making and the avoidance of systematic cognitive biases, and that, therefore, organizations should embrace decision-aiding techniques that systematically encourage effortful thought. However, this need not necessarily be the case. Less effortful thought associated with Type I (heuristic) processing may, on some occasions, be highly functional for navigating an information-rich yet highly uncertain world, enabling strategists to reduce greatly the information-processing burden that would otherwise ensue. In addition, in the context of escalation behaviour, Type II processing may serve merely to affirm an individual's extant worldview, rather than challenge it. The suggestion here is that mapping may simply act as a vehicle for elaborating existing ways of thinking, thus providing the basis for decision makers to lend increasing support to the failing course of action, rather than abandon their original decision. On the other hand, following the success of our studies of the framing bias, it may prove possible, through recourse to cognitive mapping, to overcome a range of biases that previous research has linked to the escalation phenomenon, thereby reducing the tendency to escalate. In an effort to clarify this pressing issue, the Leeds team is investigating these possibilities directly in a series of additional studies.

At the heart of this issue is the question as to when heuristic (Type I) and elaborative (Type II) processing strategies switch from being functional to being dysfunctional in terms of their respective roles in strategic decision making. While Type II processing may enable strategic decision makers to identify the pitfalls associated with one course of action over another, excessive amounts of Type II processing may result in 'paralysis by analysis'. Such an outcome is particularly likely under conditions of high decisional stress, in which the individual decision maker stands to suffer potentially serious losses, irrespective of which course of action is selected (Janis and Mann, 1977). Under other conditions, as noted above, elaborative processing may prove dysfunctional by affirming or bolstering a decision maker's inappropriate worldview, rather than challenging it.

Using the experimental method, in conjunction with cognitive mapping techniques, it should be possible to discover more about the underlying mechanisms of functional and dysfunctional Type I and Type II processing strategies and begin to understand their impact on the structure and content of decision makers' mental representations of strategic problems. In turn, these insights should help refine the use of cognitive mapping techniques as a tool for intervening in the strategy process by specifying the conditions under which such procedures are more or less appropriate.

CONCLUDING REMARKS

In 1982, Charles Schwenk published a paper entitled 'Why sacrifice rigor for relevance? A proposal for combining laboratory and field research in strategic management'. The purpose of this paper was readily encapsulated in its title: a plea for strategy scholars to ensure that their empirical studies meet the twin imperatives of scientific rigour *and* applied relevance in what is essentially a practitioner-oriented field. Twenty years later, the experimental method continues to be a much under-utilized mode of investigation within strategic management. Since the publication of Schwenk's (1982) paper, surprisingly few strategy researchers have sought to exploit the combined strengths of laboratory experimentation and field studies: rigorous control, accompanied by a fundamental concern to address directly the most pressing issues facing practitioners, with high levels of realism. In our ongoing work at Leeds we are explicitly attempting to achieve this balance, and the evidence presented in this chapter provides sufficient data for the reader to judge the extent to which we have been successful, thus far.

As noted at the outset of this chapter, there can be no doubt that the development and application of cognitive mapping techniques has enriched considerably the field of strategic management over recent years. The sheer range of topics addressed by the contributors to the present volume attests to the fact that the mapping community *en masse* is engaging with issues of fundamental concern to those responsible for the realities of making strategies happen in businesses and public sector organizations. However, in the absence of clear scientific evidence concerning the efficacy of these procedures, both as a basis for uncovering individuals' mental representations of strategic problems and as a means for intervening in processes of strategy making, there is a danger that our enthusiasm to develop theory, methods and research that are perceived as 'useful' by those engaged directly in the craft of strategizing may outstrip our capacity to deliver knowledge that is sufficiently robust to withstand the critical scrutiny of our less sympathetic colleagues, academics and practitioners alike.

At present, there is virtually no high-quality scientific evidence to support the use of cognitive mapping procedures as a basis for intervening in the strategy process. Such evidence as has been reported has been largely confined to descriptive accounts of apparent 'success stories'. In the absence of additional supporting data, gathered systematically under controlled conditions, these accounts provide little more than anecdotal evidence. Ultimately, if cognitive approaches are to win wider acceptance within the strategy field, and indeed the other organizational sciences, there is a pressing need for researchers to move beyond the uncritical application of mapping procedures in field settings *per se*. In order to demonstrate the real value-added contribution of mapping methods, it is necessary to employ these methods in conjunction with other approaches in such a way that it is possible to disentangle cause and effect. Only when we have submitted our methods to the rigours of this form of analysis will it be possible to discover the extent to which mapping techniques can truly provide useful, additional sources of insight into organizational strategy.

NOTE

1. The work reported in this chapter was funded by the UK Economic and Social Research Council (ESRC) under Phase II of its 'Risk and Human Behaviour Programme' (Grant number L211 25 2042). The contribution of Nicola Bown, Keith Glaister and Alan Pearman is gratefully acknowledged.

REFERENCES

Anderson, N., Herriot, P. and Hodgkinson, G.P. (2001) 'The practitioner-research divide in industrial, work and organizational (IWO) psychology: Where are we now and where do we go from here?' *Journal of Occupational and Organizational Psychology*, 74: 391–411.

Axelrod, R.M. (ed.) (1976) *The Structure of Decision: Cognitive Maps of Political Elites*. Princeton NJ: Princeton University Press.

Barnes, J.H. (1984) 'Cognitive biases and their impact on strategic planning', *Strategic Management Journal*, 5: 129–137.

Bateman, T.S. and Zeithaml, C.P. (1989a) 'The psychological context of strategic decisions: A model and convergent experimental findings', *Strategic Management Journal*, 10: 59–74.

Bateman, T.S. and Zeithaml, C.P. (1989b) 'The psychological context of strategic decisions: A test of relevance to practitioners', *Strategic Management Journal*, 10: 587–592.

Bazerman, M.H. (1984) 'The relevance of Kahneman and Tversky's concept of framing to organizational behavior', *Journal of Management*, 10: 333–343.

Bazerman, M.H. (1998) *Judgment in Managerial Decision Making*. 4th edn New York: Wiley.

Chaiken, S. (1980) 'Heuristic versus systematic information processing and the use of source versus message cues in persuasion', *Journal of Personality and Social Psychology*, 39: 752–756.

Chaiken, S. (1987) 'The heuristic model of persuasion', in M. Zanna, J. Olsen and C.P. Herman (eds), *Social Influence: The Ontario Symposium, Volume 5*. Hillsdale, NJ: Erlbaum. pp. 3–39.

Daniels, K., de Chernatony, L. and Johnson, G. (1995) 'Validating a method for mapping managers' mental models of competitive industry structures', *Human Relations*, 48 (9): 975–991.

Das, T.K. and Teng, B.-S. (1999) 'Cognitive biases and strategic decision processes', *Journal of Management Studies*, 36: 757–778.

Eden, C. (ed.) (1992) 'On the nature of cognitive maps', *Journal of Management Studies*, (special issue) 29: 261–265.

Eden, C. and Spender, J.-C. (eds) (1998) *Managerial and Organizational Cognition: Theory, Methods and Research*. London: Sage.

Fiske, S.T. and Taylor, S.E. (1991) *Social Cognition*. 2nd edn. New York: McGraw-Hill.

Forbes, D.P. and Milliken, F.J. (1999) 'Cognition and corporate governance: Understanding boards of directors as strategic decision-making groups', *Academy of Management Review*, 24: 489–505.

Goodwin, P. and Wright, G. (1997) *Decision Analysis for Management Judgment*. 2nd edn. Chichester: Wiley.

Green, D.W. and McManus, I.C. (1995) 'Cognitive structural models: The perception of risk and prevention in coronary heart disease', *British Journal of Psychology*, 86: 321–336.

Green, D.W., McManus, I.C. and Derrick, B.J. (1998) 'Cognitive structural models of unemployment and employment', *British Journal of Social Psychology*, 37: 415–438.

Hodgkinson, G.P. (1997a) 'Cognitive inertia in a turbulent market: The case of UK residential estate agents', *Journal of Management Studies*, 34: 921–945.

Hodgkinson, G.P. (1997b) 'The cognitive analysis of competitive structures: A review and critique', *Human Relations*, 50: 625–654.

Hodgkinson, G.P. and Bown, N.J. (1999) 'The individual in the strategy process: A cognitive model', paper presented at the Annual Conference of the British Academy of Management, Manchester, UK, September.

Hodgkinson, G.P. and Herriot, P. (in press) 'The role of psychologists in enhancing organizational effectiveness', in I. Robertson, M. Callinan and D. Bartram (eds), *Organizational Effectiveness: The Role of Psychology*. Chichester: Wiley.

Hodgkinson, G.P. and Johnson, G. (1994) 'Exploring the mental models of competitive strategists: The case for a processual approach', *Journal of Management Studies*, 31: 525–551.

Hodgkinson, G.P. and Thomas, A.B. (eds) (1997) 'Thinking in organizations', *Journal of Management Studies*, (special issue) 34: 845–952.

Hodgkinson, G.P., Padmore, J. and Tomes, A.E. (1991) 'Mapping consumers' cognitive structures: A comparison of similarity trees with multidimensional scaling and cluster analysis', *European Journal of Marketing*, 25 (7): 41–60.

Hodgkinson, G.P., Tomes, A.E. and Padmore, J. (1996) 'Using consumers' perceptions for the cognitive analysis of corporate-level competitive structures', *Journal of Strategic Marketing*, 4: 1–22.

Hodgkinson, G.P., Bown, N.J., Maule, A.J., Glaister, K.W. and Pearman, A.D. (1998) 'Dual information processing in strategic decision-making? A theoretical framework and some empirical data', paper presented at the 18th Annual International Conference of the Strategic Management Society, Orlando, USA, November.

Hodgkinson, G.P., Bown, N.J., Maule, A.J., Glaister, K.W. and Pearman, A.D. (1999a) 'Navigating an uncertain world: Strategic cognition and risk', *ESRC Risk and Human Behaviour Newsletter, Issue 5*. Swindon: Economic and Social Research Council.

Hodgkinson, G.P., Bown, N.J., Maule, A.J., Glaister, K.W. and Pearman, A.D. (1999b) 'Breaking the frame: An analysis of strategic cognition and decision making under uncertainty', *Strategic Management Journal*, 20: 977–985.

Huff, A.S. (1990) 'Mapping strategic thought', in A.S. Huff (ed.), *Mapping Strategic Thought*. Chichester: Wiley. pp. 11–49.

Huff, A.S. (2000) 'Changes in organizational knowledge production', *Academy of Management Review*, 25: 288–293.

Huff, A.S. and Schwenk, C. (1990) 'Bias and sensemaking in good times and bad', in A.S. Huff (ed.), *Mapping Strategic Thought*. Chichester: Wiley. pp. 89–108.

Janis, I. and Mann, L. (1977) *Decision Making: A Psychological Analysis of Conflict, Choice and Commitment*. New York: Free Press.

Johnson, G. (1987) *Strategic Change and the Management Process*. Oxford: Blackwell.

Kahneman, D. and Tversky, A. (1979) 'Prospect theory: An analysis of decision under risk', *Econometrica*, 47: 263–291.

Kahneman, D. and Tversky, A. (1984) 'Choices, values and frames', *American Psychologist*, 39: 341–350.

Kahneman, D., Slovic, P. and Tversky, A. (eds) (1982) *Judgment Under Uncertainty: Heuristics and Biases*. Cambridge: Cambridge University Press.

Lant, T.K., Milliken, F.J. and Batra, B. (1992) 'The role of managerial learning and interpretation in strategic persistence and reorientation: An empirical exploration', *Strategic Management Journal*, 13: 585–608.

Maule, A.J. (1995) 'Framing elaborations and their effects on choice behavior: A comparison across problem isomorphs and subjects with different levels of expertise', in J.-P. Caverni, M. Bar-Hillel, F.H. Barron and H. Jungermann (eds), *Contributions to Decision Research 1*. Amsterdam: Elsevier. pp. 281–300.

Maule, A.J. and Hodgkinson, G.P. (in press). 'Heuristics, biases and strategic decision making', *The Psychologist*.

Meindl, J.R., Stubbart, C. and Porac, J.F. (eds) (1996) *Cognition within and between organizations*. Thousand Oaks, CA: Sage.

Mintzberg, H. (1983) *Power in and around organizations*. Englewood Cliffs, NJ: Prentice Hall.

Pettigrew, A.M. (1973) *The Politics of Organizational Decision Making*. London: Tavistock.

Pettigrew, A.M. (1985) *The Awakening Giant: Continuity and Change in Imperial Chemical Industries*. Oxford: Blackwell.

Petty, R.E. (1995) 'Attitude change', in A. Tesser (ed.), *Advanced Social Psychology*. Boston: McGraw-Hill. pp. 194–255.

Petty, R.E. and Cacioppo, J.T. (1986) 'The elaboration likelihood model of persuasion', in L. Berkowitz (ed.), *Advances in Experimental Social Psychology, Volume 19*. New York: Academic Press.

Porac, J.F. and Thomas, H. (eds) (1989) 'Managerial thinking in business environments', *Journal of Management Studies*, (special issue) 26: 323–438.

Porac, J.F., Thomas, H. and Baden-Fuller, C. (1989) 'Competitive groups as cognitive communities: The case of Scottish knitwear manufacturers', *Journal of Management Studies*, 26: 397–416.

Reger, R.K. and Huff, A.S. (1993) 'Strategic groups: A cognitive perspective', *Strategic Management Journal*, 14: 103–124.

Reger, R.K. and Palmer, T.B. (1996) 'Managerial categorization of competitors: Using old maps to navigate new environments', *Organization Science*, 7: 22–39.

Schwenk, C.R. (1982) 'Why sacrifice rigor for relevance? A proposal for combining laboratory and field research in strategic management', *Strategic Management Journal*, 3: 213–225.

Schwenk, C.R. (1984) 'Cognitive simplification processes in strategic decision making', *Strategic Management Journal*, 5: 111–128.

Schwenk, C.R. (1985) 'Management illusions and biases: Their impact on strategic decisions', *Long Range Planning*, 18 (5): 74–80.

Schwenk, C.R. (1986) 'Information, cognitive biases and commitment to a course of action', *Academy of Management Review*, 11: 298–310.

Schwenk, C.R. (1989) 'Linking cognitive, organizational and political factors in explaining strategic change', *Journal of Management Studies*, 26: 177–187.

Schwenk, C.R. (1995) 'Strategic decision making', *Journal of Management*, 21: 471–493.

Sieck, W. and Yates, J.F. (1997) 'Exposition effects on decision making: Choice and confidence in choice', *Organizational Behavior and Human Decision Processes*, 70: 207–219.

Simon, H.A. (1955) 'A behavioral model of rational choice', *Quarterly Journal of Economics*, 69: 99–118.

Simon, H.A. (1956) 'Rational choice and the structure of the environment', *Psychological Review*, 63: 129–138.

Smith, S.M. and Levin, I.P. (1996) 'Need for cognition and choice framing effects', *Journal of Behavioral Decision Making*, 9: 283–290.

Spender, J.-C. and Eden, C. (1998) 'Introduction', in C. Eden and J.-C. Spender (eds), *Managerial and Organizational Cognition: Theory, Methods and Research*. London: Sage. pp. 1–12.

Staw, B.M. (1981) 'The escalation of commitment to a course of action', *Academy of Management Review*, 6: 577–87.

Takemura, K. (1994) 'Influence of elaboration on the framing of decision', *Journal of Psychology*, 128: 33–39.

Tesser, A. (ed.) (1995) *Advanced Social Psychology*. Boston: McGraw-Hill.

Tranfield, D. and Starkey, K. (1998) 'The nature, social organization and promotion of management research: Towards policy', *British Journal of Management*, 9: 341–353.

Tversky, A. and Kahneman, D. (1981) 'The framing of decisions and the psychology of choice', *Science*, 211: 453–458.

Walsh, J.P. and Fahay, L. (1986) 'The role of negotiated belief structures in strategy making', *Journal of Management*, 12: 325–338.

9

FACILITATING GROUP COGNITIVE MAPPING OF CORE COMPETENCIES

Phyllis Johnson and **Gerry Johnson**

ABSTRACT

This chapter gives an account of the theoretical, methodological and practical issues that emerged during the completion of a corporate research project. We describe how expert facilitation overcame issues encountered during the research process and suggest guiding principles for facilitating the surfacing of knowledge across large multinational organizations. The chapter concludes by discussing the impact that inappropriate assumptions about the nature of cognition can have on the outcomes of both corporate interventions and empirical work.

DESCRIPTION OF THE RESEARCH PROJECT

A similar approach and group cognitive mapping method to that described by Ambrosini and Bowman (Chapter 1 in this volume) was employed during a programme of consultancy intervention with a UK-based major multinational organization. At the time of the consultancy, this organization was engaged in the process of rethinking its corporate strategy and the role of its corporate centre. This conglomerate had businesses in consumer, commercial and industrial sectors throughout the world.

In the past, the corporate centre had seen its parenting role as one of offering guiding strategic principles and direction but with limited direct involvement. The top team of the corporation wished to explore several things: (1) why the most successful of their businesses were successful; (2) where their core competencies[1] lay within their organization as a whole; (3) to what extent there were commonalties across business units in this respect; (4) how they could build on these competencies in terms of their acquisition/divestment strategy and restructuring; and (5) what the new role of the corporate centre should be in the light of the above analyses. The impetus for the project was a need to explain clearly their strategy to their major stakeholders; in particular, could they argue they were building on synergistic threads and common competencies throughout the organization?

The top team selected 21 of their high-performing businesses from different countries to take part in a series of group core competency mapping events to be held in several locations around the world. At each workshop a maximum of four, but usually three, business units were represented.

Before attending the workshop, the management team from each unit was asked to complete a piece of work that would help identify what customers believed them to be especially good at and which set them apart from their competitors. The teams brought these data with them to the workshop.

During the workshop, the teams were asked to take each of the most important elements of their success (as identified by their customers) and rate themselves and their top three competitors against each one.[2] The units had typically provided a list of five or six elements. When the teams had plotted their ratings on a wall chart, the elements in which they surpassed their competitors were extracted and given the title *primary success factors*. The primary success factors that commonly emerged at this stage were typically broad statements such as 'customer service' or 'technical support'.

The teams from each business unit were asked to take the three most distinct (i.e. the factors in which they perceived the greatest distance between themselves and their competitors) of their primary success factors and spend several hours using group mapping to explore where they came from, and how they were achieved, maintained and embedded within organizational life. Each team was asked to map at least two primary success factors (PSFs) over one and a half days. The mapping was based on a simple process of placing post-it notes on very large blank sheets of paper pinned to the wall of the team's workspace. The teams were asked to follow a 'flowering-out principle' where they would begin with their PSF and place a set of post-its around it that described how they were able to deliver it. Each of these post-its was itself surrounded by explanatory post-its, and so on. A sample map is shown in Figure 9.1.

It is important to note that when the project began, these teams were *not* continually facilitated. It was intended that they should be left alone with one of the authors circulating between the four teams to troubleshoot and problem solve.

Once this mapping was complete, the teams were asked to distil what appeared to be their core competencies (in some ways similar to tacit routines) from their rich and detailed maps. At the end of each session the maps produced by each team were retained, along with a record of the

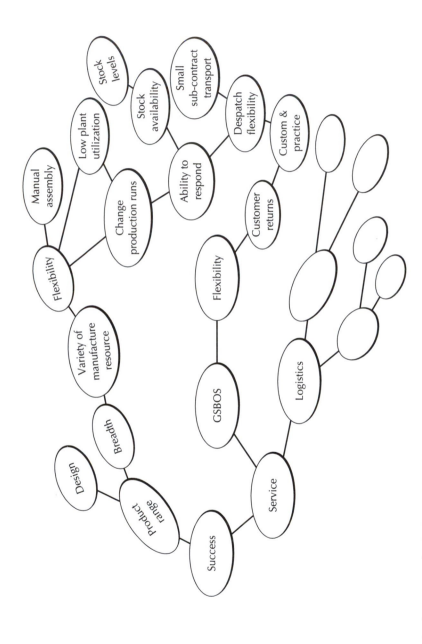

Figure 9.1 An extract of a core competence map

teams' own analysis. These were then used by the authors and senior executives at corporate centre to look for evidence of organization-wide core competencies.

ISSUES ENCOUNTERED

After the first mapping session, it became apparent that the protocol needed to be changed to ensure the company could get access to the sort of detail it required: that is, to identify patterns and routinized ways of behaving at the level of the 'everyday' that may combine and intermingle to produce a core organizational competence. It appeared that the mapping groups selected from each of the high-performing business units had difficulty carrying out the mapping task alone and needed close and expert facilitation. This became apparent when one of the authors, a facilitator also experienced in cognitive mapping, sat with one group to assist them when they encountered problems. At the end of the first day, the data provided by this group far surpassed that which the other two groups had been able to achieve working on their own, with only occasional support of the overall co-ordinator. On the second day, it was decided to give as full facilitatory support as was possible. The end result was that the output from this first session was sufficient to go forward for further analysis by the corporate centre. However, the protocol was changed for future sessions. In subsequent sessions all groups were closely facilitated throughout the two-day mapping event. Additional facilitators and cognitive mappers were proposed by corporate centre (drawn from human resources and consultative psychology departments) and trained for the purpose.

In the context of the ideas developed in this chapter, the fact the protocol was altered and corporate centre were happy with the results is not the main issue. What is important (and is the theme of this chapter) is that the groups that were not facilitated were not producing information that could be described as a *cognitive map* of the primary success factors they had decided to focus on, whereas the facilitated groups produced data that could be described as a cognitive map and therefore help to predict influences on behaviour in the organization. There were several reasons (which we explain here) to question the validity of the approach we were intending to take and, more broadly, to question the validity of *cognitive* data produced from non-facilitated groups.

The cause of the difficulties encountered by unfacilitated groups was found to be multi-factorial. These difficulties hindered the groups' ability to produce core competency maps that had real utility and more broadly highlighted problems with group-level cognitive mapping in general. These have been collapsed into and discussed under two headings: (1) mapping issues and (2) group dynamic issues.

Mapping Issues

The first, and perhaps most disabling, obstacle that the unfacilitated groups faced was their inability to move beyond a discussion of the obvious when trying to access and describe the nature of their complex and causally ambiguous core competencies. For instance, a primary success factor that emerged in many of the groups was *'customer service'*. When the groups were asked to explore this and follow the flowering-out protocol described earlier, they would not produce the kind of map shown in Figure 9.1. Instead they found themselves unable to move much beyond the level one branches shown in Figure 9.2.

When we consider the cognitive task we were presenting to our informants, it is not surprising that they are disabled in this way. They were being asked to access their own long-term memory and bring into their working memory (Baddeley and Hitch, 1974), any information that is retrieved or triggered via the parallel spread of activation (Anderson, 1983, 1990; McClelland and Rumelhart, 1986), across their neural network of nodes initially triggered by the stimulus 'why is your customer service outstanding?' There are several reasons why this cognitive task can, if left unfacilitated, produce only limited results. First, cognitive theorists suggest that information is processed in long-term memory using parallel distributed processing (see McClelland and Rumelhart, 1986, or Sternberg, 1999, for a review). During this process, a stimulus will excite and stimulate other associated nodes that contain linked information and in this way long-term memory is searched and information retrieved. This process is not serial, that is, one node stimulated after another in sequence. Rather, multiple nodes are excited and stimulated at the same time and in turn stimulate others. Hence the term 'parallel distributed processing', designed to evoke the image of a flowering out of activation from a central stimulus.

One of the major benefits of this form of information processing is its speed, with long-term memory being searched in milliseconds. Part of the ability to produce such speedy responses resides in the notion of familiarity or deeply ingrained paths. If stimuli usually spread activation to and from one another, then their propensity to continue to do so increases with each subsequent activation. For example, if the stimulus *knife* usually triggers the activation of *fork*, and vice versa, then when either is presented as a stimulus it will trigger the other – they are a familiar association.

Returning to our core competency mapping groups, we can be reasonably certain that when managers are presented with the stimulus question 'why is your customer service outstanding?', the response provided without facilitation will be that which is familiar to the group, that which has been triggered before and is more or less obvious to them. The clear difficulty that this presents in core competency mapping is that the concept of the core competency is not at all familiar to the informants. To explore what their core competencies might be requires them to move beyond the

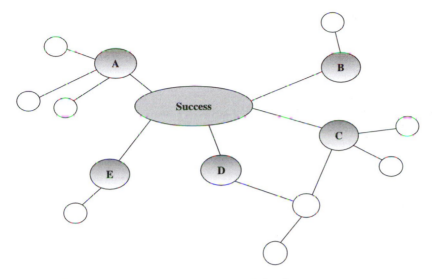

Figure 9.2   Example of a cognitive map with only level one

obvious (the taken for granted) and search their own structured knowledge of the way they do business in ways that access the unfamiliar and the unusual connections that they have perhaps never made before. It is asking the informants to do the impossible, to retrieve, verbalize and map something they do not even consciously know that they know themselves.

By facilitating group processes, informants can be helped in this process of discovery. The facilitator's role is to work as a catalytic part of the cognitive mechanism of the assembled memories available in the group. That is, the facilitators can help identify and raise to consciousness connections between concepts verbalized in the group. These verbalizations may have been made by two different people or have occurred at different times but are none the less connected and represent shared (socially constructed) cognition. The facilitator's role here is to help make the connections. Alternatively, the facilitator can focus on individuals and encourage them to say more, to explain in detail, to give examples of what they are trying to explain. In this way, other group members are offered more potential triggers for their own memory search. The facilitator's role here is in providing alternative stimuli. In this exercise, encouraging informants to tell stories was especially useful in provoking the response 'That makes me remember the time that ...', so that another series of possibly important pieces of information and connections could be produced.

Although clearly rooted in cognitive theories of information processing, this form of facilitation of the group's collective construction of their cognitive map (and in fact the whole skill of facilitation) is highly reminiscent of counselling psychology. Standard protocols and practices can be borrowed from this branch of psychology to provide a mechanism that enables the facilitators to act as the central processing unit of the group's collective cognition. That is, in order to be able to make lateral connections between verbalizations within the group and push individuals to say and discover more, facilitators actually take groups through a process of self-exploration and understanding. This same process of exploring your own ideas, values, attitudes, memories and beliefs in order to come to understand yourself better is mirrored in several schools of counselling practice (see Woolfe, 1996, for a review), but particularly in Egan's model of person-centred counselling. Egan (1994) suggests that the counsellor actively listens to the client's story and acts as a mirror reflecting back to the client what he or she seems to be saying (i.e. picking up on connections, repetitions, themes, etc., that may not be obvious to the client). In this way, and over a period of time, counsellors and therapists help individuals understand themselves and their psychological life a little better. We say more about *active listening* and general facilitation skills later in this chapter.

The second mapping issue we encountered is also linked to the task of helping each individual in a mapping group to move beyond the obvious and question his or her *taken-for-granted* ideas. Earlier, we described how this might be difficult for informants simply in terms of the cognitive logistics of the task. However, the mapping task we asked individuals to complete presented difficulties on another level. When people are asked to question what they take for granted to be true, uncertainty can be created. Where there is uncertainty, associated anxiety can often be found.

Hirschhorn (1988) discusses the relationship between uncertainty and anxiety in the workplace and describes the various ways in which individuals can seek to avoid, minimize and transfer such anxiety. In terms of our mapping groups, we found that one mechanism that workshop members employed to reduce uncertainty (and therefore anxiety) was to avoid questioning taken-for-granted assumptions and ways of doing things within the organization and to become defensive or dismissive when challenged. In some cases, we found that this *uncertainty avoidance* was led and positively re-enforced by the most senior member of the group. This in turn made it difficult for more junior members of the group to intervene and challenge what was being mapped and re-enforced anxiety about challenging in the group.

With status as an impartial outsider, a well-trained facilitator can identify and break such patterns of behaviour before they become established within a group. In addition (and this leads to our third point below), it can be helpful for the facilitator to undertake the physical task of mapping, so as to increase his or her ability to intervene when power games are taking place. In the scenario where a powerful member is taking editorial control of the mapping, the facilitator can repeatedly check with the rest of the group to make sure a map entry reflects the views of others. Overall, though, the simple awareness that challenging the taken for granted is likely to induce a degree of anxiety and reticence can enable a facilitator to recognize avoidance behaviour and work to overcome it.

The third mapping issue that we faced concerned, not the elicitation of the information to be contained in the map, but rather the construction of the map. It became apparent when observing the groups that group members were unable simultaneously to verbalize and map constructs. There was a need for a facilitator to take a faithful note of their group's verbalizations and, with the co-operation of the informants and at appropriately spaced intervals, map the constructs noted. The unfacilitated groups found that the maps that they produced showed little detail, not only because they had not explored such detail in discussion, but also because they found themselves unable to remember connections they had made in conversation when they later paused to map.

The final issue that we encountered with unfacilitated groups was concerned neither with elicitation of constructs nor map construction, but with semantics and interpretation. The groups who worked alone on the first day of our project produced maps that contained large amounts of abbreviation and company jargon that were incomprehensible to an outsider or indeed those at the corporate centre responsible for content analysing the maps. To compound this further, as our project was spread internationally, we also had to contend with cultural differences and the semantic difficulties that translation produced. Having a facilitator present helped the group to master these problems as all abbreviations, jargon and translation issues were dealt with at the time of mapping.

Group Dynamics Issues

In addition to specific mapping issues that the unfacilitated groups faced, we were also aware from the beginning of our project of the problems that can be presented by a reliance on individuals working well in groups. There were a number of issues that seemed to be endemic throughout the whole project. We believe they present themselves as problems in most forms of group-work, especially in group cognitive mapping.

In our project, we were asking teams from high-performing business units to explain what enabled them to out-perform competitors. The fact that the teams were all high performing and had been recognized as such by their selection to take part in the project led to problems. One consequence was that many of the teams we worked with were somewhat self-congratulatory. In itself this was not a problem. That is, as they were high-performing units, they understood *why* we needed to understand the basis of their success. However, on occasions, self-congratulatory tendencies led informants to conclude that the reason for their success was their own personal skills as individuals and as a management team. This may indeed have been a significant contributor and a key element of the core competencies. However, given that we know core competencies are by definition likely to be causally ambiguous and arising from multiple activities, it is unlikely to be the whole story. We found that one of the important roles of the facilitator was to push the teams beyond self-congratulation to examine other possible reasons and activities to which they could attribute their competitive advantage.

Some of the teams that attended the series of workshops also had amongst them at least one senior executive from the business unit nominated to attend. This was useful as it gave insight into each business unit's activities from a top team perspective. However, on occasions we witnessed the dynamic in the team as a whole suffering as a result of the presence of this senior member. Whether the senior executives courted it or not, more junior team members behaved in a deferent fashion towards them. In terms of the mapping exercise, this manifested itself in a reticence to challenge ideas and opinions offered by senior team members, in addition to a general wariness about disclosing some working practices that, although giving the business unit the edge over competitors, were either contrary to or a very liberal interpretation of company policy.

We found that storytelling about breaking rules was often the source of what we began to refer to as 'gold dust'. This was extremely rich data about how individuals within the company wanted and were empowered to 'go the extra mile' to win and keep customers. Again, the role of the facilitator was important. The facilitator needed to manage the dynamic to ensure that all views were heard and hierarchical deference did not take over the team. It was important continually to reiterate and check with senior team members that the team-working environment was a 'safe place' to disclose the 'gold dust' data.

As the project developed we began to find that, just as unfamiliar stories were frequently useful and to be encouraged by the facilitator, familiar stories had to be treated with some caution. The group mapping exercise was an ideal venue for 'axe grinding' and 'hobby horse' riding. Individuals, or the team as a whole, were aware that, via the research team, they had a direct line back to corporate head office. If the informants were left unfacilitated, old familiar issues could be woven into the maps and take on central importance. Again, by using a facilitator to question and challenge the group's output, it was more likely that maps were genuine representations of what the informants believed their core competencies to be.

The final issue in terms of group dynamics that we repeatedly encountered during the completion of the project was associated with the length of time that the teams spent mapping. The teams were asked to map a minimum of two primary success factors (PSFs), with most attempting to map three. This took at least a day and a half and was a tiring and at times frustrating experience for those involved. One of the most important roles that the facilitators took on was to maintain momentum, keep the teams focused and aware of their progress through the entire process.

We also found that for the facilitators themselves simultaneously managing the mapping task and managing group dynamics for hours at a time was tiring and stressful. To help them overcome 'facilitator burn-out', we made sure there was always a 'floating facilitator' available to work with groups for short periods helping the full-time facilitator pick up momentum and maintain overall direction. The entire facilitation team was trained together and met at the start and end of each day's mapping to exchange experiences and support. This helped the communication between the floating facilitator and the full-time facilitators flow more easily. We developed code-words to indicate to the floating facilitator such messages as 'Go away we're doing fine and you're disrupting the dynamic', 'Help out here, this guy's being difficult', 'We're getting stuck and I can't see how to help them; a different approach from you might help'.

There are a number of points to be made to conclude this section, which has focused purely on the issues that we faced in our own project using group-level core competency mapping. First, we are not suggesting that other unfacilitated group mapping techniques are fundamentally flawed, but rather that without facilitation, they can run the risk of failing to produce the data that they could be capable of producing. Second, we found there were two distinct categories that the majority of the issues we faced fell into: (1) mapping issues and (2) group dynamic issues. In our view, the first of these presents the greatest threat to the validity of the data obtained from the mapping technique if conducted without necessary facilitation. The third point is concerned with facilitation itself. Facilitation is a skill that requires training, development and practice. The limitations of untrained facilitation are heightened when combined with a requirement to manage a cognitive mapping exercise properly. In our view, such a task should not be undertaken lightly. Individuals who are especially well suited are those who have experience in cognitive mapping and are confident in dealing with groups and individuals facing difficult situations. We selected individuals with backgrounds in psychology and human resources, and although these worked well for us, they are not necessarily the only choices.

THE PRINCIPLES OF FACILITATION

There are several purposes of facilitation (see Redman, 1996; Westley and Waters, 1988), but in general they can be summarized as follows:

- to get the best information out of the informants;
- to help them through the entire process;
- to manage the group dynamics; and
- to help the informants make sense of the information that emerges.

The most important skills that we focused on in our own facilitation and training were: (1) active listening; (2) early diagnosis of problems in the group dynamic; and (3) intervention in restoring balance to the group dynamic. We also stressed as part of our training that it was vital to remember that the purpose of facilitation is not for the facilitator to offer his or her own view or in any way *direct* the group towards a particular line of argument, rationale or outcome.

Active listening is a skill developed by those working in many fields of organizational and one-to-one interventions. It involves the listener concentrating completely on what the individual speaking is saying, how he or she says it and what he or she is not saying. Active listening is not about a dialogue or a conversation, where part of the task of listening is to construct your own response internally. Rather, it is about total listening, so if asked, the listener could repeat or reflect back (word for word or paraphrased) what the speaker has said and meant to communicate. It is important to remember that active listening is a skill and not a naturally occurring attribute; therefore it requires practice.

Some of the common syndromes that are encountered in group facilitation are described by Westley and Waters, (1988) as 'multi-headed beast', 'feuding factions', 'dominant member' and 'sleeping meeting'. Each of these is briefly described below, along with suggested interventions. As will be apparent from the descriptions, interventions can either be direct (verbalize the problem to resolve it) or indirect (facilitator manages the dynamics without the need to verbalize the problem). Often, the use of direct or indirect intervention is a matter of which method appears appropriate to a group's own style and the facilitator's natural inclination (i.e. confrontational or not).

The 'multi-headed beast' syndrome involves group members talking past one another. Here, no one is listening to anyone else. It appears that group members are working to their own agendas. An intervention that can work well in this situation is to give the group the shared agenda that is missing: that is, to reiterate the task, where the group is and where it needs to get to. In addition, it is important with groups displaying this syndrome to ensure they are not being premature in their discussion of answers, as it is often this rush to answers that causes the lack of built consensus.

The 'feuding factions' syndrome is the manifestation of unproductive conflict between two sub-groups (or even two individuals). It is characterized by repeated cycles of arguments, perhaps with a different topic but a familiar theme. The feud might reflect 'old stuff' brought to the mapping session. It is important to recognize that the role of the facilitator is not to act as organizational analyst and solve endemic conflict. Rather it is to see through the successful completion of the mapping task. Consequently, interventions should be made with short-term goals in mind. One direct form of intervention is to encourage other group members to stop the feuding with their own intervention, for example: 'We've heard a lot about this from you Craig and Jeff, perhaps we could hear what Monica and Dave have to say.' Alternatively, the facilitator could get the group to take a coffee break and take both the feuding factions to one side and ask them to leave their differences aside for the sake of the task.

The 'dominant member' syndrome is self-explanatory. It can be directly managed by raising the issue of his or her domination with the individual concerned. This can be done in the group or perhaps during a break. An indirect intervention would also be to strongly re-enforce contributions from other group members. This can be achieved by: making repeated eye contact with them; placing your body in-between the dominant member and the rest of the group; taking any control tools (i.e. the post-its and pens) away from the dominant member; and, finally, being verbally supportive when other members offer their view.

The 'sleeping meeting' syndrome is characterized by long silences, low energy and no new ideas circulating in the group. Fear of volatile issues, general hostility, a lack of understanding of the task, and fatigue can all cause this syndrome. Depending on the cause of the syndrome, the facilitator can: take a break; reiterate aims and objectives of the task; reiterate the rules of mapping (i.e. that it is a safe place), or isolate the hostility and agree to handle it elsewhere. If all fails and the group are still 'sleeping', it can be best to move on to another task rather than sacrifice the whole of the group's time to one blockage.

Overall the most important message about facilitation is that its purpose is not for the facilitator to offer his or her own view or in any way *direct* the group towards a particular line of argument, rationale or outcome. It is to help the group find their voice and tell their own story.

OVERALL PROBLEMS WITH COGNITIVE MAPPING

In the field of managerial and organizational cognition (MOC) research, methodology has always been a problem and a matter of compromise. This results from the subject matter itself: human thinking and its relationship to and explanation of human behaviour, which is captivating and wonderfully rich but persistently illusive. The search for managers' knowledge (either singly or in groups) can yield a powerful source of explanation to help us make sense of organizational reality. However, to state that the way someone *thinks* about something (assuming one has confidence in the evidence) is likely to affect how that person *behaves* in relation to that thing is a disarmingly simple link to make. Full appreciation and understanding of this link is a task that has engaged psychologists for over one hundred and fifty years.

This development in psychological understanding is largely the result of specialized and consistent effort. For instance, cognitive scientists focus on the activity of cognition, information processing, storage, retrieval and use. Although they do not deny it is an important endeavour, they themselves are not necessarily interested in behavioural outcomes. Likewise, discursive psychologists (e.g. Edwards and Potter, 1992; Harré and Stearns, 1995) do not deny the cognitive hardwiring of the human mind, but rather choose to envisage thinking as a social activity facilitated by discourse – what people choose to say and hear. Social cognition (see Augoustinos and Walker, 1995; Nye and Bower, 1996, for reviews), born out of the advances of others, is trying to bridge the gap between cognition and behaviour. Through such specialization and focus, the field of cognitive psychology as a whole is continuing to move forward. It is important to note that no matter what their focus, none of the researchers listed above would claim to have developed a foolproof method that maps cognition or to argue that from such a map they can consistently and accurately predict behaviour.

Management research has witnessed its own cognitive revolution (Walsh, 1995). The managerial and organizational cognition literature has chosen to explore the relationship between cognition and behaviour in the context of socially complex issues in a complex environment. Many varied tools and techniques have been used to access the cognitions. These mapping techniques have been designed to approximate the contents and or structure of managers' mental models in varying degrees of detail. No matter what the intended form of map, it is crucial to recognize that maps are not actual paper or electronic transformations of managers' thinking. In other words they are not models of cognition but *approximated displays of elements of managers thoughts at a specific point in time, noted in particular ways in particular environments* that determine their format and in many instances their content. The key to the quality of the end product of cognitive mapping lies in the recognition of this and of two other associated issues: (1) the quality of the theory of cognition the researcher employs to frame his or her predictions about what is occurring when an informant attends to and interprets a stimulus presented to him or her by a researcher; and (2) the elicitation technique the researcher uses to access an informant's interpretation of the initial stimulus and in effect retrieve information from long-term memory. Both issues have been raised and discussed extensively by Eden (1992).

Embedded within these issues are the assumptions that were introduced in the second section of this chapter, that is, (1) the assumptions that researchers make about cognition and, leading from this, (2) the assumptions they then make about cognitive mapping and (3) the nature of the end product their methodology achieves.

In a discussion of the state of the art in cognitive science, Sternberg (1999) highlights the potency of the connectionist school of cognitive theory. For connectionists such as Anderson (1983, 1985) and McClelland and Rumelhart (1986), knowledge is implicit in neural connections between constructs, and working memory exists in the presence of a stimulus that triggers a specific spread of activation amongst constructs. So in connectionist models of cognition, what is important is not how constructs are stored, but how they are activated. Therefore the context in which a memory is triggered is crucial.

However, within the field of MOC research, there has not been a consistent effort to ensure that mapping methods are able to cope with the issue of context dependency. For example, there has been research published in the past that adopts a context-independent method. In each of these studies (Bougon, 1983; Markóczy, 1995; Porac et al., 1989; Reger, 1988), the parameters of context are ignored as researchers make the assumption that their results will be valid independent of the context in which their data are gathered. The cognitive assumptions that would appear to underpin this work are questionable, as is the validity of attaching the label *cognition* or *cognitive* to the output of this work.

Alternatively, there are a range of context-dependent methods (Allard-Poesi, 1995; Daniels et al., 1995; Eden, 1992; Johnson et al., 1998; Tomicic and Hellgren, 1999) in which researchers do little to predefine the contents of the map, in effect offering the informant a metaphorical blank sheet to work with. By allowing informants to define their own constructs and therefore the context in which they verbalize their current thoughts and to do so in an unstructured format (i.e. imposing no pre-defined hierarchy on the constructs elicited), such methods take account of the context dependency of cognition.

In terms of the second criterion upon which mapping efforts can be judged (the source of data), there is also a range of current practice. From what we know of the context dependency of cognition, it would be difficult to support maps that have been crafted from documented archival data such as memos, company reports and minutes of meetings (Examples of this form of archival mapping are Barr et al., 1992; Fahey and Narayanan, 1989; Fiol, 1989.) Such maps may tell us a lot about what a company wants the outside world to think it is thinking, but little about what individual managers are actually thinking about issues that are likely to predict future actions of the company and the individuals within it. (Eden, 1992 and Golden, 1992, 1997 extensively criticize the use of retrospection in management studies.)

Arguably, better mapping practice (in terms of the source of data used to elicit maps) recognizes the transient nature of cognition by accessing thoughts directly from informants. Following this basic principle produces maps that can lay claim to a better approximation of thinking than can those extrapolated from documentation of various forms. (Techniques that gather data directly from informants are: Allard-Poesi, 1995; Bougon, 1983; Daniels et al., 1995; Eden, 1992; Jenkins, 1998; Johnson et al., 1998; Walsh et al., 1988.)

Direct elicitation methods also suffer from the effect of audience. In other words, they are likely to be influenced by the informant's need for social desirability: that is, to say what they think the mapper wants to hear. The issues of audience and social desirability, although endemic in much social science research, can, to some extent, be managed (Huber and Power, 1985). It is quite probable that their effects can never be fully removed. None the less, safeguards such as assurances of anonymity, confidentiality and non-judgemental empathy projected during interview should be employed to reduce their effects.

In summary, two common pitfalls in cognitive mapping are to employ a method that is context-independent, and to use secondary data allowing the informant little or no expressive adequacy. Overall, the comment that we would make is that mappers should try to ensure that the method they choose is genuinely fit for the purpose they intend to put it to. The notion of 'fit for purpose' in mapping ought to take into account: cognitive theory; the context in which the mapping is taking place; the source of data; the philosophy being adopted; and, finally, the execution of the mapping itself to ensure the informant receives facilitation in the telling of his or her story.

CONCLUSION

This chapter has considered both competence mapping and cognitive mapping in the light of an exercise conducted within a multinational firm. It has concluded that the richness and value of a competence map is, in no small way, a function of the extent to which the process takes into account the difficulties of servicing and exploring aspects of organizational life that are typically taken for granted. Moreover, that in so doing, there are likely obstacles related to the behaviour of the group of people undertaking the task. We have argued that it needs to be recognized that effective mapping of this sort is unlikely to happen without skilled facilitation, and we have provided guidance on what such facilitation might need to entail.

We have also argued that there are related concerns here with regard to cognitive mapping. Specifically, the context dependency of cognition requires methods that take account of such context.

If we bring together these two summary observations on the challenges of competence mapping and of cognitive mapping, we must conclude a third. If researchers or consultants choose to employ cognitive mapping techniques as a means of understanding the competencies of organizations, they need to recognize the fragility of what they are exploring and take pains to triangulate their findings. For example, in the study we have reported here, the mapping exercise took place using a similar form for 21 business units with a conscious search for both convergence and divergence of findings. Whilst replication of mapping of this order may not be required, assumptions of useful findings based on one or two mapping exercises may be misguided.

NOTES

1. A core competency is defined as an activity, a messy accumulation of learning comprising both tacit and explicit knowledge (Hamel and Prahalad, 1990) that provides fundamental customer benefit yet is difficult to define.

2. The exercise corresponds to that described as the 'customer matrix' by Ambrosini and Bowman (2002).

REFERENCES

Allard-Poesi, F. (1995) 'Representations and influence processes in groups: Towards a socio-cognitive perspective of cognition in organizations', paper presented at the 3rd International Workshop on Managerial and Organizational Cognition, Glasgow, 14–16 June.

Ambrosini, V. and Bowman, C. (2002) 'Mapping successful organisational routines', in A.S. Huff and M. Jenkins (eds), *Mapping Strategy in Knowledge*. London: Sage.

Anderson, J.R. (1983) *The Architecture of Cognition*. Boston: Harvard University Press.

Anderson J.R. (1985) *Cognitive Psychology and its Implications*. 2nd edn. Melon University.

Anderson, J.R. (1990) *The Adaptive Character of Thought*. Hillsdale, NJ: Lawrence Erlbaum Associates.

Augoustinos, M. and Walker, I. (1995) *Social Cognition: An Integrated Introduction*. London: Sage.

Baddeley, A.D. and Hitch, G.J. (1974) 'Working memory', in G.H. Bower (ed.), *Advances in Learning Motivation, Vol. 8*. New York: Academic Press. pp. 117–90.

Barr, P.S., Stimpert, L.J. and Huff, A.S. (1992) 'Cognitive changes, strategic action, and organizational renewal', *Strategic Management Journal*, 13: 15–36.

Bougon, M.G. (1983) 'Uncovering cognitive maps: The Self-Q technique', in G. Morgan (ed.), *Beyond Method: Strategies for Social Research*. Beverly Hills, CA: Sage. pp. 173–188.

Daniels, K., de chernatony, L. and Johnson, G. (1995) 'Validating a method for mapping managers' mental models of competitive industry structures', *Human Relations*, 48 (9): 975–991.

Eden, C. (1992) 'On the nature of cognitive maps', *Journal of Management Studies*, 29 (3): 261–265.

Edwards, D. and Potter, J. (1992) *Discursive Psychology*. London: Sage.

Egan, G.E. (1994) *The Skilled Helper*. 5th edn. Monterey, CA: Brooks/Cole.

Fahey, L. and Narayanan, V.K. (1989) 'Linking changes in revealed causal maps and environmental change: An empirical study', *Journal of Management Studies*, 26: 361–378.

Fiol, M. (1989) 'A semiotic analysis of corporate language: Organizational boundaries and joint venturing', *Administrative Science Quarterly*, 34: 277–303.

Golden B. (1992) 'The past is the past – or is it ? The use of retrospective accounts as indicators of past strategy', *Academy of Management Journal*, 35 (4): 848–860.

Golden, B. (1997) 'Further remarks on retrospective accounts in organizational and strategic management research', *Academy of Management Journal*, 40 (5): 1243–1251.

Hamel, G. and Prahalad, C.K. (1990) 'The core competence of the corporation', *Harvard Business Review*, 72 (1): 77–86.

Harré, R. and Stearns, P. (1995) *Discursive Psychology in Practice*. London: Sage.

Hirschhorn, L. (1988) *The Workplace Within: Psychodynamics of Organizational Life*. Cambridge, MA: MIT Press.

Huber, G.P. and Power, D.J. (1985) 'Retrospective reports of strategic level managers: Guidelines for increasing their accuracy', *Strategic Management Journal*, 6: 171–180.

Jenkins, M. (1998) 'The theory and practice of comparing causal maps', in C. Eden and J.-C. Spender (eds), *Managerial and Organizational Cognition: Theory, Methods and Research*. London: Sage. pp. 231–249.

Johnson, P., Daniels, K. and Asch, R. (1998) 'Mental models of competition', in C. Eden and J.-C. Spender (eds), *Managerial and Organizational Cognition: Theory, Methods and Research*. London: Sage. pp. 130–146.

Markóczy, L. (1995) 'States and belief states', *International Journal of Human Resource Management*, 6: 249–270.

McClelland, J.L. and Rumelhart, D.E. (1986) *Parallel Distributed Processing: Explorations in the Micro-Structure of Cognition Vol. 2: Psychological and Biological Models*. Cambridge, MA: MIT Press.

Nye, J.L. and Bower, A.M. (1996) *What's Social About Social Cognition?* Thousand Oaks, CA: Sage.

Porac, J., Thomas, H. and Baden Fuller, C. (1989) 'Competitive groups as cognitive communities: The case of Scottish knitwear manufacturers', *Journal of Management Studies*, 26 (4): 397–416.

Redman, W. (1996) *Facilitation Skills for Team Development*. London: Kogan Page.

Reger, R.K. (1988) 'Competitive positioning in the Chicago banking market: Mapping the mind of the strategist', unpublished PhD thesis, University of Illinois at Urbana Champaign.

Sternberg, R.J. (1999) *Cognitive Psychology*. 2nd edn. Orlando, FL: Harcourt Brace and Co.

Tomicic, M. and Hellgren, B. (1999) 'A framework for analysing cognitive homogeneity and heterogeneity in management teams', paper presented at British Academy of Management Conference, Manchester.

Walsh, J. (1995) 'Managerial and organizational cognition: Notes from a trip down memory lane', *Organization Science*, 6 (3): 280–321.

Walsh, J.P., Henderson, C.M. and Deighton, J. (1988) 'Negotiated belief structures and decision performance: An empirical investigation', *Organizational Behaviour and Decision Processes*, 42: 194–216.

Westley, F. and Waters, J.A. (1988) 'Group facilitation skills for managers', *Management Education and Development*, 19 (2): 134–143.

Woolfe, R. (1996) 'The nature of counselling psychology', in R. Woolfe and W. Dryden (eds), *Handbook of Counselling Psychology*. London: Sage. pp. 3–20.

10

USING A KNOWLEDGE-BASED SYSTEM TO STUDY STRATEGIC OPTIONS

Dale W. Jasinski and **Anne Sigismund Huff**

ABSTRACT

Knowledge-based computer systems (KBSs) provide tools for storing, manipulating and analysing texts. These tools enable researchers to identify key concepts, define typical relations among concepts, and dynamically explore alternative definitions of these relationships. The distinctive advantages of such a system for qualitative research are two-fold. First, KBSs provide a way graphically to explore different aspects of the subjects' mental models in search of patterns or distinctive content. Second, the KBS allows researchers to develop their own mental models and document for others how these structures relate to the data. This chapter illustrates the use of such a system in a longitudinal study of strategic decision making from an options perspective.

One cannot ordinarily follow how a researcher got from 3600 pages of field notes to the final conclusions, sprinkled with vivid quotes though they may be.

(Miles and Huberman, 1994: 16)

Renewed interest in case studies and other qualitative research designs in the management sciences (Bartunek et al., 1993; Eisenhardt, 1989; Larsson, 1993; Van de Ven and Poole, 1990)[1] has elevated a number of methodological issues. First, these projects generate large data sets from field notes, interviews and documents taken directly from organizational archives (memos, presentation material, minutes of meetings, etc.). The ability to manage text data is extremely critical to the success of such research and computers are an obvious asset, but software is just now becoming commercially available and the capabilities of these packages are not widely known. Second, the aim of this kind of research is typically theory development. It is important that the researcher establish a theoretical perspective, but maintain the ability to recognize new issues suggested by the data that do not fit that theoretic framework (Miles and Huberman, 1994; Weitzman and Miles, 1995; Yin, 1993). It is not clear how computer tools interact with this double need. Finally, researchers are increasingly being asked to provide the consumer of their studies with a better understanding of how they came to their conclusions. Computer tools can increase confidence in systematic analysis, but the criteria that will convince a knowledgeable audience bear further discussion.

This chapter demonstrates that knowledge-based computer systems (KBSs)[2] are a critical tool for conducting case studies and other qualitative research by addressing each of these issues. KBSs provide organizational researchers with the ability to: (a) store large quantities of information verbatim; (b) manipulate the data in different ways to gain insights that manual techniques would find extremely cumbersome; (c) identify structures that appear to capture the mental models used by subjects, at a level of detail appropriate to the researcher's subject and ontological orientation; and (d) document the research constructs that result from this analysis.

In this chapter we illustrate these benefits by drawing on a 15-month study of strategic decision making in a high-technology firm. The purpose of the chapter is not to discuss strategic decision making in detail, but rather to provide the reader with an example of a substantive research design that uses a knowledge-based computer program to assist in the analysis of textual data. Accordingly, the remainder of this chapter is organized as follows. First, we give a brief background into mental models as a key feature of qualitative research. Next, an overview of KBSs is provided. The third section of the chapter introduces the research we conducted using one such system, ATLAS/ti™. The next section of the chapter outlines specific coding decisions, and illustrates the kind of analysis possible with this knowledge-based system. We conclude by discussing some methodological issues, including the key contributions knowledge-based systems can make to qualitative research.

MENTAL MODELS

Mental models are the mechanisms whereby humans are able to generate descriptions of system purpose (why a system exists), ... form (what a system looks like), ... functioning (how a system operates), ... observed system states (what a system is doing), and ... predictions of future system states.

(Rouse and Morris, 1986: 351)

The complicated 'how', 'what' or 'why' questions of organization participants and researchers require a framework. For example, the research reported in this chapter centres on the decisions made within a single high-technology firm that was trying to develop and choose among options for future product development. How do individual decision makers actually evaluate their options for the future? And what perceived organization and environmental factors influence the process of strategic option evaluation? Mental models must be developed by people within the company to answer such questions.

Mental models help construct a sequence of related events, processes or structures that connect concepts. To be understandable, each concept must have a relationship to some other concepts. The researcher interested in understanding what a concept means to an informant must thus seek out these connections. Meaning can be captured, at least in part, by developing a semantic network generated by an exhaustive search of all concepts connected to the subject in question (Carlson, 1993). For example, an organizational function like 'marketing' is a concept defined by the people who perform it, the organizations where those people work, the managers of those organizations, the activities that those persons and organizations are responsible for, and so forth, until all relations, and relations of relations, have been exhausted.

In the process of trying to understand such a framework, the researcher generates his or her own mental model. In theory development from a qualitative perspective the desire is typically to have a close correspondence between the informant's mental model and the researcher's mental model, but the researcher's model will also include concepts made salient by the research itself. In our view even the most inductive study cannot help but carry some marks of the researcher's past experience with academic study and with other organizations. Further, the researcher cannot be just a passive recording instrument; the experience of conducting the research will (and should) generate their own new connections. Further, the outputs of a research project typically will be more valuable if the researcher's mental models edit aspects of the models gathered from the field. The researcher should also be expected to highlight certain concepts and relationships as worth special attention from those outside the context of study.

As this brief discussion illustrates, the task of describing and documenting a mental model is likely to require much more than a couple of boxes with connecting arrows. Accordingly, researchers can benefit from tools that assist them in handling complex relationships. To minimize the problems of information processing and to provide an efficient means by which to document the models attributed to and derived from the data, this research chose to use a knowledge-based computer system.

KNOWLEDGE-BASED SYSTEMS

The use of a computerized knowledge-based system (KBS) provides the tools to create an 'audit trail' of the often implicit assumptions and decisions made during the course of a research project. Miles and Huberman argue that there are three steps in qualitative data analysis: data reduction, data display and conclusion drawing/verification. Data reduction is the 'process of selecting, focusing, simplifying, abstracting, and transforming the data' that is 'occurring as the researcher decides (*often without full awareness*) which conceptual framework, which cases, which research questions, and which data collection approaches to choose' (1994: 10, emphasis added).

KBSs require that these decisions are made more explicit than they otherwise might be. The particular brand of software we used, ATLAS/ti (Release 1.1E, Scientific Software Development, 1996), has a hypertext interface for creating and browsing networks of related concepts. Through the use of this KBS a researcher is able to identify concepts in the context of use, explore relationships among concepts, gather and assimilate knowledge (as represented by the text data collected) into a model, and browse the resulting knowledge base in search of patterns or unusual relationships. Though these activities are influenced by subjective researcher decisions, which we discuss in further detail at the end of the chapter, the KBS imposes the discipline of considering all data collected and maintaining the structure used throughout the project. Further, it efficiently displays this structure for consideration and critique by others so that they can follow the thought process that leads to a study's conclusion. The software also saves all data in a manner that allows re-analysis under alternative mental models.

Conceptually, hypertext is analogous to the creation of 3×5 notecards containing observations that are then stored simultaneously in numerous fileboxes for later retrieval. ATLAS/ti extends this filing property by allowing the researcher to establish any number of relationships among individual notecards and fileboxes. Moreover, the researcher can modify the number of relationships to any one card at any time. Thus, ATLAS/ti allows seamless revisions of relationships to account for new developments that arise during the research or new insights from analysis. All concepts affected by such a revision are then automatically updated. Searching the notecards or browsing through the model via graphical interfaces uncovers relationships and patterns among events and frameworks. The set of data and the disclosed hypertext structure clearly demonstrate the logical support for theory extensions and conclusions.

The advantage of such software over programs that merely enable text to be parsed, coded, and retrieved based on coding is that KBSs support the researcher in building theory. Weitzman and Miles point out that, 'computers don't think, and they can't understand the meaning of your qualitative data' (1995: 18). What KBSs *can* do is *assist* the researcher to: (a) build connections between various codes that enable the development of higher-order classifications and categories; (b) visually document the conceptual structure that fits the data (using specific user-specified relationships such as 'is a kind of', 'belongs to'); and (c) generate attending propositions concerning that structure, and, depending upon the design, even test those assertions (Weitzman and Miles, 1995). The KBS enables the researcher to ask questions like these:

- To what extent is a specific concept grounded in the use of other concepts?
- Thinking about a particular organizational outcome, what consequences might an actor anticipate by applying a specific strategy?
- What other roles does concept X play beside those identified in my current analysis?
- Show me all text passages that directly reference phenomena P or any other codes that play a role (via 'consequence', 'condition' or 'strategy' relations) with respect to P.
- What other codes have been used to describe these parts of the text?
- Which text passages provide evidence (or support, or contradict) the statement in text passage T?
- What are the dimensions of category C?[3]

These are exactly the kind of questions we explored in our research project.

STRATEGIC OPTIONS EXAMPLE

The substantive questions driving the research reported in this chapter grew out of our desire to further develop ideas from option theory as a means of dealing with uncertain futures affecting current firm decisions. Originally developed in finance literature, option theory was gaining currency among management researchers as a way of capturing volatile and uncertain decision contexts such as joint venture creation and research and development funding (Bowman and Hurry, 1993; Hurry, 1994; Kogut and Kulatilaka, 1994; Sanchez, 1993). The study (more fully reported in Jasinski, 1996) examined actions and decisions made by the entrepreneur/founder and 24 other experienced managers of a high-technology venture over the course of 15 months as they tried to identify the direction of future product development.

THEORETICAL FRAMEWORK AND RESEARCH DESIGN

Options theory posits that the firm's existing resources and capabilities can be positioned to capture future opportunities by either the expansion or the contraction of investments across environmental domains. In essence, the firm's resources comprise a bundle of possible options for future strategic choice (Bowman and Hurry, 1993). The interaction between a firm's existing investment, new investments in its capabilities and knowledge, and decision makers' perceptions of future environmental opportunities create the option. Creation only occurs when decisions made today provide the firm with preferential (in relation to its competitors) access to future opportunities. In these situations it is almost always necessary to make some (relatively small) investments in the present in order to delay the decision to make a more strategic investment in the future. This characteristic is a key link back to financial options theory. Another important connection involves the link between the value of an option and when it is 'called'. However, the date is specified for a financial option, and this is very often a difficult decision when working with strategic options.

The key point is that strategic decisions that have the character of *options* cannot be adequately analysed with most models of decision making and strategic planning. Option theory differs from definitions of scenario building (Schoemaker, 1995), for example, by focusing on the strategic advantage of delayed investment because the future cannot be adequately envisioned. In fact, standard tools of planning analysis (such as discounted cash flow) typically lead to different recommendations than option theory would provide.

At the time of the study the available literature on strategic options (Bowman and Hurry, 1993; Hurry, 1994; Kogut and Kulatilaka, 1994; Sanchez, 1993, etc.) was theoretic. The aim of the case study was to investigate options thinking empirically in an organizational setting. The organization chosen was not using options vocabulary, *per se*, but was following suggestions by Hamel and Prahalad (1994), as presented by an outside consultant. Hamel and Prahalad make very similar prescriptions to those put forth in the strategic options literature, emphasizing, for example, the importance of discovering 'white space' ideas – opportunities that reside between existing products – based on business definitions. We wondered whether this options orientation could be maintained, given distinctive differences from other planning ideas. If options thinking did persist, we wondered what organizational and environmental factors would influence the development of options over time.

Research Site

The research site, given the pseudonym DataCorp, is an entrepreneurial, privately held, high-technology firm, formed to design, assemble and sell computer data communication products. The firm resembles hundreds of entrepreneurial firms in the United States. It was founded in 1982 by a small group of scientists and engineers who recognized and responded to a market need for improved communication links among terminals, mainframes and mini-computers.

The early years of the company were marked by tremendous excitement generated by technical innovations and the risks and opportunities of launching the new company. The company obtained venture capital and outside board members to support further development, and introduced its first commercial data communications product line of mainframe peripheral controllers in 1984. In 1985 the firm generated its first profit and positive cash flow. Revenues grew to an all-time high in 1989, and employment peaked at nearly 350.

In late 1989, however, the company's original equipment manufacturer partner unexpectedly developed proprietary communication technology and dramatically reduced its orders from Data Corp for the following year. In response, the company redirected its distribution strategy, reduced its sales force, and began development of a new product line that would facilitate communication between networked computers and mainframe computers. These network products were still under development when the market for its mainframe communication products shrank in 1992. By the end of 1992, sales were almost half of their all-time high in 1989. The company reduced its workforce again and restructured into three groups, one of which was in charge of developing a new product that would operate on IBM's new high-speed fibre-optic access architecture. By the end of 1993, development was progressing with this product, but sales were not yet being made in any significant amount. Another lay-off was deemed necessary, this one even larger than the prior one in 1992.

It was at this point that DataCorp's top management team decided to engage in a strategic planning process markedly different from any used in the past. Up to now, the planning process had been restricted to the members of the top management team. The purpose of this new process was to provide DataCorp with an opportunity to gain input from more members of the organization. The logic behind this increased participation was that it would lead to more ideas and the development of a new technology platform that would enable DataCorp to break its dependence upon the mainframe computer. Consequently, the 7-member top management team was joined by 18 other members of the organization to form the 'Gang of 25' responsible for identifying promising 'product platforms'. There was a specific injunction against thinking about specific product ideas in favour of 'white space ideas' that very much had the character of strategic options. An initial group of five possibilities was reshaped to three, then two, with a final choice just as a buyout offer was accepted (to the surprise of many in the company). The company's demonstrated capacity to think in terms of new platforms appears to have been part of the appeal of the company to the buyer.

Using ATLAS/ti to Store and Display Qualitative Data

Although a variety of organization documents were collected and analysed following this interesting planning process, the following discussion focuses on a core set of interviews conducted at four critical points with each of the seven members of the top management team.

These 27 interviews account for 6,895 lines of text (128 pages). The way in which this data set was established and manipulated will be described in some detail before turning to the analysis of option thinking we accomplished.

data entry and sorting into 'text families'

In order to utilize the ATLAS/ti text analysis software, each interview tape was transcribed using a word-processing program. ATLAS/ti required that each document be saved in an ASCII format (with file extension .txt) with approximately 50 characters per line. This is done to facilitate the display of text in the software and eliminates the need for horizontal scrolling while reviewing the text.

To allow unambiguous reference within and among documents, each file was then reformatted with every line numbered (these files are given a .num file extension). Line numbering is used by the software to identify the chunks of coded text and can be used to move from one location in a file to another. Thus, once the coding procedure is begun, no changes should be made to the text files.

The various documents entered into ATLAS/ti are classified as primary texts. The software enables primary texts to be grouped into 'families', with the possibility that a single document can be a member of multiple families. This allows searching to be restricted to a specific subset of the data. For example, each transcript from an interview is a member of the 'interview transcript' family, while only those conducted during the first time period are members of the family 'time period 1'. It is thus possible to search for discussion of a particular topic (say the 'WAN' strategic option) during the early days of the study by using the primary text family 'time period 1' as a filter prior to beginning a search of the interviews.

All family divisions divide the text into major 'chunks' that the researcher might want to search independently. Thus, for example, the initial coding scheme also identified files in terms of which individual was being interviewed, since we knew we were interested in the development of individual mental models. The families established for the project are shown in Table 10.1.

data coding process

Once text has been transcribed and identified by text family, coding can begin. The first step in the coding process is to select a passage of text (a 'quotation' within the vernacular of ATLAS/ti) for coding. Sentences or paragraphs thus became the basic unit of coding. In no instance in the research was a quotation comprised of less than one sentence. The longest amount of text coded as a single quotation was three paragraphs (24 lines).

Coding quotations is a three-step process involving delimiting text passages, assigning one or more codes, and possibly annotating that passage

TABLE 10.1   Primary text families

Primary text family	Purpose
Time period 1	All interviews, field notes and company documentation pertaining to the first data collection time period: 1 August through 21 September 1994.
Time period 2	All interviews, field notes and company documentation pertaining to the second data collection time period: 22 September through 15 October 1994.
Time period 3	All interviews, field notes and company documentation pertaining to the third data collection time period: 16 October through 15 November 1994.
Time period 4	All interviews, field notes and company documentation pertaining to the fourth data collection time period: 16 November through 28 January 1995.
Transcripts	Only the interview transcript files.
Individual (one family for each of the repeated interviewees)	Each individual's set of interview transcripts.
Field notes	All word-processed field notes.
Company documents	All scanned company documents such as memos and presentation material.

with a memo. For example, since the core interviews in the data set included the same basic questions repeated in each of the four critical time periods, the question asked was used as an initial code.[4] Inspection of the data suggested that each of the questions asked during the interview tended to be associated with certain subjects. These became a secondary code. The questions, and the codes used to classify responses to the interview questions, are shown in Table 10.2.

The memo function, briefly illustrated in the following section of the chapter, is a very useful capability of ATLAS/ti. Memos make it possible to annotate text and codes, which encourages and facilitates capturing researcher insight throughout data entry and analysis. In the initial coding period these memos are a useful way to note tone, distractions or other aspects of the data collection process that are not clear from the transcript alone. When later considering alternative ways of combining and viewing the data, the memo feature of the software becomes a repository for theoretical insight. Memos also offer a helpful way to begin 'writing' analysis while the researcher is in the data collection phase of a project.

After identifying quotations within the interviews that related to specific questions, it was necessary to assign the secondary code(s) found at the right of Table 10.2. In ATLAS/ti coding can be done either by selecting from a menu of existing codes or by creating a new code. The codes shown in Table 10.2 are an initial set of codes established prior to beginning the coding process. These categories were quickly elaborated.

TABLE 10.2   Initial coding scheme: responses to interview questions

Question	Codes
What happens in your study group meetings?	Process: Methodology Personality Structure Study Group: Membership
What do you think your role is in the meeting?	Individual Founders
How do you think it's going?	Process: Evaluation
What factors are important when you are evaluating these scenarios?	Decision Criteria
What factors are important to the executive staff?	Decision Group: Agreement
Who is going to make the final decision?	Decision Maker
Right now, if you had to allocate 100 points among each of the scenarios, how many points would you give each? Why?	Point Allocation
How do you think the other members of the decision group would allocate their points?	Decision Group: Agreement
Evaluate the criteria on the Scenario Evaluation Form in terms of its relative importance to you in assessing the overall strength of the scenarios to be presented next week.	Decision Criteria
Are there any other criteria that you feel will be used in making the final decision regarding these scenarios?	Evaluation Sheet: Completeness
What do you feel are the top three strengths (opportunities) and weaknesses (problems) for each of the remaining scenarios?	Option Decision Criteria
For the scenarios that were not presented to the board of directors, what factors made them less attractive than the ones selected for presentation?	Decision Criteria
For each of the two remaining options, please describe the key events that will unfold over the next year for each of these scenarios. In other words, if you were to sketch out a timeline, say by quarters, what would be the milestones, and what contingencies or alternatives might exist at each of these points? In identifying the timeline, are there any key resources (people, alliances, financial, etc.) that need to be expended to pursue the option?	Milestones

coding elaborations

As all qualitative researchers are quick to point out, the coding process is highly iterative. Though many researchers now think that it makes sense to begin with some theoretic framework (Eisenhardt, 1989), rather than attempt to abandon all preconceptions in an attempt to ground codes totally in the data alone (Glasser and Strauss, 1967), these initial ideas almost always prove insufficient. Additional coding categories were added in this study and augmented with a very useful additional step to organize those categories.

coding families

At the very beginning of the coding process reported here, it became clear that additional codes were needed. First, the strategic options defined by the company (which changed over the course of the research, see Jasinski, 1996) were set up under the coding family 'option'. Coding families operate in a similar manner to primary text families in that they can be used as a means to sort or filter the data.

It was also necessary to treat individuals as a coding family. It was not necessary to assign each quotation to the individual who authored it, since this was already being tracked by the system. Rather, a new scheme was needed to capture references to other individuals. For example, during the interview with DP on 9/21, DP responded to a question concerning decision group membership by stating:

166   Initially I wasn't sure why BW was on

167   there except that JM really wanted BW to be

168   on there. We wanted LR to be on there because

169   in the strategic planning process she's the most

170   effective at implementing things that have to get

171   done. You've got JM and RE who are pretty

172   intuitive and they don't sit down and really

173   implement some of these things. They won't take

174   notes and send out minutes and do that kind of

175   stuff. So LR had to be a part of it. (11:20)

Each of the individuals referenced (BW, JM, LR and RE) was coded so that his or her role in the evaluation process could be tracked. These individuals were assigned either to the 'top management team' coding family or to the broader 25-member 'decision group' family, depending upon their position within the organization. (In addition to coding by person, the passage as a whole was coded 'decision group: membership' as it pertained to the rationale behind adding two members ([BW and LR] to the decision group.)

quotation identification

In the process of coding, each quotation from the text was also referenced parenthetically with a two-number code. The prefix indicates which primary text file the quotation is from while the suffix indicates the quotation number within that text file. Thus the above cited quotation reference is (11:20), indicating that it is from primary text file number 11 and the particular quotation is number 20 in that file. As data sets become more voluminous, and coding decisions more complicated, this 'audit trail' procedure becomes more and more important.

stabilizing the coding framework

As shown in Table 10.2, it was initially decided to use a two-part classification scheme. The prefix code would be the more general category (question, process, decision criteria, option) while the suffix would be the more specific category for that particular code. Thus, within the general code of 'process', specific factors such as personality, structure and methodology were established.

These initial codes were derived *prior* to the actual coding of the documents and were based upon a review of the strategy literature as well as from prior research at this site. For instance, the strategic planning process followed the prescripts of Hamel and Prahalad's *Competing for the Future* (1994), which stresses the importance of identifying the organization's core competencies, developing and implementing a strategic intent statement, and finding 'white space' of market opportunities. Accordingly, each of these three concepts was initially established as a sub-code within the code 'decision criteria'.

After establishing the initial codes, a sample comprising the first two interviews with RE was coded. This enabled the first author to gain familiarity with the software and gain insight into how to structure the system to best enable the software to assist in the data analysis. From this sample, it was decided to expand the coding system. Accordingly, the number of codes increased from an original 63 prior to the sample coding to 74 after coding the two interview transcripts. After the other two RE interviews were coded, the number of codes increased to 79 and a level of comfort was reached with the general structure. After five sets of interviews (total of 20 transcripts) were coded, the number of codes stabilized at 98.

The software continues to allow the development of additional coding categories, but each addition requires reconsidering all prior coding decisions. Thus, it is important to work with the coding scheme until it is fairly stable. One way to check the categorization system is to review all quotations currently given a particular code; this is particularly helpful in deciding whether or not a category needs to be subdivided, given the purposes of the research project.

Once codes are established, the number of quotations in a particular category is also of theoretic interest, but it needs to be pointed out that while programs typically provide this capability, care must be exercised in interpreting frequencies. The fact that a particular code has more or less 'hits' than another code does not in and of itself imply significance. Rather, the researcher must examine the underlying data structure (in this case the quotation and perhaps the interview) to determine the meaning of the frequency and prepare an explanation. In this research, for example, some respondents were much more verbal than others. The issues that were particularly salient to them are thus 'over-represented' in the frequency count.

TABLE 10.3   ATLAS/ti relations

Relation	Symbol	Attribute
A is associated with B	==	Symmetric
A is a part of B	[]	Transitive
A is a cause of B	>>	Transitive
A contradicts B	<>	Symmetric
A is a B	is-a	Transitive
A is a property of B	*}	Asymmetric

establishing data relationships

After the first 20 transcripts were coded with the 'stable' coding structure, data analysis was initiated using the network editor function within ATLAS/ti. The network editor enables the researcher graphically to depict relationships between the concepts discovered through textual analysis. It facilitates a major step in data analysis, and also requires additional coding decisions.

All elements of the ATLAS/ti database (codes, memos, quotations and primary text files) can be nodes within a particular network view. As further discussed in the last section of this chapter, the relationships between these nodes are both a product of the initial structuring of the data and the result of additional researcher input. For instance, the code 'option' and the designation of specific option alternatives is a fairly straightforward categorization from the text. Also rather straightforward is the subsequent relationship established between these codes, indicating that each of the individual options being evaluated by the firm has a predefined connection 'is-a' to the family code 'option'.

Other relationships are possible. Table 10.3 summarizes the types of relationships that are predefined within ATLAS/ti, where A represents the source node (code, memo, quotation or text) and B represents the target node of the relationship. The symbol indicates how the relationship will be shown when viewing the data within the graphical mode (network editor). The attributes indicate how the relationship chosen will impact searches and data displays. For example, the transitive nature of causality means that all data coded with a causal relationship will be treated in the following way: If A is a cause of B, and B is a cause of C, A will automatically be treated as a cause of C. And if a network view is created (a capability of ATLAS/ti described in the next section of this chapter) that requires examining A, relationships with both B and C will be shown as well.

With this capability to relate codes to other codes, a further nesting or hierarchy of codes is established that can then be used to examine relationships between specific elements (codes, quotations or memos) within the database. Remember, the relationships shown in Table 10.3 only specify the possible connections between data elements. Each specific occurrence of such a relationship is considered a link. In other words, while there is only one 'is-a' relation defined, there could be several links between data elements using the 'is-a' relation.

One immediately useful output from relationship coding is a more structured view of coding decisions. For the data set used as an example here, the initial application of relationships yielded the coding structure shown in Figure 10.1. Note that the higher-order codes begin on the far left of the figure (Decision Criteria, Decision Group, etc.) with their subordinate codes branching out to the right.

The parenthetical numeric reference after the code name refers to the number of quotations linked to that particular code (prefix) and the number of codes linked to that code (suffix). For example, at the time this graph was made, the code 'Decision Criteria' had no quotations but 35 codes linked to it. The code 'Decision Maker' had 19 quotations but no links to other codes.

network display of data structure

Once a relationship structure is established, analysis using the network editor can begin. To illustrate, after the first 20 transcripts were coded, a preliminary analysis of the role of competition in discussions about new product development was carried out. The code 'DC:Competition' was selected and a network view opened that asked for all quotations and their codes to be displayed. This initial view is shown in Figure 10.2.

Rich with information, this view enables the researcher to retrieve quotations in context by sizing the network view window and 'shift clicking' to display the quotation summarized by any given label. The researcher, then, is never far from the data, and can easily switch between a detailed examination of a specific piece of the data and a more holistic view of the entire database.

initial analysis and data simplification: the initiation of the researcher's mental models

Although 'rich', the direct graphic display of data rarely lends itself to direct explanation. Thus, after reviewing the relations shown in Figure 10.2, and re-examining the quotations associated with each node, a new network view was created that summarized the primary links in the data.

This in fact is a critical step in the process of analysis – which represents the move from models that are as close as possible to the mental models of respondents (given the objectives of the specific research project) to a more abstract picture that represent's the *researcher's* mental model. Such a refined view is shown in Figure 10.3, which offers a more comprehensible picture of the way competition seemed to be affecting DataCorp.

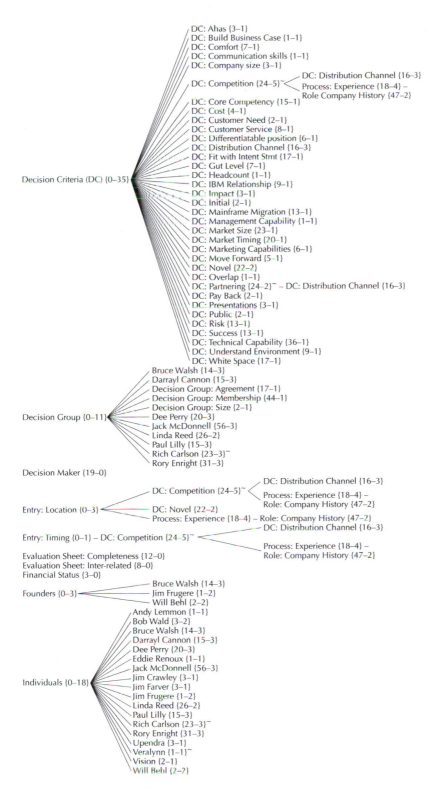

Figure 10.1 Hierarchical view of codes

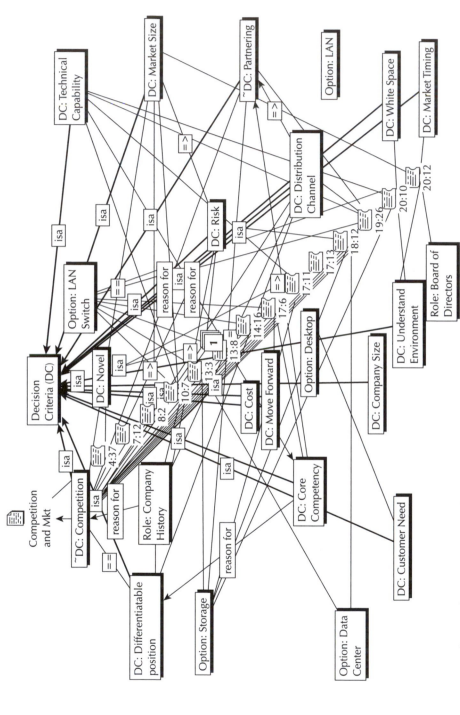

Figure 10.2 Initial network view of competition

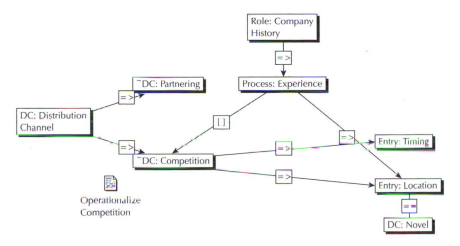

Figure 10.3 Initial analysis of the role of competition

The figure uses a new concept 'Process: Experience' (shown in the middle of the figure) as an organizing device. It also specifies details about entry into new markets that are not available in Figure 10.2. These details grew out of examining the various nodes in that figure.

The process of analysis was facilitated by the note-taking capacity of ATLAS/ti. As already mentioned, this ability to write while viewing the data is a very powerful feature of ATLAS/ti. The memo icon entitled 'Operationalize Competition' (shown at the left in Figure 10.3) allows the researcher to retrieve the details about how the various respondents described competitors (size, number, where competition would likely occur, etc.). The ability to record impressions about the data constantly while maintaining the integrity of the data themselves expedites analysis and explanation.

Options Reasoning

We now move to an abbreviated discussion of the substantive analysis being carried out with the data set just described, though it should be emphasized that other text files were also of great importance in the project itself.

One focus of theory-building endeavours involved an effort to use and possibly expand the conceptual structure of strategic option analysis. Although, as noted above, DataCorp did not directly use the language of options theory; interviews and other data satisfied us that this company was often, though not always, operating in an options framework. Tables of data (illustrated by Table 10.4) that were constructed using key concepts in the options framework facilitate this effort. *In toto*, these quotations make it possible to outline several new aspects of strategic as

TABLE 10.4   Examples of option-striking considerations

Person	Response	Code
BW	We can't hedge our bets too long, but its important for us to be ready to jump into it when we do make a decision. The passage of time will be one trigger. We need to be doing everything that is flexibly useful during that time, such as building alliances, watching for emerging markets, etc. We need to use the time to keep progressing. It could be as short as six to nine months.	External: Time
GF	We can do both for some period of time especially in an unofficial capacity. You never want to walk away from a new product idea too soon. Again, we need to come up with a compelling value-add for the one option. We can continue to look into both until we have to commit to one product or until it becomes forced upon us to do so.	External: Partner
	Its probably going to be an outside event. For example, with the 9XXX product, I can imagine DEC saying we need it yesterday and all of a sudden it will begin to snowball and gain momentum and a slew of decisions will be made. But we want to keep our options open as long as we can before we start making those decisions.	
WB	Well, I haven't made up my mind yet as to where the industry is going even after doing a lot of reading and research. Seems like we are playing a game of musical chairs with the scenarios we have examined so far; we just threw out three chairs and I'm not sure that the remaining two are really worth keeping.	Internal: Visionary
	We need a visionary to say this is where I think the market is going to be in five years and take a guess at a product and do it.	

opposed to financial options. Since this work does not draw directly on the capabilities of the ATLAS/ti program, however, we will not discuss it further.

A more detailed analysis of the reasoning behind continued investment in (or termination of) each option the company considered was also being carried out. This analysis extensively relied on the software's capabilities, and will therefore be described in some detail. For purposes of the analysis, the primary data set examined consisted of the interview transcripts, though once again company documents and notes from critical meetings were important as well. The following discussion draws primarily on the interviews. As shown in Table 10.5, these documents were coded into 723 quotations.

These data were analysed in the following way:

- As noted earlier, each member of the top management team of the organization ($N = 7$) was interviewed periodically over the course of the planning process, (four interviews per person, with the exception

TABLE 10.5   Document statistics

Primary text no.	Document name	No. of lines	No. of pages	No. of quotations
3	RE1111	555	10	61
4	RE1012	534	10	71
5	RE124	405	8	29
6	RE921	385	7	43
7	PL921	173	3	20
8	PL1012	171	3	17
9	PL1111	96	2	16
10	PL124	77	1	9
11	DP921	404	7	41
12	DP1012	86	2	20
13	DP1111	168	3	22
14	DP119	161	3	18
15	RC921	192	4	14
16	RC1012	70	1	12
17	RC1111	214	4	22
18	RC118	370	7	24
19	JM118	385	7	32
20	JM1111	224	4	26
21	JM1012	189	4	19
22	JM103	49	1	5
23	DC921	294	5	25
24	DC1012	178	3	21
25	DC1111	190	4	29
26	DC119	118	2	20
27	LR1012	323	6	24
28	LR111	151	3	24
29	LR21	733	14	59
	Total	6,895	128	723

of LR, who was interviewed three times). These interviews form a total population of 27 'explanation opportunities', which presumably were guided by more or less explicit mental models of the planning process and option opportunities.

- For each interview, text passages pertaining to the decision criteria used in judging the options currently being investigated by the company were coded by decision criteria mentioned by informants (i.e. competitors, market size, risk). When these factors were elicited from comments directly regarding the study group responsible for developing a particular option, the passage was also coded to that group (i.e. WAN, LAN, Data Centre, etc.). Thus, a matrix could be established that showed the evaluation criteria used in judging each of the firm's options.
- Next, each transcript was read to determine if the individual articulated an 'ideal future state' for the company. In other words, without referencing a particular option, did individuals express what they thought the 'ideal' option should be and/or what the consequences of that option would be for DataCorp?

- If the individual expressed relationships among decision criteria or other events that would or did occur, those statements were classified as 'causal elements'. Words like 'so', 'since', 'because', indicated a causal relationship between the elements while other statements were linked in a temporal order such as 'We'll start from the Data Centre side and work out towards the LAN.'
- A matrix was developed for each individual that compared these three items (decision criteria, ideal future state and causal elements) across each of the four time periods.

At this point it was hoped that a mental model could be constructed for each individual's explanation(s) of the information presented by each of the study groups. Drawing on previous research on jury's, medical team's and other group's decision processes (Pennington and Hastie, 1986, 1988), it was expected that the individual would construct an explanation or story about each possible action (select, reject, success, failure) that could be undertaken with respect to a given option, and that judgement would be based on the best match between the constructed explanation and the individual's favoured option.

Unfortunately, it was not possible to pursue this expectation about knowledge generation for all individuals, for each option, for each time period, because the amount of explicit reasoning about each option by each individual varied. In addition, as noted earlier, there was a great deal of variance between subjects in terms of the amount of narrative obtained from the interview, as shown in Table 10.5. The variance is partly a function of the interview schedule (some respondents were pressed for time so answers were brief), the amount of information gathered as part of each interview (a second researcher also gathered data during the interview), and the introverted personality of some of the members of the executive staff.

However, a composite explanation could be and was constructed for each DataCorp option. This composite documents that knowledge development about the company's options in the first two time periods was quite general, while in the latter two time periods, comments were directed toward each option currently being considered, although some comments still pertained to the set of options.

As an example of the rich analysis possible within this framework, one option – the LAN Switch – is now presented in some detail. The detail illustrates the kind of data available to qualitative researchers. It also illustrates the 'embedded' nature of the data, which will be discussed later as a critical issue for research interpretation and coding reliability.

LAN switch decision

The LAN Switch option group exhibited a great deal of energy and enthusiasm in the Decision Group meetings and at their presentations to the planning group. They tried to capture the imagination of the company as evidenced by this statement from their leader:

> If DataCorp wants to be something bigger than they are today, they have to diversify and enter the world market. The mainframe is not a good market. Other possible ways to go would be to acquire companies in the mainframe market. There is certainly a way to do that. But the ideas that they proposed in the mainframe market … [aren't] exciting opportunities in terms of potential growth. DataCorp could certainly acquire some other companies in the mainframe business. Become big internationally. They could do it. But still the growth is questionable. Say you buy out a $100 million company, now you have to become $200. How are you going to get from a $200 million company to $500? (30:3)

Feeding off the energy of their leader, UG, the group worked quickly to develop ideas and by the middle of December were much farther along in terms of definition than either the Data Centre group (which temporarily disbanded at this point) or the Storage group. Yet the very nature of the market demanded that the company make a quick decision on the development of this option. One month later (18 January 1995), UG expressed concern that the decision to give the group the go-ahead was taking too long:

> The problem is the time. Almost two months have passed. And in this market two months is a long time to wait. Especially when the market has already been recognized in the marketplace as an exploding market. (30:4)

An analysis of the evaluation of the LAN Switch helps to explain why the decision was delayed and points out some key process issues that impacted the ultimate decision to drop this option. Our interpretation and subsequent discussion was facilitated by initially considering the positive and negative evaluations of the LAN option separately.

LAN Switch: positive evaluation

One of the most frequently mentioned decision criteria that reflected a positive evaluation of the LAN Switch option was the size of the potential market and the fact that DataCorp's core competencies matched the skills needed to develop a product line (10:7, 19:26, 20:11, 28:11). For example:

> This is clearly a major market scenario and our skills line up pretty well with that. I think it plays well to the existing networking and switching skills. (20:11)

In addition to market size, the LAN Switch option was also perceived as providing leverage of the company's history:

> Because we know something about inter-networking, we've been in that environment. We're coming along in understanding the details of the playing field. Who's doing what with what architectures. (3:37)

It is important to note here that these skills and experiences were primarily developed for the line of business known as 'inter-operability', which had been sold off almost one and a half years prior to the research into this option. That point was noted by the respondents and is elaborated in the discussion of the negative evaluation.

In addition to being 'interesting' (18:22) and providing a good migration from mainframe dependency (28:11), the LAN Switch also was considered to have the potential to define a differentiated market position for DataCorp (3:10, 13:8) that would create value for the company:

> The network switch, as I listened to that one before I got on the team, I sat there and said 'Aren't there a ton of people in that position? How are we going to be different?' What I like about it was if we could create a position, that would probably be the best leverage of the value of this company. But that's a big if. (3:10)

If such a position could be located, it would also help in DataCorp's efforts to find a suitable partner:

> I think that there's some significant players. If we could partner with one – in other words, if we have enough specific skill competence in the switching area that they don't have – then we might have a better chance. (13:8)

JM summed up the positive evaluation in the following critique of the LAN Switch:

> LAN inter-networking is quite interesting. I think the proposal is interesting in terms of if you can break into that there's a lot of growth. This is clearly a major market scenario and our skills line up pretty well with that. I think it plays well to the existing networking and switching skills. (20:11)

This quotation by a single individual is actually very close to the mental model that we constructed for the group as a whole, as illustrated by the decision criteria used in the positive evaluation for the LAN Switch. This model is summarized in Figure 10.4.

LAN switch: negative evaluation

Although the LAN Switch emerged as the option that seemed to provide the company with the 'white space opportunity' (Hamel and Prahalad, 1994) it sought, ultimately it was rejected. The negative evaluations of this option (presented in detail in Jasinski, 1996) are theoretically interesting,

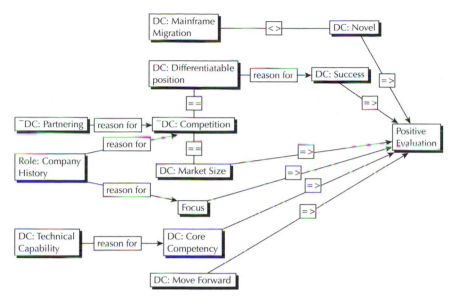

Figure 10.4   LAN Switch decision: positive evaluation model

in part, because they do not mirror the positive evaluation. When placed beside a similar analysis of decision making around other options, the study provides a very rich picture of option analysis to present to the field of strategic decision making. The ATLAS/ti database permits comparison of the structure of arguments across options, which makes it possible to think about the influence of option content. It is also possible to compare the development of arguments over time, which has led us to think about the transfer of logic between options, and partial 'collapse' of reasoning for a period of time into arguments that are not sensitive to content.

Clearly the KBS used is just a means to these ends. But if the findings are to be believed, the impact of these means has to be considered. We will therefore turn to how we evaluate the reliability of this study, and to what extent the use of KBSs affects establishing reliability.

METHODOLOGICAL ISSUES

The use of qualitative methods is channelled by the researcher's stance towards what can be known and how it can be learnt. These complexities of ontology and epistemology are too great to be reviewed here (see Blaikie, 1993) except to remark that qualitative methods can be used in many different kinds of studies and the standards of validity the researcher hopes to meet depend very much on initial assumptions, even if they are not made explicit.

This study takes an interpretive approach, which means that we assume all descriptions of the world (organization members' and researchers') are affected by the describer's place in time and space, his or her prior experience, and specific aspects of the immediate context. This epistemic starting point is less demanding than more positivist approaches in terms of establishing validity, and yet we want to communicate with others who are less inclined to an interpretive approach. Thinking about the extent to which we can meet the standards of unbiased design, systematic data collection and logical analysis that grow out of more positivist approaches facilitates such communication. We also believe such questions can facilitate interpretive work, even though an interpretive approach denies such standards can be met and their prescriptions are not essential for this approach.

The issue is basically one of trustworthiness:

> How do you persuade your audience, including most importantly yourself, that the findings of your inquiry are worth taking account of? What is it that makes the study believable...? ...This is not simply a presentational matter. ... There are fundamental issues about the inquiry itself [that must be addressed]. (Robson, 1993: 66)

The qualitative researcher trying to communicate with a broad audience has to think about establishing validity ('whether the findings are "really" about what they appear to be about' [Robson, 1993: 66]) and reliability (whether others would come to similar conclusions, given the data collected). Even though we believe that there are no ultimate arbitrators of these questions, we wanted to communicate with the reader about the match between our subject of interest and the data collected, and the non-arbitrary coding procedures and analysis applied to that data. To some extent these are design issues that precede the use of a KBS; for example, it makes sense to note the amount of time spent in DataCorp before coding began to help establish the validity of conclusions drawn. A KBS is very helpful in further addressing validity and reliability. Though the following discussion reflects an interpretive approach to these issues, the categories of concern have applicability to qualitative studies with other starting points.

Researcher Interpretation

The researcher's focus of attention affects the data gathered, as well as all subsequent research decisions. More specifically, to ATLAS/ti, that means that researcher interpretation affects the way blocks of text are demarcated, coding structures are defined and carried out, relationships are established, networks are analysed and models are configured. Other decisions are always possible. In this case, an interest in dealing with complex and confusing strategic decision-making environments led us to note and work with certain aspects of DataCorp. A researcher observing the very same meetings, and even asking the very same interview questions, might carry out these tasks quite differently if he or she was interested in the planning situation as a means of interpersonal control and influence.

The roots of researcher influences on attention and decision making are deeply embedded in socially situated past experience and current intentions. There is no way these influences can be eradicated. There are only other perspectives. On the other hand, just any interpretation is not acceptable. The reader of a study deserves to know that researchers were careful not to let initial mental models overwhelm the decisions that were made to carry out the study. Further, the reader deserves to know that we considered some of the most plausible alternative choices that might be made. There are several ways in which this might be done.

respondent verification

One of the most obvious checkpoints on validity is to interact with the sources of data themselves. Some methodologists feel that the respondent's interpretations of a given event or concept should dominate the researcher's since they are the source of the data. We take the position that the subject's perspective must be noted, but that it is not the only acceptable or valid interpretation. Every point of view has its 'blind spots' as well as its unique insights: for example, people within a context can be more focused on detail than on pattern.

Some writers on methodology also worry about the possibility that interaction between researcher and subject around constructs of interest will itself bias the data. Though always something to be aware of, we were not particularly concerned about this possibility, given that our subjects were intelligent adults with far more at stake thinking about the future of DataCorp than our study. Part of the study design therefore included discussion of interpretation to date with people in the organization. Notably, about seven months into the study the ideas behind strategic option theory were discussed with the top management team. Their responses are an interesting part of the data collected.

intercoder reliability

A frequently used method of assuring study reliability is to involve more than one individual in the coding process, comparing coding decisions to assure that significant overlap between coders exists. At the beginning of this study it was assumed that a second coder would be used in this way. However, the technical nature of much of the transcripts precluded an efficient means of accomplishing this. An attempt was made to create a translation scheme whereby a non-technical person could code the data, but it was abandoned after it became apparent that there were too many terms that had to be defined. The following two quotations are indicative of the problems encountered:

> Because we know something about inter-networking, we've been in that environment. We're coming along in understanding the details of the playing field. Who's doing what with what architectures. (3:37)
>
> On the campus backbone I think our strength there is that it's building off the switching technology that we had developed for the Conductor. (13:5)

In both cases, the respondents are referring to the LAN Switch option but in neither instance do they use that term. In quotation 3:37 the reference is to 'inter-networking' and in 13:5 it is to 'campus backbone'. Based on field notes of the interview and familiarity with the technology, the first researcher was able to make proper attribution. But it became obvious that technical knowledge and a significant amount of time spent at the research site (almost three years) provided a level of understanding and insight about the people and the planning process that could not be easily duplicated.

multilectics

A more successful attempt to establish study validity and reliability involved the use of more than one research interpreter. The people interviewed and observed in this study were in general intensely involved in their jobs, at a major turning point for their company. They had sufficient interest in the subject of the study to provide extensive access, for which we are very grateful. Their overall concerns, however, were not ours. They could not be expected to be involved in some of the details of analysis that interested us, though keeping in touch with their response to that analysis is always important. Use of a second interpreter, more closely aligned with the subject of interest and the ultimate audience of a large portion of the research, is an important additional element of the research design.

The study reported here is the dissertation research of the first author. As supervisor, the second author was significantly involved at the early stages of defining the study. During much of the data collection period the two authors met weekly. Though less involved with data coding, for reasons already described, the second author was again more involved as the findings of the study took shape. Furthermore, for a portion of the data collection period a third researcher attended meetings and interviews to carry out a second research project. She also shared notes and discussed ways in which the data could be understood.

The philosophical importance of this kind of relationship can be described as 'multilectic' (Huff, 1981), a word that is expanded from Hegel's 'dialectic'. From a multilectic perspective the inevitability of each individual's unique point of view is a strength in scientific inquiry. In a world that is taken to be ultimately undescribable from one point of view, more than one theoretical observer provides 'different ways of *logically* understanding an issue. Each individual perspective is expected to be internally consistent, and to have gained from prior use in other settings some confirmation that it is a viable way of looking at (at least parts of) the world' (Huff, 1981: 90).

ATLAS/ti was especially helpful in generating dialogue from multiple perspectives. Interaction with graphic views, and the first researcher's mental models described within the system, provided the grounds for discussion. A basic precept of multilectics is that total synthesis cannot be achieved, and richer insight is provided by maintaining alternative perspectives. The flexibility of the program made it possible to maintain alternative interpretation of the data for further development and analysis.

data triangulation

A discussion that advances some, though not all, of the multilectic argument falls under the heading of 'triangulation'. Denzin (1978) distinguishes triangulation by data source (which can include persons, times, places, etc.), method (observation, interview document), researcher (investigator A and B) and theory. Miles and Huberman (1994) add data type (qualitative text, recordings, quantitative).

Despite the focus on one data set in this article, we were in fact very much influenced by the importance of data triangulation for establishing study validity. The goal of data triangulation is to pick sources that have different biases and different strengths, so they can complement each other. 'In effect, triangulation is a way to get to the finding in the first place – by seeing or hearing multiple *instances* of it from different *sources* by using different *methods* and by squaring the finding with others it needs to be squared with' (Miles and Huberman, 1994: 297). Multilectics expects points of view to be more intrinsically incommensurate.

Following the precepts of data triangulation, we obtained information from public records (via Lexis searches of newspapers and trade magazines), as well as private company written material such as memoranda, brochures and financial statements. Moreover, information was obtained from company informants both in public settings (attendance at company meetings) and in confidence during private interviews. Using ATLAS/ti, it was possible to compare comments made during interviews to the same individual's statements during group meetings and perhaps even to subsequent written documentation in company and/or public documents.

While these procedures are in line with classic, pre-computer, principles of qualitative research design, the use of ATLAS/ti allowed much more extensive data gathering. More important, it offered multiple views and slices of the data. For example, data relationships could be viewed graphically, in text format or in numerical frequency distributions. Patterns could be gleaned from one perspective and then pursued from another.

This was especially true in constructing the decision models for each of the option decisions. Often the initial pass would be through graphical examination of the data codes and quotations and would then proceed to a review of the text passages in context of the transcript. To gain one sense of the weight of a particular decision factor, the frequency of occurrence of that criterion could be reviewed.

In short, ATLAS/ti provided us with what any computer support system should be expected to provide: the capacity to more adequately account for and deal with a complex data set. Ultimately, however, the capacity of a KBS goes beyond helping to establish the trustworthiness of a study, which is the subject of our conclusion.

CONCLUSION: DISTINCTIVE CONTRIBUTIONS OF KBSs TO QUALITATIVE RESEARCH

The basic things KBSs accomplish merely take over jobs the qualitative researcher has always done. These systems collect and code information, and can carry out systematic searches of the database (e.g. for counter-examples). Of course KBSs allow the single individual to accomplish these things much more quickly. Given the important trade-off between time and money, this in practice means that KBSs make much larger projects possible.

KBSs begin to make a more distinctive contribution to qualitative research as the researcher starts to manipulate the data collected. Time is the barrier that hinders the completion of qualitative research projects in the collection, coding and systematic search phases. As the KBS aides data manipulation, however, time is no longer the focus. KBSs are of greater value at this stage of the research process because they make it possible to consider different parts of the data simultaneously, thereby promoting discovery of patterns that otherwise might be obscured by the weight of evidence. At issue is the fact that the human brain is not very adept at keeping many bits of information in mind at once (Miller, 1956), but is uniquely suited to discovering patterns.[5] The KBS thus extends a human strength.

Of equal importance for qualitative research, KBSs allow more alternatives to be considered before a pattern is selected as meriting further analysis. However skilled the individual researcher might be in establishing such connections, KBSs again extend that reach. A system like ATLAS/ti allows the researcher to carry out an infinite number of 'what if' analyses. The potential contribution to qualitative research is as great as the spreadsheet's contribution to financial analysis.

KBSs are even more important as a tool to facilitate the development of the researcher's own mental models. Here the issue is that KBSs offer a quick connect between researcher-defined variables and structures and variables and structures more closely linked to the data. This possibility puts the central characteristic of KBSs (that they can incorporate more data, and iterate more alternatives than any human mind) in a new light. The researcher skilled in interpretation and theory building in the past typically had to move away from the data for a time in order to pursue analysis. Data sets are distracting; they easily become clay around the feet of the theorist. The KBS allows the needed distance, because it can 'hide' connections to the data. But the data are always only a click away.

The advantages of this capacity are enormous, and researchers are only just beginning to discover how to use it. The potential is matched by that derived from a second critical aspect of KBSs: their capacity to explore the consequences of researcher structures. The search for counter-examples has long been established as the hallmark of good qualitative research. KBSs allow the introduction of a new – related but more important – hallmark. Given the capabilities of this new research tool, we propose that the careful qualitative researcher should provide an audit trail back to the data of the consequences of theoretically elevating specific concepts and relationships. The KBS thus not only allows, but also demands a closer connection between theory and data. As consumers of qualitative research, we should now ask to see the larger picture; we can ask about other concepts that are attached to those being proposed as central, those that in the past have been left 'on the cutting-room floor'.

We are just beginning to establish such an audit trail for the study summarized in this chapter, but we can see the potential of the system we used. For example, a key concept in the study involves timing. 'When to call' is a central issue for strategic option theory; it was also a central issue for DataCorp as it tried to find new sources of competitive advantage and was ultimately approached with a buyout offer. ATLAS/ti allows us to explore the ways timing is defined, and summarize simple links (of the kind reviewed in the LAN option) between timing and other decision criteria. We believe that the data can suggest more complicated connections. Starting at the other end of the process, we also think that as we develop more complicated theoretic ideas on our own, ATLAS/ti will allow us to test them more adequately by returning to the complexity of the available evidence.

Having expounded on the virtues of KBSs, it is important to remember in closing that qualitative analysis continues to be an art. Qualitative studies have always suffered from the problem of 'too many trees to see the forest'. The KBS proffers yet more, and new kinds of trees. The need for artistry is thus greater than it ever has been. But KBSs are providing new raw material that promises to elevate the status of qualitative studies as a source of social science insight. Certainly these systems make qualitative analysis more exciting than it ever has been.

NOTES

1. In addition to these published reports, the 1996 Academy of Management Meetings featured a special session in the business policy and strategy section devoted entirely to analytic case-based research.

2. While this chapter uses the term 'knowledge-based system' to refer to a generic type of software, Weitzman and Miles (1995) use the terms 'code-based theory-builders' and 'conceptual network builders'. Commercially available programs include AQUAD, ATLAS/ti, HyperRESEARCH and NUDIST.

3. Examples drawn from an electronic mail discussion with the Thomas Muir, developer of ATLAS/ti.

4. Methodologically, the use of the same questions for each time period facilitated comparison of responses among individuals at a particular time period but also between time periods for the same individual. Of course, this is just one aspect of the total data set, but a particularly important part of the data being used as an example.

5. This point is frequently made by the director of the National Supercomputer Applications Center at the University of Illinois in Champaign-Urbana.

REFERENCES

Bartunek, J., Bobko, P. and Venkatraman, N. (1993) 'Toward innovation and diversity in management research methods', *Academy of Management Journal*, 36: 1362–1373.

Blaikie, N. (1993) *Approaches to Social Enquiry*. Cambridge: Polity Press.

Bowman, E. and Hurry, D. (1993) 'Strategy through the options lens: An integrated view of resource investments and the incremental choice process', *Academy of Management Review*, 18 (4): 760–782.

Carlson, D. (1993) 'Hypervision: A tool for semistructured data analysis', unpublished working paper, University of Colorado at Boulder.

Denzin, N. (1988) Sociological Methods: A Source Book, 2nd edn. New York: McGraw-Hill.

Eisenhardt, K. (1989) 'Building theories from case study research', *Academy of Management Review*, 14 (4): 532–550.

Glasser, B. and Strauss, A. (1967) *The Discovery of Grounded Theory*. Chicago: Aldine.

Hamel, G. and Prahalad, C.K. (1994) *Competing for the Future*. Boston: Harvard Business School Press.

Huff, A. (1981) 'Multilectic methods of inquiry', *Human Systems Management*, 2: 83–94.

Hurry, D. (1994) 'Shadow options and global exploration strategies', *Advances in Strategic Management*, 10A: 229–248.

Jasinski, D. (1996) 'Using strategic option theory to provide sensible problem solving for venture growth', unpublished doctoral thesis, University of Colorado at Boulder.

Kogut, B. and Kulatilaka, N. (1994) 'Options thinking and platform investments: Investing in opportunity', *California Management Review*, Winter: 52–71.

Larsson, R. (1993) 'Case survey methodology: Quantitative analysis of patterns across case studies', *Academy of Management Journal*, 36: 1515–1546.

Miles, M. and Huberman, A. (1994) *Qualitative Data Analysis*. Thousand Oaks, CA: Sage.

Miller, G.A. (1956) 'The magical number seven, plus or minus two', *Psychological Review*, 63: 81–97.

Pennington, N. and Hastie, R. (1986) 'Evidence evaluation in complex decision making', *Journal of Personality and Social Psychology*, 51: 242–258.

Pennington, N. and Hastie, R. (1988) 'Explanation-based decision making: The effects of memory structure on judgment', *Journal of Experimental Psychology: Learning, Memory and Cognition*, 14: 521–533.

Robson, C. (1993) *Real World Research*. Oxford: Blackwell.

Rouse, W. and Morris, N. (1986) 'On looking into the black box: Prospects and limits in the search for mental models', *Psychological Bulletin*, 100 (3): 349–363.

Sanchez, R. (1993) 'Strategic flexibility, firm organization, and managerial work in dynamic markets: A strategic options perspective', *Advances in Strategic Management*, 9: 251–292.

Schoemaker, P. (1995) 'Scenario planning: A tool for strategic thinking', *Sloan Management Review*, 36 (2): 25–40.

Van de Ven, A. and Poole, M. (1990) 'Methods for studying innovation development in the Minnesota innovation research program', *Organization Science*, 1 (3): 313–335.

Walsh, J. (1995) 'Managerial and organizational cognition: Notes from a trip down memory lane', *Organization Science*, 6 (30): 280–321.

Weitzman, E. and Miles, M. (1995), *Computer Programs for Qualitative Data Analysis.* Thousand Oaks, CA: Sage.

Yin, R. (1993) 'Applications of case study research', *Applied Social Research Methods Series, Vol. 34.* Newbury Park, CA: Sage.

ANNOTATED BIBLIOGRAPHY

Heidi M. Neck and Nardine Collier

Ackermann, F. and Belton, V. (1994) 'Managing corporate knowledge experiences with SODA and V.I.S.A.', *British Journal of Management*, 5 (3): 163–176.

> Two management science approaches are introduced that have been used for the effective management of knowledge, toward the development of strategy, planning and decision making in a wide variety of organizational settings. Both approaches make use of computer technology to provide a flexible and interactive environment that incorporates a visual representation of the problem. The SODA methodology is based on a multidisciplinary theoretical framework for 'action research.' Kelly's (1955) Personal Construct Theory, from which the cognitive mapping technique originated, is at the root of the framework. V.I.S.A. is a decision support system that has been developed to assist in multiple-criteria analysis. Underlying the approach is a conceptually simple, theoretically well-founded and well-validated model – an additive-weighted value function. Case studies illustrate the two approaches.

Andersen, C.R. and Paine, F.T. (1975) 'Managerial perceptions and strategic behavior', *Academy of Management Journal*, 18 (4): 811.

> The process by which the organization and the environment interact has not been firmly established. Certainly, the strategy formulation process is a crucial part of that interaction. Contributions to understanding organization-environment interaction from the policy and organization areas are integrated through a perceptual model of strategy formulation. Key inputs in the model are managerial perceptions of environmental certainty and uncertainty and low and high need for change. The resulting four quadrants present different kinds of strategy formulation problems.

Andersen, P.H. and Strandskov, J. (1998) 'International market selection: A cognitive mapping perspective', *Journal of Global Marketing*, 11 (3): 65–84.

In the international market selection literature, selecting new markets is often largely understood as an information-processing problem. The notion is that managers require extensive market information to reduce decision-making complexity. It is argued, however, that managerial cognition is more central to international market selection processes, since recognition and evaluation of strategic stimuli strongly affect the way this process is approached and executed. Market environments are not unambiguous realities, but abstractions that are given meaning through processes of selection, identification and screening. To select among international markets, managers impose mental maps to acknowledge markets proposed for mapping managerial decision making, based on the so-called 'means–end theory'.

Barnes, J.H., Jr (1984) 'Cognitive biases and their impact on strategic planning', *Strategic Management Journal*, 5 (2): 129–138.

In strategic planning, human judgement is needed to interpret the facts and determine their relevance for the future. Certain biases are inherent in any decision making as judgemental rules, or heuristics, are employed to simplify difficult mental tasks. Such heuristics as availability, hindsight, misunderstanding the sampling process, judgements of correlation and causality, and representativeness can lead to large and persistent biases with serious implications. Overconfidence results when people are insensitive to the tenuousness of the assumptions upon which their judgements are based. While nearly everyone has a desire for certainty, often some level of risk is inevitable. Experiments show that a person's cognitive limitations lead to simplifying the process of integrating information when making even the most important decisions. Bias can be dealt with by forcing planners to perform sensitivity analysis on their estimates.

Barr, P.S. and Huff, A.S. (1997) 'Seeing isn't believing: Understanding diversity in the timing of strategic response', *Journal of Management Studies*, 34 (3): 337–370.

There is general consensus in the strategy literature that successful firms alter strategy to address changes in their environments and enact more favourable conditions. Studies suggest that this adjustment is not always made in a timely manner. A new study of six pharmaceutical firms suggests that multiple concepts associated with environmental changes must be directly linked to organizational performance

> before new strategies are initiated. The results emphasize the importance of stress as a precursor to strategic response and have implications for the way firms conceptualize 'response' when referring to significant changes in strategy.

Barr, P.S., Stimpert, J.L. and Huff, A.S. (1992) 'Cognitive change, strategic action, and organizational renewal', *Strategic Management Journal*, 13 (Special issue: summer): 15–36.

> Organizational renewal requires that a firm's top managers make timely adjustments in their mental models following significant changes in the environment. The US railroad industry was selected as the subject of a study of whether similar organizations in similar contexts differ in their ability to recognize significant changes in their environments. The investigation focused on the mental models of the top managers of a matched pair of firms. The need for careful matching led to the selection of two Midwestern railroads, the C&NW and the Rock Island. Analysis of longitudinal data from these railroads suggests that renewal hinges not so much on noticing new conditions, but on being able to link environmental change to corporate strategy and to modify that linkage over time. The leaders of the C&NW not only recognize changes in their environment, they also gradually change their mental models of how organizational performance is affected by the changed environment.

Bartunek, J.M. (1984) 'Changing interpretive schemes and organizational restructuring: The example of a religious order', *Administrative Science Quarterly*, 29 (3): 355–372.

> A case study of a religious order is presented in an attempt to describe: (1) processes through which interpretive schemes undergo second order change (2) the relationship between second order change in interpretive schemes and restructuring and (3) the role of the environment and of the organization's leadership in these processes. During the course of the study, the religious order's shared interpretive schemes, particularly its understanding of its mission, were being substantially changed in terms of structure. It is suggested that major changes in interpretive schemes occur through dialectical processes in which old and new ways of understanding interact, causing a synthesis. The process of change in interpretive schemes is in a reciprocal relationship with structural changes. This relationship is mediated by the actions of organizational members and their emotional responses to change. The way organization leadership initiates or responds to alternate interpretive schemes restricts the type of change in comprehension that can occur.

Billman, B. and Courtney, J.F. (1993) 'Automated discovery in managerial problem formulation: Formation of causal hypotheses for cognitive mapping', *Decision Sciences*, 24 (1): 23–41.

Development of knowledge acquisition techniques known as automated discovery systems has occurred in deep and narrow domains of knowledge. Automated discovery is the generation of new knowledge by a computer system on its own, without the help of another knowledge source. This study describes research and validation of an automated discovery system for a wide and shallow domain – business management. The system continues recent advances in expert systems research that have enhanced cognitive mapping, a problem formulation tool. The system perceives the behaviour of distal variables in the environment through probabilistic cues-to-causality, and generates previously unknown hypotheses by aggregating the probabilities into a single criterion of causal relatedness. The system is validated against the source code of a simulated managerial environment, and causal relationships posited by decision makers experienced in the play of the gaming simulator.

Bougon, M.G. (1992) 'Congregate cognitive maps: A unified dynamic theory of organization and strategy', *Journal of Management Studies*, 29 (3): 369–389.

Independently, two dynamic approaches to organization and strategy have emerged in fields traditionally confined to static methods. One approach uses the cybernetic properties of collective cognitive maps to create a dynamic theory of organization and social system change. The other approach uses the hierarchic properties of collective cognitive maps to create a dynamic theory of strategy. A dynamic cognitive approach makes organization theory and strategy theory inseparable. The approach distinguishes between aggregate and congregate collective cognitive maps. In this unified theory, the hierarchic and cybernetic aspects of collective cognitive maps combine with the cryptic aspect of concepts and connections present in maps to further explicate the association between organization and strategy. Cryptic labels are very different from equivocal labels. Crypticality is a social phenomenon. The congregate cognitive map is the social reality; there is no other underlying or deeper social reality to discover.

Brown, S.M. (1992) 'Cognitive mapping and repertory grids for qualitative survey research: Some comparative observations', *Journal of Management Studies*, 29 (3): 287–307.

A study of business strategy was carried out in 86 organizations in the crop protection industry. A multi-operational approach was used to enable validation of data by triangulation. This provided an opportunity to conduct a comparative evaluation of interactional investigative methods in a relatively controlled manner. Some conclusions of the analysis are: (1) Cognitive mapping satisfies many more process criteria than repertory grids. (2) The data that cognitive maps produce are less comparable than the data from repertory grids. (3) Splitting maps produced under the constraints introduced for the purposes of the project (actual versus ideal states) allows the respondent to focus on specific aspects of the ideal state one at a time and in contrast to the actual. (4) Cognitive maps-as-programs possibly do not represent the cognitive structure of the client's own problem conception. (5) Skeleton entries to cognitive maps (COPE) can be preferable to full-string entry for certain purposes, such as the analysis of large survey data.

Calori, R., Johnson, G. and Sarnin, P. (1994) 'CEOs' cognitive maps and the scope of the organization', *Strategic Management Journal*, 15 (6): 437–457.

A study considers chief executive officers (CEO) as cognizers charged with integrating views in the top management team; a role that should require high cognitive complexity, especially in diversified multinational corporations. A methodology for studying top managers' cognitive complexity is described and then applied to a sample of 26 CEOs. The CEOs' cognitive maps of the structure and of the dynamics of their industry are analysed in terms of their degree of complexity, in relation to the breadth of the business portfolio of the firm, its geographic scope and the links the firms has with foreign parents. The results of this exploratory test generally confirm the principle of requisite cognitive complexity and reveal a new set of more precise hypotheses linking particular dimensions of the scope of the firm with particular dimensions of the CEOs' cognitive complexity.

Cossette, P. and Audet, M. (1992) 'Mapping of an idiosyncratic schema', *Journal of Management Studies*, 29 (3): 325–347.

Among researchers interested in organizations and management, some of those who use cognitive mapping share a common objective – to improve organizational action. Some intervene directly at the level of the organization while others prefer to achieve this indirectly, by working at the individual level. Those who work at the individual level rely on the emancipatory properties of a cognitive map, which facilitates reflectiveness. The cognitive map and its construction are characterized by the notions of: (1) natural logic, (2) schematization, (3) contextuality, (4) representation, (5) knowledge and (6) schema.

A cognitive map is built from in-depth interviews. The idiosyncratic map of the owner-manager of a small business contains 57 concepts, treated as variables, and 87 links. By studying each variable and its link with other variables, it becomes possible to consider many specific aspects of the owner-manager's vision of the firm. More than half the variables in the cognitive map are involved in at least one loop homogeneity. Specific propositions with regard to such research are drawn from the findings.

Daniels, K., Johnson, G. and de Chernatony, L. (1994) 'Differences in managerial cognitions of competition', *British Journal of Management*, 5 (Special issue): 21–29.

It has been assumed that strategic decision making and implementation are both achieved through managers' sharing homogeneous cognitions of competition (e.g. Porac and Thomas, 1990). The assumption of homogeneity of cognitions of competition was tested using a sample of 24 managers from the offshore pumps industry. A variety of cognitive mapping techniques were used and maps were compared using a self-rating methodology. The results indicated that managers' mental models of competition are diverse, rather than homogeneous, but that this diversity increases as company and functional boundaries are crossed.

Daniels, K., de Chernatony, L. and Johnson, G. (1995) 'Validating a method for mapping managers' mental models of competitive industry structures', *Human Relations*, 48 (9): 975–991.

Cognitive mapping techniques refer to methods used to elicit the structure and content of people's mental models. There is growing interest in applying these techniques to the study of managers' mental models of strategic management issues. A new method is suggested for mapping managers' mental models of competitive industry structures that is based upon recent developments in the cognitive psychology of the categorization of concepts. The method is evaluated with respect to its psychometric properties against the well-established, but potentially cumbersome, repertory grid technique. The method is demonstrated to have good validity by comparing it with the repertory grid technique.

Day, G.S. and Nedungadi, P. (1994) 'Managerial representations of competitive advantage', *Journal of Marketing*, 58 (2): 31–44.

Managers use mental models of markets to simplify and impose order on complex and ambiguous competitive environments and isolate points of competitive advantage or deficiency. In a study of senior managers of 190 businesses, four different types of mental models or representations of competitive advantage were found, varying in the emphasis placed on customer or management judgements about where and how competitors differ. These representations were influenced equally by pressure points in the environment and choice of strategy. The type of representation was also strongly associated with constrained patterns of information search and usage, raising the possibility that the necessary simplifications and narrowing of perspective may come at the cost of myopia and insensitivity to challenges from unexpected directions. There was also a strong association between the completeness of the managerial representation and relative financial performance, which supports related studies on the profitability of a market orientation.

Diffenbach, J. (1982) 'Influence diagrams for complex strategic issues', *Strategic Management Journal*, 3 (2): 133–146.

Influence diagramming is a qualitative approach to mapping the interrelationships of complex strategic issues. Because of its qualitative nature, it is a simple desktop tool, requiring no computer software or particular expertise. The influence of social, economic, technological and environmental factors can be assessed and then used in conjunction with quantitative analytical techniques. The design and interpretation of influence diagrams is illustrated and applied to a policy assessment study of peak-load electricity pricing. Influence diagrams can vary in complexity and detail, and can be refined and revised as needed. Initially, the influence diagram can provide insight into relationships requiring further examination. It can uncover counter-intuitive relationships. It can be used effectively for communication and can reveal differences in decision makers' assessments.

Duhaime, I.M. and Schwenk, C.R. (1985) 'Conjectures on cognitive simplification in acquisition and divestment decision making', *Academy of Management Review*, 10 (2): 287–296.

Acquisition and divestment decisions usually involve complexity, ambiguity and lack of structure. It is suggested that business decision makers may employ some systematic and predictable simplification processes in defining such poorly structured problems. It is further argued that four major biases, selected from the organizational behaviour and cognitive psychology literatures, may describe and explain the sorts of decision-making errors found in cases of ill-considered acquisitions followed by unsuccessful turnaround efforts and eventually by divestment. The four biases are: (1) reasoning by analogy, (2) illusion of control, (3) escalating commitment and (4) single-outcome calculation. Examples from field research and the business press support the argument, and implications for theory and research are discussed.

Dunn, W.N. and Ginsberg, A. (1986) 'A sociocognitive network approach to organizational analysis', *Human Relations*, 39 (11): 955–976.

A sociocognitive network methodology for investigating organizational dynamics is presented. The methodology allows one to uncover and quantify differences in the content of organizational reference frames. The resulting indexes of cognitive content may be merged with standard sociometric data, creating a network matrix that measures the sociocognitive connectedness of an organization's participants. When compared to other methodologies for investigating human consciousness, the sociocognitive network approach has several advantages. The grid technique is flexible, efficient, systematic and easily reproducible. Theoretically, it alleviates the establishment of subjective meanings of organizational processes to participants before an attempt is made to measure them. Finally, the grid technique permits one to monitor diverse organizational learning processes.

Dutton, J.E. (1993) 'Interpretations on automatic: A different view of strategic issue diagnosis', *Journal of Management Studies*, 30 (3): 339–358.

Models of strategic decision making and environmental scanning typically assume that decision makers diagnose issues actively, using conscious and intentional effort to identify and to interpret potentially significant events, developments and trends. When decision makers confront an issue that is novel in content, about which persons have strong evaluations, where time pressure and information load are intense, or decision makers exist in an organization that has routinized means for dealing with issues, norms for consistency are prevalent, or the organization has been successful, design and process interventions may be necessary to engage active strategic issue diagnosis.

Dutton, J.E. and Jackson, S.E. (1987) 'Categorizing strategic issues: Links to organizational action', *Academy of Management*, 12 (1): 76–91.

A general conceptual framework is presented that is concerned with how the meanings attached to strategic issues by decision makers are translated into organizational responses. The model integrates an interpretive view of organizational decision making with cognitive categorization theory, providing a framework for understanding why organizations in the same industry respond differently to the same environmental events and trends. It is believed that labelling an issue as either a threat or an opportunity affects both subsequent information processing and the motivations of key decision makers. It also is argued that decision makers' cognitions and motivations systematically affect the processing of issues and the types of organizational actions taken in response to them. The model helps researchers better understand the problem-sensing and diagnosis process in decision making.

Dutton, J.E., Fahey, L. and Narayanan, V.K. (1983) 'Toward understanding strategic issue diagnosis', *Strategic Management Journal*, 4 (4): 307–324.

A framework is presented to describe the strategic issue diagnosis (SID) process. Strategic issues are poorly defined, emerging developments. Their diagnosis requires interpretation, judgement and questioning traditional assumptions about the business environment. The outcomes of SID serve as the basis for future strategies. SID inputs include the concepts and beliefs of individual decision makers and their political interests, as well as the particular characteristics of the issue facing them. Analysis of strategic issues will be characterized by successive revisions of individuals' judgements, and negotiations among individual decision makers to reach a consensus on their assumptions about the issue, its causes and effects, its expected outcomes, and the language and labels chosen to characterize it. It is shown how the strategy formulation models of the Boston Consulting Group's growth-share matrix and the Profit Impact of Market Strategies (PIMS) can be used as tools to aid decision makers in SID.

Dutton, J.E., Walton, E.J. and Abrahamson, E. (1989) 'Important dimensions of strategic issues: Separating the wheat from the chaff', *Journal of Management Studies*, 26 (4): 379–397.

Decision makers must use dimensions to sort the wheat from the chaff in the field of potential strategic issues. The dimensions implied by 3 literatures and dimensions generated by an empirical study are compared. A search of the 3 literatures identified 26 dimensions that differentiate strategic issues. Repertory grid techniques were used to identify the range of attributes used to define the 'meaning space' for strategic issues in a sample of strategic decision makers at the Port Authority of New York and New Jersey. Dimensions in the literature overlap those in the empirical study; 13 dimensions accounted for 51 per cent of the frequency with which all attributes were mentioned over all respondents. However, these 13 dimensions exclude the one cited most often in the literature – immediacy. Also, marked differences in the relative importance of classes of dimensions emerged in the sample relative to the literature. Issue content was about 3 times as prevalent in the sample, action was about the same in both, analytic characteristics were almost twice as prevalent in the literature, and source did not emerge in the sample at all.

Eden, C. (1990) 'Strategic thinking with computers', *Long Range Planning*, 23 (6): 35–43.

Strategic options development and analysis (SODA) has been used extensively by project teams working on strategic issues. A typical program involves a SODA facilitator in capturing the views, knowledge and expertise surrounding the issue. It is important to include interviews with those who could sabotage the outcome or those who are involved in implementation. Using cognitive mapping as the core technique in work on major issues produces high levels of ownership of the model constructed and of the agreed actions. In a SODA project, it is imperative that the ownership of an action portfolio be increased by the use of cognitive maps during the early stages of the project. As the project progresses, the maps are aggregated into a single group map, which will not belong to any member of the group. It becomes a device for facilitating negotiation, synergy and creativity. Promoting a series of focused strategy workshops can ensure coherence in strategy and create logical incrementalism.

Eden, C., Ackermann, F. and Cropper, S. (1992) 'The analysis of cause maps', *Journal of Management Studies*, 29 (3): 309–324.

Cause maps are used to depict and explore the cognitive structures of members of organizations. They are coded following many different conventions. A cause map has several structural properties – the property of hierarchy and linkage. At one extreme a map can comprise several clusters of nodes and links that are each disconnected from one another. At the other extreme, a map can be highly interconnected. One important analysis of emerging features relates to the detection of clusters, where a cluster may be more or less separable from other parts of the map. Within the context of analysis of directed graphs the existence or not of feedback loops will be of interest. Nodes with a single link to other parts of the map can be deleted to strip the map of detail. The effect of this process of stripping out detail is to collapse the map to include only those nodes with a domain score of three or more, thus retaining those nodes that sit at branch points. As the analyses are completed, some nodes take on a different status from others.

Fahey, L. and Narayanan, V.K. (1989) 'Linking changes in revealed causal maps and environmental change: An empirical study', *Journal of Management Studies*, 26 (4): 361–378.

The cognitive maps of the dominant coalition of one firm over time are explored. Two key methodological issues warrant attention: (1) the process of deriving the anticipated environmental elements in the causal maps; and (2) the derivation of the causal maps themselves. The revealed causal maps of television receiver maker Zenith over the period 1960–79 were traced. The twenty-year period was grouped into five eras, based mainly on industry sales evolution. The structure of the raw and reconstructed revealed maps indicated that decision makers were cognizant of the complexity of the environment. The content of the maps changed considerably from period to period. However, little interconnectedness between elements of the macroenvironment and the industry was present in the maps. This may reflect a difficulty on the part of decision makers to construct a complex and integrated view of the environment. Results of the hypothesis-testing stage suggest that the revealed causal maps evolve over time and sometimes in tune with the environment.

Fiol, C.M. and Huff, A.S. (1992) 'Maps for managers: Where are we? Where do we go from here?', *Journal of Management Studies*, 29 (3): 267–285.

Cognitive maps are graphic representations that locate people in relation to their information environments. Cognitive maps are of potential interest to managers because they are a means of displaying graphically the firm's current strategic position and because they hold the promise of identifying alternative routes to improving that position. Broad strategic concerns of managers require a portfolio of different kinds of cognitive maps. Cognitive maps encompass not only specific choice points, but also information about the context surrounding the points. Maps can be products designed to remain relatively stable over time or tools that people expect to modify. Current knowledge of cognitive maps allows the identification of submaps of different aspects of cognitive processes. These include: (1) identity submaps, (2) categorization submaps and (3) causal and argument submaps. Taken together, these three provide a tool kit for managers who must make sense of ambiguous and changing environmental stimuli.

Fournier, V. (1996) 'Cognitive maps in the analysis of personal change during work role transition', *British Journal of Management*, 7 (1): 87–105.

The way in which personal construct psychology and repertory grids can be used to produce cognitive maps is illustrated, and psychological adjustment during the transition from college to employment is analysed. Cognitive maps are based on the principal component analysis of repertory grid data and provide a visual representation of the way in which the subjects see themselves in relation to other people and in relation to their construct. The cognitive maps produced by two graduates shortly after entry in employment and six months later are analysed and compared in order to identify trends of personal change. The case studies show that the analysis of the cognitive maps provides some valuable insights into the way in which graduates change their construction of themselves and of their work environment during the period of transition.

Gavetti, G. and Levinthal, D. (2000) 'Looking forward and looking backward: Cognitive and experiential search', *Administrative Science Quarterly*, 45 (1): 113–137.

This paper examines the role and interrelationship between search processes that are forward-looking, based on actors' cognitive map of action–outcome linkages, and those that are backward-looking, or experience-based. Results show that, although crude, these representations still act as a powerful guide to initial search efforts and usefully constrain the direction of subsequent experiential search. Changing a cognitive representation itself can act as an important mode of adaptation, effectively resulting in the sequential allocation of attention to different facets of the environment. This virtue of shifting cognitive representation, however, may be offset by the loss of tacit knowledge associated with the prior cognition.

Ginsberg, A. (1989) 'Construing the business portfolio: A cognitive model of diversification', *Journal of Management Studies*, 26 (4): 417–438.

Researchers investigating the relationship between diversification and performance have been generally inattentive to the dominant general management logics that corporate-level managers use to understand and manage strategy diversity. In response to this, the use of the repertory grid is proposed. The grid is a methodology adapted from the work of Kelly (1955) and other personal construct theorists. As an approach to operationalizing the mental maps that direct the management of strategic diversity, the business repertory grid appears to have several important advantages. It is particularly useful in assessing the ways in which top managers construe the corporate portfolio and manage strategic diversity. Grid technique is flexible, efficient and systematic. It is also highly reproducible, thus allowing researchers to validate or challenge the results of previous studies. A main goal of the application of the repertory grid to the study of strategic diversity is to measure the way in which top managers perceive relationships among businesses in their firms.

Ginsberg, A. (1990b) 'Connecting diversification to performance: A sociocognitive approach', *Academy of Management Review*, 15 (3): 514–536.

A socio-cognitive model of diversification is developed that bases the role of top managers' belief systems in the cognitive and behavioural attributes of corporate strategy. In contrast to more traditional approaches that emphasize the economies generated by diversity and relatedness, this approach emphasizes the creativity and flexibility associated with corporate-level decision-making processes. The socio-cognitive perspective of strategy proposed makes three important contributions: (1) It allows the examination of the ways in which managers' cognitive structures reflect the systemic properties of strategic position. (2) It allows the examination of the ways in which shared cognitive structures reflect the behavioural dynamics of strategic decision-making processes. (3) It allows the development of specific predictions and prescriptions regarding the influence of top management teams' socio-cognitive capacities on processes of diversification and their economic outcomes.

Ginsberg, A. (1994) 'Minding the competition: From mapping to mastery', *Strategic Management Journal*, 15 (Special issue): 153–174.

Cognitive approaches to strategy have examined the subjective nature of business environments and competitive situations, but have failed to show how managerial mental models lead to superior economic performance. In contrast, resource-based views of strategy acknowledge the importance of managerial skills in creating economic rents, but have not examined the processes through which managerial cognitions lead to sustained competitive advantage. To address this deficit, an analysis develops a socio-cognitive capability approach that integrates cognitive and economic theories. The approach: (1) identifies socio-cognitive foundations of differentiation and cost; (2) examines how these foundations emerge from the process of strategy development; (3) explains how group capabilities influence this process; and (4) shows how human and organizational resources give rise to group capabilities.

Gripsrud, G. and Gronhaug, K. (1985) 'Structure and strategy in grocery retailing: A sociometric approach', *Journal of Industrial Economics*, 33 (3): 339–348.

The objective market structure of a conventionally defined geographical market area is contrasted with the relevant structure as it appears to individual retailers. The impact of perceived competitive structure on the retailers' choice of strategy is examined. The interdependence in the strategy formulation of close competitors is emphasized. Three hypotheses treating retail competition are advanced. Consideration is given only to those grocery stores defined at the four-digit level by SIC-data in one conventional market area – a small Norwegian town encompassing 51 stores. Data are obtained from personal interviews with store managers, and a complete sociometric mapping is made. Results support the hypotheses and indicate that imitation or differentiation by close competitors is related to whether intervening competitors of less importance do or do not exist. However, the findings indicate that an adequate assessment of the subject is difficult using only objective market structure data.

Gronhaug, K. and Falkenberg, J.S. (1989) 'Exploring strategy perceptions in changing environments', *Journal of Management Studies*, 26 (4): 349–360.

How a firm perceives its own strategy and that of its competitors is explored using the forest products industry to represent the research context. Multiple data sources include semi-structured interviews with top management, annual reports, 10–K forms, articles from business periodicals and questionnaire data. Great discrepancies in self-evaluations and competitors' evaluations of the firms' strategies were seen. The reported differences between actors and observers indicate that perceptions are biased and that firms only partly understand their environments. Also, it is observed that competitors' perceptions of each other are not necessarily mutual. This indicates that firms select competitors based on their reality construction and that only a fraction of the potential objectively defined competitors may be included in the firm's evoked set of competitors. This may be interpreted as firms selecting competitors as a basis for strategy formulation and strategic actions.

Gupta, N. and Shaw, J.D. (1998) 'Let the evidence speak: Financial incentives are effective!', *Compensation and Benefits Review*, 30 (2): 26–32.

It is an inevitable fact that most of us are motivated by money – some more so than others. Behaviours that are rewarded are repeated, behaviours that are punished are eliminated. When certain behaviours are followed by money, they are more likely to be repeated. This means that employees will do the things for which they are required; it also means that they will ignore the things for which they are not rewarded. What management supports with money is given greater weight than what management supports simply with words. In short, money motivates by rewarding certain behaviours; it also motivates by showing people what is valued in the organization – it provides a cognitive map of the path people must take to succeed. There are good ways and bad ways to use financial incentives. Financial incentive programmes should: (1) be tied to valued behaviours; (2) have good measurement systems; (3) use financial incentives to supplement other rewards; and (4) have realistic goals. On the other hand, financial incentive programmes should not: (1) be idealistic and unrealistic; (2) equate rewards and punishments; or (3) violate employee expectations.

Hall, R.I. (1999) 'A study of policy formation in complex organizations: Emulating group decision-making with a simple artificial intelligence and a system model of corporate operations', *Journal of Business Research*, 45 (2): 157–171.

A process theoretic framework using a brain–body analogy is used to conceptualize the interactions between the corporate and the policy-making systems of an organization. The policy-making system is modelled as an artificial intelligence containing behavioural rules that mimic the socio-cognitive and socio-political logic used by policy-making groups in constructing a simple shared cause–effect cognitive map from which to select policy options. The study provides the paradoxical finding that a better group cognitive map containing causal relations more closely mirroring the real-world system will likely engender more internal conflict. The study also provides insight into the process by which key feedback loops of influences become overlooked in the building of a group cause map. Implications for management training and practice and future research are drawn from the analysis.

Hawes, J.M. and Crittenden, W. (1984) 'A taxonomy of competitive retailing strategies', *Strategic Management Journal*, 5 (3): 275–288.

Top managers from a national sample of grocery store chains were surveyed about adoption of generic products and the target market, marketing mix and retailing mix strategies used by their firms in retailing generics. An 18-item Likert-type scale was provided for answers. Using a multivariate clustering procedure, respondents were grouped according to their use of various strategies, leading to the development of a taxonomy of four distinct competitive patterns, including: (1) non-adopters, (2) aggressive initiators, (3) conservative reactors and (4) submissive defenders. Aggressive initiators were early adoptors and active promoters of generic products, expecting them to be a source of sales growth from new customers. Of the three adopting groups, aggressive initiators featured the largest selection and lowest prices for generic products. Conservative reactors adopted generic products in response to competitor adoption. Submissive defenders adopted generics at a low level, in fear of losing sales, and devoted little effort to promotion. The aggressive initiator strategy was found to yield superior performance.

Henderson, G.R. (1998) 'Brand diagnostics: Mapping branding effects using consumer associative networks', *European Journal of Operational Research*, 111 (2): 306–327.

Understanding consumer perceptions and associations is an important first step to understanding brand preferences and choices. The ways in which cognitive theorists would posit network representations of consumer brand associations are discussed. Several empirical examples of consumer associative networks, based on data from a variety of data collection techniques, are relied on in order to demonstrate the tools available to the brand manager using network analytic techniques. In addition to being grounded in theory, networks are shown to be quite important to mapping an extensive array of branding effects, including: (1) branded features, (2) driver brands, (3) complements, (4) co-branding, (5) cannibalization, (6) brand parity, (7) brand dilution, (8) brand confusion, (9) counter-brands and (10) segmentation.

Hodgkinson, G.P. and Johnson, G. (1994) 'Exploring the mental models of competitive strategists: The case for a processual approach', *Journal of Management Studies*, 31 (4): 525–552.

Recently there have been a number of studies published that seek to further the understanding of the competitive structures of markets. These studies have used aggregate perceptual data in an attempt to uncover industry-level mental models of business environments. It is argued that such studies are predicated on the assumption that there are high levels of consensus within and among organizations in a given industry concerning the bases of competition and the positioning of particular organizations. A recent study revealed considerable variation in terms of the nature of the cognitive categories elicited from the participants and the overall complexity of their taxonomies relating to competitive structures, both within and among the organizations.

Hodgkinson, G.P., Bown, N.J., Maule, A.J., Glaister, K.W. and Pearman, A.D. (1999) 'Breaking the frame: An analysis of strategic cognition and decision making under uncertainty', *Strategic Management Journal*, 20 (10): 977–985.

The findings of two experimental investigations are reported into the efficacy of a causal cognitive mapping procedure as a means for overcoming cognitive biases arising from the framing of strategic decision problems. In Study 1, participants in the post-choice mapping conditions succumbed to the framing bias, whereas those in the pre-choice mapping conditions did not. Study 2 replicated and extended these findings in a field setting. Taken together, the findings of these studies indicate that the framing bias is likely to be an important factor in strategic decision making, and suggest that cognitive mapping provides an effective means of limiting the damage accruing from this bias.

Hoffman, R.R., Shadbolt, N.R., Burton, A.M. and Klein, G. (1995) 'Eliciting knowledge from experts: A methodological analysis', *Organizational Behavior and Human Decision Processes*, 62 (2): 129–159.

The psychological study of expertise has a rich background and has recently gained impetus in part because of the advent of expert systems and related technologies for preserving knowledge. In the study of expertise, whether in context of applications or the context of psychological research, knowledge elicitation is a crucial step. Research in a number of traditions – judgement and decision making, human factors, cognitive science and expert systems – has utilized a variety of knowledge elicitation methods. Given the diversity of disciplines, topics, paradigms and goals, it is difficult to make the literature cohere around a methodological theme. The types and subtypes of techniques are illustrated and a discussion of research culminated that has empirically evaluated and compared techniques.

Ingoo, H. and Sangjae, L. (2000) 'Fuzzy cognitive map for the design of EDI controls', *Information and Management*, 37 (1): 37–50.

Electronic Data Interchange (EDI) control design is ill structured and demands consideration of the complex causal relationships among various components of the controls, which may be broadly classified into formal, informal and automated types. Each of these can, in turn, be categorized as internal or external. However, it is difficult even for EDI experts to predict the causal effects of one control on another. In order to aid the design of EDI controls, the application of a fuzzy cognitive map, EDIFCM (EDI-Control Design using a Fuzzy Cognitive Map), was developed. Structural equation modelling was used to identify relevant relationships among the components and indicate their direction and strength. A standardized causal coefficient from structural equation modelling was then used to create a fuzzy cognitive map, through which the state or movement of one control component was shown to have an influence on the state or movement of others. Thus, EDI auditors were able to enhance their understanding of the causal relationship of controls and effectively design them.

James, L.R., Joyce, W.F., Slocum, J.W., Jr. and Glick, W.H. (1988) 'Organizations do not cognize', *Academy of Management Review*, 13 (1): 129–132.

Glick's (1985) discussions of organizational climate (OC) contain some inconsistencies. He first defines OC as a non-psychological organizational variable that is different from a shared assignment of psychological meaning. Then he describes OC as a 'shared meaning' or a 'collective attitude'. Glick also focused attention on the need to obtain accurate descriptions of organizational characteristics in order to assess OC. However, if OC is defined in terms of shared meanings, then many of Glick's recommendations need rethinking. In a response, Glick contends that the disagreement between his views and the views of James et al. rests on the differences between two conflicting definitions of organizational climate. While Glick included shared meaning as a component of organizational climate, this does not imply that organizational climate is psychological. The individualist and macroclimate researchers disagree and should work together to clarify definitions and resolve differences.

Jenkins, M. and Johnson, G. (1997) 'Entrepreneurial intentions and outcomes: A comparative causal mapping study', *Journal of Management Studies*, 34 (6): 895–920.

A study uses a causal map methodology to consider the contrasts between entrepreneurial intentions and outcomes. In evaluating a series of propositions drawn from the extant literature, the study finds that the elicited causal maps are consistent with contrasts in entrepreneurial intentions, but not outcomes. The study develops a series of output propositions suggesting that entrepreneurial outcomes are associated with causal maps that connect the internal operations of the business with the external environment. This implies that entrepreneurial success may be the result of intuitive systems thinking in which connections are made between the environment and the internal operations of the business.

Jones, S. and Sims, D. (1985) 'Mapping as an aid to creativity', *Journal of Management Development*, 4 (1): 47–60.

Three techniques for eliciting creative problem-solving ideas include: (1) brainstorming, in which problem solvers generate as many ideas as possible about a problem without evaluating any one idea; (2) force-field analysis, in which problem solvers list the possible forces that will contribute to and inhibit solution of a problem; and (3) lateral thinking, in which problem solvers apply ideas from diverse areas to an unrelated problem situation. While these techniques are effective in generating creative ideas, translating creative ideas into practical problem solutions has been difficult. Cognitive mapping is proposed as a means for managing the creative problem-solving process. Through cognitive mapping, problem solvers' explanatory and predictive beliefs about a problem and its solution are graphically modelled so that members of a problem-solving group are better able to understand one another's positions and underlying assumptions. Therefore, members can draw upon their own and others' personal wisdom in creatively solving the problem. Examples of the practical business implementation of the technique are presented.

Kiesler, S. and Sproull, L. (1982) 'Managerial response to changing environments: Perspectives on problem sensing from social cognition', *Administrative Science Quarterly*, 27 (4): 548–571.

Managerial problem sensing is characterized as a necessary precondition for managerial activity directed toward organizational adaptation and is composed of noticing, interpreting and incorporating stimuli. The constituent social cognition processes that make some types of problem-sensing behaviour, including errors, relatively likely to occur are reviewed. Four simple ideas emerge as the conventional wisdom of problem sensing. To improve problem sensing, individuals or organizations should: (1) learn from experience; (2) plan; (3) increase the speed with which managers receive information; and (4) increase the range of information managers receive. For social perception, five theories dominate: (1) the augmentation principle, (2) the discounting principle, (3) illusory correlation, (4) illusory causation and (5) automatic scanning. The social cognition processes have organizational implications for such issues as crises, chance events and breakpoints.

Klein, J.H. and Cooper, D.F. (1982) 'Cognitive maps of decision-makers in a complex game', *Journal of the Operational Research Society*, 33 (1): 63–71.

Much attention is currently being directed towards the problems of strategic decision making and decision making in conflict and crisis. An interdisciplinary stance involving psychological research, political science and international relations would be helpful in assessing the contributions of the individual decision maker to the model. This review illustrates the use of a cognitive mapping technique to examine the behaviour and perceptions of individual decision makers, a cognitive map being a representation of the subjective decision-making environment of an individual. Seven military officers each played two scenarios in a research war game. Analysis of their communications revealed that the individual players were remarkably consistent over the two scenarios but that their perceptions of their common decision-making environment differed significantly. The differences noted focused on: (1) the size and complexity of their cognitive maps; (2) detailed interpretation of the maps; (3) players' confidence and anticipation of the future; and (4) the way in which the maps were altered as time progressed.

Kwahk, K.-Y. and Kim, Y.-G. (1995) 'Supporting business process redesign using cognitive maps', *Decision Support Systems*, 25 (2): 155–178.

Turbulent changes and competitive pressures have forced organizations to constantly change. Business process redesign has been widely adopted as an organizational change method in the 1990s. Although BPR projects provide the possibility of dramatic performance improvement, many organizations have encountered serious problems due to the lack of commitment to such projects and the difficulty of systematic targeting of critical processes. By identifying the cause–effect relationships within an organization, an attempt is made to address these issues. A cognitive map-based method, called two-phase cognitive modelling (TCM), is proposed to help organizational members identify potential organizational conflicts, capture core business activities and suggest ways to support the necessary organizational change. To apply the method in the real-world context, a prototype modelling tool, called two-phase cognitive modelling facility (TCMF), is developed. Working procedures of the TCM method and TCMF features are illustrated with their application to the real BPR project of a dairy company.

Langfield-Smith, K. (1992) 'Exploring the need for a shared cognitive map', *Journal of Management Studies*, 29 (3): 349–368.

An experiment was undertaken to elicit the shared perceptions of six individuals employed in a Fire Protection Department regarding the important aspects of the job of a fire protection officer. The experiment consisted of two stages – individual cognitive mapping sessions and group workshops. Shared perceptions were modelled in the form of a causal cognitive map. Participants were divided into subgroups of two to three people, and each subgroup was asked to cluster elements and to categorize the elements as agreed, disputed or discarded. Participants met as one group to finalize the list of agreed elements. The workshop terminated because of the lack of agreement on language and its meanings. A new model that explained the relationships between individuals' and shared belief systems and collective cognitions proposed that individuals operating as a decision-making group do not necessarily need to share an extensive system of shared beliefs.

Langfield-Smith, K. and Wirth, A. (1992) 'Measuring differences between cognitive maps', *Journal of the Operational Research Society*, 43 (12): 1135–1150.

A causal cognitive map is a directed network representation of an individual's beliefs concerning a particular domain at a point of time. The nodes and the arcs joining them indicate causal beliefs. There have been few attempts to develop quantitative measures for such maps. The measures could be used to compare the maps of different individuals and also to track the changes in the beliefs of a single individual over time. They would assist in providing a more objective basis for qualitative analysis. Current cognitive mapping research is reviewed, and some measures are proposed for computing the difference between two maps illustrating this work with a managerial example.

Larsen, E. and Lomi, A. (1999) 'System dynamics and the "New Technology" for organizational decisions: From mapping and simulation to learning and understanding', *European Management Journal*, 17 (2): 117–119.

Managers are surrounded by systems of all kinds: economic, cognitive, social and organizational. These various systems are generally characterized by a number of attributes that make them difficult to predict and control. Computer simulation is a powerful tool to help managers deal with the systematic properties of their decision environments. System dynamics offers a comprehensive approach to the integration of organizational learning, computer modelling and the creation of test-bed for evolving alternative solutions and strategies.

Laukkanen, M. (1994) 'Comparative cause mapping of organizational cognitions', *Organization Science*, 5 (3): 322–343.

> A method for comparatively studying real-life managerial thinking – defined as the respective manager's beliefs about key phenomena and their efficacy links in their strategic and operative situation – is described. A study case comparing the cognitive structures of managers in two interrelated industries in terms of their concept bases and causal beliefs is presented. It is shown that patterns of industry-typical core causal thinking, manifestations of a dominant logic or recipe, can be located, operationalized and comparatively analysed with this method. The contents of management thinking are typically products of complex long-term mechanisms.

Louis, M.R. and Sutton, R.I. (1991) 'Switching cognitive gears: From habits of mind to active thinking', *Human Relations*, 44 (1): 55–74.

> A perspective on the switch from automatic to active thinking and the conditions that provoke it is discussed. Effective thinking may be related to an individual's ability to sense when a change in thinking style is needed.

Madu, C.N. and Jacob, R.A. (1991) 'Multiple perspectives and cognitive mapping to technology transfer decisions', *Futures*, 23 (9): 978–997.

> Multiple perspectives are used to analyse the technology transfer process. The use of multiple perspectives avoids the problems encountered in using purely technical or rational models, such as management science and operational research techniques used in solving socio-technical problems. Emphasis is placed on technology transfer to less developed countries where previous rational techniques have been unsuccessful. Two case studies are used: one focusing on the development of agricultural versus oil technology, and the other focusing on the transfer of production technology. The case studies illustrate the way in which the use of multiple perspectives allows the consideration of the technical, organizational and personal perspectives in the technology transfer decision-making process, thus enhancing and facilitating the process.

Marchant, T. (1999) 'Cognitive maps and fuzzy implications', *European Journal of Operational Research*, 114 (3): 626–637.

> A cognitive map is a collection of nodes linked by some arcs. Up to this point, there is unanimity in the literature about the previous definition. However, if one looks closer at the meaning of the nodes and links, one can expect that there are crucial differences between the various authors. These differences are

not always explicit. In spite of this, it seems that many authors perform on the maps the same kind of analysis (strongly inspired by Axelrod, 1976), even if these analyses are not consistent with their conception of a cognitive map. That is why it is important to define the kind of map used clearly and formally. A formal definition of a cognitive map relying on the concept of fuzzy implication is proposed. In the framework, a node is a logical proposition and a link is an implication. Starting from the definition, some properties of this kind of maps and some analysis techniques are shown.

Morecroft, J.D.W. (1992) 'Executive knowledge, models and learning', *European Journal of Operational Research*, 59 (1): 9–27.

Modelling and simulation have come of age, extending their influence beyond the mind and desktop of the analyst into the boardroom and the mental models of managers. Increasingly, models are seen to have a role as instruments to support strategic thinking, group discussion and learning in management teams. In this respect, they are quite similar to qualitative problem-structuring approaches used by strategy advisers and process consultants. Models are described in terms of three attributes that support different cognitive and group processes in management teams. Models can be viewed as maps that capture and activate knowledge. They can also be viewed as frameworks that filter and organize knowledge. Finally, they can be viewed as microworlds for experimentation, co-operation and learning. An explanation is given of how the modelling process fits into conventional management team meetings. The value chain methodology and system dynamics are then constrasted in order to illustrate the variety of group and cognitive support provided by different maps and frameworks.

Porac, J.F. and Thomas, H. (1990a) 'Taxonomic mental models in competitor definition', *Academy of Management Review*, 15 (2): 224–241.

A cognitive approach to the problem of competitor definition is outlined. Before competitive strategies can be formulated, decision makers must have an image of who their rivals are and on what dimensions they will compete. Given the diverse range of organizational forms and decision makers' limited capacity to process complex interorganizational cues, the task of defining the competition is both important and problematic. This dilemma leads to the use of simplified mental models to define rivals. To the extent that the two can be separated conceptually, the focus is primarily on the structure of these models, rather than on the process of competitive identification. By internalizing a mental classification of organizational forms, the strategist can simplify the interorganizational environment by collapsing individual organizations into category types. Five propositions that clarify how this simplification process works in practice are provided.

Porac, J.F. and Thomas, H. (1994) 'Cognitive categorization and subjective rivalry among retailers in a small city', *Journal of Applied Psychology*, 79 (1): 54–66.

Results are reported of two studies conducted to measure the cognitive structures underlying perceived competitive relationships among retailing firms in a small city. Drawing from recent research on cognitive categorization, the theoretical importance of studying subjective rivalry is first discussed, and then an explanation of how categorization processes influence perceived competitive boundaries among firms is offered. The results of Study 1 suggest that cognitive categories of firms are perceived to be largely independent sets of organizations. The results of Study 2 suggest that middle-level categories represent a psychological inflection point differentiating rivals from non-rivals. The implications of these data for studying how managers make sense of competitive structures are discussed.

Porac, J.F., Thomas, H. and Baden-Fuller, C. (1989) 'Competitive groups as cognitive communities: The case of Scottish knitwear manufacturers', *Journal of Management Studies*, 26 (4): 397–416.

The Scottish knitwear industry was chosen to study the influence of shared beliefs because of its small size and long-standing traditions. Extensive semistructured interviews were conducted with top managers from approximately 35 per cent of these companies over a six-month period. It is suggested that the Scottish knitwear sector exists as it does today because the mental models and strategic choices of key decision makers intertwine to create a stable set of transactions in the marketplace. Core identity and causal beliefs are identified that allow managers to define competitive boundaries and make sense of interactions within these boundaries. It is suggested that such beliefs are reinforced by a mutual enactment process in which the technical choices of firms constrain the flow of information back to decision makers, thereby limiting their vision of the marketplace to that which has already been determined by existing beliefs.

Reger, R.K. and Huff, A.S. (1993) 'Strategic groups: A cognitive perspective', *Strategic Management Journal*, 14 (2): 103–124.

The strategic group concept provides an attractive middle ground between firm and industry for both theory development and empirical analysis. To date, this concept has been defined by researchers in terms of secondary accounting and financial data, and a number of critics have questioned the validity of this work. Research shows that industry participants share perceptions about strategic commonalities among firms, and that participants cluster competitors in subtle ways not reflected in extant academic research on strategic groups. Decision makers' perceptions and cognitions are phenomena that can be expected to influence industry evolution. They are of research interest as an additional source of data on firm commonalities that helps address concerns about previous strategic group research.

Reger, R.K. and Palmer, T.B. (1996) 'Managerial categorization of competitors: Using old maps to navigate new environments', *Organization Science*, 7 (1): 22–39.

The paper examines differences between automatic and controlled processing by executives in an increasingly dynamic industry. The results suggest that cognitive inertia affects judgements in both modes, but the effect is stronger with automatic processing. The longitudinal results indicate that change creates diversity of thought across managers in the same environment. Managers at competing firms are therefore apt to view competition quite differently in turbulent environments.

Reger, R.K., Gustafson, L.T., Demarie, S.M. and Mullane, J.V. (1994) 'Reframing the organization: Why implementing total quality is easier said than done', *Academy of Management Review*, 19 (3): 565–584.

A cognitive theory is presented of why planned organizational change efforts, such as total quality initiatives, often fail. The theory suggests that employees resist total quality because their beliefs about the organization's identity constrain understanding and create cognitive opposition to radical change. A dynamic model is proposed in which successful implementation of fundamental organizational transformation is partly dependent on management's ability to reframe the change over time. Implementation may best be accomplished through a series of middle-range changes that are large enough to overcome cognitive inertia and relieve organizational stress, but not so large that members believe the proposed change is unobtainable or undesirable.

Reynolds, T.J. and Gutman, J. (1988) 'Laddering theory method, analysis, and interpretation', *Journal of Advertising Research*, 28 (1): 11–32.

Laddering is an in-depth, one-on-one interviewing technique that is used to develop an understanding of how consumers translate product attributes into meaningful associations regarding the self. The underlying theory behind the technique is the Means–End Theory (Gutman, 1982). Several specific interviewing devices used to initiate the laddering process are described, including: (1) triadic sorting, (2) eliciting preference-consumption differences and (3) determining consumption differences by occasion. The value of the occasional context is stressed. The analysis of laddering data is discussed, and emphasis is placed on the crucial difference between this technique and other, more traditional, qualitative ones. With the laddering technique, the primary output is quantitative and in the form of a hierarchical value map (HVM). The construction of the HVM is reviewed in detail. Applications also are discussed, with consideration of the key research problems, including perceptual segmentation, product/brand assessment and assessment and development of advertising strategy.

Roos, L.L. Jr and Hall, R.I. (1980) 'Influence diagrams and organizational power', *Administrative Science Quarterly*, 25 (1): 57–71.

The use of influence diagrams to help understand political processes within organizations is examined and illustrated through a case study of a new extended care facility connected to a hospital. The high-cost unit was operating well below capacity, so an influence diagram was drawn to help understand why the director was unwilling to increase the occupancy rate to budgeted standards and how such action was related to his overall strategy. A particular object of this study was to discover the influences and strategies underlying the director's policies and postures in dealing with the unit's environment. Influence diagrams helped to generate an overall view of the organizational problems being considered. The influence diagram suggests ways in which innovation might be facilitated. Proper positioning within the organization, having the support of top management and establishing external support help the innovator.

Russell, R.D. (1999) 'Developing a process model of intrapreneurial systems: A cognitive mapping approach', *Entrepreneurship: Theory & Practice*, 23 (3): 65–84.

This paper uses a cognitive mapping approach to build a model of corporate entrepreneurship from an organizational perspectives. This approach analyses corporate entrepreneuring from a systems viewpoint and facilitates an understanding of the process through which entrepreneurial firms generate innovation. Additionally, the application of Maruyama's (1963) concept of 'morphogenetic' systems provides a possible explanation for the non-linear changes that are characteristic of intrapreneurship.

Salancik, G.R. and Meindl, J.R. (1984) 'Corporate attributions as strategic illusions of management control', *Administrative Science Quarterly*, 29 (2): 238–254.

This study analyses the reasons given by 18 chief executive officers to explain their firms' performance in annual stockholder reports over the 1961–78 period, comparing firms with stable and unstable performance. It is contended that the managements of unstable firms, lacking real control over organizational outputs, strategically manipulate causal attributions to manage impressions of their control. These managements claim liability for both positive and negative performances more than do the managements of firms with stable performance, and, contrary to psychological theories, seem unwilling to attribute poor performance to uncontrollable environmental events. When environmental effects are cited, they are associated with announcements of executive changes, thus implying to readers that management is prepared to do battle with its volatile environment. These attributional strategies resulted in better future performance for the firms using them.

Schwenk, C.R. (1984) 'Cognitive simplification processes in strategic decision making', *Strategic Management Journal*, 5 (2): 111–128.

Generating ideas about the ways decision makers actually deal with complexity, ambiguity and uncertainty, involves looking at cognitive simplification processes in strategic decision making. The focus on simplification processes for which laboratory and field support exists should increase the chance of identifying cognitive processes that really do affect organizational decisions, rather than processes produced only by the artificiality of the laboratory context or the political processes in organizations. A review is provided of selected cognitive simplification processes and the possible effects of these biases on strategic decision making, even though these biases are not always harmful in organizations. Future research in this area should concentrate on field settings to provide insight into the effects of these processes. Laboratory research should use tasks more representative of the ill-structured problems actually encountered in business.

Schwenk, C.R. (1985) 'The use of participant recollection in the modelling of organizational decision processes', *Academy of Management Review*, 10 (3): 496–504.

Two basic differences exist between models of organizational decision processes founded on participant recollection and those founded on other data sources, such as analysis of meeting transcripts, archival data and field observation. Specific decision-process models illustrate these differences. Possible reasons for the differences among models developed from different data sources are outlined, and implications for decision-process research are discussed. Approaches must be formulated for combining data from various sources so that they challenge and improve models developed from a single data source rather

> than merely confirming and extending them. Suggestions are offered to help minimize the biasing effects of primary reliance on a single data source and to reconcile some of the differences between decision process models based on different data sources.

Schwenk, C.R. (1988) 'The cognitive perspective on strategic decision making', *Journal of Management Studies*, 25 (1): 41–55.

> Strategic management researchers are focusing increased attention on the cognitions of key decision makers. This is an important development because: (1) the study of cognition may improve understanding of industry and competitive strategy and the ways environmental factors affect strategic decisions; and (2) sufficient attention has not been paid to the study of cognition in the past. Cognitive research can give insights into the ways decision makers with limited cognitive capacities comprehend and solve very complex strategic problems and into the types of errors they make. Recent research has explored such topics as: (1) heuristics and biases, (2) assumptions and cognitive maps, (3) analogy and metaphor, and (4) the development of strategic schemas. These separate streams of research need to be integrated in order for future research to provide a complete understanding of strategic problem solving.

Sims, D.B.P. and Doyle, J.R. (1995) 'Cognitive sculpting as a means of working with managers' metaphors', *Omega*, 23 (2): 117–124.

> A new technique is presented for helping managers to talk through and develop their views of difficult and complex issues, which are given expression by arranging a collection of objects, some of them symbolically rich, in an arrangement or 'sculpture'. At the same time, the managers describe and develop the meanings being given to, and the relationships among, the objects. The technique is in the tradition of elicitation techniques, such as cognitive mapping, in that it encourages a person or a group to dialogue with a physical representation of their ideas. Meanings are not merely described but sometimes actively constructed or negotiated. Theoretically, the technique draws on recent work in cognitive psychology and linguistics on metaphors. The use of this technique in a variety of different circumstances is described and evaluated. It is argued that, more than two-dimensional techniques, cognitive sculpting offers the requisite variety to capture and communicate the richness and metaphoric complexity of managers' views of their world.

Snaw, J.B. (1990c) 'A cognitive categorization model for the study of intercultural management', *Academy of Management Review*, 15 (4): 625–646.

A cognitive categorization model of intercultural management is developed that focuses on interaction between an expatriate manager and a host country subordinate. The model's premise is that difficulties occur between managers and subordinates from different cultures because of basic differences in how the individuals collect, process, store and use information about one another's behaviour. Some of the effects that culture may have on the content and structure of schemas are outlined. In addition, consideration is given to the extent to which automatic versus controlled information processing occurs. The use of the model to examine convergence of cognitive structures through intercultural dynamics is also discussed. The model focuses on the daily interaction between a manager and a subordinate. It does not attempt to explain culture-based differences in other important interpersonal or group relationships.

Stubbart, C.I. (1989) 'Managerial cognition: A missing link in strategic management research', *Journal of Management Studies*, 26 (4): 325–347.

The linkages between cognitive science and strategic management research are explored. Schendel and Hofer (1979) implicitly assumed a cognitive basis for much of the strategy-making process, but they did little to systematize a cognitive approach. Strategy scholars have recently focused their efforts upon describing managers' semantic networks, or cognitive maps (what managers know about their competitive situations). Semantic networks have several useful properties, including flexibility, activation, reasoning and computation. These networks also have limitations, such as: (1) there is no evidence that humans reason according to matrix algebra; (2) cognitive maps cannot easily represent temporal relations; and (3) cognitive maps used in strategy are often excessively abstract. Today, some scholars regard cognitive simplification and non-optimal heuristic inferences as a serious threat to managerial decision making. However, strategic management stands to benefit greatly from an infusion of relevant empirical findings, stronger theory and added support for strategic planning.

Swan, J. (1995) 'Exploring knowledge and cognitions in decisions about technological innovation: Mapping managerial cognitions', *Human Relations*, 48 (11): 1241–1270.

Success and failures with technological innovation can, in some cases, be attributed to the decision-making processes in the user organization. There has been a growing interest among strategy researchers in managerial cognitions. The nature and importance of knowledge bases and cognitions for decisions about technological innovation are described and a suggestion is made about how knowledge and cognitions can be explored using process research. Cognitive mapping methodologies are useful to researchers, particularly in conjunction with process research, and potentially useful to practitioners, for understanding managerial cognitions and for anticipating problems that may arise as a result of these cognitions.

Swan, J. (1997) 'Using cognitive mapping in management research: Decisions about technical innovation', *British Journal of Management*, 8 (2): 183–198.

The paper highlights the importance of cognitions in decisions about technological innovation. However, cognitive processes have been under-emphasized in empirical work on technological innovation and part of the problem may have been lack of availability of research tools and techniques with which to explore cognitions. Cognitive mapping methodologies are reviewed in terms of their potential to fill this gap in the research into technological innovation. The paper discusses these methodologies, evaluates their limitations and argues that a distinction should be made between cognitive maps and the output of mapping techniques. It is concluded that cognitive mapping may provide a useful addition to existing management research tools provided researchers are clear about what is revealed by the particular methodology used.

Swan, J.A. and Newell, S. (1994) 'Managers' beliefs about factors affecting the adoption of technological innovation: A study using cognitive maps', *Journal of Managerial Psychology*, 9 (2): 3–11.

Managers' cognitions or belief systems play an important role in the decision-making process that leads to the adoption of innovations, but research in this area has been neglected. A cognitive mapping methodology is used to reveal managers' beliefs about the causes of and effects of a particular type of technological innovation. These managers' beliefs are compared with suggestions made in the academic literature about the factors that influence a firm's level of innovation. Factors that, according to the academic literature, increase the likelihood of innovation were not believed to be important direct causes by these managers. These managers saw involvement in professional associations as a very important causal factor in innovation in production and inventory control. Other factors seen to be direct causes were the ratio of professional and technical staff to others in the firm, the promotion activities of vendors, and the competitors' levels of technology.

Thomas, J.B., Clark, S.M. and Gioia, D.A. (1993) 'Strategic sensemaking and organizational performance: Linkag', *Academy of Management Journal*, 36 (2): 239–270.

The question of how key cognitive processes (scanning, interpreting and responding) of top managers may be linked to organizational performance is examined. Scanning involves searching the environment to identify information that is pertinent to the organization. Interpretation involves comprehending the information and deciding which strategic issues to address. A response, or action, is a change in organizational practices. Using path analyses on data from 156 hospitals, the direct and indirect effects among these sensemaking processes and performance outcomes were tested and a model of their relationships developed. Top managers' attention to high levels of information during scanning was found to be related to their interpretation of strategic issues as positive and as implying potential gains. There was no link found between positive-gain interpretations of strategic issues and subsequent action. However, the interpretation of a strategic issue as controllable had a positive effect on product-service change.

Vislosky, D.M. and Fischbeck, P.S. (2000) 'A mental model approach applied to R&D decision-making', *International Journal of Technology Management*, 19 (3–5): 453–471.

A mental model approach is developed to map systematically an organization's R&D project-selection decision process from the cognitive beliefs of its key decision-makers. Respondents revealed decision-criteria maps are judged against a normative project-selection model to reveal systematic departures from rational choice. The methodology is demonstrated within an industrial R&D organization of a large production company. The results highlight the value of the mental model approach applied to R&D decision making. Application of the methodology may prove useful to managers and policy makers by providing insightful information about an industry's R&D selection process.

Walsh, J. (1988) 'Selectivity and selective perception', *Academy of Management Journal*, 31 (4): 31–35.

Dearborn and Simon's (1958) work on selectivity and selective perception was conceptually replicated and extended using data from 121 midcareer managers enrolled in a two-year, part-time executive master's degree programme at a large university. The early work was replicated and extended through measures of managers' entire work histories, their belief structures and three indexes of information processing in an ill-structured decision situation. Results indicated that, contrary to Dearborn and Simon, few managers saw their organizational worlds along narrow functional criteria. Three-quarters of the group either had no firmly held dominant conception of success or had strong conceptions of success. Little evidence was found of parochial information processing.

> Managers with a marketing belief structure identified more external management problems and asked for more external management information than did managers in human relations and generalist groups.

Walton, E.J. (1986) 'Managers' prototypes of financial firms', *Journal of Management Studies*, 23 (6): 679–699.

> The applicability of meaning giving as a categorization process of matching stimuli against prototypes to organizations was explored by focusing on prototypes as a central component of the perspective. A phenomenological analysis of 22 prominent institutions in New York City focused on the meanings that managers attach to organizations or to contents of categories and prototypes. A four-part structured interview was used to elicit managers' descriptions of their own firms and nine others. The responses were analysed linguistically, and multidimensional scaling techniques were used to uncover hidden structures in the data. The results of the study supported the premise that people endow organizations with meaning by a prototype-matching categorization. The results suggest that prototypes affect structure of information about organizations. Managers apparently used the labels provided to list prototypical attributes.

Wang, S. (1996) 'A dynamic perspective of differences between cognitive maps', *Journal of the Operational Research Society*, 47 (4): 538–549.

> To complement current methods used in measuring the differences between cognitive maps, the application of neural network tools is suggested. The neural network approach aids decision makers in the identification of dynamic aspects of target systems that are represented by the cognitive maps to be compared. A real-data application of this method shows that the proposed technique can be used to enhance the understanding of a decision environment.

Warren, K. (1995) 'Exploring competitive futures using cognitive mapping', *Long Range Planning*, 28 (5): 10–21.

> Uncertainty over the direction and scale of change in future industry conditions is one of the most intractable problems of strategic management. Anticipating the future can be hampered by misunderstanding of the driving forces at work, their relative significance and the ability of the firm to affect them. UK take-home drinks retailing is examined and it is shown how diverse forces for change may be combined in mental maps to build credible scenarios to inform a firm's strategy. An example shows the dangers of accepting conventional wisdom,

the importance of including in scenarios the responses of participating firms, and the potential to discover promising strategies in apparently unattractive competitive conditions.

ACKNOWLEDGEMENT

REFERENCES

Axelrod, R.M. (1976) *Structure of Decision: The Cognitive Maps of Political Elites*. New Jersey: Princeton University Press.

Dearborn, D.C. and Simon, H.A. (1958) 'Selective perception: A note on the department identifications of executives', *Sociometry*, 21: 140–144.

Glick, W.H. (1985) 'Conceptualizing and measuring organizational and psychological climate. Pitfalls in Multilevel Research', *Academy of Management Review*, 10 (3): 601–616.

Gutman, J. (1982) 'A means-end chain model based on consumer categorization processes', *Journal of Marketing*, 46 (2): 60–72.

Kelly, G. (1955) *Theory of Personal Constructs*. New York: Norman.

Maruyama, M. (1963) 'The second cybernetics: Deviation-amplifying mutual causal process'. *American Scientists*, 51: 164–179.

Porac, J.F. and Thomas, H. (1990) 'Taxonomic mental models in competitor definition', *Academy of Management Review*, 15 (2): 224–240.

Schendel, D.E. and Hofer, C.W. (1979) *Strategic Management: A New View of Business Policy and Planning*. Boston: Little Brown.

INDEX